2006

The American Moment
Stanley I. Kutler, *Series Editor*

America's Public Schools

From the Common School to
"No Child Left Behind"

William J. Reese

The Johns Hopkins University Press
Baltimore

© 2005 The Johns Hopkins University Press
All rights reserved. Published 2005
Printed in the United States of America on acid-free paper
9 8 7 6 5 4 3 2 1

The Johns Hopkins University Press
2715 North Charles Street
Baltimore, Maryland 21218-4363
www.press.jhu.edu

Library of Congress Cataloging-in-Publication Data
Reese, William J., 1951–
    America's public schools : from the common school to "No
Child Left Behind" / William J. Reese.
        p. cm. — (The American moment)
    Includes bibliographical references and index.
    ISBN 0-8018-8195-1 (hardcover : alk. paper) —
ISBN 0-8018-8196-X (pbk. : alk. paper)
    1. Public schools—United States—History.   2. Education
and state—United States—History.   3. Educational change—
United States—History.   I. Title.   II. Series.
    LA212.R423 2005
    371.01'0973'09—dc22   2004029625

A catalog record for this book is available from the British
Library.

To Carole and Lil, with love and affection

Contents

Series Editor's Foreword

Public education has been a constant spur for enhancing freedom and material well-being throughout American history. It has been a handmaiden to the hopes of the nation's founders for an informed, free citizenry equipped with the tools to develop its faculties and pursue opportunities. The historical role and workings of publicly financed and supported education are among the most unique American contributions to human development and enrichment.

William J. Reese's engrossing narrative succinctly and shrewdly analyzes nearly two centuries of American public schools, taking us from the pioneering efforts in the early nineteenth century through the political and cultural conflicts of today. This is not a "things were better in the old days" argument. Reese wisely recognizes that schools have always been the battleground for shaping society. For example, the battle over the role of religion in public, secular schools is hardly a phenomenon of recent decades. That issue (among others) has exerted significant influence in determining curriculum and teaching practices throughout public school history. Whether students should pray in school, or how to resolve conflicts between science and religion, are not uniquely present-day concerns. As Reese writes, throughout their history "America's schools remain central to most public debates over how to define and secure the good life for the nation's children."

Schooling also reflects the eternal quest for the proper balance between individualism and community—both "values," deeply ingrained in the American character, with substantial merit and appeal. Americans, Reese notes, vacillate between the two, yet constantly search for a useful, meaningful reconciliation of any tension between them, favoring an education system that will promote and serve both values. Reese appropriately acknowledges that the fate of our schools "remains in the hands of a citizenry that craves both continuity and change."

Reese's survey of public education is history at its best, always setting its subject as a faithful mirror of the larger societal history. The political, cultural, and economic context of given moments looms large in this thoughtful work. Reese successfully demonstrates that the staggering expansion of public education in the twentieth century reflects the country's equally staggering transformation from a rural, agriculture-oriented society to the complex urban and commercial nation of the twenty-first century.

Stanley I. Kutler

Acknowledgments

I am indebted to numerous colleagues and friends, librarians and archivists, and several institutions for their generosity. Their help and encouragement demonstrate that scholarship remains a social enterprise, though they must be absolved of responsibility for any shortcomings in my work. These I achieved all on my own.

I cannot say thank you often enough to the stream of graduate assistants who helped me locate sources and who sometimes read and criticized my work. Among them were Tony Abeln, Karen Benjamin, Matt Calvert, Christie Hanzlik-Green, Story Matkin-Rawn, Suzanne Rosenblith, Dina Stephens, Patricia Stovey, and Carole Trone. Graduate students at Indiana University at Bloomington and the University of Wisconsin–Madison helped me refine my ideas, either through private conversations or classroom discussions. A number of colleagues also offered detailed and constructive comments on various drafts of my manuscript, including David Adams, Mary Ann Dzuback, Barry Franklin, Herbert Kliebard, B. Edward McClellan, David McDonald, Adam Nelson, John Rudolph, Jeremi Suri, David B. Tyack, and Maris Vinovskis. Conversations with Richard Aldrich of the Institute of Education, University of London, helped shape my understanding of the European background to American school reform. Robert Orsi also shared the gift of friendship and the benefits of his mastery of American religious history. In addition, librarians at the University of Wisconsin–Madison and Wisconsin Historical Society have been unfailingly helpful, and I give special thanks to James Danky. I am also indebted to the countless historians and educators whose works are acknowledged in my bibliographical essay. Chapter 3 appeared in a different form in the *History of Education Quarterly,* and I am grateful to its editors for permission to draw upon it in this volume.

The timely assistance of Dean Charles Read of the School of Education and Dean Martin Cadwallader of the Graduate School of the University of Wisconsin–Madison helped accelerate the progress of my work, as did the Spencer

Foundation through various grants over the last decade. Henry Tom, my editor at the Johns Hopkins University Press, and Stanley I. Kutler, my colleague, friend, and series editor, had the patience of Job. I am extremely grateful to my outstanding manuscript editor, Susan Lantz, who labored so diligently and so well on my behalf.

America's Public Schools

"'Tis education forms the common mind / Just as the twig is bent, the tree's inclined." So wrote Alexander Pope, the eighteenth-century English poet. Turning a biblical aphorism into contemporary verse, Pope spoke to the ages, to generations of Western thinkers who emphasized the power of education and the crucial importance of socializing the young for the sober responsibilities of adulthood. Since antiquity, village elders, priests, scribes, and parents have liberally offered advice to the young. Prescriptions abound in times of social change, real or perceived, whenever fears mount that families are collapsing, young people are insolent, and disorder reigns free. In America, jeremiads about fallen youth appeared within a generation of New England settlement and continue today. Now laments of undisciplined pupils merge with anxieties fueled by the global marketplace, cultural diversity, the divisions between rich and poor, and the gnawing sense that civic participation and community cohesiveness need shoring up in a postmodern, often violent, world.

This is a history of one of America's most familiar and basic institutions: the public schools. Over the past few decades, more than a few of the nation's governors and presidents have made educational reform a political priority not only in electoral campaigns but also in far-reaching legislation, from the education of children with special needs to the academic achievement of the poor. Since the 1980s, Republican and Democratic presidents alike, as well as scores of state and local officials, have endorsed higher academic standards, championed national goals including drug-free schools and universal graduation, and, in the latest incarnation of reform, promised to "leave no child behind." The most hardheaded politicians often embrace utopian claims about what schools can accomplish, and everyone aspiring to office seems to be an educational reformer.

Historically, legally, and practically, public schools are in fact largely controlled by state laws and locally governed. Their decentralized nature makes their reform and transformation painstakingly slow and frustrating to reformers of all political stripes, especially when trying to address problems that originate outside school classrooms and corridors. But adults who are unable to solve the nation's most serious, recurrent dilemmas—poverty, racial and social injustice, and civic apathy—predictably conclude that the solution resides not in their own behavior but in the flawed practices of the schools and imperfect nature of the young. Since the early nineteenth century, public schools have often been at the center of attempts to improve the lives of individuals and to ensure the greater good of society. Whether they are caricatured or discussed intelligently, public schools remain the subject of debate among television's talking heads, in newspaper articles, at professional conferences, and in meetings of local school boards, lobbying groups, and neighborhood parent-teacher organizations. Because more and more Americans have attended schools, and for more years of their lives, everyone has an opinion, not always flattering, about what schools were once like and what they should become. Citizens who should know better routinely expect them to accomplish what is humanly impossible, complain bitterly when the schools falter, and yet turn to them again and again to cure social ills not of their making. For more than two centuries, many Americans have agreed that a better society is impossible without improved schools, yet complaint and criticism about the public system have never ceased.

In this book, I focus on two closely related phenomena: the persistent attempt by many citizens since the early nineteenth century to reform society through schools, and the ongoing battles within schools to alter their organization, curriculum, teaching practices, and overall purpose. This is a history of reformers working on the outside as well as on the inside of the school system. The first three chapters examine school and society in the nineteenth century, and they explore in turn the origins of public schools in the decades preceding the Civil War, their growth and nature across the nation in the postbellum era, and the attempts of romantic reformers throughout the century to transform the schools' curriculum and teaching practices. Chapters 4 through 6 examine the first half of the twentieth century: they present a portrait of competing visions of education and reform during that era, followed by an analysis and description of the main characteristics of elementary schools and then high schools, which were becoming mass institutions. Chapters 7 through 9, which focus on the 1950s through the early 1980s, are structured similarly. They reconstruct the vast social changes and competing reform ideals that shaped modern America and its schools, and then revisit elementary schools and high schools in the civil rights era and its aftermath. The epilogue offers a sketch of diverse reformers' ongoing efforts since the Reagan years to transform the schools.

The following outline of my narrative is to help the reader navigate this stormy history of school reform, a journey covering nearly two centuries of American aspiration, achievement, and disappointment. America's public schools were born in the nineteenth century in the northern states in an age of evangelical Protestantism, regional conflict, and dramatic social change. Established at a time when cities, industry, and immigration seemed to undermine the rural and agrarian values on which the nation was founded, the schools were expected to strengthen the moral character of children, reinvigorate the work ethic, spread civic and republican values, and along the way teach a common curriculum to ensure a literate and unified public. After the Civil War, the schools remained integrally connected to the vital public debates of the day. The nation's moral standards were on the line during Reconstruction, when four million ex-slaves sought the rights of citizenship and dreamed of a better life for their children, despite the often violent and hostile response they received. Ours is not the first generation to wonder how well the schools will address thorny issues of race and ethnicity or whether they will guarantee social cohesion and higher intellectual achievement. Nor are we the first to struggle to define the place of cities and the urban poor in the body politic.

Cities were the great hope of public school reformers throughout the nineteenth century, the site of curricular and pedagogical innovation. The familiar image of the modern elementary school class—one taught primarily by a single teacher, usually a woman, in a self-contained, age-graded classroom with standard books—is a visible legacy of urban antebellum reform. Across the course of the century, a noisy and serious debate arose between those who defended traditional classroom norms and practices and those who wanted to recast the curriculum and pedagogy through the adoption of manual training courses and two other European imports, kindergartens and object teaching. Manual training classes promoted a variety of handicraft skills, kindergartens emphasized the value of structured play and social cooperation, and object teaching, which included using natural objects such as peas and pebbles instead of books to teach addition and subtraction, also challenged educational convention. That progressive educators still labor to make schools more innovative, appealing to students, and less competitive, and that their victories have often been marginal, highlights the powerful role of tradition and the continuity of school practices.

The expansion of public education in the first half of the twentieth century was one of the wonders of the age. Overall, the period witnessed the contin-

ual growth of public schools as the nation became the world's leading industrial and military power. Before the flow of immigration from central and
southern Europe ended in the mid-1920s, America was becoming more ethnically diverse, especially outside the South. By World War I, African Americans
increasingly moved from the rural Jim Crow South to the more economically
advanced urban North, seeking a more promising future for themselves and
their children. These dramatic social changes raised even higher expectations
for public schools, themselves adopting new organizational practices that reflected a more corporate economic order, and facing the competing demands
of activists who, like earlier generations of citizen reformers, wanted to transform school and society.

Throughout the early decades of the century, cities remained the bellwether
of social change, and schools faced the painful dilemmas that confronted the
larger industrial society. Voluntary associations had been crucial in the formation of public schools in the antebellum period, and they remained vital
sources of grass-roots agitation in the Progressive Era (circa 1890–1920). Activist women drawn from settlement houses (neighborhood centers focused on
the problems of the urban poor), women's clubs, and mothers' organizations
labored to expand their political authority at a time when school boards were
centralized and big business dominated; along with a variety of other community groups, they lobbied to enhance the social functions of the schools.
This led to the expanded use of schools as social centers, the establishment of
playgrounds, provision for medical and dental inspection, and enriched summer programs and free school meals for the poor. Citizens repeatedly battled
over fundamental aspects of educational policy, including the nature of the
curriculum, the extent of social welfare programs, and the appropriateness of
more student-centered instruction. On one side of the political aisle stood
those who embraced the values of social efficiency, business ethics, and scientific management; on the other, those who resisted the sirens of economic efficiency but wanted to democratize the schools, ensure fairer representation of
ordinary people in school decision making, and otherwise expand social justice to the less privileged.

Schools underwent remarkable change but nevertheless preserved many
traditional features and practices. Elementary schools, for example, were increasingly transformed by the tools of science: the development of IQ (intelligence quotient) tests and an array of achievement tests forever undermined
rule-of-thumb measures of academic performance. Ability groups, which sep-

arated children for instructional purposes into separate classes within the same grade or subgroups within the same class, became common, as educational researchers confirmed the realities of human difference through scientific measurement. Progressives and child-centered activists stirred debates about the purposes of schools and whether the training of the mind should take precedence. They offered a flurry of proposals that attacked the continued reliance of teachers on textbooks rather than more inductive methods, memorization rather than understanding, and the needs of the bureaucratic system rather than those of the individual child. By the 1950s, traditionalists sometimes confused the triumphal rhetoric of progressivism with everyday school practice, ignoring the persistence of tradition. At the same time, like many Americans across the political spectrum, they rightly worried whether the schools had unduly sacrificed academic standards as they became mass institutions.

High schools, too, were caught in the grip of massive social change, in the tension between those who wanted to democratize them and those who would preserve them as centers of academic excellence, two goals professional educators generally viewed as mutually exclusive. Attended by a minority of students in the 1890s, the high school became a mass institution in a little more than a generation, as the Great Depression eliminated many jobs once available for youth. The high school increasingly enrolled more working-class and immigrant youth, unwittingly helped establish peer cultures, and seemed to elevate social over intellectual aims. Fears of declining standards, so common in our own times, became ubiquitous as the high school expanded its reach beyond the privileged few. The number of vocational courses grew dramatically. So did team sports. Indeed, local high schools often became better known for their basketball and football teams than for their debate clubs and honor societies.

Like elementary schools, high schools assumed broadened social responsibilities during the early twentieth century, and the larger consolidated schools sometimes downplayed academics, especially for poorer pupils not likely to attend college. Many school officials and parents nevertheless successfully resisted pressures to eliminate the teaching of basic academic subjects, and most teachers resisted the seductive charms of progressive pedagogy. But secondary schools remained a source of public concern in the decades that followed. They seemed to lack a coherent purpose. Since the 1930s, high schools have kept youth out of the workplace and often out of harm's way, have entertained pupils as well as their communities through sports, bands, and other extracurricular activities, and have tried to educate those who can barely read and those heading for the Ivy League.

From the 1950s to the recent past, public schools faced another period of remarkable social change. As in earlier moments in American history, citizens turned to public schools for solutions to familiar as well as novel problems that surfaced in contemporary society. Along with the usual fears of academic decline and immoral youth came the demands of the civil rights movement, the anxieties of the cold war, growing divisions between city and suburb, rising levels of immigration after 1965, the needs of a postindustrial economy, and the controversial role of markets and the federal government in educational policy. Schools again encountered the complaints of reformers outside of the system as well as those within it. Despite growing interest in private school alternatives, many Americans still regarded the public schools as vehicles of reform, whether they were engaged in a liberal war on poverty or a more conservative war on low standards. The inclusion of new populations of pupils—poor and minority children in high school, and an explosion of special education programs on all levels—ensured the perpetuation of hoary debates over the nature of the curriculum, academic standards, and pedagogy.

Without shedding the thick husk of social expectations they had already accumulated, the nation's schools played an expanded role in the economy. Weakened academic standards, said many critics in the 1950s, had allowed the Russians to take the lead in the cold war with the launching of Sputnik. Someone had to be responsible, and many blamed John Dewey and "progressive education," which had presumably paved the way for social promotion and semiliterate pupils who became less-than-productive adults. As jobs on farms and in factories declined, teenagers stayed in school longer. This led business organizations and other pressure groups to lobby for a more practical curriculum for the non–college bound. Champions of vocational education usually supported a more nonacademic curriculum for other people's children if not for their own. Middle-class parents, enjoying a standard of living in the suburbs that was the envy of the world, pressured teachers and administrators to ensure that their children got into the right college. "To get a good job, get a good education," claimed a popular television commercial. Educational credentials and economic success seemingly marched arm in arm.

After World War II, expectations among Americans—whether in terms of consumer goods, health care, or overall lifestyle—rose perceptibly. Expansive rhetoric about the potential of schools, and about their failures, similarly soared in the 1950s. Administrators labored to hire enough teachers and find enough classrooms to meet the demands of the baby boom, and progressives insisted upon more child-centered, innovative approaches to teaching and curriculum. But the public soon blamed them for lowering standards and for becoming too permissive, which only promoted delinquency and other social ills. Historically, most high school pupils had never received a diploma, but increasingly these "dropouts" were doomed to low-wage, low-status jobs in an expanding service economy. The price of failing at school began to rise as jobs without educational requirements declined, adding to the pressures on schools to better educate those who were previously viewed as uneducable.

Long the national symbol of opportunity, the schools were expected in the postwar years to make good on their promise for all Americans. Civil rights activists led their campaigns for racial integration by first attacking segregated schools. Middle-class parents demanded high-quality education for their own children. Parents of children with disabilities and special needs demanded more access to school programs. In the 1960s, striking when the hour was right, liberals secured more federal aid for the "disadvantaged" during the heady days of the Great Society. In the wake of the civil rights and antiwar movements, "free schools," open classrooms, and other educational choices and alternatives also became popular, as the countercultural left, like so many other groups, endorsed school innovation. Conservatives, angry that the highest court in the land forbade official prayer in the schools but welcomed Darwin, led a steady drumbeat against the evils of liberalism and permissiveness for the rest of the century. Evangelical conservatives would found Christian day schools in impressive numbers and, along with other disaffected parents would later champion "home schooling," an oxymoron.

Once the postwar economic boom ended in the early 1970s and other nations rose to industrial supremacy, romantic critics of the schools—the spiritual descendants of Johann Pestalozzi, Ralph Waldo Emerson, and other dreamers who followed—faded from view. But their criticisms of underperforming, bureaucratic, and uncaring institutions remained, adding to the condemnations of schools, which grew more deafening. Parents, school board leaders, and legislators demanded better discipline, higher standards, and back-to-basics curricula. State-mandated minimum competency tests became common. Educational choice, attractive in both left-wing and right-wing circles, gained more political support, including the once-heretical notion of tax dollars for parochial and Christian schools. From many sectors of society came the demand for tougher standards and higher expectations, especially as Scholastic Aptitude Test (SAT) scores fell. Success, everyone seemed to say, now depended on access to quality education, too often in short supply. The most noted educational manifesto of the last half century, *A Nation at Risk,* appeared in 1983 and popularized the notion that lousy schools had helped produce America's economic woes. Just as many people once blamed teachers for the embarrassment of Sputnik, they now held them accountable for the Rust Belt, a broad band of declining industrial centers in the urban North.

By the early 1990s, the schools remained front and center as the most visible target for reformers. The heightened aspirations of many different segments of society had not dissipated. Laments about school failure produced only more demands for school improvement, leading to an endless succession of management schemes, organizational plans, and pedagogical reforms, most of which failed to lift test scores high enough to satisfy anyone. Governors and presidents alike endorsed school reform, the sooner the better. Who could argue with the need for more discipline, hard work, and higher test scores? Promising not to meddle unduly with local control, Republicans set national education goals with the aid of Clinton Democrats. A national school "report card," with charts and graphs, appeared annually from the Department of Education, which Republicans otherwise regarded as the demon child of the Carter administration. Strange new phrases such as "performance indicators" rolled off the tongues of experts who vowed to measure progress ever more efficiently.

In the early twenty-first century, America's schools remain central to most public debates over how to define and secure the good life for the nation's children. The post–World War II years witnessed renewed battles between progressives and traditionalists, who fought over every basic educational issue, from curriculum to pedagogy. Despite the widespread assumption among conservatives that child-centered progressives (or liberals and secularists) had captured the educational system, traditional values about hard work, individual achievement, and curriculum and teaching often endured in the larger society and in many schools. Pupils still passively read textbooks, teachers still talked too much, and teacher educators still complained about these practices, much as they had since the nineteenth century. Educational activists on many campuses emphasized the importance of multicultural education and other left-leaning reforms. But the imperatives of efficiency and standards overshadowed everything. Standardized testing easily trumped the romantic notion, briefly revived in the 1960s, that schools should enhance children's growth, development, cooperative instincts, or other intangible, hard-to-measure qualities. President George W. Bush's recent signature education legislation, which promised universal success, reinforced the traditional view that testing and measurement are the sine qua non of education. Across the political spectrum, education remains the fundamental means of individual opportunity and social reform in America, the public schools its beleaguered institutional expression.

CHAPTER ONE

The Origins of the Common School

The year was 1845. In April the New York State Convention of County School Superintendents met in Syracuse, and among the featured speakers was none other than Horace Mann, the most prominent school reformer of his generation. A sober, upright man who endorsed temperance reform and was anti-slavery, Mann was born in Franklin, Massachusetts, in 1796 and attended district schools and Brown University. Trained as an attorney, he became a congressman for the Whig party but made his mark as an educational leader. A legendary figure in his own lifetime, thanks to his writings on public schools and his labors as secretary of the Massachusetts State Board of Education (1837–48), he was later lionized by the education profession as the leading champion of free, universal education.

Mann was still in the prime of his life as he complimented the assembled listeners for playing an integral role in the cause of school reform. Progressive citizens throughout New England, he said, wanted to perfect the schools and affirm their centrality in shaping the character, morals, and intelligence of the rising generation. They pressed for the consolidation of small schools and more state intervention into local affairs. To build a sturdy system of schools,

Mann warned, would not be easy, and the failure to do so ominous. Social class divisions had widened in recent years. Riots and public disorder were especially common in the cities, reflecting social tensions between rich and poor, native born and immigrant. Mass education, however, promised to restore social harmony to the land. Rising wealth among the few had been accompanied by rising rates of poverty among the many, but the schools could cement bonds in a world where community ties had dissolved. So said America's leading advocate of the common schools.

Before Mann finished his speech, he praised a fellow reformer, Henry Barnard. Like Mann, Barnard was a New Englander by birth, a Connecticut Yankee to be precise, a Yale alumnus also trained in the law. Professional training for educators was in its infancy, and these were amateurs, though the most famous of the day. Like many reformers, Barnard attended a private academy early in life but now championed the public sphere. The great educational question of the day was whether citizens would rally around the fledgling public system to enable all children and not just the poor to receive a free education. Most rural children attended locally controlled district schools, which were not always free but were widespread in New England, though less common in the mid-Atlantic states and scarce in the slave South. Since the 1790s, the urban poor in most regions had access to free charity schools, founded by elite philanthropic Protestants. These schools were becoming incorporated into more class-inclusive urban systems, but "free" education of any sort in the cities retained a class stigma. As Mann wrote, neither he nor Barnard wanted a system of schools that "was necessarily cheap, ordinary, inferior, or which was intended for one class of the community; but such an education as was common in the highest sense, as the air and light were common; because it was not only the cheapest but the best, not only accessible to all, but, as a general rule, enjoyed by all."

In the decades preceding the Civil War, a range of institutions—from hospitals to workhouses, children's asylums to prisons—appeared in the northern states, becoming a familiar aspect of public life. Faith in education and in the importance of schools had preceded the attempts of Mann and his allies to build a system of universal education. By the 1830s, white Americans were already among the most literate people in the world, and school attendance in a variety of institutions—charity schools for the urban poor, tuition academies and female seminaries, and rural district schools in particular—had risen dramatically in leading northern states such as Massachusetts. Though families, churches, apprenticeships, and other mechanisms of learning and socialization shared the main responsibility for nurturing and educating the young, New England's Puritans and other Protestants had promoted schools since the seventeenth century. In the eighteenth century, a growing secular emphasis on the value of literacy, numeracy, and basic knowledge further fueled support for formal education. After the American Revolution, civic leaders on the national and local levels trumpeted the importance of schools in promoting republican values and citizenship. Indeed, as historians Carl F. Kaestle and Maris A. Vinovskis revealed in their pathbreaking scholarship in 1980, for a variety of reasons enrollments in Massachusetts schools were already quite high prior to Mann's appearance as a school reformer, particularly for youth between the ages of eight and thirteen. "Per capita consumption of schooling in the American Northeast was probably increasing substantially before the reforms that began in the late 1830s," they write, "although the exact dimensions are as yet unknown."

A variety of educational reforms built upon relatively high enrollments already achieved. Mann and other reformers called for longer school terms, better daily attendance, school consolidation, the professional training of teachers, and a host of other improvements that yielded some success in the decades that followed. Thanks to Mann and his allies, the clamor for a single system of public schools soon intensified in the northern states, especially in long-settled New England. In an age that witnessed considerable support for social improvement, public schools often took center stage. By the 1830s, a chorus of reform-minded people began to sing the praises of free, tax-supported schools: Thaddeus Stevens, later a prominent Republican activist in Pennsylvania; Catharine Beecher, advocate of more educational opportunities for women; Caleb Mills, an evangelical minister who later became Indiana's leading common school advocate; and even notable Southerners, who faced the greatest opposition and whose efforts bore the least fruit. Enthusiasm for social improvement through education flourished. Since the turn of the century, countless pamphlets, speeches, reports, petitions, testimonials, newspaper editorials, books, and articles had promoted the importance of education in a republic. A few dozen educational periodicals also popularized the cause of learning by promoting a class-inclusive school system, especially for white children.

In Philadelphia, New York, and other cities, the editors of workingmen's newspapers—the voice of the skilled artisan minority—despaired over the fate of youth as apprenticeships declined and unskilled factory labor increased; they endorsed instituting a common system and eliminating the stigma attached to free schools. "I think that no such thing as *charities* should be instituted for the instruction of youth," wrote one articulate worker in the *Mechanics' Free Press* in Philadelphia in 1828. He favored free schools dependent not on "private charities" but "founded and supported by the government itself." One Ohioan added, "Unless the Common Schools can be made to educate the whole people, the poor as well as the rich, they are not worthy of the support of the patriot or the philanthropist." "Give to education . . . a clear field and fair play," said a recent immigrant in *A Treatise on American Popular Education* in 1839, "and your poor houses, lazarettos, and hospitals will stand empty, your prisons and penitentiaries will lack inmates, and the whole country will be filled with wise, industrious, and happy inhabitants. Immorality, vice and crime, disease, misery and poverty, will vanish from our regions, and morality, virtue and fidelity, with health, prosperity, and abundance, will make their permanent home amongst us."

Born in an age when millennial ideals, such as universal peace and prosperity following Christ's imminent return to earth, influenced wide sectors of the population, the common schools became a useful barometer of the extensive social changes that transformed the nation before the Civil War. Cities, factories, and foreign immigration generated moral panic and social fears among many northern reformers, whose search for solutions to public ills centered on a more expansive public school system. Reflecting the contradictory passions of the reformers, schools not only favored greater access to literacy and academic study but simultaneously downplayed intellectual achievement by elevating the moral aims of instruction. America's ambivalent attitude toward the life of the mind and scholarship thus found expression in the nation's emerging school system, where character development and moral uplift took precedence even as lifeless instruction in academic subjects predominated. Setting a pattern that long endured, reform-minded citizens increasingly assumed that individual welfare and social progress depended upon an extensive network of public schools.

✎

"School-houses and churches are the true symbols of New England civilization, as temples, pyramids and mausoleums were the symbols of ancient civilization," declared a college professor at midcentury at the New Hampshire State Constitutional Convention, where he endorsed the creation of a new state office, the superintendent of public instruction. Schools, he said, were not like clocks, once wound ticking of their own accord; someone needed to operate and guide them. Moreover, "no reform is carried in the State or the world without a reformer. Improvements originate with original minds, and are usually presented to the people by interested advocates." Whether the cause was temperance or antislavery, pacifism or women's rights, crusades for social improvement abounded in the pre–Civil War era.

Historians need a wide lens to capture the interlocking changes that shaped American economic, social, and political life during these crucial decades, changes that formed the backdrop to vigorous campaigns for school improvement. By the 1820s many Americans experienced exhilarating as well as unsettling changes that undermined a familiar rural and agrarian world. In the South, the invention of the cotton gin and rising world demand for cotton breathed new life into slavery despite the formal end of the slave trade in 1808. After a series of insurrections, frightened southern leaders by the 1830s increased the fines and penalties for anyone educating slaves, dampening regional support for the common school. The economic chasm between North and South widened, decisively shaping views on government and education. The idea of free public schools—theoretically for everyone, with boys and girls taught together—soon became associated with Yankee culture, not American culture, deepening the sectional divide.

Throughout the North, the region's integration into a larger market culture in the early national period entailed changing rhythms of work, discipline, and self-identity among farmers and urban workers alike. Most farmers still consumed most of their own crops, sold their surplus locally, and bartered for materials and services. In the 1820s, northern farmers sold around 20 percent of farm products in the marketplace, but their self-sufficiency and independence soon faded. As government (especially the states) and private individuals invested in improved roads, bridges, turnpikes, and then canals and railroads, farmers, like everyone else, felt the birth pangs of change. Cheap print and the telegraph fostered a communications revolution, which along with transportation improvements knit an expanding nation closer together. The great hope of Thomas Jefferson—the perpetuation of a nation of independent yeoman farmers, seemingly assured by the Louisiana Purchase—was dashed as survival and the lure of making money strengthened commercial market values. White Americans prided themselves on their republican heritage: they were independent and free, enabling them through hard work to provide for their families. But economic changes increasingly challenged their family authority and control over their livelihood.

The appearance of textile mills in New England in the decades following the American Revolution represented the early stages of mechanization and the factory system, even though most people still worked on farms or small shops at midcentury. Women and children fresh from the farms worked in the mills, in advance of the new world of industry that would soon change the face of work and social relations. Change seemed unrelenting as skilled craftsmen were increasingly replaced by machines, which routinized labor and dramatically increased the percentage of unskilled workers. Some age-old crafts such as shoemaking disappeared quickly, and fears of dependency, even among advantaged white workers, accelerated. This only heightened perceptions of disparities between North and South, free citizens and slaves. Deteriorating working conditions led to some of the earliest trade unions, labor newspapers, and social conflicts of the period and alarmed many, who became attracted to reform.

The decline of apprenticeships for boys was an ominous indicator of change. For centuries in Western Europe and throughout much of American history, apprenticeships were a common way for young white males to come of age, moving from a state of semidependence to independence. An apprentice lived under the roof of a master craftsman, who assumed the parental duties of teaching morals and discipline plus the "mysteries and art" of a particular trade. From early adolescence to the age of twenty-one, the apprentice was taught skills as well as values that theoretically produced a responsible, self-sufficient adult. Economic changes, however, undermined this familiar world. As historian William J. Rorabaugh has demonstrated, apprenticeships became increasingly scarce in the antebellum period. Master and apprentice had had mutual, nonremunerative obligations, but now most laborers simply competed for wages in a world of supply and demand. Traditional pathways to independence disappeared, and the life of Benjamin Franklin—who had broken his apprenticeship, run away from home, and enjoyed fame and riches—became legend, if not exactly a blueprint for what awaited those set free in the marketplace. Wage workers increasingly feared becoming "wage slaves," measuring their declining status against the lives of those further down the social scale in the slave South. Many northern mechanics would later endorse the symbols of the new Republican Party: free men, free soil, and free labor, as well as its close ally, free schools.

Cities, too, were the focal point of dramatic social changes in the generation after American independence. Into them arrived youth displaced from New England farms made less competitive by the 1825 opening of the Erie Canal, which connected the East and newer western states. Only one in five Americans lived in an urban area in 1860, but antebellum cities grew at a rate never again matched in the nation's history. Between 1840 and 1860, Boston jumped from 93,000 to 177,000 residents, Philadelphia from 220,000 to 565,000, and mammoth New York from 312,000 to 805,000. Urban issues were never far from the minds of reformers. Symbols of both economic growth and moral degradation, cities contained millionaires and paupers, demonstrating the widening gap between extremes of wealth and poverty.

The cities were home to banks, moneylenders, and middlemen: visible signs of a more interdependent, unequal society. Here lived novelists, editors, and reformers of all stripes who found tales of cheer and woe, contradictions galore. Beautiful hotels, theaters, restaurants, and fabulous homes, said some critics, heralded an emerging aristocracy, an affront to republican simplicity and virtue. As historian Steven Mintz has documented, contemporaries were terrified by the "specter of social breakdown" seen so vividly in the city. Ostentatious display contrasted sharply with the degradation of the poor, ever isolated in their own neighborhoods; the gangs of youth cut loose from traditional moorings; and the homeless ragamuffins, beggars, pickpockets, and thieves astride the city streets. Moralists who did not even live in cities talked endlessly about the evils existing there, calling out for concerted public action. When Irish Catholic immigrants—the victims of famine, brutal landlords, and British imperialism—arrived by the tens of thousands on the eastern seaboard by the 1840s, Protestant anxieties about the moral health of the nation only deepened.

A broad range of citizens responded to these developments by forming innumerable voluntary associations dedicated to social reform. These reformers recoiled at the ugliness and distortions of modern social life but were sanguine about the salutary effects of newly established public institutions. Scholars disagree sharply about how to characterize the reformers, especially their motives. Most conclude that they were largely middle class, native born, and Protestant, fearful of the consequences of social change but otherwise convinced of the fundamental goodness of an expanding market society. News reports from abroad, especially after the numerous failed revolutions in Europe in 1848, ter-rified them: the restrictions on suffrage (which had largely been eliminated here for white males), the repressive authority of church and state, and the de-fense of a fixed social order. As numerous historians make clear, reformers sought to reform the individual, not change the social system, which is why so many turned to the schools to address poverty, immoral behavior, or cor-rupt politics. They thought the solution to social ills resided in the hands of individuals, who needed discipline and self-control to succeed and improve themselves and the social order.

Evangelical Protestantism decisively shaped the world views of the ante-bellum reformers. Horace Mann abandoned the religion of his youth, Puritan Calvinism, and became a Unitarian, a largely upper-class faith that emphasized God's love, human reason, and the possibilities of universal salvation. The classroom became his pulpit. Catharine Beecher, the daughter of America's most famous preacher, failed to have a conversion experience and ultimately joined the high-church Episcopalians. But she too became a social reformer, championing the professional training of female teachers and middle-class do-mesticity. Whether working to create prisons or schools, reform leaders were mostly evangelical Christians, whose intensity and influence naturally varied in different locales. Reformers who might differ philosophically, politically, or temperamentally generally applauded the wondrous expansion of the capital-ist economy but worried about the accompanying social ills. They hoped that the fallen woman, the habitual drunkard, or the ignorant child could be set straight, sobered up, or educated by appeals to self-improvement or through the disciplinary power of institutions, which often bore the markings of reli-gious enthusiasm.

The cautious optimism of reformers came from many sources, including seemingly contradictory influences such as the Enlightenment and Romanti-cism. Various Protestant denominations had long shaped community life in the northern states, promoting literacy to ensure children's access to scriptural authority. With declining support for the Calvinist ideal of predestination and growing emphasis upon free will and salvation by good works, evangelical Christianity held out the promise of individual reformation and social im-provement, often anticipating God's ultimate return to earth. It is not surpris-ing, then, that Protestant ministers usually strongly supported the public schools, frequently wrote school textbooks, and commonly served on school boards and steering committees. Between 1838 and 1879, ten of the first eleven superintendents of public instruction in Kentucky were Protestant ministers, a pattern common elsewhere before professional educators arrived on the scene.

The Scottish Enlightenment (and not its anticlerical French cousin) decisively affected intellectual life in the early republic. Especially influential in the colleges and among well-educated Protestant leaders, it stressed the possibilities of human improvement and the common-sense striving of ordinary people for right living. Moreover, a less easily definable but palpable romantic view, evident in mainstream Protestantism by midcentury, also grew in prominence. It emphasized the goodness of the child, the power of the environment, and the benevolent work of God and His worldly emissaries, such as the local reformers. The Reverend Horace Bushnell, in sermons and popular writings on Christian nurture, popularized these ideals among his socially mobile, middle-class congregation in Hartford, Connecticut. Although cool toward revivalism as well as reform passions such as women's rights and the abolition of slavery, Bushnell idealized middle-class domesticity and praised gentle methods of child rearing and the benevolent work of public education, as did his neighbor and political ally, Henry Barnard. Critical of predestination and original sin, Bushnell called for common schools and other moral reforms to bridge the class divisions endemic in urban America, believing that *all* people could exercise their free will and "rise."

Successive waves of religious enthusiasm swept across America after the 1790s. After remarkable camp meetings on the western frontier—such as one at Cane Ridge, Kentucky in the early 1800s that attracted over twenty thousand people—revivals sporadically spread like wildfire. In the 1820s and 1830s, booming commercial towns and cities including Rochester, New York, which had been economically transformed by the Erie Canal, were set ablaze spiritually by revivalism. Evangelicalism made Baptists, Methodists, and Presbyterians the nation's largest Protestant denominations, and their members joined Unitarians, Quakers, and other religiously inspired men and women in the cause of social uplift. With the increased materialism spawned by commercial and early industrial capitalism, revivalists called for a restoration of virtue among the citizenry. The Reverend Lyman Beecher, father of famous daughters Catharine Beecher and Harriet Beecher Stowe, spoke for many kindred spirits in 1835 when he warned of the dangers of western expansion and commercial and industrial growth. Without the leavening influence of churches and schools in society, commerce would corrupt the morals of the people. "We must educate! We must educate!" Beecher thundered. "Or we must perish by our prosperity."

Protestant concern for education did not alone account for the growing citizen interest in schools and school improvement. Theorists of republican political thought traditionally juxtaposed virtue and commerce, the private good and the public good, a theme that resurfaced in public oratory as market relations spread across the growing nation. Reformers typically did not criticize the economic system that produced many failures and weakened moral restraint, leading to excessive drinking, occasional wife beating, and child abuse. Instead, they focused on the responsibilities and obligations of individuals: if people admitted their failures and softened their hearts, God's grace would rescue them from strife and eternal damnation. If they strengthened their character, they could also better ensure success in the here and now. Hard work, punctuality, honesty, and sobriety—the lessons taught in Benjamin Franklin's popular *Poor Richard's Almanack* in the eighteenth century—would prevent a downward slide into poverty and strengthen family and community during an era of profound social change. On such fundamentals evangelical reformers and secular-minded allies could easily agree.

The family was the bedrock of society, wrote many reformers who drew upon stereotyped images of middle-class homes. Jeremiads about weakened families and disobedient children are timeless, but anxieties over family decline intensified before the Civil War. As men increasingly left the farm and moved to towns and cities, writers and moralists emphasized the existence of separate spheres: men at work away from the home and women at home protecting the young from worldly temptations. In truth, of course, women's labor, paid and unpaid, everywhere remained crucial to family survival. Wives and daughters worked part time outside the home, grew and sold surplus crops, and occasionally labored in cotton mills and other factories. But the fiction of separate spheres, though never an accurate description of most middle-class homes, persisted in much reform literature. The home was characterized as a female preserve, a haven from a heartless society. While women's domestic responsibilities for child rearing intensified, men of all classes were expected to become more temperate and pious, avoiding the grog shop while attending to familial duties. Although their aim was to make individuals moral and bring them closer to God, evangelical Christians thus helped impose disciplinary values, teaching the self-restraint necessary to survive in a competitive society.

Evangelical sentiments thus colored the reformers' views of the family, gender relations, and evolving public institutions. Focusing on the faults, short-comings, and ignorance of the individual, rather than on the inequalities in the social system, these activists were reformers, not revolutionaries. Some wrote compassionately about the poor and those in distress while condemning immoral behavior. Even as soft-spoken a minister as Horace Bushnell, hearing of Catholic criticisms of the schools, exploded with fury. Bushnell told his congregation in a fast-day sermon in 1853 that if Catholics and foreigners did not like the common schools, they were welcome to leave the country. This powerful grip of Protestantism on everyday life amazed foreign visitors. They marveled at the rising church membership, rousing tent meetings, and religious impulse that spawned countless voluntary associations, including Sunday school societies, temperance groups, and missionary associations. Politicians routinely called the United States a Christian nation, despite church disestablishment. "Americans of all ages, all stations in life, and types of disposition are forever forming associations," the French writer Alexis de Tocqueville noted after a visit in 1831. "As soon as several Americans have conceived a sentiment or an idea that they want to produce before the world, they seek each other out, and when found, they unite." Joining in common cause tempered American individualism and also produced tangible results, including the founding of business corporations, churches, hospitals, and schools.

One crucial voluntary association was the political party. The so-called first party system, which pitted the Federalists, who favored a strong national government, against the Jeffersonians, who wanted strong state government, disappeared by the 1820s. By the 1830s, the newly created Whig Party attracted most contemporary reformers. Horace Mann, Henry Barnard, and many of their less famous counterparts were Whigs and sometimes very active politically. The Democrats, the party of Thomas Jefferson and Andrew Jackson, urged limited government and more personal liberty (for white people), endearing them to slaveholders and to immigrant groups such as Irish Catholics, who rightly concluded that the largely Protestant Whigs were hostile to their religion and culture. The Whigs more often endorsed state-sponsored internal improvements such as turnpikes and railroads and reform movements, including public education and temperance. Economically progressive and socially conservative, as historian Daniel Walker Howe has aptly characterized them, Whigs believed in government aid in economic development and moral uplift. Market economies, they believed, promoted a rising standard of living but weakened the social bonds of community. Many Democrats also believed in temperance, and in many communities they similarly championed the public schools. Thus, the dichotomy between the two major parties on public issues can be overdrawn. But the Whigs—whose leadership and followers were mostly native born, middle class, Protestant, and strongest in cities and in areas undergoing market development—appealed to the majority of reformers between the 1830s and early 1850s.

The birth of the Republican Party in 1854, coalescing from the remnants of the Whigs, whose party collapsed due to factional disputes over slavery, and some third parties, proved pivotal in the history of reform. Heirs to Whig views on public investment in the economy and institutions, the Republicans promoted themselves as the party of free men, free soil, free labor, and free schools. A former Whig named Abraham Lincoln endorsed public schools for their civilizing and disciplinary qualities, and Radical Republicans after the Civil War demanded more educational opportunities for ex-slaves. The party of Lincoln remained widely identified as the faithful friend of the common school. The rise of free labor in the North and intensification of southern slavery, the spread of unskilled labor among Yankee working classes, and the growth of cities with their unprecedented wealth and abysmal poverty provided the backdrop to the rising agitation for common schools and their place in party politics. Activist citizens, who gravitated toward the Whig and then Republican parties, wanted to provide each individual with guidance and direction, the stewardship that evangelical ministers preached about in their sermons. In 1838 a Jacksonian Democrat typically moaned that "a peaceable man can hardly venture to eat or drink or to go to bed or to get up, to correct his children or kiss his wife, without obtaining the permission and the direction of some moral or other reform society." Reforming society by reforming the schools had increasingly become a northern, Yankee ideal, supported by those who welcomed economic growth and expansion yet worried about the fate of morals and tradition in a divisive age.

✎

Before the Civil War, common school reformers throughout the northern states promised to solve an array of grave social problems. In a multitude of speeches, articles, editorials, reports, and books, antebellum reformers highlighted the positive benefits of the common school. "Education is a social want: its costs therefore ought to be sustained by society," declared the Reverend Benjamin O. Peers in a speech printed in 1838. "Popular education is a common good," and government should provide every child access to an elementary education in basic subjects and Christian morality, without which the republic would disintegrate. "In a society where every man may do pretty much as he pleases, it is of utmost importance that its members should be so educated that they shall choose to do right." As countless writers stated, corruption and immorality caused even mighty Greece and Rome to fall. At a time when economic divisions had widened, public schools offered common ground and the prospect of social harmony.

According to Peers and other reform-minded citizens, the common schools promised social stability, so visibly absent in times of labor strife, and access to knowledge and values essential to the rise of talent in America. As Thomas Jefferson and other theorists had so eloquently written, this would prevent the hardening of social classes, especially for the white citizenry. Contrary to Calvinist precepts, children did not enter the world fully formed or with a certain destiny; even if some children had vicious parents, moral education might save them from a life of vice and crime. "The germs of morality must be planted in the moral nature of children at an early period of their life," said a typical contributor in the *Common School Journal*. The journal's editor, Horace Mann, agreed that sound mental and moral training countered the tendency toward rampant individualism and wayward behavior so evident in a more urban, commercial society. In Europe, autocratic governments had "thousand-eyed police to detect transgression and crush it in the germ," said Mann in a lecture in 1840, a time of severe economic depression just before most U.S. cities hired their first professional police officers. "Forts, arsenals, garrisons, armies, navies, are means of security and defense, which were invented in half-civilized times and in feudal or despotic countries," he wrote in a report the following year, "but schoolhouses are the Republican line of fortifications, and if they are dismantled and dilapidated, ignorance and vice will pour in their legions through every breach." The young needed self-control and moral restraint, essential in a republic without a standing army or state-sponsored church to monitor personal behavior. To check the influence of "the mobs, the riots, the burnings, the lynchings perpetrated by the *men* of the present day" required widespread support for free and universal education.

Mann left an abundant written record of his views on school and society. As biographer Jonathan Messerli concluded, Mann was a "circuit rider to the next generation," a tireless champion of an expanding system of public education. Yet he often sank into despair, privately brooded, and had a moralizing demeanor. Humans, he concluded, were by nature selfish. "From our very constitution," Mann wrote in 1840, "there is a downward gratification forever to be overcome. The perpetual bias of our instincts is, from competency and temperance to luxury and inebriation; from frugality to avarice; from honest earnings to fraudulent gains; from a laudable desire for reputation, and a reasonable self-estimate, to unhallowed ambition." The young therefore needed to learn socially redeeming virtues at the earliest opportunity.

Happily, Mann wrote, the human capacity for good works revealed itself through temperance crusades, prison reform, and other social causes. But Mann was ever the watchful pedagogue, alert to disorder in the classroom and immorality in the wider world. "Even in the present state of society," he continued, "and with all our boastings of civilization and Christianity, if all men were certain that they could, with entire impunity, indulge their wishes for a single night, what a world would be revealed to us in the morning? Should all selfish desires at once burst their confines, and swell to the extent of their capacity, it would be as though each drop of the morning dew were suddenly enlarged into an ocean." Just as the Luddites destroyed machinery in Britain, race riots and ethnic disturbances scarred American cities, where arsonists too often plagued society. But it was a loving God, said Mann, who planted the seed of benevolence in the human breast. Vice and immorality would persist in the darkest corners of society, but well-managed families, schools, and other benevolent institutions would nurture the best within the citizenry. They were the American substitute for the "thousand-eyed police" of aristocratic nations.

Republican values seemed precarious in a world of brutal class conflict, ethnic and racial divisions, and unimaginable riches and unspeakable poverty, but public schools vowed to teach a core of common values and to promote social cohesion. To strengthen the republic in a growing free market society, citizens, said many northern Whigs and Republicans, required the systematic training of the young, not the accident of birth. Private schools separated the rich from everyone else: they were antirepublican to the core. Catholic schools, rising in prominence in many cities after the 1840s, served a different, poorer population but were even less republican, pledging allegiance to a pope who opposed freedom of conscience and political liberty. In contrast, as the editor of the *Common School Assistant* claimed in 1839, teaching pupils "in the same house, the same class, and out of the same book, and by the same teacher" reflected the best in republican values, an essential way to shore up morals and ensure greater opportunity for everyone. Honoring personal merit in such schools was the highest good and gave the lie to critics of the social order. The curriculum would enhance literacy and character development, weakening the specter of social conflict or class war while promoting a fluid social order and the common weal. So believed many northern educational leaders, who shared a fairly coherent mentality about the aims and purposes of public schooling in the pre–Civil War era.

Bands of citizens after the 1820s debated anew the purposes of education and community responsibility for the schools. Horace Mann and Henry Barnard called these citizens the "friends of education." On village greens, from Protestant pulpits, and in long-forgotten town meetings far from the glare of city lights, they lectured, debated, and otherwise urged citizens to strengthen and reform the schools. School trustees, local ministers, and prominent teachers and community leaders realized that theirs was not the first generation to value formal schooling. Many of them believed that the Pilgrims and Puritans had planted the common school on American shores, and that the current generation needed to restore public support for education, which they said had slackened in recent decades. This trope on the alleged decline of the schools and the need for revival was commonly heard in New England. In a series of lectures and writings in the 1820s, James Carter, a prominent New England reformer, depicted the state of schools as calamitous. The ubiquitous lament of cultural decline was the secular analogue to original sin, a cry for repentance after the Fall. Such appeals to time-honored ideas would recur in subsequent eras of profound social change.

Among the keywords that dominated educational discourse in the antebellum period, none was so ubiquitous as republicanism. Hardly a local school report, stump speech, or appeal for a graded school, nicer building, or better textbooks escaped the embrace of this hallowed word. It underpinned the civic purposes of the common school and became a tiresome cliché. Robert Rantoul Jr., a Massachusetts Democrat and school activist, spoke before the Beverly Mechanics' Association in 1839. Echoing Thomas Jefferson and the Founding Fathers, he reminded his audience that "Intelligence and Virtue are the only safe foundation of Republics." Since the Revolution, every political faction and social group had claimed to uphold the principles of 1776, when brave republicans fought against monarchical tyranny. White mechanics invoked the image to explain why moneylenders had to be vanquished and the credit system reformed to allow working men to earn a decent living and not become like slaves. Jacksonians said only less government would preserve republicanism, while the Whigs and then the Republicans often argued that proper moral guidance and government investment in internal improvements would promote greater prosperity and freedom. Southern plantation owners used the word to justify their ownership of slaves, invoking the rights of property owners.

Discussions of republicanism in educational writing superseded more open discussions of social class but reinforced the common fear that America was on a collision course with history, which was unkind to republics. "Americans of the 1830s and the 1840s," writes Carl F. Kaestle, "inherited from the revolutionary generation an anxious sense of the fragility of republican government." That republics were short-lived and threatened by unfair privileges, corrupt politics, and private interests was a staple of political oratory between the Revolution and the Civil War. Jacksonians lashed out at the conspirators poised to rob the people of their liberties: bankers, monopolists, and college-educated Whigs, whom they viewed as modern-day Federalists and aristocrats. Nothing less than the safety and perpetuation of the republic was at stake, ordinary citizens were told in political broadsides and Thanksgiving-day sermons. Cheaply printed reading material of every variety, the product of technological advances and new distribution networks, flooded the marketplace. New ideas about how to shape the common mind competed for public favor.

Alpheus Packard spoke to the Teachers' Association of Bowdoin College at a meeting in Freeport, Maine in the winter of 1837, and his speech proved so popular he delivered it again in North Yarmouth. The title of the talk was "Characteristics of a Good District School," referring to the tiny one- and two-room schools that dotted the New England countryside. The "district" had become the legal basis for local school organization in the North outside of the cities after the American Revolution, but Packard typically traced the idea to the wisdom of the Pilgrims. The pride of New England, "the school house . . . is one of the characteristic features of the land of the Pilgrims. Wherever the New Englander may roam over the face of the earth, next to his father's fireside, the school house is one of the familiar objects that come up most frequently in his visions of home. There are comparatively few hearts in which the District school has not a place."

But these were dangerous times. Class divisions threatened the harmony of the people. Universal male suffrage was almost a reality, a momentous political change that required stepped-up efforts to educate the masses. "Now, what is the ground of our confidence, that anarchy and misrule will not prevail, and our beloved constitution of government be overthrown?" asked Packard. "I put it to every one present, what is your security, that mob-law, which has exhibited such frightful scenes of violence and lawlessness in many parts of our land, will not extend over the whole country, sweeping before it the barriers which have hitherto guarded the rights of property and the comforts and privileges of social and civil life, and mingle all in one common ruin?" Only religion and education, he and countless reformers said, could address these dire problems.

Charity schools were no answer, as citizens were discovering in the cities. In New York City and other places that once had free schools for the poor alone, "a feeling of self-respect and a sort of pride" kept many parents from sending their children, who frequently hustled on the streets and stole from the greengrocers and from the docks, adding to the woes of city life. But by the late 1830s and 1840s the charity schools were losing some of their stigma, as city authorities increasingly took them over from private, quasi-public voluntary societies. Now these free schools would receive only public funding and draw children from all backgrounds. While the South lagged behind in provisions for mass education, many northern states were actively encouraging more public support for the common schools. It was often said that education deterred crime, and Packard added that the movement to educate all classes together would make the system "manifestly *republican,* entirely republican." If "the sons of wealth and of poverty" sat side by side in school, they would learn mutual respect. At school the only "distinction" that mattered was individual merit, "superior worth. The child of the cottage may bear home, exulting, the little badge of merit which she has won from her companions, as frequently, and probably more frequently so, than those who have been brought up in luxury."

Republicanism colored the passionate political debates of the antebellum period. Irish Catholic immigration in the 1840s and 1850s aroused the hostility of native Protestants, who exuded anti-immigrant rhetoric that linked the common schools with liberty and freedom for everyone and accused private schools of dishonoring the memory of the Pilgrims and Founding Fathers. "Common schools," announced Horace Bushnell from the pulpit in 1853, "are nurseries . . . of a free republic, private schools of factions, cabals, agrarian laws and contests of force." A contributor to the *Pennsylvania School Journal* similarly praised the common schools for preventing the hardening of social classes. "The high and the low, the favorite child of fortune and the offspring of the pauper, have equal right to pluck the rich fruit from this tree of knowledge, planted in the very midst of the garden, and to experience alike its enlightening, its elevating influences." Sensitive to the stigmas associated with free education, especially in the cities, he echoed Horace Mann, adding that common schools (despite their name) were not "of a lower order than other institutions established for the education of children, but common as the air we breathe is common,—its benefits are free to all who choose to partake of them."

Much republican rhetoric substituted for frank deliberations on social class, just as later generations were more comfortable discussing the "culturally disadvantaged" or those "at risk" than "the poor." But writers sometimes offered sensitive commentaries on economic deprivation, fears of moral decline, and the fragility of the republic. That very rich citizens did not patronize public schools discouraged reformers throughout the century. Whig politicians, aware that the wealthy feared their children's contamination by association with the poor, often lectured the well-to-do on their civic responsibilities. In the 1830s the governor of Maine spoke optimistically: "I want to see the children of the rich and the poor sit down side by side on equal terms, as members of one family—a great brotherhood." In the classroom, only individual merit mattered, not family wealth, and poor but talented and hard-working students could rise to the top and preserve a fluid social order. "The different classes are so much separated when young," he added, "that they greatly misunderstand each other when they grow up." Without closer "bonds of sympathy . . . society is well nigh rent asunder by distrust, envy, and all hateful passions."

As the gap between rich and poor widened and periodic economic panics and depressions took their toll, educational rhetoric accelerated regarding the role of schools in guaranteeing social stability but also opportunity for the most talented. An essayist in the *Common School Journal* in 1840 attacked the elitism of private schools and wanted to infuse public schools with the spirit of Christian brotherhood and republicanism to enhance "an equality among the people; not by depressing those who are exalted, but by lifting up those who are bowed down." Horace Mann realized that many citizens wanted social uplift but not a hint of revolution. He thus emphasized that public schools would not level social distinctions but strengthen republicanism by guaranteeing that merit alone counted in life.

But even Mann editorialized that both Sunday schools and common schools were *"the great leveling institutions of this age. What is the secret of aristocracy? It is that knowledge is power."* The challenge of the day was to diffuse knowledge, create excellence in a common system, and make the schools "good enough for the richest, open to the poorest." In a celebrated report on the ties between education and economics, Mann carefully chose his metaphors, saying that people could have social stability and economic mobility simultaneously. For education was "the great equalizer of the conditions of men—the balance-wheel of the social machinery." Schools would uplift the poor, protect the property and wealth of the successful, and obliterate "factitious distinctions in society." Some Americans were beginning to think the schools could do all this and more.

To attain such lofty ends, educators in the antebellum period waxed enthusiastic about how the schools would fulfill their promise. First, reluctant taxpayers whose bills were rising in an age of dramatic spending on improvements in transportation and communication had to open their pockets wider. By midcentury, U.S. investment in mass education surpassed that of any other Western nation, but the pedagogical collection plate was never full. To offer every child, at least every white child, a common experience at school would mean huge investments in buildings, textbooks, and teacher salaries. After all, it was a youthful country. In 1830 one-third of the white populace was under the age of ten. With few alternatives for respectable employment outside the home before the Civil War, women increasingly became elementary school teachers in the urban North and, in later decades, in the countryside. Mann, Beecher, and other reformers applauded the domestic qualities of women, who were described as naturally talented teachers of young children especially and, since they were paid less than men, easy on the budget. On their shoulders rested the responsibility for teaching a common course of study as well as the moral values and sensibilities that would preserve and perpetuate the republic.

By the 1830s, the common curriculum usually included a handful of elementary subjects. Rural district schools, the typical schools most children in the North attended, taught at least reading, writing, and arithmetic. Though ungraded schools had many similar characteristics, there were thousands of them in the expanding rural republic, and local variation ensured some unique features. For example, some schools might have only five or ten pupils, all siblings or cousins; others were crowded with an assortment of children, some shoeless and undisciplined, others more prosperous, ambitious, and likely to excel. Common district schools were initially located in barns, prosperous farmers' living rooms, or new churches, which were often the first community institutions built in newly settled areas. Some schools were well maintained and in bucolic settings; typically, they were basic, plain buildings, what local farmers thought suitable and affordable. By the early nineteenth century, male teachers in the countryside usually taught in the winter terms, which were frequently crowded since the older boys, who could be unruly, had fewer chores on the farm. Young women, seen as more delicate, more often taught in the summer terms.

Yet teachers everywhere, including the majority laboring in small ungraded country schools, mostly pursued the same goals through the same means. Few schoolmasters in 1830 had ever studied pedagogy or thought much about the curriculum, and didactic teaching practices had long been common in all types of schools. Reminiscing in 1833 about his childhood experiences in a district school in Massachusetts, the Reverend Warren Burton, who later applauded more European-style, child-centered teaching methods, could recall the names of the handful of prominent, well-known textbooks that he and most children read and memorized. He also remembered that "we occasionally had our hair pulled, our noses tweaked," and "our ears pinched and boxed" by one particularly cruel master. Horace Mann became a major champion of better teacher training and urged the creation of normal schools, teacher training institutions that soon opened in Massachusetts. But most teaching and disciplinary practices still resembled the world Burton remembered. The purpose of the common school remained the same: to teach Christian morality, discipline, and a handful of academic subjects, a process sometimes reinforced by the generous use of the rod. Despite local variations in the size of schools, background of children, and character of teachers, most pupils at midcentury spent their school days memorizing material and reciting it while standing beside their barebacked desks. And everywhere children studied in whatever textbooks—no matter how tattered or out-of-date—their families owned or could afford.

Teachers usually taught this bare course of study in ungraded, one-room buildings. As Tocqueville noted in *Democracy in America*, Americans valued useful learning and practical subjects but denounced the metaphysics of medieval scholasticism, Catholicism, and aristocratic education. An observer in Maine said that local communities generally agreed upon the core of the curriculum. "If inquiry is made regarding the branches to be taught in our district schools, the reply is obvious," he wrote in 1838. "Every thing should be taught which may be of use in the common business of life. There is no question about Reading, Writing, Grammar, Arithmetic, and Geography. These branches are established in all our schools." Some schools also taught history, but the observer's assessment otherwise aptly highlighted the usual subjects.

The curriculum was a product of tradition, and it anchored schools amid massive changes in the larger society. Since colonial times, Protestants valued reading as essential to exposure to the Bible and religious print. "Knowledge is power" had become a familiar adage by the eighteenth century, and antebellum writers extolled the genius of free institutions and the multiple uses of reading for traditional religious ends as well as for widening secular purposes. Newspapers, magazines, and books inundated a growing reading public. Numerous politicians and educators in the early nineteenth century insisted that good reading skills enabled citizens, particularly recently enfranchised white males, to understand the laws, vote wisely, and function well in the marketplace. Noah Webster's blue-backed spellers gained renown by opening up a world of letters and then words that provided the foundations for more advanced accomplishments. As school enrollments expanded, salesmen of spellers, primers, and readers abounded, hawking the titles of previously unknown authors including the Reverend William Holmes McGuffey, whose first textbooks appeared in the 1830s and whose sales ultimately trailed only those of the Bible.

Born in western Pennsylvania in 1800, McGuffey was an ordained Presbyterian minister, whose name became synonymous with his popular textbooks. According to historian Elliot J. Gorn, McGuffey's books in their various editions may have sold fifty million copies, and they were frequently handed down to siblings, relatives, and neighbors, adding to their influence. They thus introduced reading and writing to countless children, offering some semblance of a common curriculum in America's tens of thousands of ungraded schools. The readers included excerpts from the Bible such as the Sermon on the Mount, speeches by Patrick Henry as well as Hamlet's soliloquy, and selections by American writers including Washington Irving and William Cullen Bryant. They explicitly taught moral and religious values and included stories about the importance of honesty and virtue, courage and patriotism, diligence and hard work. In addition, like most textbooks of the day, they offered a vision of a social order where proper behavior multiplied the chances of personal happiness and social mobility, or at least respectability. An 1866 edition of a McGuffey Reader included a story about a barber who refuses to work on Sundays, despite the resultant economic hardship. One Saturday night, as the barber tells his sad tale of economic woe to an equally pious customer, he learns that he is heir to a fortune, one currently claimed by "an imposter"! Young children encountered numerous tales, many less fantastic, that showed that hard work, discipline, and doing right often led to self-respect, public honor, and economic success.

In previous centuries, writing was particularly important for men working in the public sphere. Often taught in colonial New England by special teachers, writing was less important than reading for the majority of people, who were farmers. Pens, ink, and paper were expensive and traditionally associated with the labors of clerics, merchants, government officials, and lawyers. In the modest schools of the early nineteenth century, the hiring of separate writing masters was largely unknown. Teachers in ungraded classrooms, the most common before the Civil War outside the cities, taught all ages and all subjects. Yet writing, while less important than reading, also enhanced communication in an expanding nation, as Native Americans and foreign challenges to manifest destiny were eliminated or defeated, and as postal delivery and transportation quickened and became more reliable. Steel pens were neither cheap nor easily available until after the 1830s, and the quill and slate had to suffice in writing instruction. Enough was already being spent, thought many parents, on costly textbooks, dear to any beleaguered family.

Arithmetic, in contrast, had been a fit subject for children since the early modern period, when commerce and trade gave birth to expanding capitalist relations and business transactions. The third "R" became basic to survival in a commercial and industrial society and was the quintessential useful subject. "Perhaps the importance of no other Common School study can be made more obvious and palpable to all pupils than that of Arithmetic," said an editorial in a school journal in 1843. "Almost every week, if not every day, the young arithmetician in solving his imaginary questions, disposes of such quantities of goods as would make or ruin the fortune of a wholesale dealer; he makes calculations respecting such sums of money as but few capitalists have the disposal of." Among the many competing arithmetic and mathematics texts, the most popular were by Joseph Ray, a high school and college teacher in Cincinnati. His books introduced the young to the mysteries of computation, compound interest, and the conversion of British sterling to American dollars. Ray tried to teach youngsters how to determine crop yields in a particular field, the height of a tree as determined by its shadow, and profits turned on so many bales of cotton.

While given less overall attention, history and geography helped to round out the basic elementary curriculum. Both subjects had had their advocates since the colonial period, when imperialism and revolution nurtured curiosity about the larger world. Ethnocentric and heavily patriotic to modern eyes, these textbooks extolled the glorious struggle for political independence, the treachery of Benedict Arnold, the superiority of America's institutions, and the grandeur of its natural resources. Children in Hartford or New Haven and in rural Maine or Ohio read of the striking contrasts to their happy fate: Africa was a benighted continent, full of savages deprived of Christianity; Italy a land with a great artistic heritage but made servile by the papacy; and Ireland an unhappy place thanks to the imperial British and the power of Catholicism.

By the 1830s the major authors of school textbooks were native-born Protestants, frequently ordained ministers, often college presidents, and Whigs. Not surprisingly, most of the authors after the 1850s were Republicans. While the common school curriculum was modest, many school principals and superintendents boasted that it reflected republican simplicity, the foundation stones of a house built on the idea of equality. Globes, maps, chalk and blackboards, and other new school apparatus appeared on the market after the 1820s, but textbooks formed the main course of study. Textbooks aimed to diffuse knowledge, emphasize personal responsibility, and ensure social stability by teaching all students a common core of beliefs. At the dedication of a new school in San Francisco in 1854, a speaker said that though the public schools were "the most unassuming places in the world," they "lay the groundwork of the man— and that is everything because it amounts to everything." Schools would help make men moral, productive, and free people who would prosper in a free land.

Educational leaders wanted to create graded classrooms to replace the highly individualized instruction in the typical country school. Guides on how to organize such classrooms appeared in Boston as early as 1831, and city-based educators across the country soon offered detailed blueprints for reform. In an ideal school, children of roughly the same age proceeded through school together, read the same books, and encountered more difficult material as they climbed the academic ladder. Without a concentration of students of the same age, however, this was difficult. Small, ungraded or only partially graded schools remained the norm outside of the cities. In many northern states, schools in little villages and adjacent rural areas by the 1840s consolidated independent districts into larger "union" schools, where some age grading was achieved. These were proudly featured in northern school reports issued by villages, small towns, and the state superintendent's office, but remained a small percentage of the system into the late nineteenth century.

In her memoirs, teacher and city school superintendent Mary D. Bradford reminded readers of the nature of rural education in Wisconsin at midcentury, describing a fairly common situation in most states. "There was no grading which would afford parents and teachers a standard or proper measure of progress," she wrote. Instead, "students started a particular study and went ahead as fast as they could. Progress made was reported to the next teacher, who, either doubting the ability of his predecessor, or realizing the devastating effect on a child's memory of a long intervening vacation, would often put the child back in work, to do it all over again." Some of the children, bored with all the memorization and repetition, became obstreperous. But Bradford, unlike most reformers at the time, actually saw at least one redeeming feature of the multi-age classroom. "It afforded the opportunity for younger pupils, when unoccupied, to listen to the recitations of the older ones—to listen, to wonder, admire, and catch a vision of similar future achievement for themselves; also to pick up information which they were apperceptively prepared for."

Only the large cities had the potential to form actual age-graded classrooms. In the cities came the first innovations: early attempts at graded classrooms, the hiring of superintendents without teaching responsibilities and women as elementary school teachers, more uniform textbooks, and more access to advanced knowledge in high schools, the first of which opened in Boston (though only for boys) in 1821. Cities had the concentration of wealth and the tax base to construct larger schools, pay higher salaries, and build rudimentary bureaucracies with administrative posts to attract ambitious educators, especially after the Civil War when the office of school superintendent became common and well paid. For the majority of pupils, however, the common district school in the country, with its modest curriculum in a modest building, was their reality. Many educators and reformers believed it still made vital contributions to republican America.

Despite considerable talk that "knowledge is power" and basic literacy a practical tool, antebellum educators were more interested in training children's character. The founders of the public schools were often well-educated academy or college graduates who loved to read and write and reflect upon society and its problems. But theirs was a moral mission. They did not believe that the schools should focus only on intellectual training, however important. Even Ralph Waldo Emerson, who found many of the reformers distasteful, frequently told his lyceum audiences that the aim of education was to make a life, not a living. Character was everything in an age of fast deals, confidence men, geographical mobility, and changes that battered body and soul. Like republicanism, character was a slippery word, an indirect way of talking about, say, the morals of the poor. It nevertheless remained an integral facet of republican education, a way to ensure that economic success remained a possibility for the hard-working, intelligent student. Success depended upon how one behaved. Most jobs did not require high educational attainment or school credentials, and leading educators, whether teachers or administrators, believed that while useful knowledge promoted economic success and personal happiness, the values learned at school were far more valuable than any textbook knowledge. The formal curriculum was "but a small part of the teachings in a school," most educators assumed. "The rudiments of feeling are taught not less than the rudiments of thinking. The sentiments and passions get more lessons than the intellect." Honesty would outshine any academic prize on graduation day.

Antebellum Americans were certain that morally upright behavior strongly shaped academic achievement. In speech after speech, Whigs and Republicans linked intelligence and virtue with the survival of the republic. Still, they knew that immorality flourished even during this time of overall economic expansion, rising church membership, and the spread of libraries and schools. Everyone marveled at the growth of popular education and availability of inexpensive reading materials. Yet, according to the reformers, simultaneously came a rise in excessive drinking, juvenile delinquency, and overall crime. How had this occurred? They concluded that there had obviously been a breakdown in character and that academic learning alone, apart from moral instruction, was insufficient to ensure social order and human improvement.

According to prominent reformers and educators, the diffusion of basic knowledge, republicanism, Christianity, and character formation were among the many benefits of public education. Consider, for example, the speech George B. Emerson delivered at a school dedication in Somerville, Massachusetts, in 1848. Emerson was a revered teacher in Boston, a pious Protestant who had taught in America's first high school before opening a prominent girl's academy. He stressed character formation and elevated Christian piety and morality above worldly knowledge. A huge turnout at the local ceremony forced the overflow crowd from the school to a nearby church. There Emerson invoked sentiments heard throughout the northern states in countless speeches, addresses, and books on education. "The Common School is preeminently a Christian institution," Emerson told his listeners, who were proud of their new school. "The friends of the common school feel that they stand on Christian ground, when they promise to regard with equal favor the poorest child from the poorest cottage, and the child who is clad in soft garments and comes from the palace of a prince." Public schools could be as good as the best private schools, and to participate in social uplift was a sacred duty. The health of the individual, family, and nation depended upon steadfast Christian values. In *Reminiscences of a Teacher* (1878), Emerson would recall: "I taught as well as I could, but always considered this teaching of little consequence with that of the formation in my pupils of a single and noble character. . . . To be able to speak confidently to the effect of teaching, I must be able to look into the hearts of my pupils."

Public school activists and educators never strayed beyond a few core beliefs: that the soundest morals came from Christianity in general and Protestantism in particular; that learning without piety was dangerous; and that schools, while concerned with training the mind, should preeminently focus on shaping character. "What is your education, with all its intellectual completeness," said a primer on teaching, "if it does not secure that the child shall become the true man, the pure friend, the worthy parent, the noble citizen, to say nothing of the Christian?" Whether in tiny villages or expansive cities, the moral aims of instruction predominated. Common schools, said one Philadelphian in 1830, should promote "the advancement of private interest, the maintenance of public virtue, the due appreciation of talents, the preservation of a sacred regard to principle, and a high tone of moral sentiment."

Pre–Civil War reformers often assumed that Americans would succeed and improve as a people, especially if schools imparted the right values and sentiments to the rising generation. In *American Education* (1838), the Reverend Benjamin Peers prophesied national ruin if teachers forgot that pupils had "hearts as well as heads." "Education without religion, is education without virtue," said Horace Bushnell in the 1850s. "Religion without education, or apart from it, is a cold, unpaternal principle, dying without propagation." In a world where vice and dissipation threatened individual morality and public order, cautionary tales abounded about the evil paths onto which youth could stray. Writers excelled at painting the stark choices facing the citizenry. In 1842, Orville Taylor, a self-styled patriot, public school zealot, and publicist said that "to govern men, there must be either Soldiers or Schoolmasters, Books or Bayonets, Camps and Campaigns, or Schools and Churches—*the cartridge or the ballot box.*"

Heavy moralizing came with the territory. In a special report in 1848 on moral instruction, the State Board of Education in Maine recommended hiring teachers with only the highest ethical character. "Those teachers who most successfully enforce the precepts of morality, are, usually, the most successful in promoting the intellectual advancement of their scholars. And the reason," the committee continued, "is evident. Morality is the parent of order; and order is indispensable to intellectual success." A North Carolinian explained in the 1850s that only when schools taught more Christian values would the "godless creeds" of spiritualism and socialism disappear as well as "the mental hallucinations" of feminists, "the ravages of Mobocracy and Filibusterism, and the terrors and disgraces of Mormonism and Abolitionism."

By custom, teachers began the school day with the Lord's Prayer and excerpts from the King James version of the Bible, usually read without comment. Protestants congratulated themselves for their magnanimity and open-mindedness in doing so, since this was part of their celebrated non-denominational ethos. While Protestants had subdivided into numerous denominations, they usually agreed on certain fundamental truths. Catholics, agnostics, and atheists, of course, saw things differently. Catholics, whose numbers swelled with German and especially Irish immigration, were the most vocal and numerous critics of teaching Protestant values in schools. This led to infamous school wars and two main demands: to end what were viewed as sectarian practices in the common schools, and to allow tax dollars to help support an emerging parochial system. Both ideas angered and horrified the Protestant reformers. They occasionally compromised on the most insulting of school practices, such as forcing a Catholic child to read from the Protestant Bible, but they absolutely refused to budge on the question of tax support, which Catholic schools had sometimes received earlier in the century. By the 1850s, in the midst of a rising tide of immigration, even Protestant ministers such as Bushnell, who wrote so lovingly on Christian nurture, denounced Catholics from the pulpit. The common school should be a Christian, non-denominational institution, reflecting shared Protestant values.

"I regret exceedingly that the principal opposition to the school systems of the country, comes from a single religious body, a very large proportion of whom were not born on our soil; and who necessarily bring with them many opinions and habits entirely foreign to the spirit of our institutions." So wrote a minister in 1853 in a typical reaction to the newcomers in the *Pennsylvania School Journal*. In New York City (most famously), Pittsburgh, Louisville, and countless towns and cities with growing numbers of immigrants, Catholic leaders were labeled "whining sectarian bigots," the enemies of the common schools. A Thanksgiving sermon in Newark, New Jersey, warned of a vile "plot" to undermine America: "The poisonous stream arises in the seven hills of Rome." That the common school should "Americanize" the foreign born was abundantly clear to the Protestant majority. Another minister, who taught Latin at the University of Michigan, said the schools had a solemn duty to teach the basic subjects and only impart common Christian values. "We do not want Methodist, or Protestant common schools . . . we should as soon think of asking for a Methodist post-office, or an Episcopal court-house, or a Presbyterian road." Angry Catholics were wrong to believe that schools were sectarian, when according to Protestant reformers, classrooms simply promoted "that homogeneity of character so essential to safety in a democratic republic."

The whole point of common schools, after all, was to teach the same things to every white child of a neighborhood or area, in the same classroom, with the same teacher. Majority rule dictated that Christian (though not sectarian Protestant) values would dominate, as antebellum writers and public school activists insisted. Protestants quarreled over whether to use the Bible as a textbook, and practices varied in the many tens of thousands of schools across the nation. But to exclude "Christian" instruction was unthinkable to most citizens. Catholics did not want a morally neutral school, but one that reflected their own church teachings and version of the Bible, taught in catechetical style by priests and nuns.

Usually written by ministers or deeply religious men (and sometimes women), school textbooks frequently reflected the common faith of the Protestant majority. Public school history books thus praised the Protestant Reformation and condemned the followers of Rome. In addition to prayers and Bible reading, religious sentiments flowed from songbooks and hymnals, which often included adaptations of traditional Protestant hymns or popular tunes. Asa Fitz, a leading compiler of school hymnals and songbooks, provided pupils with words and music to sing the Lord's Prayer, among other religiously inspired materials. These, too, helped shape the character of the young. So said the reformers, with greater intensity as Catholic migration swelled.

School textbooks, which largely defined the curriculum and determined classroom instruction, abounded with lessons on morality and character development. Textbooks were part of a larger disciplinary process that tried to reinforce adult authority, morals, and literacy. The McGuffey Readers, whose first editions in the 1830s were fairly sectarian, soon moderated their religious tone but continued to teach about the kindness of Jesus and value of the Golden Rule, honesty, and fair play, in a context that emphasized the majority Protestant faith. They provided explicit moral lessons about the contrasting fates of memorable characters such as Hugh Idle and Mr. Toil as well as a taste of Edgar Allen Poe, William Shakespeare, and *Ivanhoe*. Joseph Ray's arithmetic series was not theistic but contained numerous story problems that assumed the superiority of private property and capitalism to any alternatives and taught a language of money and investment. The future farmer, artisan, factory worker, or housewife could learn the benefits of saving for old age, how to balance a budget, or even measurements for cooking. Similarly, history was a moral tale of the goodness of the Pilgrims, Founding Fathers, and pioneers, and of the treachery of loyalists, Indians, and Romanists (Catholics). Schoolbooks offered the young guidance in a world where traditional controls on human behavior seemed undermined by impersonal economic and social forces that made Americans rich but not necessarily contented or always morally upright.

Most school officials, whether local worthies or nationally prominent, shared common ideas on political economy, a constellation of views about capital and labor that informed, in unpredictable and uneven ways, the lives of children in classrooms. This found expression in the formal structure of the school day, which often began with prayer and was governed throughout by rules and regulations not always honored dutifully by children. Punctuality, like deportment and scholarship, was seen as a moral as well as a practical concern in the nineteenth century. The need to show up on time signaled one of the profound changes altering the workplace. Many lives were now governed by the ticking of the clock rather than customary rhythms of work, once determined by the seasons, the rising and setting of the sun, or the task in question. Time-consciousness became a ubiquitous concern of educators, whose school reports included statistics on daily attendance, enrollment, and punctuality. Many a forest fell to keep the tally.

Increasingly cheap and mass produced, clocks and watches became more common in the schools, especially in wealthier urban districts. Early public schools were often held in rented rooms, church halls and basements, or other buildings that resembled Protestant churches. Soon the ringing of the school bell and church bell became as familiar as the ticking and chime of the clock. "There ought to be a Timepiece, of some kind, in every schoolroom, so placed that all the children can see it," thought one typical reformer in 1839. "It relieves their bodies by its assurance that the time of relaxation is approaching; and it stimulates their minds by its admonition, that the sands of time are wasting." In modest country schools without a clock, teachers rang cowbells or struck iron triangles, announcing that play must stop and work begin.

Songbooks added their own meter to the school day. Singing likely broke the boredom of silent study and the endless string of recitations heard by the teacher and fellow students. The singing books also explicitly taught punctuality, perseverance, honesty, and other virtues undergirding the work ethic. The lyrics thus connected youth to seemingly timeless values, reminiscent of the homilies of Benjamin Franklin. Traditional values might provide moral ballast in a society governed by the rhythms of supply and demand and the sounds of whistles and bells. *The School Harp* (1855) characteristically drove home familiar messages about duty and responsibility, hardy values for the rising generation. Like many songs, "Haste to the School Room" was sung to a popular tune, "Wait for the Wagon," thus connecting past and present.

> Will you come to me, my schoolmates, to yonder schoolhouse free,
> Where our lessons are recited, O come along with me;
> Yes, every schoolday morning, happy faces bright,
> We'll hasten to the schoolroom, where we all take delight.
> Haste to the schoolroom, Haste to the schoolroom,
> Where we all take delight.
> Haste to the schoolroom, Haste to the schoolroom,
> Where we all take delight.

Other songs in *The School Harp*, with similar didactic intent, included "O, Yes, I Must Study My Arithmetic Now," "Seek the Schoolroom," and "The Temperance Song." "The Truant's Soliloquy" added a cautionary tale, a lament by a misguided lad whose "wayward heart" could only be mended by returning to school.

This was the great age of etiquette books, themselves expressions of bourgeois respectability. Use your handkerchief, not your sleeve, when blowing your nose, do not belch or worse in public, and practice common courtesies, the children were told, as adults combated the specter of cultural decline. Cockfights, fistfights, eye gouging, race riots, and common thievery and disorder seemed ascendant. Teachers and children alike were constantly warned to mind their manners and to live morally. Indeed, the annual reports of local school trustees, from Maine to Wisconsin, read like a sermon on republicanism, Christian ethics, and the duty to prepare youth for upright behavior. Manners and morals, hard work and diligence, honesty and punctuality were the only sure routes to success, the only safe pathways to national prosperity and personal happiness.

Every prominent textbook on political economy written for high school and college students underscored the importance of showing up to work, church, and school on time. Working hard was the only antidote to penury and public disgrace. As a contributor to the *Common School Journal* affirmed at midcentury, "laziness has been the parent of all the sins that have been committed since the morning of creation. Eve was in a lazy fit at the time Satan tempted her; if Adam had been kept busy, she would have been kept out of mischief, and we should all have been as innocent as young lambkins." Contemporaries debated whether labor was a curse, required to discipline humanity after the Fall. The alternatives to diligence, they said, were the almshouse, workhouse, and asylum, all less attractive than learning to live by the sweat of one's brow.

While "it is sometimes said that labor is a curse," wrote Horace Mann in 1843, "it is an inevitable condition of our well-being in this life," and "those who strive to avoid this curse, always incur a greater one." Like most educational leaders, Mann argued that people lacked equal talent and ambition. To anticipate the charge that he was a utopian or socialist, he emphatically stated that children would not leave school equal. Schools, however, should offer everyone a chance, and those who worked hard would do better than the lazy, even if the hard workers never won an academic medal. Mann believed that God had instituted labor as an act of love. In 1845, he said that, in a land blessed with abundant resources and opportunities, hard work ensured that America honored a "Divine Economy" in which "the privilege of primogeniture attaches to all; and every son and daughter of Adam are heirs to an infinite patrimony." Drawing upon the teachings of Adam Smith and classical economics, Mann linked divine and secular knowledge, concluding that more education made "a more industrious and productive people. Knowledge and abundance sustain to each other the relation of cause and effect. Intelligence is a primary ingredient in the Wealth of Nations."

The rising generation could only gain from long evenings of study. Self-improvement was an inevitable outcome, with moral, intellectual, and material benefits. Primers on how to teach multiplied during these years, as numerous writers offered new approaches to pedagogy. The followers of Johann Pestalozzi, a European romantic, published solemn treatises on the virtues of "object teaching," contending that little children in particular should not read as much as learn from solid, real objects and contact with the natural world, to lay the basis for higher-order thinking later. Many writers complained loudly about the dull, monotonous character of the typical school, based on sing-song drill and heroic feats of memorization and recitation. Despite recurrent complaints, pupils still memorized the rules of grammar, the names of mountain ranges, the capitals of distant nations, the facts, names, and dates of important military battles, and lists of words ordinary people almost never used. At the end of grammar school, said officials in Cincinnati in the 1840s, pupils should be able to spell not only *refugee* and *drawl* but also *thanatopsis, orgies,* and *ennui.* In Chicago, *effluvia, inimical,* and *trisyllable* helped build a good vocabulary. Throughout the nation, educational periodicals were filled with points and counterpoints on the alleged evils of "emulation," the desire to excel by surpassing others. Those who reached the top of the class, said the naysayers, were often smug and without regard for the hurt feelings of the less talented. However, in practice, as in the spelling bee, only one scholar was called the best. And study and recitation were the only sure way to learn, for they were the alpha and omega of the classroom.

Hiram Orcutt offered the usual sober advice on how to best shape character and promote a good school in *Hints to Common School Teachers, Parents, and Pupils; Or, Gleanings from School-Life Experience,* published in Vermont in 1859. Typical for his generation, the author explained that of all the traits needed in a teacher—common sense, love of children, and mastery of subject matter—having a "moral and Christian character" was indispensable. "Every arrangement in the school should be systematic," he asserted. "There should be a time for everything, and everything in its time; a time to open the school, which should never vary; a definite time for every school exercise; a time for study and a time for recess; a time to whisper and a time to keep silent." Only quacks and theorists, he said, thought moral suasion "*alone* will govern schools." Like most educators, Orcutt assumed that corporal punishments to fit the crime were permissible as a last resort. Barbaric practices occasionally found in some schools were indefensible: "Holding weights in extending arms, 'sitting upon nothing,' bending forward with the arm extended to the floor, all blows on or about the head with stick or ferule, and all violent shaking of children by the shoulders, endangering their health and life, are entirely improper." As for study, Orcutt felt that the Bible was unparalleled for teaching moral truths, and the various school subjects all "abound in moral sentiments. Indeed, there is a moral in everything; in every lesson recited, in every school-exercise, in every action, thought, and feeling of school-life."

Antebellum reformers agreed that the public schools stood as the antidote to crime, the defense of republicanism, and a bulwark against atheism, socialism, and alien ideologies that threatened private property and public morals. Self-discipline and moral character mattered more than anything else. Schools provided republican alternatives to the repressive social controls that regulated and governed the masses in despotic lands. Hard work was among the chief virtues taught in common schools, and despite many complaints about memorization and recitation, about too much homework and too many rules and restrictions, the specter of anarchy or irreligion, as Orcutt noted, was the alternative. "Study and recitation are the principal means by which the desirable results of education are secured. These constitute the business of the schoolroom."

After the Civil War, criticisms of teachers would intensify. The curriculum would seem outmoded and out of touch with industrial culture, and a new generation of educators would try to redefine the aims and purposes of public education. Anticipating debates that would revive in every generation, Orcutt warned about soft pedagogical approaches that took away the incentive for children to study and work hard. While countless educators condemned the parrot-like recitations heard in school, year after year the practices continued. To most educators, the mind was a muscle strengthened through use, like the strong arms of workers laboring in fields and factories. "How many lessons would be learned in any school if no recitation were required?" Orcutt asked in his book. "How much knowledge or discipline would be gained by hard study, if the pupils understood beforehand that the hour for recitation would be occupied by the teacher in lecturing or asking questions?"

By the 1850s, northern Whigs, Republicans, and other activist citizens had turned to the common school in their search for a positive force in a nation that had undergone rapid social, economic, and political change. White children might attend school for only four or five months a year and a few years of their life, but the majority did so, and reformers predicted even longer school terms and more consolidation and graded classrooms in the coming years. Rallying behind the call of free men, free labor, and free schools, many educators later concluded that the Civil War could have been prevented if the South had also built common schools. They would have taught the young that theirs was a common national destiny. Throughout the antebellum South, however, the idea of free schools retained its traditional association with the children of the poor. The only notable exception, as historian Joseph W. Newman has written, was in a handful of southern port cities, including New Orleans, Charleston, Mobile, and Savannah. There a concentration of New Englanders, often Unionist Whigs, constructed a fledgling system of public schools for whites only in the decades preceding secession.

More typically, Southern states meagerly attended to the education of their poorest white citizens and warned against cultural imposition from the North. As James Henry Hammond, the governor of South Carolina, wrote in 1843, despite some provision for the education of poor whites, "the paupers, for whose children it is intended, but slightly appreciate the advantages of education; their pride revolts at the idea of sending their children to school as *'poor scholars';* and besides, they need them at home to work. These sentiments and wants can, in the main, be only countervailed by force." And no one proposed forcing anyone to go to school, something even Northerners opposed, as evidenced by poorly enforced compulsory education laws late in the century.

To Southerners, the specter of blacks learning to read and write raised terrifying thoughts about the notion of human equality, and it united whites of all social classes into a deadly defense of slavery. In the 1840s and 1850s, champions of free public schools for white children existed in the South, especially in North Carolina and Virginia. But the southern sparseness of settlement, fear of government intrusion in existing social arrangements, and the hostility of the planter class to the education either of poor whites or black slaves meant that common schools were largely a Yankee ideal. In a culture dedicated to preserving both a racial and social hierarchy, the notion of common schools for everyone in the South, even in theory, was repugnant. Southern leaders smirked at the idea that free schools, North or South, would change the hard realities of life. Social class and racial differences, they insisted, would always

CHAPTER TWO

Postbellum America and the Common School

America's preoccupation with public education fascinated foreign visitors in the late nineteenth century. During a two-month tour in the 1870s, R. W. Dale, an Englishman, visited several schools and engaged in numerous conversations with educators. His *Impressions of America* (1878) included a description of "the common school" as "one of the most characteristic of American institutions." Dale had arrived during the depths of a severe economic depression and in the immediate aftermath of the Civil War. Scandals in Washington, D.C., unemployment, labor riots, communist agitation, and the struggle to build common schools for the freedmen all stirred passionate debates. With the northern victory, Yankee assumptions about the salutary role of public education were strengthened and even revitalized.

Like many European visitors, Dale tried to unravel an apparent contradiction: America's professed love of freedom from government strictures and general willingness to fund public schools. Citizens frequently attacked centralized authority and government intrusion, exemplified by the lack of an established church or strong federal presence in everyday life. The Founding Fathers had largely relegated education to the states, and the U.S. Bureau of Education (founded in 1867) lacked the policy-setting authority common in European ministries of education. Yet public schools had spread to many corners of the land. Whether one traveled through rural Vermont or Minnesota or towns and cities in New England or the Old Northwest, schools were a familiar part of neighborhood and community life. In the 1890s, another visitor from England, one of Her Majesty's Inspectors of Schools, also commented on the contrast between the Old World and the New. He found the concept of local control unique but the basis of the American educational system. England's great public schools, he said, were bastions of aristocratic privilege, while America's characteristic secondary school—the free high school—seemed fairly accessible to any ambitious grammar school graduate who could delay entering the work force.

The millennial expectations of Horace Mann's generation had somehow retained their salience as America expanded from the Atlantic to the Pacific, became a more industrial nation, and even suffered the trauma of civil war. Despite their promise, schools had obviously not been an antidote for social disorder, radical agitation, or poverty, yet they remained central to mainstream thinking about cultural cohesion and social improvement. The importance of literacy, moral training, and education for citizenship seemed clear, as exemplified by the struggle to educate ex-slaves. "Common Schools: The Hope of Our Country" read the pithy epigraph to an 1872 school report in an Indiana town. The fate of the republic still rested in the people's hands, said the editors of *The Common School* in Grafton, North Dakota, in the early 1890s. Only a broad diffusion of knowledge, available in free schools, they concluded, could counter the forces of anarchy and despotism: "To Build High Make the Foundation Broad."

Historians have traditionally regarded the final three decades of the nineteenth century as an interlude in the grand procession of school reform, less significant than the eras personified by Horace Mann or John Dewey. But the postbellum decades were fascinating in their own right and central to the course of common school development and unfolding reform movements of long-range importance. Public schools remained vital to the great human drama of American history. The nation had survived a bloody civil war, and cities, industry, and immigration helped transform some aspects of life beyond recognition. It was inconceivable, many citizens thought, that schools would not play some role in addressing the vital questions of the day, from the rising presence of Catholics to concerns about training for industrial employment to the reintegration of the rebel South into the Union.

The postbellum decades thus contributed to the making of the modern public school system. The schools were basic to nation building, cultural and geographical integration, and socialization of the young to the dominant values of the age. Like their predecessors in the antebellum period, educational leaders and a host of reformers frequently debated the place of schools in a changing society. Without question, schools remained central to public discourse about how to build a stable but also better society. In the cities, which remained the center of economic and social change, school officials dismissed ongoing Catholic complaints about the Protestant values undergirding the system and solidified their political authority. By the 1890s they also pressed for organizational reforms that reflected a more hierarchical industrial world. The cities remained the great hope of most educational leaders, who labored to build a uniform, well-funded system. Along the way they often created careers for themselves within an expanding system. In the countryside, where the majority of families and children lived, citizens were bombarded with ideas for educational improvement that originated in the city. And schools were also integral to the explosive events surrounding southern Reconstruction. The decades after the Civil War were no mere interlude.

Late nineteenth-century educators were proud of the heritage of the common school. They admired Horace Mann's generation and watched with pride as free public schools spread across the nation. Like other citizens, they were nevertheless anxious about the future and the specter of change. Locally controlled, schools were open to all sorts of political influence, from the ward-heeling politician in the city to the farmer in the countryside who wanted to keep taxes low and the curriculum bare. Whether one accepted Charles Darwin's theories of evolution, natural selection, and fight-to-the-death competition, many citizens agreed that the common school, born in a more rural and agrarian past, would have to adapt to prosper in a modern age.

In 1869, Albert N. Raub, the superintendent of the Lock Haven, Pennsylvania, schools, echoed the concerns of many citizens worried about the dizzying pace of social change. In *Plain Educational Talks with Teachers and Parents,* he underscored the role of education in a republic, the centrality of moral training, and the need to transcend dry-as-dust teaching methods. Like earlier commentators, Raub recognized the ambiguous influences of economic and technological change. Americans enjoyed the fruits of technology, but the machine age continually undermined tradition and familiar ways of life. Raub wrote, "Everywhere the click of the hammer and the sharp, shrill scream of the whistle, or the buzz and whirr of the busy spindle resound in our ears." Throughout the Western world, the Industrial Revolution had unleashed social forces that reshaped everything in their path. Americans from all walks of life were fascinated by inventions. The memory of the enterprising Ben Franklin was alive in the industrial age, as citizens flocked to industrial expositions to see the latest labor-saving marvels, whether in Philadelphia or Birmingham. Not especially known as philosophers or social theorists, Americans were a practical-minded people, who tinkered rather than speculated. By 1860, they had already taken out twenty-seven thousand patents, and that number would grow to a million forty years later, though increasingly under corporate sponsorship.

The first great corporations were the railroads, central to nation building and market expansion. Federal land grants, extensive private investment, and ties to emerging corporate interests in oil, coal, and other extractive industries made the railroads powerful. Cheap federal land and the completion of the transcontinental railroad in 1869 opened the West to a massive migration of white settlers, killing or displacing thousands of native peoples. Railroads helped integrate the national economy. They transported Texas cattle to the Kansas City stockyards, sent a cornucopia of farm goods to cities such as Chicago for processing and distribution, and shipped countless raw materials and finished products—Alabama cotton and Pittsburgh steel, Dakota wheat and Carolina pines—to expanding domestic and international markets. Through the railroads, a modern economy was born.

Virtually every industrial monopoly associated with modern economies, including coal, oil, gas, steel, the telephone, electricity, and food processing and distribution, came into existence after the Civil War. Pools, trusts, and other legal and extralegal strategies ensured monopoly control. Rockefeller, Westinghouse, Edison, Vanderbilt, and Carnegie all became household names, revered or despised for their fabulous wealth and power. The face of working America also changed dramatically. The manufacturing workforce quadrupled between 1860 and 1900, when a quarter of all workers labored in factories, mostly in unskilled jobs. Change came quickly and furiously. Writing from the most industrialized state, the editor of the *Pennsylvania School Journal* observed in 1890 that "whole forests are swept away as by magic, till our mountains even are becoming treeless and our streams fishless." Major coal deposits in the Keystone State had literally helped stoke the Industrial Revolution, and Pittsburgh became the great symbol of national economic strength. In different parts of America, mining towns came and went, coal mines were dug and soon abandoned, exhausted soils forsaken for the next forty acres. It was, said the editor, a "wild race for riches."

Postwar industrial expansion concentrated in the North and followed an upward economic curve, but with devastating pendular swings. The worst depression the nation had seen hit with savage force between 1873 and 1877, a recession followed between 1884 and 1886, and another depression—the most serious before the 1930s—struck a severe blow between 1893 and 1897. All were tied to similar economic downturns in Western Europe, reflecting more integrated international markets. In 1900 the South produced only a small fraction of the nation's industrial goods. But it too had increasingly industrialized, though it remained heavily rural and agricultural and America's poorest region. However uneven, industrial growth in the postbellum years was spectacular. In 1870, the U.S. trailed behind the great industrial titans of Europe: Great Britain, Germany, and France. Within a generation its industrial output exceeded theirs combined.

America's industrial development had begun modestly in rural areas in the early nineteenth century, along New England rivers and streams. Early textile mills and factories often depended on the labor of women and children fresh from the farms. In much of Western Europe, the enclosure of common lands and farm consolidation forced millions of people from the countryside, turning peasants into an urban industrial work force. But America was land rich. After the Civil War, as plows cut through Midwestern prairies and broke sod on the Great Plains, industry and agriculture expanded as population spread to the Pacific. The number of farmers increased until the early twentieth century, though the percentage of agricultural laborers declined from 53 percent to 42 percent between 1870 and 1890.

Citizens often worried about the rise of the city, increasingly the home to most industry and to rising numbers of immigrants. One leading educator, A. E. Winship, spoke before the Vermont Teachers Association in 1894, a year of intense labor conflict in the cities. Winship opened his talk by explaining that the world had been "born in the country but humanized in the city." He claimed that "both the fears of Christianity and the hope of humanity are in the large cities," where commerce and industry often flourished. Centers of concentrated wealth and cultural opportunities, they were also home to vice and crime and political machines such as Tammany, a powerful Democratic organization in New York. "The mission of the coming statesman, philosopher, philanthropist, and churchman is to winnow the vices of the city from its virtues, to clarify its official life, purify its municipal suffrage, harness the commercial, industrial, and social energy of the city to the car of human progress." Even in largely rural Vermont, eyes were drawn to the city.

Traditionally, urban areas were centers of commerce, shipping, and government administration. But the city's industrial cast soon became its most visible characteristic. By the 1880s, for example, 60 percent of Ohio's workforce was in manufacturing, concentrated in towns and cities. Historian Walter Licht has explained that there as elsewhere the mix of jobs, market niches, and other factors made industrial development uneven. Late in the century, anthracite coal dominated northeastern Pennsylvania, while textile mills shaped the southern Piedmont. New York, Chicago, and various major cities had several leading industries but overall were quite diversified. Railroads, postal delivery, the telegraph, and later the telephone connected urban areas to an intricate web of markets, with their unpredictable rhythm of bust and boom. Citizens everywhere worried about the social consequences of urban growth: the separation of home from work, the isolation of immigrants in distinct neighborhoods, the widening gap between rich and poor. By 1900, cities produced about 90 percent of all manufactured goods, resulting in a higher standard of living but also rising fears of class conflict.

Social change was thus experienced differently in various times and places. Technological innovations, mechanization, urban growth, immigration, market conditions, and government policy interacted to transform the familiar outlines of a more rural, agrarian nation. Within a few decades, America had become heavily industrial, its manufacturing workforce primarily immigrant and urban. Eleven million newcomers arrived between 1870 and 1900. European immigrants still migrated to rural areas and small towns, such as Scandinavians and Germans to Minnesota and Wisconsin and Czechs to Texas. But northern industrial cities became home to millions of people looking for work. Low wage and nonunion, the South attracted relatively few newcomers.

By 1878, B. A. Hinsdale, a prominent northern educator who was president of Hiram College in Ohio, repeated what was on everyone's mind: "Society is every day becoming more complex; the problems of life are daily becoming more difficult," especially in the teeming industrial cities. Social war seemed imminent. During the depression of the 1870s, a national railroad strike prompted the use of federal troops to restore order. Over ten thousand strikes, lockouts, and other work stoppages, usually over wages and working conditions, occurred in the 1880s. The 1886 Haymarket Square riot in Chicago, in which several policemen were killed by a bomb thrown by unknown assailants at a labor demonstration, brought the bogeyman of anarchism to life. Despite the lack of any evidence that they were guilty, eight anarchists were tried in court and convicted. Four were hung, one committed suicide, and the other three were imprisoned. In 1894, a half-million railroad workers struck against the Pullman Company, leading to more government repression of labor activists. To political economists, depressions and panics were a natural part of the capitalist business cycle. Workers forced to depend on child labor for up to 40 percent of family income thought greed, government corruption, and unfair labor practices better explained their distress. Old republican assumptions about the dignity of work, a fair wage for honest labor, and the dream of economic independence for the worker thus collided with new realities. Most jobs were unskilled and dead end, worker turnover was very high, and families lacked security, though union leaders and radical activists pressed for justice for those who labored in fields, factories, and mines.

That so many industrial workers were foreign born posed a unique set of problems for native-born Protestants. Many educators, school officials, and citizens, however, were confident that the common school would absorb and assimilate the children of the newcomers. In *The Free School System of the United States* (1875), Francis Adams claimed that the public school "draws children from all nations together, and marks them with the impress of [American] nationality." Similarly, the *Educational Weekly* in Indianapolis assumed in 1883 that "the obliteration of caste and the extinction of all class distinctions are in the hands of the common school." Even an anti-Catholic minister on the West Coast whose prose reeked of ethnocentric bigotry still argued in 1890 that nothing could stop the process of assimilation. "Children go into" the schools, he said, "English, Scottish, Irish, German, Danish, Norwegian, Italian, French,—and all come out American!" A Chicagoan typically added that social cohesion would result once the Old and New World met at school.

Beneath such optimism, dark fears lingered. James A. Garfield, a prominent

Ohio Republican congressman in the 1860s and later a martyred president, fervently championed public education and even helped create the U.S. Bureau of Education. Like many Republicans, he believed educating immigrants was imperative: "We must pour upon them all the light of the public schools. We must make them intelligent, industrious, patriotic citizens, or they will drag us down to their level." While xenophobia intensified during economic downturns and labor disturbances, educators and social commentators worried about the fragility of the republic. Like anxious citizens earlier, they often imagined a simpler, better time when America was more homogeneous and respected honesty, hard work, and personal responsibility. In 1887, an educator from La Crosse, a small town on the Mississippi, wrote in the *Wisconsin Journal of Education* that America, like ancient Rome, might fall as a "vast horde" of newcomers arrived, modern-day barbarians who were "the off-scourings of Europe," the alumni of "her alms-houses and prisons."

State and local reports sent to the U.S. commissioner of education in the postbellum era revealed widespread nervousness. It was bad enough that many thousands of Irish, German, and other European Catholics were arriving on the East Coast, but Asian immigration to the West Coast, particularly Chinese immigration, also frightened the native born. John Eaton Jr., the commissioner during Reconstruction and a fervent Republican, had long supported public education. Regarding the Chinese, however, he noted in 1872 that reports from California and other western states indicated that "their industry is wanted, but in many respects their presence is abhorred." Eaton cited a Nevada law requiring that "negroes, Mongolians, and Indians shall not be admitted into the public schools," though local districts could establish segregated ones. Nevada's superintendent of public instruction said at a National Education Association meeting that certain groups should not study the common curriculum: "A knowledge of English literature, architecture, or jurisprudence could serve a Chinaman little purpose, while by his knowledge of gardening, laundry work, or cooking he derives his sustenance."

"The prejudice against the race is so strong," said a woman correspondent from California in 1876, that the "Chinese are not permitted a place in the public schools, with only a rare exception, here and there, in some lonely mountain district; and school directors, when petitioned to provide in some way for the education of Chinese children, pass the subject by, although the Chinese pay their full proportion of the taxes." In San Francisco in the 1860s and 1870s, Chinese American children were often excluded from public schools, and Japanese children later faced exclusion and severe discrimination as immigration increased their numbers. Assimilation was not a universal policy, since some marginalized groups were segregated into often inferior school facilities or were excluded entirely. The Chinese Exclusion Act of 1882, which ultimately became a national embarrassment, reflected popular attitudes. In 1885 the California Supreme Court ruled in favor of the legal right of Chinese children to receive an education but did not mandate integrated schools.

For all the fears about Asian peoples, for the native-born American "immigrant" usually conjured up the image of Catholic newcomers arriving from Europe, generally from Ireland, a German state, or Austria-Hungary, and settling in northern cities. Their labor enriched the nation but hardly softened prejudice against them. Catholic immigrants had already transformed the ethnic and political complexion of many towns and cities on the East Coast, and Catholics horrified many citizens by building more parochial schools and reviving demands for a share of public monies for them. It takes some imagination, given the collapse of most overt anti-Catholicism today, to recall its virulence in the nineteenth century. Hostility ranged from outright mockery of the Catholic religion from many respectable middle- and upper-class Protestant pulpits, to lurid novels about priests and nuns, to the resurgence of nativist political movements after the Civil War. References to "Romanists" abounded in mainstream periodicals, newspapers, and political broadsides, as did caricatures of the Irish. In 1889 and 1890 the Reverend Richard Harcourt lectured on the Catholic menace to overflow crowds in San Francisco. His book, *Conspiracy: The American Public Schools* (1890), recounted the grand history of common schools, tracing their origins to the Pilgrims and outlining recurring plots by the Vatican against them. He mocked everything from praying with rosaries to parochial school pedagogy and called Catholicism "A MENACE TO REPUBLICANISM." Thomas Nast, the celebrated political cartoonist, prepared the volume's illustrations. One depicted the year 2000, when Irish apes would run the country.

Vigilance had become second nature to some leading Republicans. Anti-Catholicism was granted a new lease on life, partly as a reaction to the bolder, more confident character of some Catholic leaders after the 1860s. Some outspoken bishops and priests demanded more parish schools, the division of the school fund, and the end to mandatory Bible reading and removal of offensive textbooks from the public system. This bore educational fruit but made more than a few enemies. In a celebrated legal decision, Cincinnati lost a prolonged battle to retain Bible reading in its schools. In the 1870s, school officials in Poughkeepsie, New York, faced with severe overcrowding and the imminent closure of parochial schools that mostly served the poor, began a unique experiment. They rented the Catholic schools for a nominal fee, provided for their upkeep, and cooperated with church leaders to hire well-qualified Catholics to teach in them. This continued until the late 1890s, horrifying those who called it a compromise with the Devil. Nativist temperatures also boiled as Catholic immigrants grew more powerful within the Democratic Party. Besides opposing temperance laws and other intrusions on personal liberty, northern Democrats often demanded fairer treatment of Catholic schoolchildren, most of whom remained enrolled in the public, not parochial, system.

Nativism accelerated in the New Mexico territory and nearby areas populated by Mexican Americans, who were often Catholic. One writer complained that Jesuits diverted tax monies to their own sectarian institutions, where helpless school children bowed before "clerical robes." Histrionics aside, schools in which the Spanish language prevailed were often recognized as public schools until the 1890s. Throughout California, the Southwest, and other conquered territories, many Mexican Americans nevertheless faced considerable discrimination due to their religion, poverty, and skin color as Anglo-American migration to these territories intensified after the Civil War. Mexican Americans in urban areas frequently lived in segregated barrios with meager educational provision. In El Paso, Texas, public schools opened in the early 1880s but only admitted children who knew English, forcing those speaking Spanish to a Mexican Preparatory School. Students often mastered English and the basics but then ended up in lower-class jobs. Once public school systems became better developed in California and the Southwest, poorly funded, segregated schools were common. While poverty, cultural alienation, and ethnic and religious discrimination kept many from attending, the children of Spanish-speaking citizens and alien residents in Tucson and other communities sometimes attended school in impressive numbers, as circumstances allowed, to learn English and some elementary subjects. Many parents also turned to parochial schools, which promoted literacy and traditional Catholic doctrines.

The growth of Catholic schools in different parts of the country was uneven but angered the defenders of public education. Since the antebellum period, pastoral letters had warned Catholics about the dangers of secular, godless education—as represented by the public schools—and the need for catechetical instruction. Parish schools opened in some towns and cities, but poverty and immigrant support for common schools dampened their progress. At the Third Plenary Council of Baltimore (1884), however, American bishops urged local parishes to build more parochial schools, which was made easier after the war as immigration accelerated. Hoping to preserve their language, culture, and religion, German Catholics were especially prominent in building parish schools, while the Irish, like the Italians later, often invested in beautiful churches but were less interested in constructing schools. Nativists did not usually notice these distinctions.

Anti-Catholicism helped revive the fortunes of the Republican Party. By the mid-1870s, the nation tired of Reconstruction, Democrats grew more powerful, and the taint of corruption surrounding the administration of Ulysses S. Grant overshadowed his victories on the battlefield. In 1875 Grant sent a bill to Congress forbidding the use of public monies for religious schools. While the bill did not pass, its basic provisions later became law in nearly thirty states, often as amendments to state constitutions. In an earlier gubernatorial race in Ohio, Grant's successor, Rutherford B. Hayes, called Democrats the shills of Rome. In such poisoned soil, nativism sprouted in different parts of the nation in the 1880s and 1890s. Republicans in Illinois and Wisconsin in 1889 endorsed state regulation of private education that required English as the language of instruction, which mobilized German-American Lutherans, Catholics, and the Democratic Party to help squash the laws and the enemy at the polls. Anti-Catholicism waxed and waned but revived as the war with Spain in 1898 reignited old prejudices. Another presidential hopeful from Ohio, William McKinley, rode to power in part on the broad coattails of ethnic and religious prejudice.

Even southern educators, in a region that had relatively few immigrants and was often preoccupied with suppressing the freedmen, cast rhetorical stones at the newcomers. Southern newspapers reported on northern industrial strife and the spread of Catholicism in the North. In 1888, the Reverend John F. Crowell, president of Trinity College (later Duke University), spoke at the dedication of a new graded school in Winston, North Carolina, far from the industrial North. "The immigrant problem," he warned, "is a big one and the biggest end of it falls upon the public schools." Whether of Polish, Italian, or English descent, he said, all children belonged in the common school. Otherwise they might end up in "that last and most hopeless institution . . . the penitentiary." The following year, the editor of a journal called *The Teacher at Work,* published in Huntsville, Alabama, did not mince his words: "For the peace and order of society, and the safety of our American institutions, one of two things must be done, and that speedily: either stop the tide of alien immigration, or provide schools where they can be educated up to our standard of thinking."

The city—teeming with immigrants, industry, and untold wealth and poverty—captivated the imagination of countless educators, moralists, and politicians in the last three decades of the century. The city had helped make America the world's richest industrial nation. But many citizens perceived it as a site of political corruption, declining public morals, and assaults on the tried and true ways of an older America. As A. E. Winship had told his audience in Vermont, the city was nevertheless filled with potential. When the nation was founded, the Puritans wanted America to become a "city on a hill." For a new generation of school reformers, the burgeoning city became a new promised land, home to new ideas about how to organize, administer, and strengthen a system of public education during an era of immense social change.

"It is frequently remarked by students of political history that some of the greatest defects of our form of government are developed in connection with municipal administration," claimed U.S. commissioner of education John Eaton in 1885. "Fortunately, in spite of this fact, some of the best school work in our country is found in the cities." Cities were the laboratories for new educational ideas such as graded classrooms, free high schools, and professionalized school administration. For women, until marriage intervened, there were often jobs galore as low-paid elementary teachers. For men, the ladders of opportunity widened for the exceptional few and could even lead to appointment as superintendent.

Eaton did better than most. Born in Sutton, New Hampshire, in 1829, Eaton was reared on a farm and educated at the district school and academy, graduating from Dartmouth College in 1854. After two years as a principal in Cleveland, he became superintendent of Toledo's public schools, where he learned to gather statistics, a skill that proved useful in Washington. He entered Andover Theological Seminary in 1859 and was ordained, then served as a Union army chaplain during the war and worked in the early stages of Reconstruction in the South before becoming U.S. commissioner in 1870. Few educators who became famous after the Civil War did not have an association, sometimes long lasting, with the city. Most prominent educators were, like Eaton, male Republicans who had risen through the urban ranks and pledged allegiance to the common school.

The city offered more opportunities than the countryside for professional educators, but it always occupied an ambiguous place in a nation that extolled rural simplicity and farm life. Home to immigrants, Catholics, and industry, cities stood in contrast to an imagined and more agreeable past when community bonded people in harmony and prosperity. In the late 1860s, Horace Greeley feared people would rush to the city to enjoy indoor plumbing, "baker's bread, gas, the theatre, and the streetcars," forgetting the God-given beauties of the countryside: "Long valleys with independence and health whispering among the oaks and pines speak of a more vigorous race." The Reverend Josiah Strong spoke for many native Protestants when in 1885 he called cities a "serious menace to our civilization." Even the more fair-minded British visitor, James Bryce, wrote a few years later that "there is no denying that the government of cities is the one conspicuous failure of the United States."

While the popular stereotype of urban politics was the venal, cigar-smoking, corpulent Tammany Democrat, Eaton defended the men even on the big-city school boards as usually honest, civic-minded public servants. Indeed, "some of the most eminent educators of the land or world have been engaged as superintendent of instruction in the cities." William T. Harris, for example, had helped make the St. Louis school system a pedagogical showplace during his tenure as superintendent between 1868 and 1880. The imposing list of educational luminaries also included the aging John D. Philbrick, long-time teacher and superintendent in Boston, who pioneered the construction of graded classrooms in a local school in the late 1840s. While they had their share of corruption and partisan politics, city schools attracted distinguished leaders with a penchant for innovation and creativity.

In 1885, Philbrick helped publicize their broad achievements and potential in a major report on the urban schools. Like other educators, he emphasized that cities, factories, and immigration had fundamentally changed the contours of American life. Cities could not build schools fast enough for the swelling numbers of children. Yet the city seemed to Philbrick a place of hope and innovation. Moreover, the Bostons and Chicagos of the world, he maintained, shaped "the general welfare . . . beyond the numbers of their population," for they were "the centers of wealth, culture, science, business enterprise, and social and political influence. The role of cities is, no doubt, to become in the future far more important, relatively, than it is now." Some self-seeking people—the "patientless doctors" or "clientless lawyers"—occasionally used their election to the local school board as a stepping stone to something more powerful and lucrative. Like Eaton, however, Philbrick insisted that, overall, it was honest men with good intentions who served on school boards, which increasingly required the expertise of superintendents to address complex educational issues.

Educational leaders who sought enhanced authority lamented the power of laypeople in the schools. School governance everywhere rested upon local control. The governing boards were variously called school boards, school trustees, commissioners, visitors, or directors. Whatever their name, a contributor to *Educational Review* in 1897 noted that in some urban areas a bewildering array of them were in charge. At one extreme, Pittsburgh had a central board of education of thirty-seven members elected to office from thirty-seven local school boards. Typically, towns and cities had a single, fairly large school board whose members were popularly elected and represented a particular ward. Cincinnati had an elected, ward-based, central board with thirty members. In most communities, candidates ran on political tickets and served a two- or three-year term, guaranteeing high turnover. Everywhere, those elected had the ultimate authority in hiring teachers, adopting textbooks, and awarding construction contracts.

By the 1890s, some cities began to reduce the size of the school board, change elections from ward based to at large, and even allow the mayor or city council to appoint its members, all in the name of reform and presumably to remove "politics" from educational decision making. As historian David B. Tyack has affirmed, events would demonstrate the futility of trying to separate education and politics, but the process of centralizing authority and enhancing expertise seemed irresistible to many elite reformers. Denver had a board with only six members, elected at large. In Kansas City and Cleveland, the local superintendent increasingly gained more decision-making authority. Typically, however, the laypeople on the board (mostly men, even after women gained the right to serve in some states) had the legal authority to make most important decisions. Critics then and later said that many members were far below the angels: they simply lined their own pockets, curried favor with voters through shady business deals, and cared little about the quality of education in the schools. Some people surely lacked any notion of disinterested public service and sought only a path to higher office. But this negative portrait is not the final word.

School board members and superintendents alike should be viewed in their historical context. Superintendents with an eye on more professional power ultimately favored every mechanism possible to centralize authority, much like their counterparts in commerce and industry. Philbrick of Boston claimed that "in the matter of administration the tendency is towards a greater centralization and permanency of authority. . . . No doubt excessive decentralization of administration has been one of the chief obstacles to improvement in every department of our free school system." Reflecting this perspective, the *New England Journal of Education* in 1881 complained that in many urban areas "the school-board has been captured by the politicians, who have used the schools to nurse fat jobs, sprout municipal fathers, and fill the school-rooms with incompetent favorites of the ward trustees. This petty favoritism is still the curse of the village and country schools everywhere, and like a poisonous malaria, inflicts the whole system of education with a general debility to effective work."

Although superintendents would consistently claim that their expertise allowed them to be apolitical—concerned only with the welfare of children—they were often intensely political, favoring centralized authority and hierarchical structures similar to those of large-scale industry. As many scholars have discovered, a growing alliance of elite reformers by the 1880s and 1890s demanded greater centralization and smaller school boards, the elimination of ward representation, and the empowerment of superintendents. By the turn of the century, magazines and newspapers could feature a photo of an urban superintendent such as William Maxwell of New York City decked out in a three-piece suit with gold watch and chain, a veritable captain of erudition.

In an age of political scandal—of Credit Mobilier, Boss Tweed, and the abandonment of Reconstruction by the Republican Party in the 1870s—some elite citizens lost faith in democracy and universal male suffrage and regularly implicated cities in the decline of the republic. Middle- and upper-class native-born citizens often scorned mass politics generally and the urban immigrant wing of the Democratic Party specifically. They pointed to the ills of democracy and endorsed civil service reform, restrictions on suffrage, and "good government," meaning deference to the well born and well educated. School superintendents seeking greater authority embraced such sentiments. Why, they asked, should dozens of laypeople without special competence in education have such influence? After all, superintendents and their subordinates actually managed the schools, and the local attorney, businessman, or skilled worker from Ward Twelve elected to the school board worried too often about parochial issues rooted in neighborhood, not citywide, concerns.

Urban school boards in postbellum America had enormous, decisive power in hiring teachers, awarding contracts for buildings and supplies, and overall policy making. Some reformers said that city systems were becoming too complicated for laypeople alone to administer and govern. Cities required greater reliance upon experts and managers. Thus a member of the school committee of Portland, Maine, reported in 1891 that cities faced more complex social problems than country schools, leading educators to embrace innovations such as better grading, classification, and curriculum design. Superintendents increasingly argued that only experts, not laypeople on school boards, could keep apprised of the latest pedagogical ideas through wide reading, professional correspondence, and association with other urban leaders. Others called for small school boards, elected at large, to improve the caliber of board membership.

What was happening to the administration and governance of urban schools reflected larger changes in municipal government. Elected officials everywhere faced continual pressure to improve and expand public services. Engineers, scientists, and other experts were essential to building and maintaining the urban infrastructure, one which often compared favorably with that of European cities. Taxpayers often grumbled about the expense but usually insisted upon the extension of sewers, paved roads, street lighting, better bridges, safe drinking water, parks and playgrounds, and more schools for neighborhood children, with education taking the lion's share of local budgets. Thus the enhanced power of highly paid school superintendents occurred within a larger urban context, in which the Industrial Revolution had made the division of labor, hierarchy, and centralization seem natural and most efficient.

The sheer growth of the population through internal migration and foreign immigration made the building of enough schools a serious problem in many cities. America still teemed with children, sending the costs of education upward. Just over half of the population was under the age of nineteen in 1850, and in 1900 the figure stood at 46 percent. Declining fertility among middle-class, native-born white women since around 1800 was more than offset by a burgeoning native working-class and immigrant population after the Civil War. As workers migrated from rural areas to the city, from farm to factory, many people wondered how best to prepare the young for a world in which smokestacks were now as familiar as the church on the village green. In the 1880s, thousands of children in Chicago, New York, and Philadelphia could not find a place in the schools. The policy was first come, first served. Children absent too often lost their seat to the next person on the waiting list. Those in attendance in many big cities often faced overcrowded classrooms and shortened sessions.

Despite such dire problems, cities still led the way in educational innovation, continuing the pattern begun before the Civil War. The construction of the first free high schools in the 1820s, the slow addition of age-graded classrooms, the hiring of women as elementary teachers, and the appointment of superintendents to supervise and administer the system all first arose in northern towns and cities. After 1865 these reforms were extended to a growing network of urban areas and even touted as the great hope for rural schools across the nation. A common course of study and perfect age grading were never fully achieved, and educators faced constant pressure to construct more classrooms and buildings while holding the line on spending. Teachers often discovered that the children pouring into the classroom were a heterogeneous lot, not all destined for academic success. A second grade class in Cincinnati in 1870 could enroll children born in Appalachian poverty and second-generation middle-class students of German descent. Some children appeared indifferent to learning, others worked against the odds to succeed. In the Queen City as elsewhere, some neighborhood schools were attended predominately by the native born and middle class while others had few native speakers. This helps explain the persistent demand for age-graded classrooms, which promised fairness but also some order and predictability. The model of one-room schools seemed antiquated, hardly a panacea for the pressing numbers of children in the booming city. Industry had advanced through specialization of function and managerial control, so why not apply this formula to schools?

The geographical mobility of families made better age grading and classification attractive, however difficult to achieve. Since the days of Horace Mann, a uniform, common course of study had been seen as a democratic aim and republican right, for all white children at least, and a standard curriculum was appealing given high pupil turnover. As towns mushroomed in the South after the Civil War, local champions of the public schools regarded graded classrooms as an essential innovation that could help attract new residents. Echoing claims once made in the antebellum North, *The North Carolina Teacher* announced in 1883 that graded schools testified to an area's general prosperity: "The advantage of good instruction, free to all, will always draw new residents to a town where these advantages exist."

One particularly important innovation, despite its appeal to only a small fraction of students, was the free high school, which formed the pinnacle of the graded system. In the antebellum period, it was a key reform that aimed to draw the respectable classes into the system. If the high school could offer as good a secondary education as private alternatives, and do so for free, it would ensure widespread middle-class support, essential to uplifting and maintaining the status of the public system. Offering mostly a modern rather than classical curriculum (despite Latin classes in many schools), high schools built upon the basic subjects in the grades below. As they grew more popular with a broad range of middle-class families in the North, they helped undermine the private sector, a process that proceeded more slowly in the postbellum South. Moreover, southern high schools were largely for whites only and were mostly found in larger towns and cities. In the North, they were more widely available and usually open to any scholar who could pass a demanding admission exam, which symbolized a public commitment to academic rigor and the fulfillment of republican aims. For no one, not even the rich, could enter the high school without passing the entrance test. To even qualify for the test, applicants needed a note from their grammar school principal that attested to their scholastic achievement, academic promise, and moral character.

Standing at the apex of the hierarchical system, high schools remained controversial institutions throughout the century: they educated a small percentage of the white middle and upper classes, catered mostly to female students (who lacked suitable job opportunities and often wanted to become elementary teachers), and were expensive. Urban high schools were among the most beautiful contemporary examples of civic architecture, derided by their critics as wasteful and antirepublican for educating the few at high cost. They were especially condemned during hard times, leading to lawsuits that unsuccessfully tried to limit public schools to instruction in the lower branches. Though only a small percentage of secondary school graduates attended college before 1900, critics said the high schools were dominated by colleges and universities, which did indeed increasingly turn to high schools to recruit students. Throughout the century some outspoken Democrats especially denounced the free high school as emblematic of Whig and Republican policies: it was a centralized, hierarchical institution that in theory was open to all but in reality was attended by only the few, at taxpayer expense.

Despite these criticisms, when educators envisioned a place of pedagogical promise they looked to the city, home to graded schools, high schools, and curriculum innovation. To an emerging class of educational leaders, the city was central to any aspirations to influence. No one proved more important or better exemplified this than William T. Harris, a Connecticut Yankee who was born in East Killingly in 1835. Educated in a variety of schools before attending Yale, Harris left without earning a degree and headed west to seek a new life. After several false starts, he became a teacher in St. Louis, quickly moving up to principal and then leaping to superintendent, serving from 1868 to 1880. Public school enrollment in St. Louis boomed from 12,166 students in 1860 to 51,241 twenty years later. Harris's rise to national fame was synonymous with the growth of the local system, which gained national attention.

Now largely forgotten or dismissed as a conservative, Harris was the nation's premier school leader between the age of Horace Mann and John Dewey, whose early work he published as editor of the highbrow *Journal of Speculative Philosophy*. A student of Hegel and of German idealist philosophy, Harris was not typical of contemporary school superintendents in terms of his intellectual interests, but he too gained prominence through his labors in the city. A defender of the idea of a common school and common curriculum for everyone, including African Americans, this pro-Union Republican later served a record term as U.S. commissioner of education (1889–1906). He was a member of virtually every national blue-ribbon educational committee, and his prolific writings and public speeches made him an international figure. When Harris died in 1909, the mantle of educational leadership had already passed to a new generation of leaders, most of whom rejected his defense of common schooling as antiquated and reactionary. In his prime, however, Harris was an intellectual force, and he was not alone in support of the principle of common education. His reports as school superintendent in St. Louis were required reading for aspiring educational professionals, essential guides to the new organizational and educational practices that had taken root in the city.

Like most educators coming of age at midcentury, Harris was heir to the legacy of the common school ideal and the belief that free, tax-supported public education was a grand republican achievement. He marveled at the spread of literacy and, with the advent of cheaper newsprint and publishing, the growth of an enlarged reading public. "The printed page," he wrote, "is the mighty Aladdin's lamp, which gives to the meanest citizen the power to lay a spell on time and space." He was close enough in time to the formation of free public education to share an earlier generation's excitement about its promise. Indeed, the St. Louis schools, like other urban systems, had begun as charity schools, and they had only become attractive to a wider range of social classes and been made free in the 1850s. According to Harris, the nation's public schools helped promote literacy and learning and aimed to reward the most talented individuals, thus preventing the hardening of social classes, the plague of Europe. And cities, he thought, were exciting places in which to work and live, their institutions vital in the preservation of the republic and in the shaping of modern society. Attuned to issues of political economy, Harris believed that the division of labor in industry that had led to greater prosperity should also guide the organization and administration of urban school systems.

In words that John Dewey would repeat a generation later, Harris claimed in 1872 that the public school was a "miniature community." Schools should thus offer students access to a basic academic curriculum, where they would imbibe a "common stock of ideas" and compete on a "common ground." In a world where industrialization increasingly shaped everyday life, Harris, like many Hegelians, thought the individual would find greater freedom and opportunity through association with large-scale public institutions. Harris eloquently defended coeducation against conservative critics, supported racial integration, championed the free high school, and agreed with Catholics, despite the enemies he made, that Bible reading and school prayer had no place in the secular public system. As a devotee of German philosophy and culture, he championed new pedagogical ideals from the Continent, especially in the area of early childhood education. Harris helped make St. Louis famous by opening some of the nation's first public kindergartens, which provided moral training and early opportunities for academic learning in a less competitive environment than the regular classroom. In alliance with Republicans (often German Americans) on the school board, he repeatedly defended foreign-language instruction in public schools. Schools could not be common, he reasoned, unless everyone attended, and the addition of German instruction seriously depleted attendance in private schools; this strategy worked in many cities with sizeable German populations. More importantly, Harris was sympathetic to immigrant parents who took pride in their past yet wanted their children to learn English well and succeed in their new home.

Access to German-language classes thus helped immigrant children adjust to American culture, by respecting their native language while ensuring their cultural assimilation through school attendance. It also added to the intellectual wealth of schools, since it promoted a wider appreciation of German achievements in literature, philosophy, science, and history. Harris did not fear the immigrants flooding into the United States. He was confident, as he wrote in 1874, that "we are all to live in one community, and the relations of family, commerce, social intercourse, and fellow citizenship shall bind us together." Like reformers in an earlier generation, he believed that public, not private, schools were the best way to build community and social cohesiveness in the complex, culturally diverse city. Not all groups were as successful as the Germans in shaping school policy in St. Louis or in other cities. St. Louis Democrats, in an attempt to undermine Harris and German language instruction, said it was unjust to not teach other foreign languages. In 1878 they called for the introduction of Gaelic, French, and Hebrew, knowing full well that this would be prohibitively expensive but hoping that it would rouse the public to demand the elimination of all foreign language classes. Historian Selwyn K. Troen has emphasized how spectacularly this political strategy backfired. The response of St. Louis's German community and their friends was swift and impressive: forty thousand people signed a petition to retain German in the schools, vindicating Harris's policy.

Harris's fame grew thanks to the opportunities provided by the city. By 1875 he was already the president of the National Education Association, a fixture at its annual meetings, and a national figure. The St. Louis school board boosted his reputation, too, by printing a few thousand copies of his annual, bulky reports, which covered an array of educational topics; the reports were distributed across the country and even published in German-language editions. Harris represented a new generation of educational leadership centered in the city, a unique place for experimentation and reform. Without question, city schools had their critics, who especially found the curriculum and teaching practices wanting. To an emerging class of male professionals, however, they offered a place to test new ideas, build careers, and adapt education to a changing world. Even those laboring in the nation's country schools and villages were told that their salvation rested in the hands of educational leaders based in the city.

"Modern civilization," wrote John D. Philbrick in 1885, "is rapidly tending to uniformity and unity." This was a common perspective among urban leaders. Nationalism intensified with the northern victory, cities and factories transformed the political economy, and railroads penetrated the upland South and various western frontiers. Indian tribes on the Great Plains mightily resisted the encroachment of the Anglo-American civilization and its cavalry, but white settlement, the destruction of the great bison herds, and the American military ultimately resulted in their defeat, death, or placement on reservations. National integration, while never complete, appeared irresistible, as did the trend toward "uniformity and unity," whether represented by machine production or graded schools.

The rise of an urban, industrial society was making America a world power, but most Americans still lived in rural areas or villages. As historian David B. Danbom has written, between 1870 and 1900 farms multiplied from 2.66 million to 5.74 million and farm acreage more than doubled. While less impressive than urban and industrial expansion, farming had hardly retreated in the wake of social transformation but had fundamentally changed. It was increasingly part of a world of commercialized agriculture tied to complex transportation and distribution networks, middlemen, and credit systems, which made self-sufficiency illusory and investment in expensive machinery such as McCormick reapers more common. By the 1870s, Montgomery Ward brought manufactured goods from curtains to pianos into more living rooms, as urban tastes spread beyond the city. Farmers fed the expanding armies of urban workers, who in turn produced a surfeit of consumer goods.

Despite urban growth, most people late in the century lived outside of major urban areas, and their children attended small, modest schools. These schools were largely ungraded, lacked a uniform curriculum, and usually provided teachers with short-term jobs, not careers. Speaker upon speaker at state teachers' conventions and at the National Education Association bemoaned the shortcomings of the country schools. These professionals dominated educational discourse, which usually began with respectful commentaries on the importance of farming as a virtuous way of life and ended with a litany of complaints about the "rural school problem."

Fixing the problem was another matter. Vast expanses of the South, Southwest, Great Plains, Far West, and even the Old Northwest remained very rural despite the forces of national integration. Western boom towns based on mining, the cattle industry, and commerce and industry sometimes flourished, as did growing towns and cities at the juncture of railroad lines that now encircled the frontier. Even the South, where the war, falling cotton prices, and recurrent depression devastated the economy, was caught up in change. Debates about slavery and free labor helped define national politics for decades, and the South's reintegration into the Union consumed many politicians. Southern towns mushroomed in the 1870s, encouraging many local educators and national observers to predict the adoption of northern ideas on school organization, administration, and pedagogy.

By the late 1870s, the South had reached a crossroads. Federal troops withdrew from civil rights enforcement, Radical Republicans declined in influence within Congress, southern Democrats regained power over state government, and racial segregation reigned supreme, reinforced in the following decades by custom and law. Thus much of the talk about "uniformity and unity" among northern educational leaders clashed with the hard realities of rural life everywhere, especially in the former Confederacy. Even Philbrick recognized the difference between urban blueprints and the facts of rural existence when he rather limply observed that "urban and rural schools are not and cannot be, and perhaps need not be, the same in all respects." Indeed, the "rural school problem" would not disappear.

In 1882, a writer in the *New England Homestead* warned about the poor quality of many country schools. Quite a few of them were "fairly, indifferently, or badly taught" and, in contrast with the cities, most districts had only "a poor, straggling high school in which some of the 'higher branches' are taught." Most country schools lacked a formal or standard course of study or a uniform means of measuring academic progress. As a result, rural educators usually did not issue report cards or diplomas, as in the city; judgments of individual progress rested upon subjective estimates and rule-of-thumb measures, now discredited in a world of science and industry where precision and uniformity counted. Rural pupils worked their way through the available textbooks, recited what they knew to the teacher, and called it an education. Financing better schools became especially difficult as rural populations declined precipitously in some New England counties, but concerns about rural education were widespread. In 1883, an educator typically derided the country schools before the Southern Indiana Teachers' Association. In the Hoosier state, 80 percent of all school children "were enrolled in the country schools. Ohio and Michigan have $\frac{2}{3}$, Tennessee, $\frac{7}{8}$, and Iowa, $\frac{9}{10}$ of their enrollments in the country schools; 85 percent of eleven states attend ungraded schools." And, he added with obvious frustration: "The question is often asked, Who ever finishes anything in a country school?" Other educators with an eye on urban developments also called for better trained teachers, uniform standards, and the elimination of every small school district.

"The district system," said the editor of the *Journal of Education* in 1889, "is a relic of the Dark Ages of school life. It has all the vices of which selfishness and prejudice are capable. Every man who loves America should wage war upon it. There have sometimes been good schools under its regime, but they have been despite it and not because of it." School districts outside of urban areas usually constituted small geographical regions whose residents often fiercely resisted consolidation, exemplifying America's faith in local control and suspicions about centralized power. But intemperate views of the district system by professional educators informed many contemporary articles, speeches, and books on education. In addition, state departments of public instruction distributed guides to show rural educators how to grade schools, select textbooks, and improve their practices. This bore some fruit, but local residents often resisted innovation, higher taxes, and the consolidation of districts, the usual advice from educational leaders and government officials. In 1883 commissioner Eaton in Washington characteristically called for more consolidated schools, including the adoption of township or county-level administration, which did occur in some states, though often without the desired results. Michigan (not exactly a frontier state) had 411 graded schools to 6,115 ungraded ones. Since consolidation was rarely popular, Eaton did not think the proportion wildly different in most states.

Writers commonly compared the promise of the city with the worst abuses of the country schools. Northerners relished the opportunity to demean rural education, especially in the South. Thus, a contributor to the *Wisconsin Journal of Education* in 1886 called southern rural schools "unspeakably bad." Georgia's teachers, he insisted, were "utterly unfit." "But little is taught beyond the Fourth Reader and the Multiplication Table and even this is execrably done." Throughout the rural South, "the school houses are often small, windowless cabins, too well ventilated, nevertheless, by the open chinks. Often the schools are taught in rude churches, especially the colored schools, with no desks or apparatus, even the most necessary." More careful writers recognized the great diversity of rural America and realized that schools could vary tremendously even within the same township or county. In some rural communities, particular immigrant groups formed a majority and foreign tongues resounded in the classroom without much controversy; elsewhere, most rural children were taught in English only.

Millions of children passed through the doors of the nation's public schools, ensuring that the experiences of teachers and pupils in different times and places inevitably varied. To speak of rural children was to generalize about those whose families grew potatoes in Maine, wheat on the Great Plains, and raised cattle in Texas, who were white, African American, native born, and immigrant, and whose personal fortunes differed. For many students, going to school was deadening, confining the body and human spirit. Rural teachers late in the century still mostly taught by the textbook and emphasized memorization and recitation, dulling the children's senses. For other students, however, school was a godsend. America's one-room schools not only expanded literacy, they also inspired some pupils, even if their experiences were not universal. In *A Son of the Middle Border* (1917), the novelist Hamlin Garland fondly recalled how his modest country school opened new intellectual vistas to him as a child growing up in Iowa after the Civil War. "Our readers were almost the only counterchecks to the current of vulgarity and baseness which ran through the talk of the older boys," he wrote, "and I wish to acknowledge my deep affection to Professor McGuffey, whoever he may have been, for the dignity and literary grace of his selections." His imagination set afire by literature and poetry, Garland remembered becoming "a page in the train of Ivanhoe, or a bowman in the army of Richard the Lion Heart battling the Saracen in the Holy Land." Herbert Quick, who became an educator and writer, also had warm memories about his district school education in Iowa, where he "was inoculated with a little of the virus of good literature," thanks to the selections in his tattered copy of a McGuffey Reader.

Whether schooling opened minds or kept them shut, whether the inoculation was successful or failed, district schools continued to increase as population moved west. And, as in the antebellum period, rural children everywhere attended schools that had similar characteristics. Laypeople still controlled—and local taxes primarily supported—the schools. Compared with the cities, the curriculum was not uniform and was often bare, classes were ungraded, teachers mostly unsupervised, and scholars attended as weather, farm chores, parental interest, and other personal factors dictated. One contributor to the *Educational Review* in 1896, however, thought that those who cast aspersions on country schools should remember that cities were not exactly perfect. "The great metropolis, New York," he wrote, "has tens of thousands of children for whom there is no room in her schoolhouses. Some pictures of her schools make a benighted rural district a paradise besides them."

By the 1890s, many state, regional, and national educational organizations proposed similar ways to improve the country schools. They included hiring more normal school graduates as teachers (despite the lure of more lucrative urban positions), creating a more uniform curriculum, appointing county or township superintendents, and consolidating districts. Demographic realities made much of this moot, as rural populations and the sheer number of farms increased in the postbellum decades. Villages and small towns, in contrast, often tried to follow the example of the cities, however imperfectly. Towns with a few thousand residents hired superintendents, who taught in the high school part time and made concerted efforts to grade the schools, establish a sequenced course of study, publish elaborate rules and regulations for teachers and students, and teach more of the higher branches such as algebra, chemistry, or Latin, staples in city high schools. In rural areas, however, one- or two-room schools remained the norm, since farmers wanted small, locally controlled schools within walking distance, even if the building was a rude structure such as a restored barn. Many farmers lived on the edge of poverty, fighting locusts, drought, poor soils, overproduction, and falling crop prices in an age of deflation and tight money.

In 1895, a committee on state school systems told the National Council of Education that while the statistics were imperfect, the percentage of ungraded schools remained high in many states: 80 percent in Texas, 65 percent in Indiana, 58 percent in Wisconsin. In Massachusetts, which was heavily urban, the figure was only 10 percent. Elsewhere the "rural school problem"—the title of countless speeches and articles in the 1880s and 1890s—was a ubiquitous concern. The president of the University of Minnesota in 1897 contrasted America's city schools and rural schools, arguing that the former had all the advantages. Country schools, he said, had the most poorly trained teachers, the worst facilities, the shortest terms. "In States as old and rich as New York and Ohio," he lamented, "from twenty-five to fifty percent of the schools have an enrollment of ten pupils or less. In this there is much waste." He urged idealistic young college students to fan out into the countryside, much like settlement house volunteers in the city, to pursue good works among the downtrodden. Many educators expected little improvement without outside intervention. Another Minnesotan, from St. Cloud, typically believed that "if there is to be reform, it must come from the normal schools, institutes, and the county superintendency."

To leading educators active in major teacher organizations, no region seemed more backward than the postbellum South. In its various expressions, Reconstruction was the centerpiece of governmental efforts at national reintegration, and it was played out in one of most rural parts of America. After early slave revolts, antebellum southern legislatures had legally prohibited teaching slaves to read and write. Even though slaves and some sympathetic whites created numerous clandestine schools in slave quarters, and free blacks promoted literacy in whatever ways possible, black illiteracy rates at the time of emancipation approached 95 percent. The absence of public schools also helped limit the access of poor whites to the world of books and modern communication. White elites were hardly interested in educating them either, since the need for their labor and shared interest in white supremacy overrode all other concerns.

After the war, ex-slaves—the poorest and most despised Southerners—fought for free public education throughout the former Confederacy. The future seemed bright in the early 1870s. Through the Freedmen's Bureau, the federal government helped coordinate the establishment of numerous schools; northern Protestant missionary groups sponsored many Yankee teachers (often women) to work in southern schools; and southern Republicans helped rewrite state constitutions to mandate public education. In addition, African American support for education was remarkable. The first desire after emancipation was land ownership, the traditional basis of white economic freedom and independence. Closely following that was access to education and the means to literacy. Harriet Beecher Stowe remarked in 1879 that following emancipation southern blacks "rushed not to the grog-shop but to the schoolroom—they cried for the spelling book as bread, and pleaded for teachers as a necessity of life." African Americans made up for lost time, often sending their children to school at higher rates than poor whites.

With the collapse of federal interest in southern affairs and the decline in Radical Republican influence in the North, southern Democrats began to "redeem" the region in the 1870s. They largely regained control over state and local government by 1877, the year of the famous railroad strikes and federal military withdrawal from southern affairs. Thaddeus Stevens and other radicals wanted to create a world based not on social equality among the races per se, but one in which everyone was judged on their "merit and conduct." That was not to be. Southern schools, except for a brief period in New Orleans after the war, were racially segregated, and by the end of the century Jim Crow had established itself throughout southern society.

When James A. Garfield, steadfast Republican and loyal friend of public education, gave his inaugural address as president in 1881, he invoked faded dreams that had evaporated like an apparition in a Shakespearean tragedy.

"The elevation of the Negro race from slavery to the full rights of citizenship is the most important political change we have known since the adoption of the Constitution of 1787," he told his listeners. Both races believed in hard work and self-help, many poor African Americans were already rising from poverty to respectability, and many more would if granted equal protection of the law. Universal education, Garfield insisted, had a "savory influence." He said, "It is the high privilege and sacred duty of those now living to educate their successors and fit them, by intelligence and virtue, for the inheritance which awaits them. In this beneficent work sections and race should be forgotten and partisanship should be unknown. Let us find a new meaning in the divine oracle which declares that 'a little child shall lead them,' for our own little children will control the destinies of the Republic."

How children were treated did help guide the destiny of the republic, but not in the ways Garfield prophesied. By 1896, when the U.S. Supreme Court put its stamp of approval on racial segregation on railroad trains, asserting that segregation was permissible if facilities were equal, white Southerners had already constructed elaborate means of racial suppression. White teachers, especially from the North, were occasionally terrorized, beaten, and killed, along with African Americans; the Ku Klux Klan and other vigilantes burned school buildings; and the federal government failed to protect the newly won civil rights of the ex-slaves once southern Democrats regained power. Black citizens struggled to provide their children with access to schools and other avenues to learning. Poverty and the doctrine of white supremacy ensured that the northern radical dream of integrated, common schools withered on the inhospitable soil of racial politics.

The horrible poverty of African Americans as well as millions of whites ensured widespread suffering. Historian Edward L. Ayers and other scholars have documented that the "New South" was industrializing, as the mill towns in the Piedmont, mines in West Virginia and Tennessee, and steel mills in Birmingham testified. As in the past, however, most Southerners worked the land. Those who had owned the great plantations revived their economic and political power, ensuring that black ownership of land, access to industrial jobs, and other forms of opportunity remained minimal. By not heavily industrializing the region, southern leaders ensured that the region remained poor, its economic woes exacerbated by the lingering economic consequences of the Civil War, shortage of credit, and the agricultural depression that hit the Western world beginning in the 1870s. Share-cropping and the crop-lien system tied poor blacks and whites alike to the soil, providing some independence from richer whites with the best land but ensuring a hand-to-mouth existence when agricultural prices plummeted. While racism largely explains the failure of states to invest in African American schools, which were nonexistent in many rural areas, economic conditions generally were dismal. The South was the poorest part of the nation in 1900, with less than half the per capita income of the North but twice as many children. Having a dual system of schools made no economic sense and especially imperiled black children, whose segregated schools were chronically underfunded. The taxes of African Americans were often used to support white schools, adding further insult to injury in a region with a time-honored hostility to taxation and state provision for education.

The North had never been hospitable to black migration and black equality. Northern blacks in the antebellum period often lived in very poor neighborhoods, had inadequate health care, faced job discrimination, and attended poorly staffed, segregated schools. Midwestern states, dominated by farmers who, like Jefferson had, linked land ownership with freedom, by law prohibited or otherwise discouraged black migration and offered limited black access to public schools in the countryside. Many feared that the emancipation of slaves would lead to heavy migration north. After the war, most northern educators, following rather than leading public opinion, acquiesced in or endorsed racial segregation. Those who spoke so earnestly about assimilating immigrants usually drew the line where African Americans were involved.

In 1884, the editor of New England's *Journal of Education* smugly noted that a southern "colored" girl had won the highest academic honors at Buffalo High School. Indeed, "we rarely visit an important school, normal, high, or collegiate, that does not contain promising students of this class. Many of these are sent North by the more prosperous class of the southern colored folk, and return to become influential leaders in the educational and social uplifting at home." But the same journal opened its pages to southern racists, who said that if forced to integrate the South would simply close every public school. Occasionally northern educators and journalists raised the issue, however obliquely, of northern hypocrisy. In 1882 a black parent in Brooklyn, where schools were segregated, requested a transfer for his daughter to a white school. The editor sympathized, noting that the girl's current school "has a morgue on one side, the jail on the other, and steam carpet-beating establishment in the rear, and the neighborhood generally is reprehensible." The petition was denied. The editor then took the position that "it is quite time that the question of color should be settled in our northern towns and cities where it has not been. Until it is, the advocates of a no-color line in the public school should have little to say to the people of the South, where real and substantial reasons exist for the separation."

These "real and substantial reasons" for segregation were paraded before the nation by prominent southern as well as northern journalists, politicians, and educators. Those who favored and those who opposed educating African Americans at public expense mostly accepted an indelible color line south of Mason-Dixon. Southerners who endorsed more common schools for blacks made similar claims for educating them that Yankees made for immigrants: to teach responsibility, self-help, morality, and respect for private property and law and order. But white southern educational leaders shared the widespread belief that the freedpeople, one step removed from slavery, had a long way to travel on the evolutionary ladder. Slavery, they said, despite its immoral qualities, had helped teach blacks to work, follow orders, and become Christians. Modern institutions, the product of Anglo-Saxon ingenuity, had to pick up where slavery left off. Segregation was essential. "Even the Italian, or the lowest and meanest of the Slavic race, may in time be assimilated," said a speaker at the all-white Alabama Educational Association meetings in 1891. But whites and blacks "are separated by as broad a gulf as divides Dives and Lazarus, and as impassable." The leopard could not change its spots, and "the Ethiopian cannot change his skin."

Writing in *Scribner's Magazine* in 1874, the Reverend William H. Ruffner, Virginia's superintendent of public instruction, wrote that "an act of Congress requiring the south poles of all magnets to attract each other, would not be a whit more absurd than one requiring education to be conducted on a race mixture in the late slave states." Speaking to the National Education Association, Ruffner later added that Negroes were a "highly improvable race," with some individuals responding exceptionally well to the message of social uplift. But "as a class, they are in character weak and ignorant—and hence to that extent a very dangerous element in society." He felt the same about poor whites, whose miserable existence also meant that their social progress would take many generations. Ruffner predicted that some day whites and blacks would live in social harmony, even intermarry, but that the evolutionary process would take centuries. That African Americans were weak minded, overly sensual, immoral, and superstitious was often an article of faith among whites who debated whether to educate African American children.

Opponents were unwaveringly racist, warning that a race war would result if educators foolishly tried to uplift ex-slaves, educating them for high paying jobs when they belonged in the cotton field. A Presbyterian minister in South Carolina opined in 1889 that an educated Negro "is just as much Negro as before, just the same raw hide volume with the incongruous addition of a gilt edge; he is only a little more aggressively offensive than his less ornate brother." Many claimed that black crime had risen with more literacy, which Northerners sometimes said about poor whites. Other skeptical Southerners believed that African Americans had smaller brains, which had once been said about women. They dismissed Ruffner's claims about black academic progress and achievement, which was remarkable given the impediments placed in their path. The Charleston *News and Observer* bluntly summed up white racist sentiments after the turn of the century. "Let us be frank and honest. The great mass of the white people of the South have no idea of educating the Negro to be a citizen—their equal, either social or political. They want him to be the white man's help, and if he is not willing to occupy a subordinate position in this country, the sooner he leaves it, or the southern part of it at least, the better for all concerned."

The vast majority of African Americans remained in the South, tied to the land, struggling for self-determination, access to education, and some realization of the American dream despite the legal, social, and economic obstacles. Leon F. Litwack and other scholars have emphasized that black parents were not naive about education, but recognized the scant economic opportunities for well-educated black youth. But becoming literate had multiple benefits. Knowing arithmetic might protect people from being cheated by literate, dishonest whites, and reading ensured a better understanding of the law and contracts as well as access to the Bible and the pleasures of print. Some children of ex-slaves recalled that their parents worried about the harsh realities after school ended. Who would hire an educated black person? Only teachers needed any formal education, and neither farming nor preaching required a school credential.

Yet the more whites blocked access to schools, the more the freedpeople assumed education was worth pursuing. The idea of free land, free labor, and free education had triumphed on the Civil War battlefields, and the association of common schools with northern notions of respectability, freedom, and opportunity was not lost on African Americans. Though it hardly guaranteed a better life, education might potentially open new vistas to their children. While ex-slaves fought for the right of their children to attend integrated schools, they saw the benefits of black-controlled schools and during Reconstruction often demanded black teachers instead of white instructors for their children. If integration was not possible or always desirable, they valued education enough to conclude that even white-enforced segregation was better than exclusion. Learning was better than ignorance of the basics. Although advanced schooling often did not lead to better jobs or weaken racism, which actually intensified as the century came to a close, African Americans respected those who championed education despite the meager or nonexistent opportunities of many ordinary citizens.

Booker T. Washington, born into slavery, inspired many by his rise to freedom and determination to use education to better his lot, as he recounted in his famous autobiography, *Up from Slavery* (1901). Among his earliest memories of his Virginia childhood, Washington told his readers, was the desire to read, so he could understand "common books and newspapers." Following emancipation, he reported, African Americans of all ages flocked to every teacher and available school to learn to read and write. It was, he said, "a whole race trying to go to school." Washington's great rival, W. E. B. Du Bois, less accommodating to segregation and an inspiring defender of civil rights, had been born in the North, had graduated from high school, and held a Ph.D. from Harvard. With a different emphasis, he also publicized the importance of education, poignantly describing his experiences as a teacher in a rural black school in Tennessee. The school was a rude log cabin, which stored a farmer's corn. "I loved my school," Du Bois recalled, "and the fine faith the children had in the wisdom of their teacher was truly marvelous." Despite their disagreements about the type of education best suited for their people, Washington, Du Bois, and other black leaders realized that access to education could contribute to a better life. Mary Jane McCleod Bethune, born free in a large family to parents who had been slaves, said simply: "The whole world opened to me when I learned to read."

Whether education was a boon or dangerous experiment remained unclear to many white Southerners in the postbellum years, when the "rural school problem" took on a pronounced racial tenor in the former Confederacy. Like most of their northern brethren, southern white educators openly endorsed the color line and joined in the national debate over how best to construct a common school system. Forward-thinking educators everywhere concluded that the town and city systems were superior. There one found all the modern (Yankee) ideals: graded classrooms, high schools, a more uniform curriculum, and professional supervision. The rural schools were the worst, while the urban schools were the best, said an educator from Clinton, Mississippi, at the state teachers' association meeting in 1884. The same thing was said in Alabama, North Carolina, and other southern states in convocations of educators and in books and school periodicals. The towns had more concentrated wealth, a greater density of pupils, and seemed to be drawing rural children off the farm, a complaint that became very common across the nation. In 1888, one white Georgian, startled at the flight of rural residents to towns and cities, urged the construction of better schools to halt the flow. Upgrading country schools became one of the central aims of reformers throughout the early decades of the twentieth century, as both races increasingly abandoned the countryside.

Social change had dramatically altered the face of America and its common schools in the postbellum era. Regional differences would long characterize American life, despite the rise of nationalism and an urban-industrial, more economically integrated economy. Yankees would continue to applaud the virtues of the common school and downplay racial problems at home while calling the South a cultural and educational backwater. Despite progress, the South continued to lag behind the North educationally, even though it spent a larger share of its smaller economic base on its schools. Southern children on average attended school for far fewer days per year and years in total than Northerners, and despite all the educational progress made, access to schools for African Americans was often meager and sometimes nonexistent. It is also easy to forget that schooling remained a small part of most people's lives. Black children, like working-class children everywhere, generally were lucky to receive a few years of schooling before entering the workforce, whether in field or factory. Yet thanks to the zeal of Radical Republicans and missionaries and the impressive labors of ex-slaves, public schools had emerged in the South, however imperfectly, in a few short decades.

By 1900, common schools were a familiar presence in Virginia, North Carolina, and other rural states, and the spread of towns meant that graded schools, high schools, and other innovations were within the grasp of more children. In his annual report to the nation at the turn of the century, Commissioner Harris applauded the remarkable growth of the common schools. In 1870, 57 percent of all five- to eighteen-year-olds were enrolled in school; thirty years later the percentage had jumped to 72 percent. The total number of days annually spent in school varied by region and within regions, with the

South still lagging behind. The national average length of the school year, however, grew from 132 to 144 days, and high school enrollment boomed in the 1890s. Schools were typically the largest part of the local budget, and public school property was now valued at over a half-billion dollars. At the dawn of the twentieth century, a quarter of a million public schoolhouses stood as testimony to faith in the power of formal education.

The expansion of public schools after 1865 was inextricably linked to the major social, political, and economic convulsions of an industrial and urbanizing age. Even the South joined in national debates about the nature, purposes, and destiny of the common school in a world of cities, factories, and commercialized agriculture. Many observers in the postbellum years were convinced that the common school was one of the great achievements of the age. New ways of teaching, new courses of study, and new ideas about the purposes of mass education vied for attention over the course of the nineteenth century and made their claims on educational thought and practice.

CHAPTER THREE

The "New Education"

Over the course of the nineteenth century, a new way of thinking about the nature of children, classroom methods, and the purposes of schools increasingly dominated educational discourse. Something loosely called progressive education, which emphasized child-centered pedagogy and curricular experimentation, became part of a larger assault on tradition and revolt against the formalism of the schools. Variously defined, progressive education still has its champions and critics, the latter blaming it for low economic productivity, immorality among the young, and the decline of academic standards. In the popular press, John Dewey's name is often invoked as the evil genius behind the movement, even though he criticized sugar-coated education and letting children do as they please, or abandoning adult authority in teaching or child rearing. Originally called the "new education" by the 1870s, progressive (or child-centered) education was controversial from the outset and continues to arouse debate among laypeople and within the education profession.

Without question, something fascinating had emerged in educational thought by the nineteenth century. Critics of traditional forms of child rearing and classroom instruction condemned what they saw as insidious notions about the nature of children and the antediluvian practices of the emerging public school system. In often evangelical and apocalyptic prose, an assortment of citizens ranging from poets to political philosophers, educators to psychologists, proclaimed the discovery of new insights into children and how they best learned. Despite many differences among them, they together produced an impressive canon. They declared that children were active, not passive, learners; that children were innocent and good, not fallen; that women, not men, best reared and educated the young; that early education, without question, made all the difference; that nature, not books, taught best; that kindness and benevolence, not stern discipline or harsh rebukes, should reign in the home and classroom; and, finally, that the curriculum needed serious reform to remove the vestiges of antiquated practices. All agreed that what usually passed for education was mind numbing, unnatural, and pernicious, a sin against childhood.

These views were expressed in books, educational magazines, and public addresses across the span of the nineteenth century. While it was easier to condemn schools than perfect them, the spirit of the "new education" reflected well a nation continually revitalized by waves of religious revivalism and utopian experiments during the antebellum period. After the Civil War, voices for pedagogical change multiplied and formed a mighty chorus, singing in praise of the child and insisting that a "new education" must supplant an "old education" based on false and wicked ideas. Writers gradually substituted the word "progressive" for "new," adding the phrase "progressive education" to the nation's pedagogical lexicon without always defining it clearly or consistently.

The sources of this new education were passionately debated from the start. The English poet William Blake, publishing his *Songs of Innocence* at the outbreak of the French Revolution, pointed to religious visions since childhood as central to his inspiration. Other champions of the child said they were simply following nature's laws. The Swiss reformer Johann Heinrich Pestalozzi, whose words became Holy Writ to many, was frankly unsure of where his ideas originated. Acknowledging the influence of Rousseau's *Emile* (1762) and his own learning by doing, Pestalozzi wrote in 1801 that "to my grave I shall remain in a kind of fog about most of my views." But, he concluded, "it is a holy fog to me." His classic volume, *How Gertrude Teaches Her Children* (1801) evoked the empiricism of Bacon, the mechanistic views of Newton, and also the contradictory claims of his mentor Jean Jacques. Like most pedagogical pilgrims, however, Pestalozzi regarded his mission as God-given. Shrouded in a holy fog, he nonetheless emitted celestial light.

Lifting some of the historical clouds that have obscured the origins of child-centered progressivism remains a challenge. In its American phase, it was part of a larger humanitarian movement led by men and women of the northern middle classes in the antebellum and postbellum periods. This was made possible by changes in family size, new gender roles within bourgeois culture, and the softening of religious orthodoxy within Protestantism. Like other reforms such as temperance and antislavery that arose during the antebellum period, the new education sought the alleviation of pain and suffering, moral and intellectual advancement, and social stability and uplift. In addition, child-centered ideas gained currency as activists drew selectively upon romantic traditions emanating from Europe. A transatlantic crossing of ideas from the Swiss Alps, German forests, and English lake district left its imprint upon these reformers. As a result, some teachers experimented with new forms of pedagogy and some school systems adopted kindergarten and other new innovations to undermine the traditional classroom regimen. Ultimately, the hopes of many child-centered educators crashed on the jagged rocks of educational tradition. But their moral crusade permanently changed the nature of educational thought in the modern world.

Child-centered progressivism emerged amid the momentous social and intellectual changes that began to alter European and American society by the early nineteenth century. By midcentury, the shift from a rural, agrarian, mercantilist world to one of markets, commercial and industrial capitalism, and cities proceeded apace. The American and French Revolutions led many citizens to dream of a more just world based on Enlightenment precepts of reason, universal law, science, and progress. Historian Thomas L. Haskell has persuasively argued in his study of Anglo-American reform movements that dissenting religious groups such as the Quakers, among the most successful capitalists of the age of Adam Smith, disproportionately led movements for moral reform and uplift. With other Protestant groups and a variety of secular reformers, they championed many unpopular causes: pacifism, women's rights, the abolition of slavery, and the more humane treatment of children, criminals, and the mentally ill. Haskell causally locates this rising ethos of caring within an emergent capitalism, which increased human misery but also made social ties more expansive and intense, promoting empathy, compassion, and social action.

Whatever the multiple causes of this growing humanitarianism, reform movements on both sides of the Atlantic reflected activist strains within Protestantism and the secular promise of social change and human improvement spawned by the political revolutions of the late eighteenth century. Thus the rise of a child-centered ethos among a minority of vocal, middle-class activists by the middle of the nineteenth century emerged during an era of sweeping change. Consider, for example, the evolving nature of northern middle-class family life and culture. In the decades after the American Revolution, middle-class families shrank in size, enabling parents to focus more on the individual child. Gender roles in such homes became more starkly separated in urban areas, the locus of social change, which intensified the domestic labors of mothers, including child rearing. By midcentury, more middle- and upper-class Protestant congregations downplayed original sin and emphasized Christian nurture over hellish damnation; more moderate, non-Calvinist views were heard from the pulpit and registered in child rearing manuals. The convergence of changes in demography, gender roles, economics, and religious ideology helped make some members of the northern middle classes receptive to new ideas about children and their education.

The growing fascination with child-centered education often deteriorated into pure sentimentality in the Victorian era, or was transmuted into a revived effort at discovering the scientific laws of physical and human development reminiscent of the eighteenth century. The discovery of the child owed an enormous debt to the rational thought of Locke and Newton as well as to the romanticism of Rousseau and Wordsworth. Progressive education was the child of Europe. As historian Hugh Cunningham has argued, Locke had challenged the seemingly timeless Christian precept of infant damnation by arguing that children's ideas, if not exactly their talents and destiny, were capable of change and improvement through education and the environment. Locke also stressed the need to observe the individual child to determine the most suitable education, a foundation of child-centered thinking. Newton, in turn, held out the promise of finding the natural laws that governed the universe, which also generated hopefulness of the human capacity to know the world and possibly improve its fate. Before the so-called romantic poets and novelists penned their odes to childhood, English evangelical Protestants by the mid-eighteenth century had created a new genre of reading materials, from reason, equally disliked Rousseau for his materialism and religious apostasy. And yet he shared Rousseau's hostility to institutions, likening schools to cages where teachers tried to teach birds to sing, and believing other institutions— like marriage, government, and the military—were satanic. Blake and Wordsworth assumed that children were good and innocent, and the American and French Revolutions set their dissenting politics aflame. After the Terror, Blake retained his radical politics but wrote a parody of his *Songs of Innocence* entitled *Songs of Experience,* printing them together by 1794 to show the "Two Contrary States of the Human Soul." London born and bred, he never shared Wordsworth's views on nature, nor did he become politically conservative like the famous bard from the Lake District.

A wide variety of European romantics influenced American child-centered ideas in the nineteenth century. The inspiring words of Rousseau or Wordsworth were pressed into service to attack the old education and demand more humane treatment of the innocent child. Yet the romantics had conflicting views on human nature, society, and social improvement. They were sometimes individually inconsistent and offered few blueprints for any educational utopias. European romantic writers, poets, and artists had also come of age in a different time and place than those who struggled to make emerging school systems in the American North more humane and child centered. They could provide insights into the evil past of child rearing and education, and inspiration for reformers. But the romantics, who were suspicious of institutions, usually did not face the challenging problems of teaching, raising school funds, or dealing with parents regularly. The romantics mattered on American shores. But only those who wrote specifically and extensively about education and schools, especially Johann Pestalozzi (1746–1827) and Friedrich Froebel (1782–1852), had a visible impact. Even then, their disciples adapted their ideas to the perceived needs of northern urban culture, tearing them from their original context.

American romantics in the mid-nineteenth century eloquently and movingly described the sweetness, harmony, and holiness of childhood, views that echoed among native poets, progressive ministers, and assorted visionaries. The transcendentalists Ralph Waldo Emerson and Henry David Thoreau, among others, saw something artificial about the schools, which ironically bore their names by the thousands in the twentieth century. Poets such as Walt Whitman, whose genius belies easy literary classification, similarly praised a more natural, not institutionally deadening, form of learning. Like Emerson

children's hymns to an array of children's literature, whose content an
dactic approach differed considerably from romanticism but heightene
tention toward the young. Children also became more prominent in n
and popular writing generally. And, as markets expanded, toy shops pro
ated, peddling their wares to the middle and upper classes.

The motives of utilitarians, rationalists, shopkeepers, and revivalists c
ously varied enormously. Still, the ascending importance of childhood
clear by the end of the eighteenth century, when democratic ideals spaw
by political revolution and various strains of romanticism together wo
veritable cult of childhood. Increasingly within enlightened circles—am
artists, poets, and educators—new ideas about childhood burst onto soc
Some, following Rousseau's lead, assumed that the child, naturally good,
corrupted not by Adam's fall but by human institutions. Even some thin
appalled by Rousseau's shocking criticisms of religion questioned whet
childhood was preparation for salvation, or even for adulthood. Those l
known to the world as romantics or transcendentalists often viewed childh
as holy and mystical, superior to the corrupted lives of adults. Blake invo
children's innocence, Wordsworth their "natural piety." Childhood becam
metaphor for goodness, a special time of life, or even a timeless, subli
essence worthy of contemplation. In his first book, *Nature* (1836), Ralph Wa
Emerson wrote that "the sun illuminates only the eye of the man, but shi
into the eye and the heart of the child." Infants, in his view, were a "perpet
Messiah."

The relationship of European romanticism to the rise of American chi
centered thought nevertheless was very complicated. The very vocabulary
dinarily associated with romanticism remained ambiguous. As the cultu
historian Raymond Williams has explained, by the seventeenth century t
adjective romantic, derived from the word romance, referred specifically
medieval verse dealing with "adventure, chivalry, and love," but soon had tl
added connotations of sentimentality, extravagance, and an appeal to tl
imagination. Only in the 1880s did scholars routinely mean by romanticism
distinctive movement of European writers, poets, and artists who lived b
tween the 1790s and 1830s. And few people defined the key word "nature
clearly. Since there was never any unified or single romantic movement, it
not surprising that historians have failed to discover a unified, single progre
sive movement in education.

William Blake, who despised Locke, Newton, and Voltaire for their faith i and Thoreau a former teacher, Whitman excoriated corporal punishment and demanded better teaching methods as the editor of the *Brooklyn Eagle*. In his poems he favored the contemplation of morning glories over memorizing facts in books, elevated human intuition over intellect, delighted in the joys of play, and snickered at the arrogance of the educated.

Yet Whitman realized that schools were here to stay. At the dedication of a new one in Camden, New Jersey, in 1874, he offered "An Old Man's Thought of School."

> And these I see, these sparkling eyes,
> These stores of mystic meaning, these young lives,
> Building, equipping like a fleet of ships, immortal ships,
> Soon to sail out over the measureless seas,
> On the soul's voyage.
> Only the lot of boys and girls?
> Only the tiresome spelling, writing, ciphering classes?
> Only a public school?

No, Whitman answered, the school, like the church, was not simply "brick and mortar," but a place of "living souls," "the lights and shadows of the future. . . . To girlhood, boyhood look, the teacher and the school."

American advocates of the new education drew as they pleased from a large corpus of romantic writings, foreign and domestic. Few Europeans were as influential as Pestalozzi and Froebel, whose ideas at times were rejected in practice even by those inspired by them. The Swiss-born Pestalozzi and German-born Froebel had emphasized the importance of motherhood, spirituality, and natural methods in educating young children, sentiments soon embraced by many progressive thinkers. Emerson E. White, who had recently retired as Cincinnati's school superintendent, told high school graduates in 1889 that "the theories and methods of Pestalozzi and Froebel have permeated elementary schools, and science and other modern knowledges, have entered the universities and are working their way downward through secondary education." This likely surprised the graduates, whose academic success depended upon endless rounds of memorization and recitation. But many educators such as Ralph Waldo Emerson, hoping to improve their craft, thought change was imminent thanks to new ideas from abroad. As a contributor to *The School Journal,* based in New York and Chicago, said in 1895, educational improvement only seemed possible after "the Pestalozzian wave struck our shores."

Indeed, decades earlier, Horace Mann, Henry Barnard, and other promoters of a gentler pedagogy had eagerly publicized the romantic ideals emanating from Europe, which assailed memorization, textbooks, physical discipline, and the usual features of the neighborhood school. Children, as Whitman said, were "stores of mystic meaning," not empty vessels to be filled with useless knowledge. But something had obviously gone wrong. Otherwise he could not have alluded to the "tiresome" methods of the school in his poem in 1874. Changing school practices became no simple matter. Despite his romantic leanings, Mann anticipated the standardized testing of the future by sponsoring citywide examinations in Boston in 1845 to demonstrate what children had learned at school, knowledge acquired by memorizing facts in textbooks. Written tests had become the rage after the Civil War, especially in the cities, where admission to high school still required passing a rigorous test based on heavy doses of rote material. Recitations, too, were pervasive on all levels of instruction in the 1870s. Learning the value of work, not play, and discipline, not doing as one pleased, remained the grand objectives of most schools. Textbook salesmen continued to hawk their ubiquitous stock, as teachers trained caged birds to sing.

To American child-centered activists, Pestalozzi and Froebel promised relief from the pedagogical status quo. Born to middle-class parents in 1746, Pestalozzi extolled nature and elevated the spiritual and practical significance of womanhood and motherhood through his idealized views of peasant women. This was sweet music to some northern middle-class Americans in the nineteenth century, as cities and factories transformed the landscape. An early enthusiast of the French Revolution, Pestalozzi recoiled just like other early romantics against its violent turn, centering his hope for the future in education and social cooperation, not political radicalism and conflict. That, too, made him palatable to urban reformers. In the early 1800s, the socialist Robert Owen found Pestalozzi's writings and model schools on the continent a source of inspiration for his own innovative schools and communitarian experiments in the villages of New Lanark, Scotland and New Harmony, Indiana. But the famous Swiss educator held a mystical but clearly Christian world view, which furthered his appeal among middle-class reformers building schools in capitalist America. His writings had a pantheistic flavor, a blend of naturalism and

Christian imagery, common to other romantics. Besides criticizing traditional, adult-centered education and invoking the child's innocence, Pestalozzi wanted every mother to teach the child "to lisp the name of God on her bosom" and to see "him the All-loving in the rising sun, in the rippling brook, in the branches of the trees, in the splendor of the flower, in the dewdrops."

Like many romantics, Pestalozzi personified Nature as female, the giver of life, synonymous with holy and good. Elevating women's roles as educators made sense to many Americans, who helped transform the elementary school teaching force from largely male to female. Pestalozzi's garden-variety slurs on Jesuits and the papacy as the source of many evil school practices hardly undermined his popularity among educational reformers. Finally, because he said that children learned best through the senses, experience, and contact with familiar, concrete objects, Pestalozzi's popularity seemed assured. To the northern Protestant middle classes, there was something practical and comforting in his message.

However, those who visited Pestalozzi's model schools in Europe, read his writings, or taught with him found inspiration, not an infallible guide. His followers soon insisted that the grand master's ideals were more important than how they were implemented. Despite the fame of his schools, Pestalozzi emphasized educating better mothers and improving home-based education, but that did not stop those seeking to spread his ideals into schools. And the inconsistencies in his writings allowed individuals on opposite sides of a question to embrace him. His insistence upon educating the head, heart, and hand led some reformers to demand vocational education for the masses. Others, like Ralph Waldo Emerson, endorsed manual labor schools but said one educated for life, not merely for work. In addition, Pestalozzi's search for a science of education, where he conjured up the spirit of empiricism and rationalism, inspired disciples on both sides of the Atlantic to create variations on a formal method—object teaching—that proved as rigid as any other pedagogical system.

Object teaching promised to cure many an educational ill and became a rallying cry among romantic educators in Europe and the U.S. As Pestalozzi explained in his famous semi-autobiographical volume, *How Gertrude Teaches Her Children,* in language that romantics everywhere repeated, young children should be taught by "*things* more than by *words*." By this, he meant that enlightened adults should downplay books, memorization, and the usual pedagogies inherited from the past. Instead, they should draw upon the natural world and familiar objects, using materials from everyday life to teach the young. Abstractions in books had no meaning for children, who learned through their senses, a point made by various educational theorists earlier but something Pestalozzi seemed to claim as his own. To teach science, why not take children on a trip to a duck pond, to draw out their innate curiosity about nature? Why not learn arithmetic by counting the number of chickens in the barnyard rather than calculating figures from some dull textbook? Why not teach geography or even history by letting children use their own powers to observe, explore, and see the world around them? To Pestalozzi this was more natural than, and superior to, forcing the young to memorize the names of rivers, the heights of mountain chains, the rules of grammar, the dates of historical battles, and the arcane names for the common minerals in the ground beneath their feet.

As Pestalozzians insisted in the coming years, just about any familiar object could replace a textbook. An instructor, for example, could bring an ordinary basket to class as a springboard to learning. One could ask children to name and describe this object: it has a lid, it has a certain width and certain shape, it is brown, it is used to store things. One of Pestalozzi's followers added that a teacher showing students a pocket watch could reveal the wonders of the new education: "The teacher, holding up a watch, asks, What is this? It is a watch. Now look well at it, and tell me the name of some part of it. The hands. Yes. Tell me another part. The glass. All repeat,—'The watch has hands and it has a glass.'" Sing-song drill under the teacher's direction could obviously coexist with object teaching, but Pestalozzi taught that the training of the senses, an interaction with things, must precede the mastery of words. Thus a drawing of a pig, a pail of milk, a collection of sea shells, writing paper and sandpaper, or a map of Europe could awaken the child's natural interest in learning. These lessons taught about size and shape, color and texture, liquids and solids, and all manner of "real," not simply textbook, knowledge.

Like any educational rebel, however, Pestalozzi often found the world resistant to change. *How Gertrude Teaches Her Children* includes discussions of his rows with working-class parents, who believed he used their children as guinea pigs, and with staff at his model schools, who among other things complained of his inability to balance the books. Pestalozzi hardly romanticized the poor. He wrote that their diction was bad and that parents favored traditional discipline and religious orthodoxy. "Let him who lives among such people come forward and bear witness, if he has not experienced how troublesome it is to get any idea into the poor creatures." When he tried to dispense with the standard books or catechism, parents "decided at a meeting that they did not wish experiments made on their children with the new teaching; the burghers might try on their own." Most ordinary parents, especially the poor, favored traditional pedagogy, words over things, at school. To this day, progressive educators encounter apathy, indifference, and resistance from the poor, who are often moored to tradition and suspicious of bourgeois reform.

Froebelian ideas and practices also inspired child-centered advocates and were continually reshaped after midcentury, when German emigres spread the kindergarten gospel after the abortive Revolution of 1848. Born in 1782 in Thuringia, one of the German states, Froebel fashioned his ideas from an eclectic mix of Enlightenment and romantic writings and from a variety of experiences, including an apprenticeship to a forester and military service against Napoleon. He studied with Pestalozzi, taught in several schools, and like Pestalozzi gave heightened significance to motherhood, womanhood, and early education along natural lines. Inventing an elaborate, highly symbolic, graduated series of classroom lessons, Froebel cast the kindergarten in the red hot glow of Christian pantheism. The child of a Lutheran minister, Froebel had an unhappy childhood but grew up in a spiritual world rich in symbolism. More bookish than his Swiss counterpart, he became a teacher when "he accepted the call from Providence." Put the concrete before the abstract, and experience before books, in the education of young children, both men and their disciples said. Blending naturalism and Christian piety, he thus described the kindergarten: "As in a garden, under God's favor, and by the care of a skilled, intelligent gardener, growing plants are cultivated in accordance with Nature's laws."

Ironically, the German state of Prussia temporarily banned the kindergarten in 1851, the year before Froebel's death, since religious and political radicals and women activists had mostly championed the innovation. Froebel's kindergarten, melding the sweet sounds of nature, human goodness, social harmony, holiness, and maternalism into a pedagogical symphony, soon proved as appealing and flexible in America as Pestalozzi's broader educational philosophy. Middle- and upper-class women, whether moralizing reformers or those who wanted to liberate the child, found in Froebel what they wanted. The well-known transcendentalist Elizabeth Peabody became a leading advocate of the kindergarten, yet hardly read any of Froebel's writings, which could be alternatively obtuse and highly prescriptive. Directly influenced by Pestalozzi and other romantic educators as well as by German idealist philosophers, Froebel devised nearly two dozen "gifts" and "occupations," a set of sequenced learning materials that promised to go beyond object teaching. He employed various familiar objects—balls, blocks, sticks, and clay—everyday materials that children had played with and learned from through the ages. But Froebel conceived of their use in novel ways, hoping to teach young children about more than color, shape, or motion. He believed that, rightly organized, kindergartens taught creativity and self-expression but also a sense of social order and recognition of the divinity within.

Even if some of Froebel's followers were confused by his often dense prose, they were understandably attracted to the genius behind the various gifts and occupations. Grasping his philosophical beliefs fully often proved elusive, but the pedagogical exercises, even if not taught in the proper sequence or exactly as the master intended, were concrete, something one could introduce into a classroom setting. For example, the first gift—a ball, perhaps made of yarn—was a familiar enough object, found even in the poorest home. It could teach about form, motion, color, or, as Froebel wrote: "In the first plays with the ball the life of the child makes itself known, and the outer world makes itself known to the child in unity." Building upon the first gift, teachers would proceed to utilize blocks, spheres, cones, sticks, peas, clay, and other materials as part of a system of learning materials that grew ever complex. Children might have simply thought that this, along with games and stories, was fun, but they were supposedly being taught about metaphysics and the divinity, the unity, of the inner child and the outer world, and self-expression and self-control. Beneath the apparent simplicity of an activity lay a deeper lesson.

Just as Pestalozzi's followers sometimes adhered to the spirit if not the exact form of his original ideas, when they could be discerned, so too did Froebel's followers substantially revise the master's highly formalized gifts and occupations. America's kindergarten enthusiasts divided into rival camps, all claiming true discipleship. Some tried to follow Froebel step by step, others improvised. And the sale of kindergarten materials (principally to make money, not to produce pantheists) could not guarantee uniform pedagogical practices. Froebel wanted kindergartens to reach all children, but America's public schools, despite important exceptions, adopted them very slowly. Moreover, those built for the urban poor often wore the badge of class stigma. To the northern middle classes, the private kindergarten might help advance their own children, since it shielded them from early contact with the poorer classes.

But for the laboring, increasingly immigrant masses, whether in charity or public kindergartens, the emphasis was on discipline and moral uplift. Thanks to Pestalozzi, Froebel, and their acolytes, games, stories, play, and more informal learning experiences became part of a widened educational repertoire. But the traditional ways of the typical school and the blight of social class bias in child-centered education long endured.

After the Civil War, American reformers frequently invoked the names of Pestalozzi, Froebel, and other European romantics, along with a wider range of more conservative writers and theorists who also stressed the importance of education in the lives of children. Despite their many differences, advocates of a new education insisted that young children, who should be educated in kindly and natural ways, learned best not through books but through sensory experience and contact with real objects. To those who wanted to humanize and enliven instruction in the expanding public schools, Pestalozzian object teaching was the answer. Advocates of kindergartens soon debated how best to plant and cultivate children's gardens. And an even wider range of reformers demanded manual training classes in the schools, challenging traditional pedagogy and learning. All of these activists would face an uphill battle, as European reformers had earlier discovered.

And yet the champions of the child persevered. The great European thinkers had helped demonstrate that most educational maladies could be corrected, said Calvin M. Woodward, America's leading advocate of manual training, if young people worked with their hands in the nation's schools. This would help eliminate class conflict, industrial alienation, and urban violence. "Did you ever see one whose mind was nauseated with spelling books, lexicons, and grammars, and an endless hash of words and definitions?" Woodward asked in 1885, "And did you, in such a case, call in the two doctors, Johann Pestalozzi and Friedrich Froebel? And did you watch the magic influence of a diet of *things* prescribed by the former in the place of words, and a little various practice in *doing,* in the place of talking, under the direction of the latter?"

Like other northern activists, the charismatic Francis W. Parker also wanted to break "the chains of the old education." A former teacher and principal who became school superintendent in Quincy, Massachusetts, in the 1870s, Parker had fought for the Union, risen to the rank of lieutenant-colonel, and become a nationally prominent champion of the new education. He was widely quoted for condemning parrot-like teaching and the emotional slaughter of the innocents in the classroom. Too many teachers, he reported, worried about trivial matters such as a shortage of teaching apparatus (maps, globes, and so forth) when natural methods were superior. In a clear reference to the Swiss master, Parker asked, "Have we not pebbles, and shells, and leaves, and flowers, and the free skies?" Edward Sheldon, who established a model normal school in Oswego, New York, that became a mecca for progressive teachers, saw object teaching as a panacea. Reportedly devising his theories before learning about Pestalozzi, he observed children closely to discover the "laws of childhood." Like his counterparts across the sea, he assailed the old education's exaggerated interest in books and words rather than nature and things.

Pestalozzi, Froebel, Sheldon, and their allies all hoped to uncover children's natural development and to fashion a veritable science of education. According to Sheldon, existing teaching methods were "very defective," since they were not based on a real understanding of the child and of nature. This emphasis on laws and methods seems contradictory in those who venerated intuition and feeling and called each individual a unique spiritual being. But the zeal of reformers to dispense with the old and herald the new blinded them from seeing any conflict. Like educators working in emerging school systems, they too applauded order and predictability but believed that most teachers had erroneous notions about curriculum and pedagogy. Through observation and keen insight, reformers had devised systematic ways to teach along natural lines.

Attempting to make Oswego a showplace of the new education, Sheldon appointed enthusiastic and like-minded assistants to help usher in a new pedagogical order. One of his co-workers, M. E. M. Jones, who had extensive teaching experience in London, typically applauded learning by doing and interacting with things rather than reading books. "For many years the sentiment has been gaining ground in this country," she said in 1869, "that there is something to do in our schools besides simply teaching children to 'read, write, and cipher.'" A familiarity "with Nature, in her varied forms, is also an important educational attainment, and . . . a knowledge of things does in its natural order precede a knowledge of *words*."

Rival primers on how to teach had existed in the antebellum period, and pedagogical wars continued throughout the century. Advocates of the new education disparaged the traditional common school curriculum, accused its defenders of mental cruelty to children, and berated familiar practices such as the mastery of textbooks, the use of corporal punishment, and the emphasis upon memorization, recitation, and written tests. Pestalozzi inspired many educational leaders, especially at the new normal schools being established in different states. From her post at Michigan's teacher training school at Ypsilanti, A. S. Welch championed the new education and published *Object Teaching* (1862) to help guide future elementary teachers. Like many primers, hers often relied upon a question-and-answer format but promised better and more lively instruction. One example—on how to teach by studying a readily available object, one's nose—illuminates the new pedagogy in action.

> *Teacher:* Today, children, we will have a lesson on noses. First, let us print the word on the board and pronounce it until we know it thoroughly. Very well. Now we will name some parts of the nose. This long part, just below where your nose meets your forehead, is called the bridge of the nose. What is the part called, children?
>
> *Children:* The nose.
>
> *T.* And the end here is called the tip of the nose. What is it called?
>
> *C.* The tip of the nose.
>
> *T.* And these two holes are called the nostrils. What are they called?
>
> *C.* The nostrils.

Other progressive textbooks similarly presented hundreds of innovative lessons—on spheres and cones, addition and subtraction, and other familiar classroom topics—a veritable godsend to those who believed that the old educational methods had failed. "Words, words, words; little black, immovable images, which [the child] can not get his fingers under. What cares he for them?" asked one critic in 1865 who said traditional instruction was "an abuse of nature."

While primers on object teaching proliferated—often appearing in multiple editions—competing authors conceded that the schools needed improvement but thought that playing with pebbles, examining baskets, and communing with nature were outside the school's purview. They regarded pronouncements about identifying "the laws of childhood" as especially pompous. As early as 1865, Frederick S. Jewell published a volume entitled *School Government,* with a ponderous subtitle that promised readers some *Critiques upon Current Theories of Punishment and Schemes of Administration.* In what became the standard slur on progressive education, Jewell wrote: "No thoughtful educator can have failed to observe that the entire tendency of our assumed improvement is to simplify books, to elaborate all the processes of reasoning for the pupil, and to make the teacher more minutely helpful. In short, we are practically running a system of study made easy." How, he wondered, could children learn self-reliance? Jewell found object teaching sometimes helpful but hardly a panacea. "Not that which is the easiest and more agreeable, is always the wisest or the best."

During this same period, right before becoming superintendent in St. Louis, William T. Harris pondered the ongoing debates on the nature of the child, the curriculum, and teaching. America had no more serious student of continental philosophy than Harris, who mastered German philosophy, literature, science, and pedagogics. Because of his alleged atheism, radical politics, and misogynist views, Rousseau was much less influential in America than Pestalozzi and Froebel, whose assumptions about children were more compatible with bourgeois Protestantism by midcentury. Harris openly dismissed Rousseau's views as reprehensible, but he also found reformers too starry-eyed and without self-criticism.

Harris agreed with the champions of object teaching that children learned by doing and that the handling of specimens could help improve, for example, the teaching of natural science, a subject which he later added to the elementary curriculum in St. Louis. He nevertheless concluded that the new pedagogy had serious limitations. "But how is it," Harris wrote in 1866, "with objects that possess universal necessity? Can we present to universal perception, God, Mind, Reason, or Truth? If not then the Science of Government, of Religion, & of Mind cannot be helped much by object lessons. On the contrary these require the profound reflection of the soul into itself." Like other methods, object teaching had some real value but also real shortcomings. Visionaries were often attracted to education, Harris realized, and they often turned genuine insights into grand schemes and confused "idiosyncrasy with originality."

Schools, Harris insisted, should teach the inherited wisdom of the past and provide everyone with common knowledge and basic intellectual skills. In time each generation made its contributions to the store of human knowledge. Would object teaching promote these ends? Admittedly, textbooks were often boring, teachers uninspiring, and the task of learning difficult, often unpleasant and frequently unrealized. However, nearing the end of his superintendency in the late 1870s, Harris concluded that people who searched for panaceas had too often embraced the new methods uncritically. "Since it has become common in this country to blame the text-book method . . . most schools seem to prefer to let some form of object lesson pass as the type of instruction method; and a teacher is prouder of his collection of bugs of 'native woods' or specimens of rocks and fossils than he is of a method of teaching to read and write. It is fashionable to speak of the 'objective method' as applicable to all branches, even those of grammar and arithmetic."

The disciples of Pestalozzi and Froebel seemed bedazzled by their discovery that children learned from more than books. They often mocked the printed word and were blind to their own pedagogical fetishes. To criticize books remained a staple of the new education, accompanying nearly every critique of the schools or advocacy of a new program, from kindergartens to manual training. Activists saw an array of sensory experiences as the basis of education and often emphasized transcendence, intuition, and feeling. They could ably cite European romantics who questioned the importance of books, grammars, and catechisms in the instruction of the young. In *Emile,* Rousseau had called reading "the greatest plague of childhood." In 1801, Pestalozzi boasted that he had not read a book in thirty years. Wordsworth playfully told everyone to put away their books: "Books! Tis a dull and endless strife / Come, hear the woodland linnet. . . . Come forth into the light of things / Let nature be your teacher." The antiacademic strain within child-centered education never disappeared.

✎

Despite Harris's biting comments on object teaching, which helped solidify his reputation as a conservative, he helped establish the nation's first comprehensive system of public kindergartens. His disdain for child-centered, romantic views hardly dimmed his interest in early childhood instruction. The leading American expert on the German philosopher Hegel, Harris worked well with German Republicans on the St. Louis school board, impressed with a reform conceived in their homeland. Only a handful of districts established public kindergartens in the late nineteenth century, since most states restricted school admission to children six years or older. For various reasons, many educators, physicians, teachers, and community leaders opposed formal schooling for very young children. Despite recurrent opposition, the first public kindergarten opened in St. Louis in 1873, followed by other Midwestern cities heavily populated with Germans. Communities in Massachusetts, long a leader in educational innovation, also funded some of the first public kindergartens. Cities led the way in building both public and private kindergartens, though most were still private ventures at the end of the century. After object teaching, the kindergarten was a prime example of the new education, and St. Louis became one of its major testing grounds.

Popular guides to the kindergarten spoke of a "paradise for children" that honored the harmonious development of the hand, heart, and mind. Activists saw a utopia in the making. Critics of educational reform often formed their judgments of the schools not from first-hand knowledge but from reading or hearing such overblown rhetoric. St. Louis's first public kindergartens opened in the poorest areas, along the levees and in the manufacturing districts. There, according to Harris and his allies, family and community had broken down as effective agencies of education and socialization. Kindergartens would help rescue the poor from crime, vice, and vicious parents, reaffirming part of the familiar mission of the urban schools. Children would learn self-control, punctuality, moral values, respect for authority, and social cooperation. In response to exaggerated claims about the importance of play and the natural goodness of children learning in Edenic settings, Harris drew upon Hegel, not Froebel, when he succinctly wrote: "The Apotheosis of childhood and infancy is a very dangerous idea to put into practice." Never enthralled by romantic imagery, Harris lived and worked in urban areas and, by conviction and political necessity, wed the kindergarten to the traditional goals of mass education.

The key figure in the success of the St. Louis experiment was Susan Blow, who began teaching as a volunteer in the early 1870s. Deeply religious, like many of the missionaries of the new education, Blow was from an elite family, taught by private tutors, educated in the finest private schools, and converted to the gospel according to Froebel. Everywhere elite women were central to the establishment, maintenance, and survival of the kindergarten. In St. Louis, teachers initially volunteered to learn kindergarten methods before joining the regular staff. By 1880 there were 166 kindergarten teachers on the payroll, assisted by 60 volunteers. Visitors peering into their classes saw brightly colored, home-like classrooms that experimented with different methods of instruction: from singing to paper folding, from the handling of cubes and spheres to weaving and clay modeling. Learning was an active process. Froebel, his disciples, and various kindergarten rivals promoted diverse methods to teach children social cooperation, manual skills, and concepts such as time, spatial relationships, and hand and eye coordination. If not exactly a "paradise for children," the kindergarten still differed from traditional instruction, with its didactic methods, rote style, and emphasis upon textbooks.

Opposition as well as public indifference to the kindergarten was common. Most urban kindergartens were controlled by charity organizations for the poor or were private schools for the rich. They did not become an integral part of mass education until the second half of the twentieth century. Even in St. Louis, site of the most famous experiment in the 1870s, trouble loomed. Angry taxpayers and political opponents launched vocal campaigns against the kindergartens, claiming their establishment exceeded the legal boundaries and original intent of public education. They seemed to some a needless expense and a form of day care that weakened parental responsibilities. Concerns deepened as the world depression weakened the local economy. The Supreme Court of Missouri ultimately sided with the opposition in 1883, narrowing the reach of the kindergartens by severely limiting the use of funds in educating the very young.

Before then, however, the kindergartens thrived and proved immensely popular. By the end of the 1870s they had expanded to every district in the city. Eight thousand children attended in 1880, an impressive achievement. Harris and Blow put St. Louis on the map forever in the annals of early childhood education. The local kindergartens received national attention, and those elsewhere were also controversial. One pundit in the *New England Journal of Education* dismissed them as "disorderly nurseries," not realizing that the rationale behind them was akin to social control. Whatever their nature in local communities, those in St. Louis were studied closely and influenced trends throughout the nation. Women were vital to the spread of kindergartens, and many teachers and supervisors in Boston, Baltimore, Chicago, and other cities were St. Louis alumnae. Charity workers, settlement house activists, and leaders in the Women's Christian Temperance Union endorsed kindergartens for diverse reasons: to save the child, to experiment with teaching methods, or to provide day care for the children of working mothers.

Like most innovations, kindergartens thus promised many things to many people. Transcendentalists and romantics beheld a place where nature's laws might be honored, in an environment that respected the goodness of the child, nurtured in harmonious ways. They believed that artifice could not take root in a carefully tilled garden. Harris and Blow, in contrast, scoffed at sentimentality and wanted kindergartens to teach all the social classes the values and skills needed for success in the elementary grades and for living cooperatively in a complex industrial society. Along with other pioneers in the mail-order business, toy manufacturer Milton Bradley was also smitten by the prospects of social reform, and he began selling instructional packets for kindergartens in 1871. Profits and progress were not incompatible in romantic reform.

In an age of recurrent Protestant revivalism, child-centered reformers actually deepened the wider evangelical faith among countless educators and citizens that schools could improve and perhaps perfect society. The mystical, quasi-religious, and Christian imagery that found prominence in European romanticism (especially in Pestalozzi and Froebel) also found ample expression in America. Many activists traveled to Europe to examine model schools that taught orphans and young children, much like religious pilgrims seeking inspiration, personal salvation, and human redemption. A religious aura frequently surrounded those who lobbied for kindergartens or manual training, or who wrote extensively on behalf of the new education. A beautiful, radiant Madonna graced the cover of one kindergarten manual by William Hailmann, among the nation's leading proponents of kindergartens and object teaching. Taught by Pestalozzian teachers in his native Switzerland, Hailmann emigrated to the U.S. at midcentury and taught in a variety of public and private schools, becoming a prolific author, prominent school administrator, and tireless champion of Froebel.

By the 1890s, the debates over the old and new education became increasingly ritualized and almost passé. In 1892, Louisa Parsons Hopkins, a supervisor of teachers in Boston, published *The Spirit of the New Education*. Like other reformers, she attacked the "medievalism" of the schools and their unnatural preoccupation with "an exclusively book education." In addition, upon visiting one kindergarten, she experienced an epiphany. The teacher and her tender charges sang joyfully and playfully engaged in their classroom activities, fostering a "baptism of the spirit." "There was an ineffable sweetness, and almost holiness, about the atmosphere of the place," according to Hopkins. "The children's faces were lighted up with real inspiration and interest, and one could almost see a tongue of flame on the forehead of the teachers." On the classroom wall hung a fine reproduction of the Madonna, a fitting image of the mother's role as savior.

Whether they were teachers or administrators, school board members or activist citizens attracted to every new social cause, reformers endorsed object teaching, kindergartens, and other innovations with such single-mindedness that more traditional educators called them arrogant and irresponsible. Labeling Francis Parker an "apostle of the new education," a writer in the *Pennsylvania School Journal* simply remarked that "if Col. Parker is right, nearly all of us are wrong." Even though William T. Harris led the nation in establishing public kindergartens and science instruction in the primary grades in the 1870s, child-centered progressives attacked him as a conservative. He remained suspicious of the utopian claims of the new education and recoiled at sugary views of the child. It did not help his reputation among the progressives when he defended the common school curriculum and refused to accept the idea that manual training, another aspect of the new education, deserved a prominent place in the nation's schools.

America's leading advocates of the new education assumed that they were on the cusp of a pedagogical and curricular revolution. In addition to promoting object teaching and kindergartens, they endorsed manual training, industrial education, and related reforms to tie schools more closely to the so-called real world. Despite disparaging those who insisted that books and academic instruction were central to the schools, many of the advocates of child-centered education themselves usually had a superior academic education. Their lives had been enriched through books, yet they ridiculed those who endorsed a basic humanistic or liberal education for the masses. Most of these reformers were very well educated indeed: the men had often attended college, even graduate school by the late nineteenth century, and the women often enjoyed tuition at the best academies. Yet they were certain that society had an exaggerated faith in book learning. Calvin Woodward, a long-time professor of polytechnics and mathematics in St. Louis, was a nationally renowned champion of the new education, especially manual training. Having received a B.A. from Harvard, he defended some aspects of academic education, correctly assuming that if taught outside of the regular curriculum, manual training was destined for second-class status. Like G. Stanley Hall, one of the founding fathers of psychology and one of Dewey's professors in graduate school, Colonel Parker continued his studies at German universities, then regarded as the most advanced in the western world. William Hailmann, Susan Blow, and other reformers received excellent academic training and spent their lives reading and pondering the meaning of education in the cosmos.

The anti-intellectual strain within the new education was nevertheless pronounced. Some critics, placed on the defensive for assailing tradition, insisted that they loved books but were opposed to reliance upon textbooks, the predominant means of school instruction. Others made little distinction between textbooks and books in general. In a typical rhetorical flourish in *The Spirit of the New Education,* Louisa Hopkins of Boston condemned "the traditions of an exclusively book education," writing that schools had "tied the child to the dead past, and confined him to the medieval form of brain activity and thought expression," making the child a passive recipient of much useless book knowledge. Only kindergarten, nature study, and wood working for boys and cooking and sewing for girls would reconnect the mind, heart, and hand. "We no longer want mere bookworms coming out of our schools," Hopkins concluded, "but live boys and girls, awake at every pore. " The old-time school would have to go.

More than a little utopianism characterized the new education. This was certainly true of its most widely discussed reform, manual training, even though the concept lacked a uniform definition or set of programs. Books and articles galore on the new education complained about the heavy hand of academic tradition, which they hoped manual training would undermine. One superintendent told *Century Magazine* in 1888 that manual training was "the greatest advance" in education in fifty years. A Philadelphian said that it would teach children about beauty, workmanship, and the value of concentration. "If the object of education is efficiency in all its relations of life," said William Hailmann, "it can be best developed by manual training." It taught personal responsibility and respect for others. Cincinnati's school superintendent, Emerson E. White, wryly observed that "I shall not be surprised to hear some enthusiast say that manual training is the only road to heaven. Every other possible claim has been made for it."

Schools since the antebellum period had often promised to heal the nation's ills. Unifying the body, mind, and heart appealed to a people ravaged by civil war and racial and class divisions. Faith in the redemptive powers of manual training was also a reaction to ancient divisions within western philosophy, which rested upon a metaphysics that divided the mind and the body, which the new education promised to reunite. Moreover, education had a hallowed place in the utopian imagination, as exemplified by Plato's *Republic,* Francis Bacon's *New Atlantis,* and Thomas More's *Utopia.* The children on More's fabled island all mastered a trade and not simply books. Few proceeded to advanced studies to join the intelligentsia, but in that mythical land the separation between mental and physical labor for the masses had mostly disappeared.

Before the Civil War, citizens with differing visions of the common good often favored some form of manual training. Ralph Waldo Emerson included manual labor schools in his transcendentalist vision; evangelical reformers among others espoused basket weaving, broom making, and wood carving for orphans, juvenile delinquents, and hardened criminals; and early advocates of object teaching and then of kindergartens said education should supersede or transcend mere books. After the Civil War, manual training and industrial education, terms sometimes used synonymously, attracted a variety of citizens searching for solutions to numerous industrial ills. They often confused learning how to use common tools with real work, and otherwise intelligent people began saying that many children were "hand-minded" and thought with things, not words. That manual training later evolved into mundane courses in leathercraft obscures its phenomenal appeal in the nineteenth century. The leading utopian novel of the late nineteenth century, and one of the century's best-selling books was Edward Bellamy's *Looking Backward* (1888). It told the fabulous tale of a Boston gentleman, Julian West, an insomniac whose mesmerist succeeds so well that he does not awaken until the year 2000. By then the labor question had been solved and manual training was taught in harmony with academic subjects. Dr. Leete, West's host in this paradise of cradle-to-grave socialism, explained to the time traveler that young men were even educated through age twenty-one, "instead of turning [them] loose at fourteen or fifteen with no mental equipment beyond reading, writing, and the multiplication table."

By the 1870s and 1880s, manual training and industrial education were the rage in many urban communities. Well-to-do women and voluntary organizations established free sewing and cooking classes, which local school boards sometimes adopted. Such classes were sometimes targeted at the poor, sometimes at every female. One visitor at a cooking class in Boston in 1886 saw real knowledge being taught to girls through "industrial education." Cooking tapped the students' interests, making learning fun and useful. "Their eager faces were pleasant to see as they stood round the stove watching their kettle of boiling fat," the guest recalled. By trial and error, the girls learned when the "fat was just right for the fish balls and muffins." Goodbye to "soggy doughnuts and greasy potatoes."

As the depression of the 1870s hit local communities and workers lost their jobs, went on strike, and sometimes engaged in mass violence, capitalists conveniently blamed unemployment on the laziness of employees and on the overly "literary" qualities of the school. The curriculum indeed centered on academic subjects, but educators still emphasized hard work, punctuality, and morally upright behavior. Business leaders, especially large manufacturers, nevertheless complained throughout the postbellum era that schools no longer produced tractable and responsible workers. Evangelical preachers and many businessmen enjoined schools to teach the dignity of work (at a time when factory labor was doing the opposite) and to restore the values of a happier and more prosperous time.

In the industrializing North, reformers were uncertain whether shop class, welding class, or other fruits of the new education should serve everyone or particular groups of children. According to some writers, manual training was best for poor Irish immigrants and French Canadians, the core of the industrial proletariat in some New England towns. The *Chicago Inter-Ocean* explained in 1892 that labor disturbances at Homestead and Pittsburgh had revived interest among employers in undermining skilled workers, who refused to train more apprentices than markets could absorb. None other than J. P. Morgan gave a half-million dollars to the New York Trade Schools, which union leaders said trained scabs. "If the American boy is to have a chance in skilled labor," said the news reporter, "we must have more and better trade schools, where the hand, the eye, and the mind are all educated together. When we have these we shall have fewer strikes and labor riots."

Northern business leaders consistently argued that America's chief industrial competitor, Germany, had a superior system of vocational schools, an unfair advantage in the global economy. Industrial expositions publicized the latest inventions and examples of manual training from Europe, reinforcing the message that America's schools had slipped. With other voluntary associations, business groups often petitioned school boards for manual training courses in the elementary grades and for manual training high schools, and also funded private ventures. At the onset of the horrible depression of 1893, the American Bankers' Association paid a professor to travel to Europe to study the latest advances in technical and vocational education. Upon his return, he predictably questioned the strictly academic features of high schools and urged the establishment of commercial high schools, at least for some children.

Fears of immigrants, union radicals, and undisciplined and volatile workers haunted northern employers. In the South, however, the labor question centered on the ex-slaves and their children. Most African Americans wanted an academic course of study in the schools. They understandably embraced the common school, long associated with freedom, opportunity, and respectability. Though they failed to invest very much in segregated black schools, whether literary or industrial, numerous white Southerners applauded manual training and industrial education for the children of the freedpeople. Educators, like other community leaders, continually complained about the flight of white and black workers from the cotton fields to the cities and the poor work habits of those left behind. Slavery, said many whites, had been a moral evil but at least had taught the "heathen," "lazy" Africans the value of hard work. Without the constant threat of the lash, new forms of discipline were necessary. A speaker at the (white) Alabama Teachers' Association in 1889 concluded that blacks could be uplifted if they learned "the ten commandments and a handicraft."

Maintaining the color line while denying equal (or any) education to blacks remained the predominant southern concern. But the new education clearly had its place below the Mason-Dixon line. The Reverend Charles L. Fry, a Yankee who attended an educational and industrial convention in New Orleans in 1888, recalled that speakers there were as worried about African Americans as Yankees were about immigrants. Southerners wanted to ensure that blacks had access to more than book learning. Instead, they believed that African Americans needed "practical information about the soil and the crops, and various trades, and horses and cattle," and, most importantly, to learn how to work, and work hard. African Americans were capable of improvement, said the Reverend, but they hardly needed a "smattering of superficial, impracticable, and worse-than-useless *book*-knowledge."

"Manual training," noted the *Dixie School Journal* in 1895, "has recently been suggested as one of the means of combating the criminal tendency in the young, and this suggestion is being received with increasing favor." State teachers' associations, as in the North, passed resolutions favoring the reform to provide African Americans and poor whites with a more realistic education and to combat laziness and crime. Many whites in the former Confederacy believed Yankees had planted dangerous, ridiculous ideas into the heads of the ex-slaves during Reconstruction. "Some of them," said one North Carolinian in 1898, "were extreme fanatics and did more harm than good, by inculcating false notions of freedom, inflaming race prejudices, and circulating the most romantic notions as to the mental capabilities of the poor Negroes and their passionate desire for the spelling book and the Bible." Other writers said blacks needed an agricultural or "industrial education" to compete for jobs, avoid "chain-gangs, jails, and penitentiaries," and stay away from the vices of the "madding towns."

Southern educators adapted romantic ideas to a region that systematically stripped African Americans of all vestiges of citizenship. Pestalozzi, it was alleged, had once faced a similar challenge: how to turn the "poor, shiftless, helpless Swiss peasantry" into good, hard-working citizens. "For all the world, especially for us in North Carolina, and especially for the Negro," said one Southerner, "must this Pestalozzian principle be a guiding and formative one." Throughout the nation, advocates of the new education often shared the widespread belief that African Americans were childlike, though capable of some improvement. "To whom is the burden and complaint of incompetent servants not known?" asked one writer in the *North Carolina Journal of Education* in 1899. According to some Southerners, the serving skills black girls once learned in slavery would now have to be taught in school.

Since 1868, when he opened Hampton Institute in Virginia, Samuel C. Armstrong above all white leaders had popularized "industrial education" as the most promising reform in the education and training of southern black citizens. Innumerable educators, business leaders, and philanthropists applauded Armstrong's missionary zeal, faith in racial uplift, and endorsement of white supremacy. A Williams College alumnus and former Union general, Armstrong was the son of Protestant missionaries in Hawaii, where the Hilo Manual Labor School well symbolized the new education. Like many white contemporaries, he characterized African Americans as simple, docile, superstitious, immoral, and inherently lazy—but, with the right guidance, candidates for social uplift. Offering courses in agriculture, domestic science, carpentry, and bricklaying, Hampton typically downplayed academic instruction. Hampton's most famous alumnus, Booker T. Washington, became the leading black prophet of self-help, hard work, and industrial education. Completing his studies in 1875, Washington told blacks to ignore politics and to become indispensable to the southern economy. That meant internalizing the Yankee work ethic by learning a trade and embracing temperance, industry, and similar virtues. Washington recalled in his 1901 autobiography that ever since his Hampton days he "had no patience with any school for my race in the South which did not teach its students the dignity of labor." Too many blacks desired a classical education, dreaming of jobs as professionals. While respectful of black aspirations, he penned the usual slurs on academic striving common among many reformers.

Up from Slavery, Washington's autobiography, in part recounted the founding of Tuskegee Institute in the Black Belt in Alabama in 1881. The school became synonymous with Washington and reflected Armstrong's lasting paternal influence. Washington certainly believed that some blacks should study classical or modern advanced subjects, but nonetheless ridiculed ex-slaves who read many "big books" and pursued "many high-sounding subjects," including foreign languages. One of "the saddest things" he observed traveling in the South was a "young man, who had attended some high school, sitting down in a one-room cabin, with grease on his clothing, filth all around him and weeds in the yard and garden, engaged in studying a French grammar." Too many students enjoyed "memorizing long and complicated 'rules' in grammar and mathematics, but had little thought or knowledge of applying these rules to the everyday affairs of their life." In contrast, Tuskegee and Hampton taught "practical knowledge" as well as thrift, honesty, and hygiene.

Across the nation, manual training and industrial education had become a panacea. They would teach the work ethic, end vagrancy, tame the labor force, reconnect the mind and body, make schools practical, and rescue listless children from boring textbooks. Everywhere the schools had trained the mind but ignored the body. Both needed attention, as the advocates of object teaching, kindergartens, and manual training noisily and repeatedly argued. This did not always lead to any agreed-upon curricular program or rationale. But it foreshadowed heated debates in the early 1900s between the defenders of academic instruction and commonality and admirers of a more experimental, child-centered pedagogy for everyone, with vocational courses for certain groups.

"Perhaps no subject elicited greater interest, or provoked sharper and more critical debate, than that of industrial or manual training in the schools," said one participant after attending the meetings of the National Education Association in 1884. No one could agree on a clear definition of manual training or industrial education. "Partisans" exhibited everything from "a wooden hatchet to a steam-engine in actual operation." Calvin Woodward prominently insisted upon wedding manual training tightly to a strong English, academic education, but the exhibitors included displays from schools for the blind, deaf and dumb, and "feeble minded." Long associated with the education of the physically or mentally ill, violent criminals, and juvenile delinquents, manual training clearly had some negative associations to overcome. However, manual training and industrial education promised to keep all schools up to date, to teach the best values, and to undermine the bookish curriculum.

Like Booker T. Washington, advocates of this aspect of the new education painted caricatures of well-educated youth out of work or unfit to plow a field. Manual training, they said, was more democratic than academic studies since it prepared pupils for the mundane but essential work of the world. As one contributor to the *Educational Weekly* opined in 1883, "it is as possible to train a boy mentally and spiritually by teaching him and requiring him to solve problems in the use of a plane or square, as in the analysis of questions in mental arithmetic, or a drill in the infinitive." Far better to learn how to build a wagon than study grammar, said one speaker at a national convention. When Woodward's Manual Training School opened in St. Louis in 1880, its motto was "The Cultured Mind—The Skilled Hand," and reflected his difficult-to-refute rejection of the belief that "all the activities of life may be learned from books."

By the late 1880s, many urban school systems had established experimental programs such as woodworking for boys, cooking and sewing for girls, and manual training high schools, which opened in Toledo, Chicago, and some other cities, initially under private patronage. The idea of learning by doing, of actively engaging students in the study of things and not just words or books, grew directly out of the romantic tradition and slowly shaped more urban schools. And, as one activist wrote in 1886 in the *Age of Steel*, a trade publication, once "head and hand" were educated together, children would leave school "better prepared to make a living." Whether one read a report from Portland, Maine, or Indianapolis, Indiana, or little Green Bay, Wisconsin, in the 1880s and 1890s it was clear that the new education had arrived in many schools. The U.S. commissioner of education reported in 1888 that twenty-five thousand girls had taken sewing classes in Philadelphia that year. Drawing courses were common in many towns and cities, teaching manual dexterity and a sense of spatial relationships. Numerous places taught wood turning, metalworking, and leathercraft. Exactly how a class in drawing, paper folding (in kindergarten), and sewing and woodworking constituted actual "industrial education" remained unclear.

Thousands of schools nationwide added manual training and industrial courses, but there was also powerful resistance to change. Many educators, Harris of St. Louis among them, thought the curriculum was already overcrowded, preferred spending money on new buildings or teachers' salaries, and doubted that the practical courses reformers desired were really very practical. Even Ralph Waldo Emerson, the hero to many romantic educators, had eloquently written that the purpose of education is to make a life, not a living. Writing in the *Alabama Teachers' Journal* in 1887, J. H. Phillips, the superintendent in Birmingham in the heart of the "New South" and no romantic, attacked the growth of a "bread and butter view of education" as a "false idea of the practical and useful." He called industrial education the latest fad, likely only to promote "gross materialism," of which America hardly had a shortage.

While manual training and industrial education made visible headway late in the century, tradition was not easily pushed aside. Many educators and citizens went on record opposing them, even if they agreed that schools were often boring and textbooks deadening. Conventional teachers, always in the majority, were understandably offended when called old fogies or meanspirited for insisting that children concentrate on academics. Like Harris, many educators and ordinary citizens still believed that schools should stay focused on training character and teaching the basic subjects. In her widely-discussed volume *Our Common School System* (1880), Mary Abigail Dodge, a former teacher who became a popular essayist and wrote under the pseudonym of Gail Hamilton, questioned the aims of the romantic educators, who sometimes started out extolling nature and childhood innocence but ended up calling for trade schools for the urban working classes. To prepare children for particular trades seemed absurd and undemocratic, said many writers. The school code hardly required teachers to "fit a man to be a gardener or a blacksmith" or "a woman to be milliner or sick-nurse." Emerson E. White pointed out that the 1870 federal census listed 338 different occupations, so which trades should schools teach? Harris predictably denounced any attempt to turn the common schools into trade schools, underscoring the arrogance of the proposal. "Who can tell, on seeing a child, what special vocation he will best follow when he grows up?" he asked in 1880.

Dodge and other defenders of the common school emphasized that most children only went to school for a few years. "For the larger part of our youth," she concluded, "this is the only time that can be devoted to intellectual pursuits. When they grow up they must go into the bread-winning trades. I should feel sorry to see the short time they have for mental culture abbreviated by the thrusting in of mechanical work before its time. Let them have all the learning they will take." The most zealous advocates of manual training wanted industrial schools for the masses, held utopian views on object teaching, kindergartens, and shop class, and wanted to connect schools directly to the workplace. In the majority of schools, however, educators often added some manual training courses but essentially agreed with Dodge that the common curriculum should not be dislodged.

Yet those who favored manual training, industrial education, or vocational education believed that while battles were being lost, the war would inevitably be won. In 1887, Woodward announced that a "great tidal wave of conviction is sweeping over our whole land," and "we continue to battle for the new and true till our banners are the only ones flying." Two years later, the editor of the *Journal of Education* argued that kindergartens, manual training, and industrial education were here to stay. He wrote that, without question, "the historic school curriculum must be adjusted to the new order of things," and "industrial education must be directed to the greatest good of the greatest number, with a view of fitting them in the best way mentally and morally for the work of life." An editorial in 1897 in the same journal asserted that "'Manual Training' is the one great triumph of the New Education. The wise men slighted it, then scoffed at it, then ridiculed it, and finally shouted for it as though they were its original champions." This belied the power of tradition, which held firm despite the clamor for change.

✎

By the 1890s, the defenders of the old and partisans for the new had spent at least a generation fighting over the nature of the curriculum, the culture of teaching, and the place of schools in an industrial society. Depending on what books or journals they read, industrial or educational conventions they attended, or classrooms they visited, citizens could conclude that the schools had witnessed an educational revolution, or the very opposite. In a diverse and sprawling nation, America had examples aplenty to confirm or deny educational change, the watchword of the period. In 1896 a dejected contributor to the *School Journal* wrote that "the study of pedagogy has been, and still is, derided by what may be termed the 3 R men. They have said and still say that it is enough to know the subjects to be taught, and how to keep order." Pestalozzians could only weep, then return to battle. Visitors to many classrooms found that a "dead common school tone" still prevailed. How had the new education affected the curriculum and pedagogy?

The highly decentralized nature of educational governance meant that changes occurred slowly, district by district. Observers disagreed whether change came too slowly or too quickly, but trial and error, said one educator in 1888, ruled. Reasonably dispassionate assessments of what pupils actually studied revealed that, though the "three R men" were hardly invincible, academic subjects remained central to most schools. Some reformers began to praise rural schools for respecting the individual, conveniently forgetting that the pedagogy there—based on textbooks, memorization, and recitation—epitomized tradition. In the cities, where social change was most dramatic and critics now regularly lamented their stultifying rules and regulations, the old course of study proved resilient.

In 1882, John M. Gregory issued a report sponsored by the U.S. commissioner of education on the basic "common school studies." Gregory highlighted what many people already knew: seven basic subjects comprised the heart of the course of study, including spelling, reading, writing, arithmetic, geography, English grammar, and occasionally United States history. The cities had a somewhat broader curriculum than the typical country school, but these basics endured. Like so many critics, Gregory regretted their staying power. How much arithmetic, he asked, did an adult really need to know? How much geography? Too much of instruction was still "the guessing of so many riddles." Gregory called for better pedagogy and the addition of more sciences such as chemistry, botany, and physics. It mattered not that anyone informed about contemporary high schools knew that the sciences were also taught not in Pestalozzian fashion but through textbooks and old-fashioned pedagogy. To condemn the old and welcome the new had assumed a ritualized style among some educators but was a poor guide to classroom practice.

The heated discussions among reformers about the "course of study" obscured the reality that everywhere the stuff of learning depended upon memorization, recitation, and textbooks. The three Rs and a handful of related subjects still dominated. Only in the graded classrooms of the larger towns and cities was there anything approaching a uniform curriculum. And even there age-grading was confounded as ill-prepared rural youth, the children of immigrants, and home-grown youngsters of uneven preparation and differing ambition made teaching anything but uniform. During his tenure as commissioner, Harris directed a staff member to study the elementary curriculum of twenty-nine different cities. As in the countryside, reading, writing, spelling, grammar, and arithmetic took up most classroom time in elementary schools in the early 1890s. The amount of time spent on various subjects varied by district, but the trends were clear. In Mobile, Alabama, for example, 19 percent of the classroom day was spent on reading, 16 percent on spelling, 7 percent on writing, 10 percent on English grammar, and 19 percent on arithmetic. That left 7 percent for drawing, 5 percent for U.S. history, 11 percent for geography, 6 percent for natural science, and nothing for the other subjects surveyed: music, morals and manners, foreign languages, physical education, and civil government.

Everywhere the school day in graded urban systems, as in the countryside, was still devoted to academics. Drawing, science, physical education, and music had joined the curriculum, fueling the common complaint that it was overcrowded and that educators added new courses without deleting old ones. But most elementary schools in the national sampling of cities concentrated on the three Rs. In Minneapolis, music reportedly consumed over 7 percent of the children's time, on the high end, while Elizabeth, New Jersey, was more typical, with 4 percent. Both allowed 6 to 7 percent of the time for drawing, about the middle range in the survey. Like Mobile, both cities concentrated on reading, writing, and its close allies, spelling, grammar, and arithmetic.

Debates had long raged about what schools should teach, how teachers should motivate, instruct, and evaluate children, and how best to educate and socialize children for the future. While the curriculum was not static but grew by accretion, older subjects prevailed. As in the past, educators still believed that schools should produce literate, law abiding, morally upright citizens, pieties heard on all sides of every debate about the schools. With the resurgence of nationalism after the Civil War, flags flew above most schools, and the Pledge of Allegiance and other patriotic rituals also grew popular. Photographic reproductions of national heroes hung on classroom walls, especially iconic figures such as Washington and Lincoln. Robert E. Lee Day added a Confederate twist below the Mason-Dixon line. Temperance instruction became almost universal, another in a growing list of school responsibilities. Despite this veneration of the past and efforts at nation building, critics loudly insisted upon various school improvements. But there was no consensus on how to proceed.

Critics in the late nineteenth century frequently complained that schools were not as rigorous as when they had attended school. Employers often said that prospective workers were lazy, could not spell, and wrote illegible, garbled prose. Many educators in response promised improvements and added new subjects on the margins of the traditional course of study. Citizens wanted evidence of change but bowed to the familiar. By the 1890s, when high schools still served a minority of pupils, one expert typically insisted that entering students should "have familiarity with the elements of arithmetic, geography, American history, grammar, including spelling, and the writing of a fair hand." Such knowledge usually came from textbooks, and was memorized by pupils, recited by each scholar before the entire class, and increasingly written down in competitive, timed examinations.

Written examinations, which grew popular in urban, graded systems by the 1870s, countered romantic reform and emerged as a favorite bugbear of child-centered activists. Nothing better stirred their emotions than these tests. If supervisors judged teachers largely on student performance on common written exams, the classroom could not become a garden where natural methods and diverse pedagogies might bloom. Instead, schools would become factory-like, barren of life; children would become cogs in the machine. Romantic critics imagined worlds that did not exist: factories where workers were routinely treated with dignity and received decent pay, and schools where teachers taught in natural ways and allowed every child to blossom. Written tests, with right and wrong answers, symbolized the old education, a prop to mind-numbing pedagogy, and a staid course of study.

The vast majority of schools before the Civil War had used a variety of methods to determine student progress. Mostly, however, each pupil memorized material, recited it to the teacher's satisfaction, and advanced to more difficult material or to a new subject. Oral methods made the subjective judgments of teachers central to evaluation in most schools, especially in the tens of thousands of rural classrooms. Teachers often sponsored a spelling bee or school exhibition to highlight a school's academic prowess before parents and local worthies. Often teachers provided their students with the questions before a public examination, a practice sometimes ridiculed but rarely abandoned. After the Civil War, when factories adopted more precise ways to measure productivity, schools, especially in the cities, also began devising more objective measures of student achievement. By the 1870s and 1880s, cities used a variety of tests—written and oral, given on a daily, weekly, or monthly basis—to help determine individual progress and annual promotion to the next grade. High school admission tests also remained common.

Written tests became something of a craze. G. Stanley Hall, still in the embrace of romantic idealism, added a new twist to the fad in 1882 when he surveyed the "contents of children's minds," learning that Boston's young lacked basic knowledge about cows and farm animals. Complaints about excessive testing and the misuse of tests led various urban systems to lessen their reliance upon them, but something important was happening whose full import only became clear in the early twentieth century. From the railroads to other major industries, measurement, communication, and quantitative analysis became more sophisticated after the Civil War. It inevitably led to the idea that student comprehension of knowledge could also be measured precisely, with more numerical assessments and comparisons with others. This ultimately had a lasting influence on how Americans would judge their schools. That rule of thumb methods, a teacher's personal or professional judgments, and reliance on oral recitation would suffice in the public's estimate of the schools was forever undermined. Romantic educators henceforth would find themselves challenged to prove empirically that new pedagogies were superior to the old and were not just pie in the sky.

By the 1870s, however, defenders of the new education saw real hope for progressive pedagogy, especially in the cities. Charles Francis Adams Jr., a reform-minded progressive on the local school board who helped publicize Colonel Parker's labors as superintendent in suburban Quincy, Massachusetts, assailed prevailing teaching methods. Before Parker arrived in town, Adams wrote, the typical teacher "unconsciously turned his scholars into parrots, and made a meaningful farce of education." He saw Parker as a charismatic, messianic figure whose advocacy of object teaching might end this nonsense, where "child after child glibly chatter out the boundaries and capitals, and principal towns and rivers of States and nation, and enumerate the waters you pass through and the ports you would make in a voyage from Boston to Calcutta, or New York to St. Petersburg." But traditional pedagogy proved hardy everywhere. Parker's stay in Quincy was short-lived; he was off to Boston by 1880, facing another round of battles on behalf of the new education. By then, written tests in many towns and cities helped assess how well young scholars grasped the mysteries hidden in their ubiquitous textbooks.

Complaints against the tests rolled effortlessly off the tongues of reformers. Teachers taught in "mechanical" ways through "grooved" methods that applied the pedagogical thumb-screw to the child. Others invoked romantic metaphors, saying that "hothouse methods" caused youth to wither on the vine. Written examinations, claimed a writer in the *Carolina Teacher* in 1887, crushed the life out of every child, a point repeatedly heard in professional circles. This traditional, almost religious reverence for the individual permeated the heavily Protestant culture of the day, which emphasized duty and personal responsibility. Romanticism and transcendentalism reinforced this idealization of the individual. Urban school superintendents, rising in influence after the Civil War, told critics that test scores actually honored the individual, whose merits would be revealed once the grades were posted.

Urban schools increasingly relied on written scores for grades on report cards, class rank, promotion, and academic honors. As a result, they were pilloried for making pupils too passive and turning teachers into "marking machines." In the long and painful transition from the world of the craftsman to that of the unskilled laborer, from yeoman farmer to urban dweller, hostility to the "machine" in the garden of learning tapped a populist, democratic sentiment. "Percent fever" had struck the schools, said many weary critics. Mary Abigail Dodge complained in 1880 that the cities drifted toward "more supervision" and "more machinery." Bombarded with tests, the pupil "is held up to study, as a factory hand is held up to the loom." It was all cram, cram, cram. In 1893, the author Edward Everett Hale asked whether the aim of the Boston schools was to prepare fifty thousand identical clothespins.

Whether romantics, realists, or of mixed pedigree, reformers too often expected educators to do the impossible. In an 1887 essay entitled "Public School Machines," an educator from Winnetka, Illinois, rightly argued that society gave schools very mixed messages. Citizens wanted equal rights for everyone but special attention for their own children. They sometimes revered the teacher as a Madonna-like figure but also hired incompetents, or the school commissioner's relatives, to teach. So "what is a teacher to do?" How could a teacher honor the individual in an urban setting where organization, hierarchy, and the division of labor were the guiding forces of political economy?

Throughout the 1880s and 1890s, educators in many school systems ultimately defended examinations and the competitive ethos of the schools. In 1884, a superintendent in a small New England city noted that passing tests, like every hurdle in life, simply required discipline and hard work. Overuse of written tests should be checked, but oral exams, after all, were subjectively graded by teachers and not above criticism. A speaker at the 1889 state teacher's convention in Florence, Alabama, believed that critics should stop complaining about the rising popularity of written competitive tests, because "adult life is one unceasing examination." The speaker pointed out that struggle for survival and preferment was common in American society, and "in school, as in social classes, some one must be first." A year later, Chicago's former school superintendent used romantic language to describe school competition: "As pupils advance in grade, if well rooted and pruned, they may be expected to bear fruit. By examination, the fruit may appear." Success was "refreshing," and failure a spur to exertion and future growth.

Criticisms of written tests accelerated in the late 1880s and early 1890s, which led to some rethinking about their uses. As a result, most pupils in graded systems were promoted and judged on a range of indicators, including test scores, daily recitations, and the opinion of their teachers. Emerson E. White, author of a detailed report on the controversy in the 1890s, believed there was, thanks to the critics, greater understanding of the limitations of written examinations. But drill, memorization, and mechanical methods of instruction were still very common everywhere. For example, however much one might extol how ungraded rural schools honored the individual, they too emphasized cramming, even if common written examinations were generally impossible there given the absence of a uniform, graded curriculum. And rural teachers continued to hear the siren call of the city due to its reputation for higher pay, innovation (including graded classes), and better overall quality of life. In 1895, a National Education Association report on rural education concluded that most normal school graduates—the teachers most sought after and best informed on progressive pedagogy—flocked to the cities, where hierarchy and order were the pillars of the system.

Throughout the 1890s, critics continued to lambast traditional pedagogy. After observing numerous classrooms, a foreign visitor was struck by the heavy reliance upon memorization. "I heard in one class the boys get up one after another recording the names, dates, and chief performances of the eighteen presidents of the United States. In another, the girls recited in order the names of principal inventors and discoverers, with a description of the exploits of each." By the time Joseph Mayer Rice published his celebrated 1893 book attacking the old education, *The Public School System of the United States,* a generation of reformers already realized that tradition was difficult to uproot. A pediatrician, Rice catalogued the usual litany of problems in the urban graded schools, where children memorized materials they did not understand, teachers resembled Gradgrind, the oppressively fact-obsessed schoolmaster of Charles Dickens's *Hard Times,* and cram was king. Readers of educational periodicals also learned of an exhaustive study of industrial education in Pennsylvania, a heavily industrial state, which concluded that most schools did not teach a "practical" curriculum or prepare youth well for industrial jobs.

The advocates of the new education could point to some triumphs but continued problems as the century drew to a close. The curriculum in some urban districts had been enriched by object teaching, occasionally by kindergarten classes, and even more by manual training classes of great variety and quality. Nature study and field trips were not unknown. Even Rice noticed an occasional ray of light in the city systems. In Indianapolis, Nebraska Cropsey, the supervisor of elementary schools and a devotee of object teaching (learned in part at Oswego), helped bring humane, natural teaching methods to the "Crossroads of America." Maybe other places would take heed. Early progressives had also stimulated national debates that reached down to nearly every village, town, and city about whether to change the curriculum and instructional methods. Yet the champions of the new education knew that the seeds of reform often failed to germinate. Sing-song drill, an expanded version of the three Rs, question-and-answer teaching methods, and the heavy use of textbooks remained common in most schools.

Writing as U.S. commissioner of education in 1891, Harris observed that an overemphasis on memorization was still the chief criticism of the schools. Teacher training books were available on object teaching, but so were many that showed not how to abandon recitations but the various ways to conduct them: individually, in small groups, or with whole classes chirping together. Question books still abounded for those trying to prepare for classroom combat, whether the Regents' tests in New York or annual promotion examinations. And critics of the new education continued to flay its anti-intellectual assumptions about textbooks and academic instruction in general. As one observer wrote in 1893, despite what all the "apostles" had said about the benefits of "sandpiles and mudpiles," traditional instruction still made the most sense. Noting that champions of the new education routinely ridiculed "the mastery of books," the editor of the *Journal of Education* emphasized that "much of this talk of substituting the real in nature and workmanship for the ideal in books, is degrading in its tendencies. . . . It is always put forward with a spiritual flavor, is always spoken of as seeing God in his handiwork; but to what child or ordinary mortal did a landscape, a river, lake, or mountain, a flower, or bird ever bring God so vividly near as in the Scripture reference to nature and her teachings, or even in the prose of Beecher or Drummand, or the verse of Bonar or Whittier?" No matter what those favoring things over words believed, "the wealth of the world's knowledge . . . is in books. . . . No school has ever taught too much of books."

The heralds of the new education were often carried away by their own apocalyptic, utopian, messianic visions. Most were frustrated that many school trustees and teachers so valued the traditional curriculum, books, and pedagogy. That was how most teachers had once been taught. Ironically, primers on object teaching, kindergartens, and manual training tended to deteriorate into formula, rules and regulations, and question-and-answer formats, an odd result in a movement that began as an assault on formalism and expressed supreme faith in intuition and individual expression. Turning romantic ideas into a program was a contradiction in terms, and critics noticed that many kindergarten and manual training teachers taught step by step, from guides and primers. In addition, when a modern "science of education" emerged in the early twentieth century, its advocates similarly promised a new educational millennium, based upon a fact-finding empiricism that would have made Pestalozzi and his disciples shudder.

It is not coincidental that the most famous theorists of the new education were not teachers, or if so left the classroom quickly. Susan Blow apparently influenced hundreds of teachers through her lectures. Edward Sheldon spent decades at the helm of a famous normal school. William Hailmann lectured and administered in a variety of prestigious posts. When asked to reminisce about her teacher, a woman recalled vividly that the young John Dewey was unable to control the unruly boys but led a school prayer that was unusually long. Charismatic reformers like Colonel Parker, however, were not called apostles and prophets for nothing. They inspired many who found the classroom experience, whether as students or as teachers, dull and deadening. Reformers assumed at times that their charisma would infect others and thus help transform bureaucracies. Institutions, which grew in size and complexity after the Civil War, nevertheless had a contradictory influence upon the lives of these leaders. Large-scale institutions empowered them personally in terms of careers and gave them the potential to leave an impact on the world, but they also simultaneously constrained their authority over real schools, which grew in number but often ignored the central office.

Perhaps it was good that many reformers left the classroom. These men and women were leaders on the lecture circuit and on the convention platform and, especially in the case of men, were destined for positions as principals, superintendents, and professors at normal schools, colleges, or universities. There they could stand above the fray, survey the educational landscape, and propose how to help set things straight. Whether one favored the old or new education, that was the common upward path—out of the classroom—for those seeking more influence, money, and status. Ironically, the very career move that made it impossible for him to transform actual schools was usually one of the proudest moments of a reformer's life. Only Harris among the chief male combatants of the postbellum school wars did not turn from teaching to professing, though the bespectacled, much-published Hegelian had the longest vitae among his contemporaries. Yet he too never returned to the classroom.

By the end of the nineteenth century, the advocates of the new education had nevertheless invented a whole new vocabulary and way of thinking about the child, the curriculum, and the purposes of schooling. What they said and attempted to implement left an important legacy for future child-centered activists. By the turn of the century, many school critics would say that the child should be an active, not passive, learner, that the teacher should be a helpful guide, not master, that the curriculum should adapt to a changing society, not stay lodged in the past, and that something needed to be done about the many incompetent teachers who sent their pupils to sleep. When he published "My Pedagogical Creed" in 1897, Dewey exemplified the highly spiritual, mystical, quasi-religious side of the new education when he concluded that "the teacher is always the prophet of the true God and the usherer in of the true Kingdom of God." The language of reform became more secular in the new century, but a millennial faith in education never disappeared.

CHAPTER FOUR

Democracy, Efficiency, and School Expansion

"Education is the common creed of the American people," Nathan C. Schaeffer, Pennsylvania state superintendent of public instruction, wrote in 1906. While citizens disagreed on many educational policies, the school was "the one institution in which all Americans believe." That same year, a young professor of education named William C. Bagley agreed that knowledge was the key factor in society's evolutionary growth and improvement and that "education is the largest word in the vocabulary of life." Countless educators, editors of newspapers and popular magazines, and social reformers at the turn of the century predicted that schools would soon increase their social and economic functions. Homes and churches alone, they said, could not possibly teach children the values and skills necessary to survive and prosper in a more complex world, one remade by cities, industrialization, and massive immigration. In Tallahassee, Florida, the masthead of *Southern School and Home* optimistically stated that "Everything in the South Waits Upon the General Education of the People."

Foreign visitors marveled at this faith in education and in the extensive reach of the public school system. Perhaps Americans tended to exaggerate the role of the public schools "in the national welfare," one European concluded in 1903 after touring the United States with a delegation studying education and industrial development. But the citizens he met often spoke enthusiastically about the importance of public education. Yet even they could not have imagined its spectacular growth in the coming decades. Between 1900 and 1950, the average school year in America grew from 144 to 178 days. Combined enrollments of elementary and secondary schools expanded from 15.5 to 25.7 million students. Per capita investment of national income in public education increased dramatically from 1.2 to 2 percent, and schools were typically the largest budget item in most communities. Sensing the trends, one of America's leading radical educators, George Counts, wrote in 1930 that Americans had a "profound" if naive faith in education and in "the potentialities of the individual man."

A few years earlier, Counts had written that "we are already hearing murmurings about universal secondary education." To the surprise of many, high school enrollments had doubled every decade since the 1890s. In the nineteenth century, most educators had assumed that the high school would remain a fairly selective institution. Child labor, common in many families, precluded an extended education, and only a handful of white-collar jobs and professions required any advanced schooling. By the 1930s, however, the labor market for youth collapsed, and child labor and compulsory education laws were strengthened and increasingly enforced. As a result, high schools— once fairly distinctive from the lower grades—joined the lengthening ladder of mass education. Educators boasted that some large American *cities* had more secondary students than some European *nations*. An estimated 519,000 pupils were in high school in 1900, a figure that had amazed foreign visitors. Incredibly, 5.7 *million* youngsters enrolled a half-century later.

Few Americans thought they had built a perfect system. Dissatisfaction with the schools in the first half of the twentieth century was common, often intensifying as attendance increased and schools assumed wider social and economic functions. States had increased their support for schools during the Great Depression, as declining property values, lower tax collections, and high unemployment weakened local budgets. Spending gaps between rich and poor districts, however, often remained wide. By the end of the 1940s, rural areas, the South, and some declining northern industrial cities had the poorest schools, with no immediate relief in sight. The federal government's share of educational spending amounted to about 1 percent, mostly earmarked for vocational programs. A few prescient critics also highlighted the wide division between some suburban and city schools and the chasm separating African American and white schools, especially in the Jim Crow South. Concerns about racial integration, federal authority in education, and the contrasting fate of city and suburb would march to the center of the public stage in the postwar era.

The impressive growth of the school system by midcentury hardly led to a uniformly satisfied public. Many citizens understandably took pride in the sheer expansion of school enrollments, curricular offerings, and social services. But criticisms abounded. A few critics realized that schools reflected society, not the other way around, and doubted their ability to ameliorate difficult economic, racial, and social problems they had not created. Could schools promote the public good or only reinforce general social tendencies, including the advantages of children from more privileged families? A range of reformers, despite their claims that schools were deeply conservative institutions, nevertheless tried to change them, whether by altering the curriculum or implementing more pupil-friendly teaching methods. In addition, despite the expansion of schooling in every region, many parents and taxpayers worried about familiar issues: whether children were well socialized, obedient, and had mastered the three Rs, whether academic standards had declined, and whether child-centered pedagogy (popularly labeled "progressive education") had undermined respect for authority, hard work, and personal responsibility. In an era of dramatic growth and change, schools received intense scrutiny and, occasionally, condemnation.

Debates over the nature of the child, the curriculum, the aims of instruction, and the prospects for reform seemed endemic after the turn of the century. Traditionalists squared off against self-styled progressives, debating each other at professional gatherings, in school board meetings, and in newspapers and magazines. As the twentieth century dawned, school reform was already a national preoccupation. As young John Dewey noted in 1897, outlining his "pedagogical creed," education was America's "fundamental method of social progress and reform." In subsequent decades, the mission of the public schools remained eclectic if not blurred as they confronted sometimes contradictory and utopian demands for reform, both from outside and inside the system. Schools were expected to firm up the social order, teach group norms, and maintain high standards, while identifying and promoting the needs, interests, and potential of each individual. They were also supposed to keep youth on the farms, African Americans from moving North, young people out of the unemployment lines, and everyone out of trouble, while ensuring that youth had mastered the three Rs. As one educational pundit wrote in 1906, "whenever anything goes wrong in the life of the nation the public looks to the school for a remedy."

Before closely examining its expanding network of elementary and secondary schools, one must first appreciate the vast changes that reshaped the nation in the early decades of the twentieth century. A new America was in the making. As in the past, school reform was part of a larger national conversation about what constituted core values and a decent society. On the local level, educational reform was embedded in diverse movements for social improvement. Citizens with different views of school and society clashed: some wanted to make schools more democratic and humane, others to better reflect business efficiency and scientific management. These were the major fault lines in school improvement in the first half of the twentieth century, and they divided local school reformers as well as nationally prominent intellectuals and educational leaders. This became evident as debates about schooling intensified in the early 1900s. Reform was in the air, wrote Ellwood P. Cubberley, a prominent professor of education at Stanford University, who announced in 1909 that Americans were "standing on the threshold of a new era in educational progress."

Historians have traditionally referred to the period between roughly the 1890s and World War I as the Progressive Era. This was an age characterized by diverse, shifting coalitions of reform parties, voluntary associations, and activist citizens, and it continues to defy easy explanation or description. Trying to account for the motivations of reformers at the turn of the century has led historians down many interpretive paths. Before the 1960s some historians believed that most progressive reformers were displaced members of an older native-born middle class, suffering from status anxieties in a world of cities, factories, and foreign immigration. Scholars later emphasized the occupational goals of a "new middle class" of professionals and experts who helped build and manage expanding white-collar bureaucracies, which grew in size and complexity by the 1890s, first in industry and then in various institutions such as schools. By the 1980s, another strand of scholarship focused on the moral and religious impulses underlying progressivism; many reformers, reared in pious, small-town, Republican households, believed in the reality of sin and social injustice and ultimately embraced good works and social reform.

Virtually every historian doubts the existence of any single progressive movement, and the search for a typical progressive reformer remains quixotic. Like romanticism and other useful labels for complex phenomena, progressivism lacked a monolithic character. It included national figures as diverse as Theodore Roosevelt, pacifist and settlement house worker Jane Addams, and journalist Lincoln Steffens. The same complexity existed on the state and local levels. Reformers came from a variety of family backgrounds and had varying psychic needs, social aims, and personal attributes. At the same time, countless reformers before World War I used words like "progress" and "progressive" in their writings. In education, for example, John Dewey regularly generalized about the "new" or "progressive education"—a carryover in language from the nineteenth century—which he contrasted with the "old education" or "traditional" schooling. Subsequent educators and theorists never used these words and phrases with perfect clarity and consistency, but they drew upon them regularly to reduce the complexity of reality to manageable terms.

Education and school reform, like other reform passions, attracted a wide range of activists. Reformers often separated, however, into two broad camps: those who emphasized education's role in promoting social justice and democracy, and those who emphasized business efficiency and scientific management. Both sides believed in the centrality of schools in furthering progress and human betterment. But they often held contrasting views about human nature, democracy and efficiency, and what a good society entailed. People who called themselves reformers looked at the same innovation and saw different realities. For example, a socialist labor leader in Milwaukee might join with settlement house workers and liberals to fund school lunch programs to help counteract the injustices of capitalism; a banker who controlled the majority on the school board, however, might worry more about costs and support free lunches not as a human right but as an investment in human capital. These competing strands of reform—emphasizing democracy or efficiency— often struggled for dominance.

Reform was the touchstone of the era. It came from many sources and assumed diverse expressions. Without question, however, the most important arena for school reform in the first half of the twentieth century was in the cities, the traditional site of educational experimentation. What happened in New York and Chicago, Detroit and Milwaukee, and Louisville and Birmingham was widely publicized at state, regional, and national education conferences and in numerous books, articles, and addresses that tried to direct the course of school improvement. There were multiple reasons for this. Cities since the antebellum period had been the crucible of social change and educational innovation. As education became a research subject at major universities, usually in newly formed departments of education, the city became an important site of inquiry for an expanding number of professors and graduate students. Education also attracted the attention of prominent scholars from many academic disciplines: the sociologist Edward A. Ross, the political economist Richard T. Ely, and the historian Frederick Jackson Turner, to mention only a few at one school, the University of Wisconsin.

Pivotal administrative and organizational reforms had already occurred in many city systems by the 1890s, and the swelling enrollments of children from diverse backgrounds provided exciting venues for investigation. By the turn of the century, most urban school boards were centralized and dominated by more elite social classes; laypeople on the board, admiring of corporate models of governance, frequently delegated supervisory and policy-setting authority to the superintendents, who were often university trained and enamored of scientific management and business efficiency. Like many of their nineteenth-century forebears, educational leaders in most state departments of public instruction, editors of professional journals, and influential school administrators often assumed that city schools were harbingers of the future. So did most prominent university professors. Together they further believed that urban practices—hierarchical models of organization, the elevation of expertise, and the elimination of small schools—needed emulation everywhere, especially in the countryside, still home to tens of thousands of one-room schools on the eve of the Great Depression.

When U.S. census officials announced in 1890 that the "frontier line" had finally disappeared, it highlighted an accelerating movement from the countryside to the city. Thomas Jefferson's old warnings about vice, luxury, and economic dependency notwithstanding, urban growth in the next thirty years was nothing less than astounding. While urban development occurred most visibly in the northern and midwestern states, no region was immune; in the still heavily rural South, many politicians and writers also bemoaned the steady migration from the countryside. By 1920, for the first time, more Americans lived in areas classified as urban (having a minimum of 2,500 residents) than rural. Obviously the nature and texture of lives varied tremendously in places as diverse as mammoth New York and Chicago as compared with Scranton, Pennsylvania and Dubuque, Iowa. Urban areas included an elastic range of human experience: from the lives of Slovaks, Italians, and other newcomers in northeastern Pennsylvania coal towns, to the Piedmont's more homogeneous native white mill workers, to the sometimes combustible mixture of Anglos, Mexican Americans, and other immigrants in southwestern mining camps and border towns.

All the world was not Chicago, but the spread of cities in their infinite varieties and regional expressions changed the face of America. The absolute number of farms grew until about 1910 but comprised a declining percentage of the occupational whole. Farms generally became larger and farming more capital intensive and competitive. Rising food prices brought relative prosperity to northern farmers during the Progressive Era, though Southerners did not equally share in this bounty as the price of tobacco and cotton rose briefly and then collapsed. Whites everywhere steadily moved to the cities, as did an impressive wave of African Americans in the South by World War I. Fears about the health of rural America multiplied as it lost its grip on the young. Living on the farm was romantically equated with the virtuous life, as if hard work, initiative, and self-reliance naturally sprouted in so many American Edens. The Country Life Commission, appointed in 1908 by Theodore Roosevelt, studied why so many bright young people left home. Poor schools and services, economic pressures and declining fortunes, and the lure of urban amenities and jobs helped empty the countryside.

Urban growth before 1920 came from many sources. Like other citizens, educators frequently worried about the situation of farmers and country folk and their fate in the city, home to vice and temptation. This paled in comparison to the public alarm at the masses of foreign immigrants who poured into the cities after the 1880s. Between 1890 and 1920, 18.2 million came to America, principally from central and southern Europe. Driven from their homelands by a variety of factors including population pressures, the commercialization of agriculture, and political repression, these immigrants arrived at the very time when corporations and modern industry had come of age. Skilled workers now formed a smaller percentage of an industrial work force increasingly based on unskilled or semi-skilled labor. All of the major extractive industries that undergirded modern industry consolidated their power through pools, trusts, and monopolies, and they often worked ruthlessly to destroy labor unions and to make factory hands more compliant, not always successfully. High labor turnover, strikes, and industrial tension were common throughout the Progressive Era, leading to widespread fears of class war and spurring the creation of socialist parties and radical labor unions.

These "new" immigrants settled predominantly in urban areas in the Northeast and Midwest, the process frequently eased by family and friends who helped them find employment, mostly in working-class jobs. The needle trades in New York City, the steel mills in Bethlehem and Pittsburgh, and the endless variety of machine shops and factories less famous than the Ford plants in Detroit were for many the ultimate destination. The immigrants also hauled coal, unloaded wagons, mended shoes, picked rags, cleaned the streets and other people's homes or, if better educated than most, found white-collar positions as clerks, salespeople, or teachers in a burgeoning urban and industrial America. While finding the low-wage, agrarian South less appealing, immigrants were still numerous enough in New Orleans and Atlanta to inflame hostility among many native white leaders, otherwise focused on oppressing blacks.

Everything about the newcomers—their religion (often Catholic, sometimes Jewish), their customs, and their languages—struck a fearful chord. Then commonly regarded as members of different races, Slavs, Italians, Greeks, and Jews often lived in separate urban neighborhoods, which only aggravated fears that they would not assimilate to "American" life. Ellwood P. Cubberley was one of many who found the newcomers morally degraded and culturally offensive. "These southern and eastern Europeans are of a very different type from the north Europeans who preceded them," he wrote in 1909. "Illiterate, docile, lacking in self-reliance and initiative, and not possessing the Anglo-Teutonic conceptions of law, order, and government, their coming has served to dilute tremendously our national stock, and to corrupt our civic life." Cubberley's were not the last words on the subject, but they typified the ethnocentric thinking that shaped landmark immigrant restriction laws in the early 1920s, which sharply reduced the overall flow of immigration and virtually ended it from central and southern Europe.

Like many contemporaries, Cubberley realized that most of the new arrivals settled in urban areas where, as he disapprovingly wrote, they "tend to settle in groups and settlements, and to set up here their national manners, customs, and observances." Parochial schools enrolled over 1.5 million children in 1910. Scholars who have studied the 1910 census have discovered that children born in the U.S. to native or immigrant parents often enrolled at high rates in school (whether parochial or public), usually until about the age of thirteen. (The figures were much lower for children born outside of the U.S.) For example, in 1910 an average of 92.9 percent of all native white ten- to thirteen-year-olds were enrolled in school. The only groups of children born in the U.S. falling below that percentage were African Americans (with 70.1 percent in school), American Indians (72.1 percent), and Hispanics (62.9 percent). These three groups were disproportionally poor, politically powerless, and usually lived in heavily rural areas without much public investment in their education.

School enrollment rates for children between the ages of ten and thirteen born in the U.S. to British, Irish, Scandinavian, Jewish, and English Canadian parents registered above 95 percent, and the figures for native-born children of French Canadians, Germans, Italians, Poles, and Russians (all above 90 percent) were also very impressive. By their middle teens, native-born youth of native parents more frequently attended school than children born in the U.S. to immigrant parents, who often insisted that their children leave school for work. But such generalizations ignore America's immigrant mosaic. Jewish Americans often emphasized school achievement and more prolonged schooling for religious and cultural reasons compared to other groups that downplayed social mobility and expected teens to contribute sooner to the family economy. Similarly, Japanese and Romanian families also greatly valued school achievement, having emigrated from nations that had impressively invested in state schooling.

Asian immigrants, who principally settled in the Hawaiian islands and on the West Coast, were an integral part of the transformation of American life during the Progressive Era. Like the more numerous immigrants from Europe, they were a diverse group, but they also often viewed public schools as a means of acculturation, English-language acquisition, and possible social mobility for the young. While the official policy of the schools was "Americanization" and assimilation, a goal that intensified during World War I, local prejudices by majority whites ensured that Asians and Asian Americans, like blacks in the South or Mexicans in the Southwest, often attended segregated schools. In 1906, the San Francisco school board ordered Japanese children who had previously attended neighborhood schools with whites to transfer to the "Oriental School," which principally served Chinese pupils and some Koreans. Protests from Japan provoked an international incident. Cognizant of Japan's military prowess and ambition and concerned about growing hostility to immigrants in California, president Theodore Roosevelt persuaded local officials to rescind the segregation of the Japanese children while he simultaneously privately negotiated with leaders in Tokyo to voluntarily reduce the level of immigration, negotiations which proved successful. Despite the virulent racism of the white majority and its political leadership, second-generation Japanese Americans (Nisei) in the coming decades would often excel in the public schools, notwithstanding widespread discriminatory hiring practices in white society.

The powerful effects of the movement to the cities, the massive waves of immigration, and the swelling industrial labor force clearly meant that America was leaving its rural and agrarian past farther behind. While industrialization was an uneven process, the changing economic and social landscape inevitably raised important and difficult questions about the place of basic institutions such as public schools in the social order. In the classroom as well as on the shop floor, ideals of democracy and justice, and efficiency and social order, vied for dominance. Familiar battles between the champions of the new and old education often resurfaced and stayed heated.

While city systems adopted more centralized governing structures and elevated the authority of expertise, a host of reform-minded citizens joined voluntary associations to counter these developments. Concerned more with social justice and democracy than with economic and social efficiency, they attempted to better link schools with local neighborhoods and the community. In the process they added a distinctive flavor to reform movements throughout the Progressive Era.

Citizens who fought against elite control of the schools sometimes saw themselves engaged in a dialectical struggle. Socialists, of course, often saw the world through the lens of class conflict, and in many cities they condemned what they saw as the narrow-minded schemes of elite businessmen and professionals, now empowered in school boards and in the central offices of school districts. By 1910, for example, radicals in Milwaukee, Wisconsin, began to elect members of the Social Democratic Party, the political arm of the trade unions, to the school board, ultimately forming one-third of the board's membership. Victor Berger, who became America's first Socialist congressman, saw the fight for democracy in the schools as a microcosm of the larger war between labor (and its liberal allies) against capital. "Two ideas are fighting for mastery in the educational world," Berger wrote in 1915. One movement, led by capitalists, "would make the schools into 'efficient,' card catalogued, time clocked, well bossed factories for the manufacture of standardized wage slaves." Opposed to the forces of privilege was a polyglot assortment of settlement house workers, unions, women's clubs, and urban liberals who, he said, "would have the schools a part of our social life, specialized to hasten the development of children into free human beings."

Urban activists, who were not usually socialists, promoted numerous reforms. And they realized that unless they formed alliances with other community groups, they would have little impact upon the school board, city council, or the mayor's office. Milwaukee's socialists were non-doctrinaire, often joining hands when necessary with settlement house and other civic leaders, women's and parent groups, and former members of the defunct Populist Party, which had fused with the Democrats and was defeated by William McKinley's Republican Party in 1896. Together they fielded candidates to the school board and drafted petitions to officials to build more playgrounds, start summer programs for the poor, and hold adult evening courses for the working classes, demanding what contemporaries called "the wider use of schools." The motives of the members of these groups varied enormously. Middle-class club women, socialist leaders, left-wing labor leaders, liberal settlement house workers, and those inspired by religious ideals such as the social gospel, which called for social action in Jesus's name to help the poor, assumed they were fighting for the best interests of the child, as did the business elites and professionals they often quarreled with. Socialists usually linked their demands for school reform to larger protests against capitalism. Most of their grass-roots allies, however, wanted to work within the system and improve it, hoping to tip the balance scales toward democracy and away from the numbing calculus of business efficiency.

Organized women played an essential role in child welfare and school reform in the early decades of the twentieth century. As early as 1902, Richard T. Ely perceptively remarked in *The Coming City* that "whenever you see any peculiarly excellent work going forward in the twentieth-century city you may be sure that the women have something to do with it." "They are cold and unmoved," he added, "when we talk about municipal government as business, but when we bring forward the household ideal they think of the children, and when they are once aroused you may be sure that something is going to happen!" Long active in urban charity organizations, women became more self-consciously political during the Progressive Era, even when they said that they were "non-partisan" and only cared about children's welfare. The national General Federation of Women's Clubs, formed in 1890, had over one million members early in the new century, and that was only the beginning. Whether in Akron or Omaha, some local affiliates promoted school suffrage, the right of women to vote in local school elections and serve on the school board, which was legal in several states before passage of the Nineteenth Amendment in 1920. Moreover, various local, state, and regional groups affiliated with the General Federation actively influenced innumerable civic reforms, including education.

By 1900 the Federation president found it difficult to keep track of the thousands of local clubs, which ranged from genteel literary groups to feminist activists. But it was clear that "more women are finding out each day, that the world's business is their business and that good housekeeping is not confined to four walls." From the Jim Crow South, a female activist later invoked what she called an old proverb, "What you would have appear in the Nation's life, you must introduce into the public schools." In Massachusetts as in countless states, club women lobbied for (and often funded) school gardens, playgrounds, and manual training and sewing classes; like their sisters everywhere, they raised money to paint and decorate classrooms, feed the poor, and petition for school improvements. In 1904 Ohio women reported a "great awakening" of female activism on all education fronts. They advocated more lending libraries, more effective child labor laws, and juvenile courts (to separate youthful offenders from wayward adults). Jane Addams flattered Federation members in 1914 when, as a featured speaker at the national convention, she said that organized women were almost single handedly responsible "for the kindergarten and domestic science for the public schools, prohibition of child labor, civil service reform, immigration, forestry, pure food, protective legislation for women, conservation of water and mineral resources, vocational training, preservation of birds, traveling libraries and art galleries, the suppression of commercialized vice" and other social improvements. Beneath the hyperbole was some bedrock of truth. On the eve of World War I, the governor of New York praised the women for pressuring male politicians to expand state responsibility for human welfare, though some club members likely winced when he called theirs a "broad minded socialism."

Many of the middle-class women who joined various voluntary groups had cut their political teeth in the Woman's Christian Temperance Union, the largest women's group in the nineteenth century. Others were former teachers who had lost their jobs due to bans on married women teaching but had not lost their interest in the schools. Women generally were excited by the spirit of reform and camaraderie that characterized many mother's clubs, early parent teacher organizations (which they dominated), and other civic associations. The National Congress of Mothers, the forerunner to the national Parent Teacher Association (PTA), formed in 1897, reflecting rising middle class interest in educational improvement among grass-roots laypeople. Its president, Alice McLellan Birney, said women had a special role in improving children's lives. "For every kindergarten there are a hundred, nay, a thousand prisons, jails, reformatories, asylums, and hospitals. And yet society cries out that there is need for more of these." The maternal impulse seemed undeniable. "Men have a thousand imperative outside interests and pursuits, while Nature has set her seal upon woman as the caretaker of the child; therefore it is natural that woman should lead in awakening mankind to the sense of the responsibilities resting upon the race to provide each new-born soul with an environment which will foster its highest development."

Some leading female activists also came out of the settlement house movement, which originated when Jane Addams and Ellen Gates Starr opened Hull House in a poor immigrant neighborhood in Chicago in 1889. In city after city, settlement house workers, including some men but especially women, helped stimulate interest in the new education. Hundreds of urban settlement houses opened by the early twentieth century; many of them offered neighborhood children, often the immigrant poor, free kindergartens, breakfasts and lunches, sewing and manual training classes, supervised playgrounds, and vacation schools. Often college educated, these missionaries to the city also established reading rooms, evening lecture series, English-language classes for adults, and labor bureaus. More than a few settlement workers, including Addams, served on school boards. By the early twentieth century, settlement activists and women's organizations joined with labor unions, socialists, and other urban liberals to establish similar programs in the public schools.

As Birney had told the National Congress of Mothers, children's nurture and welfare were traditional female responsibilities. Yet cities had never seen women so publicly active. The minutes and published proceedings of many urban school boards for the period are filled with examples of their lobbying campaigns, whether against corporal punishment, in favor of school breakfast or lunch programs, or other social welfare reforms. *Child Welfare Magazine* regularly documented the activist role of local mother's groups and PTAs. Mothers' clubs in Denver actively endorsed social centers in 1911, while the Atlanta Congress of Mothers, an all-white group, sponsored public lectures on infant mortality, childhood nutrition, and "social uplift." In Des Moines, one mothers' group helped establish a branch library and then school baths in 1912. Clubs elsewhere gathered petitions for mothers' pensions and to save new programs from parsimonious school boards. In Erie, Pennsylvania, the local PTAs buttonholed voters to support school bonds to fund more playgrounds, social centers, sanitary drinking fountains, and kindergartens. Like numerous parent and women's groups, the Austin, Texas, mothers' circles strongly favored school medical inspection, another new welfare program. In 1919 in Springfield, Missouri, the Bowerman School Circle served hot lunches at cost to seventy-five to one hundred children; the school board provided the cooking equipment but the group "manages everything."

What caused women to get involved? Some women were deeply religious, motivated by a powerful sense of social obligation to the poor; some were distressed by the destructive effects of poverty and feared rising crime and social disorder, especially in immigrant communities. Most believed in some basic way in the power of environment, though some certainly shared the nativist view that heredity predisposed immigrants and the poor more generally toward vice and crime. Still other women turned traditional norms of female nurture and caring to their own professional advantage; for example, settlement work evolved into social work. Club women and settlement workers widened women's social sphere to include politics and schools, leading some to become feminists and proponents of full suffrage. Many typically emphasized maternal values and simply declared that the public should feed hungry children, establish supervised playgrounds, and otherwise expand the social obligations of municipal government.

Voluntary associations were the lifeblood of school reform throughout the Progressive Era. In Toledo, Ohio, as in most cities, mothers' clubs, parent organizations, and a variety of civic groups lobbied for the wider use of the schools and a more liberalized curriculum. In 1900 a group formed called the Complete Education League, which pressured the recently centralized school board to raise spending on kindergartens, playgrounds, manual training classes, and other features of the new education. When board members refused, it helped vote them out of office. League members outspokenly attacked "traditional education," meaning the usual classroom emphasis on textbooks, memorization, and recitation. The inaugural issue of its magazine, *Complete Education*, featured an editorial by Stoyan V. Tsanoff, a Bulgarian immigrant hired by Toledo's radical mayor, Samuel M. "Golden Rule" Jones, to help lead an educational crusade. Too much emphasis had been placed on the development of the intellectual faculties, Tsanoff complained. "The League considers its supreme duty," he said, "to bring into prominence the fact that the acquirement of knowledge constitutes but one part of education, and that playgrounds, kindergartens, concerts, picture exhibitions, and entertainments of all kinds for invigorating and training the faculties and emotions are a necessary part of human culture." The issue also featured an article by Jones, who lavished praise on the poet of American democracy, Walt Whitman, and concluded with his trademark hymns to "Brotherhood and Sisterhood" and to the fatherhood of God.

The deeply spiritual and religious side of progressivism found no greater expression than in Toledo's eccentric mayor. Born in Wales in 1846, Jones moved with his family to New York State at the age of three, received very little schooling, and became a classic case of rags to riches, with unanticipated consequences. He worked in the Pennsylvania oil and Ohio gas fields, where good fortune enabled him to buy a gas company in Lima, Ohio, that was later purchased from him by the Rockefeller conglomerate. In Toledo he opened the Acme Sucker Rod Company to manufacture one of his inventions, an oil well pump, that made him very wealthy. Then the depression of 1893 struck. By his own accounts, he was horrified at the plight of so many honest men seeking work. It brought back painful memories of his early years in the oil fields, when he was often hungry and without a roof over his head.

Jones's spiritual crisis, like Jane Addams's after her college graduation, led to a dramatic life change. After removing the time clocks at his factory, he hung a sign on a wall that read: "THE RULE THAT GOVERNS THIS COMPANY: 'Therefore Whatsoever Ye Would That Men Should Do Unto You, Do Ye So Unto Them.'" Jones implemented higher pay, shorter working hours, and paid vacations, endorsed labor unions and women's suffrage, condemned capitalism, and dreamed of a heaven on earth. Elected mayor as a dark-horse Republican in 1897, he soon refused to belong to any political party, running as an independent and serving in office until his death in 1904. He was regularly attacked by the city's major newspapers, the Democratic and Republican parties, and the Chamber of Commerce. He quipped that the only union that did not formally endorse him was the Minister's Union.

Jones's eccentricities attracted the national press, and the Golden Rule Mayor became one of the era's legendary champions of social justice. He spoke out against corporate greed, fought for cheaper transit fares, took clubs from the police, gave away a considerable amount of his fortune, and donated his salary as mayor to the poor, demonstrating the power of the golden rule. Jones had attacked the efficiencies represented by time clocks and preached human brotherhood and democracy in little sermons he placed in his employees' pay envelopes. At his factory, he also established a playground, social center (Golden Rule House), and community band, and he enjoyed teaching children the latest exercises and singing his own lyrics about human brotherhood, set to traditional Methodist hymns. Jones invited socialists and anarchists, settlement workers and social-gospel ministers, to speak at Golden Rule House. Jane Addams was among the many guests invited to speak, and he returned the favor. In *Twenty Years at Hull House,* Addams remembered that Jones was the only person ever to receive a standing ovation after addressing a local radical study group.

Like many activists of his generation, Jones assumed that a good society was impossible without new educational practices. His Complete Education League, which attracted many club women, activist parents, and other reformers, elected candidates to office and successfully lobbied for playgrounds and school extension, which found expression in more breakfast and lunch programs and in the wider use of schools as voting centers and meeting halls. In his speeches and mayoral reports, Jones championed playgrounds, kindergartens, manual training and sewing classes, and more active roles for children in the learning process. The *Complete Education* magazine attacked cramming, memorization, corporal punishment, and an exaggerated sense of the intellectual purposes of education. When not quoting Tolstoy, Emerson, Whitman, and other romantic writers, Jones crafted his own poetry, which united nature with the divine, in the tradition of Pestalozzi and Froebel:

> The budding trees, the singing birds,
> The opening flowers of springtime tell.
> The story old made new again,
> God's in his heaven and all is well.

Throughout urban America, cities that lacked such charismatic leadership still witnessed a visible upsurge of interest in educational change and improvement. Books and articles proliferated in the early 1900s that emphasized the "social" role of public schooling, whether to enhance democracy or produce more productive workers. Clarence A. Perry, who wrote extensively about the expansion of social welfare programs in the schools, discovered that numerous towns and cities had funded evening schools, vacation schools, playgrounds, recreation halls, and social centers. Some schools taught folk dancing or woodworking, offered English-language classes or short courses on history, and had lecture series that featured local experts on the water supply, public health, and other civic concerns. Others served as polling places on election day. The title of Perry's popular book, *Wider Use of the School Plant* (1910), showed the appeal of business metaphors in educational writing, but he too was impressed with all of the civic dynamism. A bewildering variety of groups now met at schools. Examples included the frequent public events of the thousands of parents in the Home and School League of Philadelphia, meetings sponsored by the Boston Home and School Association (which drew twenty-five thousand people annually), the countless athletic teams that played in the local gym, and the school extension leagues and educational and industrial unions that demanded more public funding of social centers and various educational innovations.

For some activists, the wider use of school buildings (also called school plants) made them synonymous with social centers, and was a reaction against the dominant centralizing trends in education. School systems embraced these welfare ideas with varying levels of enthusiasm. "Different cities are working out the Social Center idea along different lines," said one Midwestern superintendent in 1909. "The term Social Center does not as yet mean any one thing: no 'type' has been developed." In most towns and cities, social centers meant the after-hours use of the schools by children and adults in diverse activities, including intramural athletic games, public lecture series, experimental courses, or a mix of traditional classes. And, as with every other innovation, those favoring social centers had varying motivations and expectations. The movement began outside of the schools, and superintendents and elites on centralized school boards were always somewhat leery of lay influence. Nevertheless, Clarence Perry, who applauded the efficient use of resources, believed that the businessmen serving on school boards were "beginning to see that the utilization of the expensive school plant less than half the time . . . does not jibe with the policy followed in their places of business." Though they sometimes supported the same reforms, proponents of democracy and efficiency would continue their tug of war.

The most famous social center experiment occurred in Rochester, New York.

Responding to pressure from an impressive variety of voluntary groups—women, labor, socialists, playground enthusiasts, and the like—the local city council and school board approved the wider use of the schools in 1907, making public access easier in the evenings and on weekends. Edward J. Ward was appointed supervisor of the centers, quickly becoming a national figure as he became embroiled in local controversies. A local news reporter called his allies "a motley array of Socialists, free thinkers, and apostles of discontent." A Christian Socialist and former minister, Ward believed deeply in free speech and in neighborhood input in shaping the local social centers. To maximize participation, he encouraged adults to form neighborhood civic clubs, which helped direct many of the evening activities, including deciding whom to invite as public speakers. The social centers proved very popular, attracting thousands of children and adults, as the wider use of schools came to Rochester.

Ward's support for free speech and his own left-wing social views ultimately proved very controversial. In some towns and cities, social centers primarily attempted to Americanize and uplift immigrants. Many school boards also banned religious or "partisan" debates. Ward, however, established social centers in neighborhoods across the city and favored open discussion. Rochester's centers were also racially integrated, a policy only "Golden Rule" Jones and a few urban radicals endorsed. The local civic clubs helped frame their own lecture programs, and controversy quickly brewed when the socialists and anarchists showed up and attacked local politicians, including the mayor and school officials. That, Ward maintained, was the price of free speech and democracy. All it took, however, was a few controversial activities at the social centers—including a Sunday masquerade ball in 1909 (leading to accusations of defiling the Sabbath as well as cross-dressing)—and Ward was fired, free speech shackled, and the social center budgets slashed, thus ending the Rochester experiment. The Milwaukee socialists hired Ward as a social center advisor, and he later worked for several years in the Extension Division of the University of Wisconsin, where he tried to promote his ideas across the Badger State.

Like many educational reformers between the 1890s and World War I, Ward had been drawn to the city, the great center of innovation. He was part of a larger movement of citizen activists who promoted neighborhood-oriented educational improvements and welfare reforms and debated the purpose and meaning of education in an increasingly complex industrial world. In his survey of changing ideas and practices in the schools, *The New Education* (1915), the radical economist Scott Nearing concluded that such Americans were living through a time of social transformation that would ultimately make the old education obsolete and the new or progressive alternative more appealing. "The new basis of education," he realized, "lies in the changes which the nineteenth century wrought in industry, transforming village life into city dwelling, and substituting for the skilled mechanic, using a tool, the machine employing the unskilled worker." Examples of positive change abounded, but movement seemed glacial. "Is it too much to ask," he wondered, "that the school stand foremost in this recognition of change, when it is in the school that the ideas of a new generation are molded, tempered, and burnished?"

The image of cities undergoing dramatic change was ever present in the minds of reformers, who struggled to define the precise role of democracy and efficiency in the schools. Many innovations originated with the grass roots and only later came under the authority of the experts and professionals who ran the schools. The cities were the locus of educational reform, where a variety of settlement house workers and assorted voluntary groups engaged in educational experimentation and social action. No one benefited more from this exciting environment than a young academic who arrived to teach at the University of Chicago in 1894. His name was John Dewey, and he wrote some of the most searching inquiries into the relationship between school and society, democracy and education, and educational theory and practice. Like many small-town boys of his generation, Dewey had moved to the city. It proved exhilarating.

John Dewey was born in Burlington, Vermont, in 1859, the same year that Charles Darwin published *The Origin of Species*. While Dewey's actual influence upon schooling was less revolutionary than Darwin's upon biology and science, he would become America's most renowned philosopher. After graduating from high school, Dewey earned a degree at the University of Vermont, taught school, and then completed a Ph.D. in psychology at the Johns Hopkins University in Baltimore. After teaching at the University of Michigan and the University of Minnesota, he moved to the newly established University of Chicago in 1894. Like other northern cities, Chicago was becoming industrialized, its population skyrocketing as it attracted immigrants and rural folk seeking work and a better life. The Haymarket Square riot of 1886 had made Chicago notorious to many citizens, but Dewey drew upon the rich intellectual and social resources of the city as he fashioned his philosophical thought. As historian Robert Westbrook reminds us, Dewey found Chicago captivating. He told his wife Alice that "the town seems filled with problems holding out their hands and asking somebody to please solve them—or else dump them in the lake. I had no conception that things could be so much more phenomenal and objective than they are in a country village, and simply stick themselves at you, instead of leaving you to think about them." For Dewey, philosophy became not the study of abstract ideas but a way of engaging life and its problems.

In a biographical portrait of her father, published in 1939, Jane Dewey (who had been named for the co-founder of Hull House) wrote that his "faith in democracy as a guiding force in education took on a sharper and a deeper meaning because of Hull House and Jane Addams." Hull House had experimented with an array of social services and innovative courses for parents and children, and Dewey occasionally lectured there before settling in Chicago. Actively interested in educational reform at the settlement house and in the city schools, Dewey established the Laboratory School at the university in 1896. He was actively involved with his wife at the Lab School until 1904 when, following a dispute with the university president, Dewey joined the philosophy department at Columbia University, where he taught until retiring in 1930.

Dewey's name became synonymous with educational experimentation and reform. Some people persisted in calling him the father of progressive education. And he enjoyed the dubious distinction of being revered or despised by people who rarely read him or who reduced his philosophy to slogans such as "learning by doing" or "child-centered education." Even some of his disciples failed to see that he criticized both the old and the new education. In his writings, Dewey typically juxtaposed contrasting positions, criticizing them and offering a new synthesis or way of looking at an educational issue. Perhaps because they saw what they wanted to, friends of the new education often quoted his criticisms of traditional schooling while they ignored or downplayed his criticisms of child-centered ideals. Never a great stylist, Dewey nevertheless presented his educational ideas fairly clearly in a series of lectures to local parents and neighbors that appeared in 1899 in a little book entitled *School and Society*. Outlining the broad context and rationale for the innovative practices at the Lab School, it was often reprinted and serves as a useful portal into his evolving intellectual world.

Like countless books written about education at the time, Dewey began by emphasizing the dramatic social transformations of recent decades. Industrialism had destroyed crafts, technology had quickened production, and transportation systems had accelerated access to global markets. This posed enormous problems for education. In the rural past, most children learned about production, about earning a living, and about social relationships in the home and often on the family farm. Schools had been created to teach the accumulated wisdom of the ages, but historically they played a small role in children's lives. As critics of the old education rightly emphasized, however, there was increasingly something artificial about schools, which had grown more important but often became "a place set apart in which to learn lessons." How to create schools less isolated from children's experience, the community, and larger society was the basic dilemma of modern education.

Throughout his lectures, Dewey presented familiar criticisms of public schools. Teacher authority and student passivity, he said, dominated. Textbooks were ubiquitous and contained knowledge far removed from children's interests or experience. Teachers told children what pages to memorize, the children rose when called upon, recited what they knew, sat down, and received a grade; the pattern and routine were numbing and commonplace. Discipline was enforced by external threats of punishment by the teacher or parent, and achievement encouraged not by tapping the child's natural interest in learning but through the fear of failure and desire for promotion. Everyone recognized the typical classroom with "its rows of ugly desks placed in geometrical order, crowded together so that there shall be as little moving room as possible, desks almost all of the same size, with just space enough to hold books, paper, and pencils." Local parents who heard Dewey's lectures or read his book perhaps nodded in agreement. Only a few years earlier, Joseph Mayer Rice had claimed in a muckraking book that drill and mechanical teaching were the norm in Chicago's public schools, which he called the worst in the nation.

Textbooks conveniently presented students with knowledge, the product of countless human experiences and social interactions, sometimes going back centuries. But as pedagogical tools they had distinct limitations. Children were far removed from the activities that had produced the world's accumulated knowledge, and textbooks presented material that was also fairly remote from their immediate lives. How could teachers connect the young to the sources of knowledge and then unite learning with daily life? Eliminating the mechanical teaching found in many schools did not mean dispensing with knowledge, which was critical for all citizens in a democracy, but discovering new pedagogical strategies. For too long the "pouring in" of facts into children's heads rather than the "drawing out" of their interest in learning had dominated instruction.

At the Lab School, in contrast, children studied and participated in learning about various occupations, examples of how people in the past earned a living and made a life. It helped to restore life to the abstract knowledge about this past that city children only read about in books. It might seem odd, Dewey explained, that children at his school among other things raised sheep, sheared wool, spun it, and made clothing. But this was not a diversion from the real work of the school, a bow to the romantic educators, or simple fun. Rather, what was more basic than learning where wool came from? Or how clothes were made? Children also worked together on projects, teaching them not just academic subjects but also social cooperation, traditionally essential to life on the family farm. At the Lab School children planted gardens and grew crops not to become farmers but to learn about food, chemistry, and geography. These students, who came from fairly affluent families in Hyde Park, acquired considerable knowledge, but they were creatively and actively involved in their education and less dependent on textbooks and traditional instruction. Children could read a cookbook to learn how to boil an egg, but experimenting on their own drew upon their interests and strengthened their powers of observation. Efficiency was sacrificed, but active engagement in learning, as in democracy, required time and patience.

Pupils who learned about occupations were not being groomed to become sheep herders, cooks, or even laboratory scientists, but to gain insight into the nature of work. Neither these classroom experiments nor the manual training at the Lab School, however, were to be confused with vocational education. Dewey explicitly divorced the study of occupations from job preparation, even if some champions of narrow trade training for the working classes missed the distinction. In *School and Society,* and more emphatically in later writings, he said that children should learn how people in the past and present earned a living, but public schools should not "prepare the child for any particular business." School gardening, for example, simultaneously taught many things—chemistry, geography, and history—but did not aim to produce horticulturists. Neither was woodworking a form of job training for the new industrial order.

Even though Dewey penned memorable images of the old education—the sterile classrooms, the bolted-down seats, the listless students—*School and Society* also subtly critiqued the new education. Dewey clearly agreed with the major criticisms of traditional schooling. He realized that people often framed their ideas in direct opposition to others, with often adverse results. For instance, reformers making the reasonable point that the schools had an exaggerated faith in teacher authority and in drill could end up wallowing in childhood sentimentality and favoring doing as one pleased. Aimless instruction was hardly an improvement upon a steady diet of rote memorization, but one extreme idea easily begat its opposite. Despite what some people believed, Dewey was never a romantic educator. He certainly respected the contributions of the European child-centered romantics and their American disciples. Much had been learned from them and from the Herbartians, who in the 1890s emphasized the centrality of children's interests in the learning process and the value of teaching subjects in closer association with each other. But they too had turned insights into panaceas, and Dewey doubted that earlier innovations such as object lessons were likely to transform the schools. Young children might learn much from concrete objects but, as other critics noted, these lessons had often become formulaic, taught step by step from primers. Froebel's kindergarten, shrouded in mysticism and symbolism, had suffered a similar fate.

In a number of writings, Dewey elaborated upon important themes first presented in *School and Society*. He consistently sought a clear path apart from traditionalists who wanted a textbook-dominated classroom filled with passive students and romantics who glorified the child's freedom unchecked by teacher guidance and authority. In *The Child and the Curriculum* (1902), Dewey stated his position clearly: "Just as, upon the whole, it was the weakness of the 'old education' that it made invidious comparisons between the immaturity of the child and the maturity of the adult, regarding the former as something to be got away from as soon as possible and as much as possible; so it is the danger of the 'new education' that it regard the child's present powers and interests as something finally significant in themselves. In truth, his learnings and achievements are fluid and moving. They change from day to day and from hour to hour."

While Dewey often lamented the tiresome methods of most classrooms, criticisms of the new education were a staple of his scholarship. In *Interest and Effort in Education* (1913), he outlined the fallacies of dualistic thinking about the contrasting ideals named in the title and also devoted several pages to criticisms of romantic educators. As before, he warned against "sugar-coated" education, sentimentality, and the impossible notion that effort could disappear from the learning process. He applauded the insights of Pestalozzi and Froebel, who were trying to end dry-as-dust pedagogy, but then found the former's ideas too rigid and formal and the latter's too mystical and abstract. In his magnum opus, *Democracy and Education* (1916), Dewey provided one of the fullest statements of his philosophy of education. He again criticized dualistic thinking and affirmed that the school not only transmitted knowledge to the young but was also the "chief agency" to help build a "better future society."

In the years preceding the publication of *Democracy and Education,* Dewey had gone on record against various undemocratic school initiatives. He wryly noted that, after removing corrupt ward leaders from urban school boards in the 1890s, administrative reformers had simply shifted power to the office of school superintendent, at the expense of the teachers. He loudly opposed the advocates of "social efficiency" who were uncritical of big business and who wanted to stream working-class children into separate vocational high schools. More explicitly than some of his earlier books, *Democracy and Education* attacked economic inequalities and injustice. Democracy, Dewey emphasized, was not a set of abstract principles but a "mode of associated living," a way of life. A democratic school, he insisted, should make all children "masters of their own economic and social" fate. To direct certain children toward courses of study that limited their growth and potential and channeled them to the most marginal jobs was a travesty. "Democratic society," Dewey concluded, "is peculiarly dependent for its maintenance upon the use in forming a course of study of criteria which are broadly human. Democracy cannot flourish where the chief influences in selecting subject matter of instruction are utilitarian ends narrowly conceived for the masses, and, for the higher education of the few, the traditions of a specialized cultivated class." As usual, the prose did not sparkle, but the meaning was clear. He had long maintained that schools were centers of academic instruction but also social institutions, where children should learn to respect the rights and opinions of others and gain exposure to the common values and ideals necessary for living in a democracy.

While Dewey turned to other philosophical concerns after World War I, he continued to inspire many who criticized the hidebound ways of the schools. A number of private "progressive schools" flourished in the 1920s, and their founders sometimes saw him as their inspiration and guide. In a major address before the Progressive Education Association in 1928, however, Dewey told the audience that many child-centered schools could benefit from a more sequenced curriculum and more adult authority. These schools did not particularly please him or reflect his philosophy of education. A decade later, at the age of seventy-eight, Dewey published his last book on education and once more tried to set the record straight. *Experience and Education* returned to themes that Dewey had first explored systematically in the late nineteenth century. Again he highlighted the shortcomings of the old and new education, the former identified with memorization and recitation, "fixed rows of desks," and "chain-gang procedures," the latter with undisciplined freedom, aimless activities, and glorification of childish impulse. Dewey nevertheless remained linked with progressive, child-centered education despite a lifetime of writing about its excesses as well as those of the traditional school. Many individuals had trouble understanding what he said or believed. In 1920, for example, the nation's leading historian of education associated Dewey's philosophy not only with "social efficiency" but also with Froebel and "learning by doing."

What everyone forgot, however, was that Dewey, like so many of his contemporaries, had forged his ideas in an urban environment. The center of social and economic change, cities became an important laboratory for testing educational ideas, whether at the Laboratory School, settlement house, or public school. As they expanded their reach, urban schools attracted a diversity of reformers who wanted to shape, improve, and control them. Dewey's urban experiences only reinforced his belief that schools were vital to social progress and human betterment and essential to the preservation and extension of American democracy. Others who looked to the city and its manifold social changes, however, learned very different lessons.

His biographers noted that Ellwood P. Cubberley had never been confused with John Dewey or with the philosopher's radical or misguided followers. He was, as David B. Tyack explains, a power broker: training administrators, writing textbooks, conducting school surveys, and advising local districts. His prose was also clearer, his meaning less contested. Dewey wanted philosophy to engage with down-to-earth problems, but Cubberley never doubted his thorough engagement with them. Cubberley represented an opposing strand of reform in the early decades of the twentieth century and was a counterpoint to the famous philosopher. Both men were prolific writers and believed in progress, in evolutionary growth, and in the importance of public schools in the social order. Both men's thinking was heavily shaped by the consequences of social developments and economic growth concentrated in the cities. After that, however, the similarities ended. Dewey looked at the emerging industrial order and found it wanting. To paraphrase Lincoln Steffens, Cubberley saw the future and it worked. So would the schools, if guided by the principles of social efficiency, business models of governance, and expert supervision and management.

Born in a village in northeastern Indiana in 1868, Cubberley attended the local schools and graduated from Indiana University at Bloomington in 1891. During his college years, he taught for a time in a country school. After graduation, he taught briefly at a college before moving to Vincennes University, also in Indiana, and quickly becoming its president. His ascent up the professional ladder was rapid. He became superintendent of the San Diego public schools, where he tangled with some board members and came to dislike lay interference in professional matters. In short order, David Starr Jordan—his former teacher and mentor at Bloomington, a prominent evolutionary biologist, and then president of Stanford Leland Jr. University—hired him in 1898 as a professor of education at the new Palo Alto campus. Earning a doctorate at Teachers College, Columbia University, in 1905, Cubberley helped establish and strengthen Stanford's college of education, serving as professor and also as dean during a long career. While he taught a variety of courses, his main writings and influence were in the fields of history of education and school administration.

At college, Cubberley had majored in physics and at Vincennes he continued teaching and studying geology, a favorite subject, before he concentrated on the field of education. Like many contemporaries, he was awestruck by the economic and social transformations that occurred during his lifetime and saw them as an expression of evolutionary growth and progress. Biology taught that life was a constant struggle for survival and preferment; social organizations, like individuals, also endured and prospered if they adapted to a world of competition and change. Business corporations utilized the division of labor, specialization of function, administrative hierarchies, and centralized authority to maximize productivity and profit. How to apply these scientific and economic truths to educational administration, organization, and supervision was central to Cubberley's large corpus of writings.

In an early and succinct statement of his social and educational views, *Changing Conceptions of Education* (1909), Cubberley emphasized how technology, industrialization, immigration, and urbanization had transformed the nation. America had become "a vastly more complex civilization, with a great and an ever increasing specialization of human effort, and new and ever more difficult social and industrial problems awaiting solution." Other contemporaries, including Dewey in *School and Society,* had said the same thing. But how differently these two men viewed education, the city, and American democracy! In the mid-1890s, while Dewey was learning about educational experimentation at Hull House and opening the Laboratory School, Cubberley was working as a superintendent in San Diego, trying to persuade the lay people on the school board to defer to his authority. Cubberley never lost his top-down view of the world. In *Changing Conceptions,* he complained about the character of the new immigrants, lay governance, and the many "evils and shortcomings of democracy." Revised editions of his textbooks in history and administration did not soften these prejudices. The city remained for him the prime site for social efficiency and scientific management, not a laboratory for democracy as Dewey and many grass-roots reformers believed.

To Cubberley, major business corporations, which were largely located in the cities, were the highest form of social evolution. Like many elite reformers, he wanted schools to imitate big business as much as possible. He consistently applauded the centralization of school boards, the elimination of ward representation, and the appointment of credentialed superintendents enthralled by the insights of scientific management. In the first edition of his popular textbook, *Public School Administration,* in 1916, Cubberley emphasized that the schools "are, in a sense, factories in which the raw products (children) are to be shaped and fashioned into products to meet the various demands of life." That was "social efficiency," a phrase he and other educators employed after the turn of the century to characterize their position. "The specifications for manufacturing," he went on to say, "come from the demands of twentieth-century civilization, and it is the business of the school to build its pupils according to the specifications laid down. This demands good tools, specialized machinery, continuous measurement of production to see if it is according to specifications, the elimination of waste in manufacture, and a large variety in the output." Such were the guiding assumptions of modern school administration, a field in which Cubberley pioneered.

Cities played a special role in Cubberley's view of education. Despite their huge potential for disorder, they were the place where schools, and especially their administrative apparatus, had reached their evolutionary apogee. The major educational achievements of recent decades, he repeatedly wrote, occurred there, unsurprising since the best talent flocked to the cities. Rural schools, which reformers often described as backward, had much to learn from them. As Cubberley wrote in *Rural Life and Education* (1914), unless country schools consolidated their independent districts, centralized authority, and elevated administrative authority, they would languish "in a state of arrested development." Progress came to the city schools through their conscious emulation of big business and successful adaptation to social change.

No wonder rural America was in a state of steady decline, Cubberley often said. Unlike those in the countryside, city schools were graded, had better trained teachers, an expanding and enriched curriculum, vocational programs, special education classes and, most importantly, trained experts who supervised the whole enterprise like a skillful military commander. "In an army good drill sergeants and lieutenants are, of course, necessary," he agreed, "but an army would prove ineffective in action if there were no captains. . . . It is the lack of captains and colonels of larger grasp and insight that is to-day the greatest single weakness of our rural and village educational army. When matched against the city educational army, with its many captains and colonels, and under generals of large insight and effective personal force, the city army easily outgenerals its opponent." Inevitably, the best rural teachers grew tired of the low pay and poor working conditions, abandoned their posts, and moved to the city. Who could blame them? And of all city officials, Cubberley boasted in 1929, the superintendent was usually among the best paid and, in his mind, the most important.

While many teachers, grass-roots reformers, and dissidents such as John Dewey were less enamored with elite governance, Cubberley applauded consolidation and centralization. He believed that the elimination of ward-based elections elevated the better class of citizens to the school board, who rightly delegated more executive and independent decision making to the superintendent and his staff. The superior quality of the people elected in at-large elections was pronounced, according to Cubberley. Gone were the rabble from the "socialistic ninth" or "red-light fourth," the ward heelers, party hacks, and patronage hunters. Now, Cubberley happily noted, school boards had "men who are successful in the handling of large business undertakings—manufacturers, merchants, bankers, contractors, and professional men of large practice." They were more likely to run the schools on business principles. Cubberley warned against any return to the old system. Who would prefer an electoral system that favored "teamsters" or "politicians, saloon-keepers, uneducated or relatively ignorant men, men in minor business positions, and women," never mind someone from the "Negro ward" near the river?

Not surprisingly given his admiration of business corporations and their governing hierarchies, the Stanford professor doubted that ordinary people had great potential or worth beyond assuming their proper place in the existing social order. While Dewey worried about the misuses of intelligence tests, narrow vocational training, and other undemocratic trends, Cubberley applauded them as desirable innovations and reforms. He did not view democracy as an extension of community life but rule by supposedly disinterested experts, and he was skeptical of public participation, including voting, in school affairs. As he wrote in 1914, "democracy ought to mean good government and efficient administration—the best and the most efficient that the taxes we pay can secure. This, however, does not of necessity mean that the people should vote for all, or even for any large number, of those who are to secure such government."

Cubberley's colleague Lewis Terman became world famous for the development of intelligence tests that emphasized the hereditary basis of human achievement and potential. Cubberley's landmark history of American education, *Public Education in the United States* (1916), a tale of "administrative progress," explained that science had demonstrated that "instead of being born free and equal, we are born free and unequal, and unequal we shall ever remain. The school, we now see, cannot make intelligence; it can only train and develop and make useful the intelligence that the child brings with him to school. This is a matter of his racial and family inheritance, and nothing within the gift of the schools or our democratic form of government." This textbook went through multiple editions and sold over 100,000 copies by World War II.

By the 1920s, national debates exploded over the misuses of intelligence tests and their class, racial, and ethnic biases. William Bagley, John Dewey, and the journalist Walter Lippmann notably attacked the questionable application of test results, including the tracking of poor and minority children into a less academic course of study. Some left-wing critics also continued to attack the unrepresentative character of centralized school boards and the undemocratic nature of some vocational programs. Now at the height of his career, Cubberley shrugged off the criticisms. He was confident that intelligence tests were reliable, that vocational education promoted social efficiency, and that society's leaders knew what was best for everyone. In *State School Administration*

(1927), Cubberley acknowledged that some critics accused vocational education of narrowing children's lives and limiting their "growth or development." But he repeated earlier claims that most children needed "an education in practical things as contrasted with book learning." An enlarged edition of his best-selling *Public School Administration* in 1929 asserted that the differentiated curriculum, vocational education, and expert leadership commonly found in the city schools constituted the hope of the nation's schools.

In his popular textbooks, Cubberley projected an image of city schools that resembled smooth-running engines, built by the best engineers and maintained by well-educated efficiency experts and administrators. It was neither an accurate view of reality nor universally accepted. And it was easily parodied. For Sinclair Lewis, the popular novelist who debunked small-town life, Protestant pieties, and business culture, the superintendent was an easy target. In *Main Street* (1920), he likened "Professor" George Edwin Mott, Gopher Prairie's superintendent, to a "Chinese mandarin." In *It Can't Happen Here* (1935), the story of a fascist takeover of a New England village, the minister of information and propaganda is the former school superintendent, Emil Staubmeyer. He is a "rule-slapper . . . a Squeers with certificates in 'pedagogy'" who "should now be able to cuff grown men instead of urchins." He edits the former village newspaper, aptly named the *Informer,* and is referred to as a "human blackboard."

Others besides novelists assailed the puffed-up mandarins. William Bagley, who had championed the cause of "social efficiency" as early as 1906, noted its pretensions a decade later and announced that administrative reformers had not led anyone to the "Promised Land." He attacked the abuses of intelligence tests in the 1920s, made fun of college deans seated at their rolltop desks, and called the economic and status gap between public school teachers and administrators shameful and "unknown elsewhere in the civilized world." George Counts, who was Bagley's left-wing colleague at Teachers College, denounced the elite nature of centralized school boards, which Cubberley so admired. In 1930, Counts also attacked the "idolatry of efficiency" and the uncritical acceptance of business models for school organization, obvious targets as the Depression worsened. He found it disgraceful that "the ambitious school administrator covets a reputation for efficiency and feels complimented if he is mistaken for a banker or the director of some large corporation."

In 1932, in a stinging attack on the quality of high schools, William S. Learned, the head of the Carnegie Foundation for the Advancement of Teaching, took time at an invited lecture at Harvard University to add a fine point to these criticisms. More than ever before, educational experts talked about efficiency and printed fancy administrative flow charts, naively assuming that their utopian schemes reflected sound educational thinking and could actually be implemented. "The point escapes us," the speaker told his audience, "that education can rarely be genuine and also tidy in the administrator's sense. He thinks of school and college as a sort of formal garden. The close-cut lawn, the precisely trimmed hedge, the standardized tulips set in patterns are an administrative delight. Educationally, they are impossible, and would be hideous to contemplate even if we could achieve them."

Hideous or beautiful, the administrative reforms that Cubberley and other founders of school administration championed nevertheless left a visible imprint on American schools in the first half of the twentieth century. These men were system builders, interested above all in efficiency and in professional management. Ultimately schools may have been a pale imitation of factories, but new schemes of testing, pupil classification, curriculum reforms, and administrative specialization and control clearly had considerable influence, particularly in the cities. As the crucible of social change, the cities were the testing ground of educational innovation. By the 1890s, many grass-roots citizens battled against the centralizing tendencies of urban governance and the tiresome quality of the old education. They fought for new school programs, teaching methods, and social services. This enabled intellectuals such as John Dewey to gain insights into the role of schools in a democratic society undergoing dramatic change. He often stood apart from the two sides striving for dominance, but on a few specific issues—administrative centralization, testing, and vocationalism—he opposed the precipitous rush to remake schools in the image of corporate enterprise and industrial management. Between the time of his arrival in Chicago and death in 1952, enrollments in urban elementary schools and especially high schools grew remarkably, providing reformers both inside and outside the system with abundant opportunities to transform modern education.

CHAPTER FIVE

A Democracy of Differences

"Butterfly-hunting, and in regular schooltime! There was a time when this would have been called truancy," read the opening lines of *Modern Practices of the Elementary School*, published in 1938. Thirty years earlier, this might have been called "extra-curricular, but today we take it for granted that a school without such activities as a vital part of its curriculum is backward." Thus wrote John A. Hockett of the Department of Education at the University of California, Berkeley, and E. W. Jacobsen, superintendent of the Oakland, California schools. To illustrate their point, an accompanying photo showed two boys in knickers walking along a bucolic path, butterfly nets in hand, part of the "transformation in education that is taking place before our very eyes." Other photos showed boys building a covered wagon; boys and girls working with hammers and saws, assembling dolls, and building a musical instrument; and girls making animals out of paper-mache, pressing flowers, and sewing kimonos. Only one illustration showed children reading books. Spared the proverbial bolted-down seats, they sat around a table, relaxed but engaged. Hockett and Jacobsen were confident that "a new conception of the functions and objectives of elementary education is rapidly gaining acceptance," contributing to "the best development of each individual child."

Indeed, *Modern Practices* hoped to sound a death knell for the "limited vision and narrow program of yesterday's school." The authors asserted: "Emphasis is indeed shifting from the mere acquisition of skills and information to the development of understanding through experiences that build desirable interests, attitudes, and ideals simultaneously." But it would not be easy. While "forward looking" teachers favored the "development of each child," tradition and the worshiping of familiar educational aims stood in the way. In the past, children went to school primarily to acquire knowledge. Teachers controlled the pace of instruction, which was dominated by textbooks. They assumed that "the prescribed lessons must be distasteful," so "a system of rewards and penalties was built up, involving grading, marking, promoting, and failing." Since the turn of the century, better informed individuals had discredited these ideas. Unfortunately, countervailing developments undermined this noble attempt to enhance every child's individual growth, Hockett and Jacobsen wrote. Schoolrooms and buildings were standardized, school leadership became autocratic (imitating military oligarchies), and teachers were often subordinates expected to "carry out the dictates of administrators, supervisors, and courses of study." Indeed, they wrote, "insidious connotations of the old, static point of view" remained popular, as evidenced by the continued use of traditional terms: "For instance, *teach, learn, subject matter, course of study, assignment, motivation, training of teachers, discipline.*" Simply put, traditional classrooms and old-fashioned pedagogy remained common.

Without question, the battle between the "old" and the "new" education was ubiquitous in America's elementary schools in the first half of the twentieth century. During this period, the enrollments of children below ninth grade in the public schools grew steadily: from 14.9 million in 1900 to 19.3 million fifty years later. In the 1930s, elementary school enrollments occasionally declined as a result of earlier restrictions on immigration from central and southern Europe and declining fertility rates during hard times. While elementary schools were not growing at the torrid pace of high schools, their presence was increasingly universal despite their varied quality. For example, African American children in the South often received less schooling than whites, and a specialist in the U.S. Office of Education claimed that around one million blacks did not attend any school in 1929–30, an injustice that was rectified, albeit in segregated settings, in the coming years. The progressive pieties of *Modern Practices* were irrelevant to their lives and to those in difficult straits, such as the Okies heading to California or the rural poor in the Southwest. Mexican American children routinely studied in inferior, poorly equipped, squalid facilities. In 1928, future president Lyndon Baines Johnson landed his first teaching job, in a segregated Mexican school in Cotulla, Texas. A strict but inspiring teacher, he personally provided free toothpaste and athletic equipment for the children and never forgot the grinding poverty and injustice surrounding their lives.

Ultimately all children had a stake in the outcome of ongoing debates about the aims and purposes of the elementary school. The nineteenth-century ideal that all children should have access to the same curriculum faced a relentless assault. Indeed, teachers and parents who defended traditional courses of study and pedagogy had few allies among educational reformers. Whether they primarily believed in democracy or efficiency, most reformers hoped tradition would yield to modernity. A variety of progressive educators wanted the child to replace academic subjects as the center of the educational experience, and they favored the new teaching methods highlighted in *Modern Practices*. More efficiency-minded reformers also focused their sights on the individual and disparaged traditional subject matter and conventional teaching. They, too, in the jargon of the times, wanted to make "the system fit the child." However, they took their cues less from the butterflies in the fields than from hardheaded business practices and the sober results of scientific testing, which made huge inroads in urban school policy.

While romantics prized the individual's growth and freedom, the efficiency-minded administrators who frequently ran urban school systems, the trendsetters of the period, spoke a very different language and had different objectives. They often talked about addressing children's individual differences. That meant statistically verifying children's innate capacities, to predict their school performance and likely social destination. Fitting the system to the child meant recognizing that some children might not profit from serious academic instruction; they might need slower tracks, a less academic curriculum, or even segregation into special classes. It was a very unromantic view of life, and it had ominous consequences. Urban administrators tried to change classroom organization, set varying intellectual expectations for different children, and implement new promotion schemes. The Ellwood Cubberleys of the age knew that certain obstacles hindered progress, particularly teachers and parents, who were often conservative and sometimes opposed innovation. Once the cities fell in line, however, perhaps the rest of the nation would follow.

Whether the new education had actually supplanted the old was intensely debated throughout the period. An unresolved tension existed between the de-

tion." Despite this weighty catalogue of failed remedies, the superintendent accepted the challenge on behalf of the teaching profession. After all, "the schools exist for the sake of the children, and everything possible should be done to fit them for citizenship, for gainful occupations, and for complete living."

In the decades that followed, first in the cities and then in consolidated districts in the countryside, elementary schools were expected to enhance their social obligations to children, families, and communities. A steady stream of speeches, articles, and books addressed the proper role of the modern elementary school, and they usually applauded its expanding social nature. In 1922, John Louis Horn, a professor of education at Mills College, published a textbook on the subject that typically underscored the unique quality of every child. He wrote that, in addition, changing expectations raised a basic though difficult question: "What is a school?" "School plants," he answered, "are now in various places centers of both mental training and bodily training, and for adults as well as children. But also they are becoming the place where neighbors vote, discuss common affairs, view beautiful pictures, hear music, dance, and play." In many cities schools inspected children for dental caries and poor eyesight. In Cleveland and other places poor children were fed and given baths. Hundreds of towns and cities and many rural districts struggled to improve vocational guidance and training for the work place. According to the professor, many people still embraced "mere learning" as the central aim of education, but the "social goals" of the school were rising in importance.

Reflecting upon recent educational changes at the end of World War II, Bessie Lee Gambrill of Yale University applauded the presumably weakened grip of academic instruction in many elementary schools. Now the lower grades were concerned "not merely with the academic accomplishments of children but with their all-round growth." Schools emphasized "personal enrichment" and "happiness" (hopeful sentiments during the war years) and seemed poised to transcend their scholastic orientation. Traditionalists feared this prospect, while progressives of various stripes lamented the glacial pace of change. And the crux of the issue remained: exactly how would modern schools honor the individuality of each child and deal with human differences?

Nineteenth-century educators realized that children differed in their capacity to learn. In the typical one-room school that most pupils attended, individuals worked their way through their textbooks, and only cities had roughly age-graded classrooms with a more uniform curriculum. Pupils in most classrooms therefore mastered their textbooks and course of study (which were virtually synonymous) as quickly as their talents and ambition allowed. While many antebellum and postbellum reformers applauded age-graded classrooms, criticisms steadily increased after the Civil War. Child-centered educators lamented the excessive competitive testing and higher academic expectations in graded settings, believing they smothered individual expression and hindered personal attention. Schools sacrificed children to the machine, tied them to a Procrustean bed, or sacrificed them on the altar of the common curriculum, said a variety of critics. Many children during the Progressive Era struggled with their studies and prematurely dropped out of school; along the way, many failed several subjects and endured the humiliation of repeating a grade.

Romantics as well as efficiency-minded educators and administrators condemned the soul-crushing qualities of the public school. Both sides quoted John Dewey selectively and insisted that schools connect themselves "to life" and abandon rote teaching, as the philosopher had suggested in *School and Society*. In *A Modern School* (1904), Paul Hanus, professor of the History and Art of Teaching at Harvard, stressed the importance of "efficiency" and the expanding social role of schools. The schools, he said, should broaden their vocational, social, and cultural training and reduce academic instruction in favor of more sewing, manual training, and practical subjects. Moreover, teachers had to recognize the folly of a common curriculum and ensure that "each individual best promotes his own development and his capacity for social service by adapting his education to his own tastes, capacities, and future needs." Hanus believed that more elective courses and vocational training in high school were imperative, but would be impossible without notable improvements in the lower grades.

Charles B. Gilbert, the former superintendent of schools in several eastern and midwestern cities, concurred. "The test of the efficiency of a school system, or a school," he argued in 1906, "is the excellence of the training given the individual children." By teaching moral values and social skills essential to succeed in the industrial world, where the division of labor ruled, schools also provided vital service to society. An academic education was fine but often overrated. "The individual who can answer the most deftly the greatest number of questions," Gilbert believed, "is by no means always the most successful or useful member of society, and the school whose pupils can secure the highest marks in examination is by no means always the best school." Knowledge was important but "nearly useless" if children lacked "acuteness of perception, judgement, reasoning power, alertness, breadth" and other skills. Traditional educators, of course, hardly disagreed with this assessment, though they wondered how these virtues could be taught apart from academic instruction.

As the decades passed, the importance of the individual and individual differences seemed irresistible. In 1910, an Alabama city school superintendent wrote in the local *Educational Exchange* that "one of the principal themes of educational programs these days is the training of the individual child." Modern schools had to educate not only "normal" children but also "the incorrigible, the backward, the physically defective, the mentally defective, and the child whose abnormal development is due to an unpropitious environment." Efficiency was everywhere the "watch-word," wrote the superintendent of schools in Punxsutawney, Pennsylvania. A more practical curriculum and medical inspection (to uncover the sources of learning problems), he thought, would help meet the needs of every pupil. By 1924, the president of the University of Washington was amazed by the expanded mission of the elementary schools. Countless school districts, especially in towns and cities, had established special classes to teach "the lame, the deaf, the blind, and the feeble of mind." Budgets swelled as schools adopted new social services and curricular innovations. Moreover, even in the regular classroom, educators now realized that students exhibited "every variation short of dramatic incompetency both special and general. Their cultural, social, and moral backgrounds are as varied as their mental capacities; their interests are as wide as their gifts. The narrow curriculum and the restricted pedagogical procedure of the past could not have coped with the situation."

Students earning an elementary teaching certificate at a normal school certainly encountered these themes in their course work. General textbooks on teaching and elementary education spoke the language of individual differences ad nauseam. "The teacher who would do his work intelligently must from the very first day of school think in terms of the individual differences of his class group," wrote George D. Strayer and N. L. Engelhardt, both of whom taught school administration at Teachers College, Columbia University, in 1920. Everything about individual students differed: their ambition, heredity, native intelligence, and social destination. Children arrived at school unequal and left the same way. "Nothing that education can do will enable a non-selected group of individuals to approach equality either in ability or in achievement. Indeed, it may be confidently asserted that the net result of education is to magnify differences rather than eliminate them." Social-efficiency educators were hardly egalitarians. Accordingly, a primer on elementary school teaching later explained that the difference between "the potential statesman and the child whose utmost capacity will be taxed by the vocation of garbage-collecting, is marked and measurable before either of them enters the school. It is a political but not a psychological truth that 'any boy may become president of the United States.'" Children's differences "are basic and permanent, not merely differences in rate of attaining similar ends."

The doctrine of individual differences seriously questioned the utility of a common curriculum. In *How to Teach* (1917), Strayer and his colleague Naomi Norsworthy typically asserted that the weight of scientific evidence and practical experience pointed only in one direction. "Individuals," they wrote, "differ from each other to a much greater degree than has been allowed for in our public education. The common school system is constructed on the theory that children are closely similar in their abilities, type of mental make-up, and capacities in any given time." But research showed that these assumptions were "false. So far as general ability goes, children vary from the genius to the feeble-minded with all the grades between, even in the same school class." Like many other administrative reformers, Ellwood Cubberley endorsed a differentiated curriculum. He saw it as the only sound policy, given innate differences in human capacity and potential, and the only way to reduce dropout and failure rates, given the desirability of running school plants smoothly. As early as 1909, Cubberley had emphasized in *Changing Conceptions of Education* that the ideal of democracy clashed with the realities of industrial society, whose division of labor contradicted sentimental though popular beliefs about human equality.

This was a far cry from the romantics extolling the inherent worth of the individual and enjoying flights of fancy in the fields. But antipopulist sentiments were pronounced with equal vigor and conviction. Some individuals who embraced social efficiency were not so pessimistic about human potential. Before the early 1920s, for example, William Bagley was a reliable champion of social efficiency but outspokenly defended the three Rs and mass instruction in basic subjects. He also frequently questioned whether heredity determined human destiny as much as many psychologists and administrative reformers assumed. In the 1920s and 1930s, this most traditional of educators loudly defended academic instruction while undermining the hereditarian assumptions of intelligence testing. Schools, he repeatedly wrote, ensured the evolutionary development of the individual and of society, part of the collective transit from ignorance to knowledge, barbarism to civilization.

In *School Discipline* (1916), Bagley admitted that a differentiated curriculum sounded reasonable until one remembered that democracy demanded "a common basis of habits, ideas, and ideals." Many people asked: "Why should the 'motor-minded' child be compelled to occupy his time with books when his whole being calls out for a different type of activity?" Bagley differed from many educationists since he thought even the less gifted deserved access to an academic curriculum. Educational inclusion supported the larger democratic and social goals of mass education. For "the function of public education (and especially the function of elementary education)" was to lay a "*common* basis among *all* of the future citizens of the land. It is a price that must be paid for social solidarity—and not a heavy price compared with what a lack of mutual understanding among the people would inevitably involve." In 1926 a writer for *Time* magazine attended the meetings of the National Education Association, where he heard a principal from Trenton, New Jersey, endorse a differentiated over a common curriculum, asserting that the latter produced a "common level of mediocrity." In contrast, Bagley insisted at the meeting that mass education was the hope of democracy.

By defending the basic principles underlying the common school, Bagley increasingly gained a reputation as a conservative. But educational politics often yield strange bedfellows. Those repelled by Bagley's views nevertheless shared his disdain for certain elitist philosophies, from vocational education to testing. William Kilpatrick, who was both Bagley's and Strayer's colleague at Teachers College, Columbia, was one of the nation's leading progressive educators after World War I. Greatly influenced by John Dewey, Kilpatrick complained in *Education for a Changing Civilization* (1926) about "the stranglehold of tradition" in the classroom but nevertheless opposed socializing children for a preordained niche in the industrial order. Industrial laborers frequently occupied a "narrow groove" at work, but that hardly justified a "corresponding narrowness" in the curriculum. Fearful of class conflict, Kilpatrick believed that narrow trade training would only aggravate social tensions.

In 1927, Boyd H. Bode, a philosopher of education and occasional critic of progressive schools, pointed out in *Modern Educational Theories* that educators piously intoned that schools prepared the young "for life," forgetting that "there is less agreement than formerly on the meaning of life or the meaning of education." Too many people forgot that "the first obligation of our public school system is to provide common interests and a common understanding as an indispensable basis for democracy." Bode wrote that children may have recognizable and scientifically demonstrable "capacities and talents . . . but none of these differences should be made an excuse for overlooking the fact that we are, first of all, members of the human race." Far too much had been made of individual differences. If the old-time school was too preoccupied with academic instruction, champions of human differences too often held "aristocratic" assumptions about who could benefit from the schools. Bode therefore feared "the tyranny of a new aristocracy, based on a caste system of vocational interests."

Like many educators with democratic inclinations, Bode sensed imminent danger as administrative leaders popularized the idea of innate human differences. Belief in human inequality received an enormous boost from the testing movement, which caught fire in the early 1900s and made extravagant claims about the hereditary basis of intelligence. Americans, Bode realized, had a "reverential attitude toward science." Technological advances spurred industrial productivity and laid the basis for a consumer society and rising standard of living. Scientific views of intelligence nevertheless undermined traditional assumptions about human worth and potential. Mental tests, said some writers, showed that the average adult had the mentality of a thirteen-year-old! Bode hailed the many critics of intelligence testing in the 1920s who highlighted environment factors in human development and achievement. But an emphasis on human difference remained popular among leading educational professionals and left a lasting imprint on elementary school practices throughout the first half of the twentieth century.

In 1929 George Counts predicted that when historians in the twenty-first century assessed the major educational developments of the early 1900s, they would be struck by the era's rising faith in science. In *The American Road to Culture* (1930), Counts elaborated upon this insight, showing how an initial interest in the scientific measurement of native intelligence and the development of achievement tests had exploded into "an orgy of testing" on every conceivable aspect of learning and human development. By the 1930s and 1940s, there were literally thousands of tests—on intelligence, on innumerable classroom subjects, on personality traits, on vocational predispositions, on how to rate living-room furniture. Counts believed that the popularity of scientific testing reflected the dominant values of business culture and social efficiency embraced by elite urban administrators. Armed with test results, intelligence ratings, and predictions about vocational aptitude, experts in the schools finally had the tools to better classify pupils, create a more differentiated curriculum, recognize individual needs in instruction and promotion, and prepare youth for a preordained place in the industrial system. Tests held promise for aiding objective, apolitical decision making, that is, in harmony with the needs of hierarchical school organizations and a free market economy.

Some of the ardor cooled in the 1920s, but a utopian strain was long evident within the testing movement. New measures, tests, and standards of evaluation would eliminate rule-of-thumb methods, subjectivity, and professional teachers' guesswork. Science would uncover irrefutable knowledge about each individual who, if placed in the correct course of study, would be efficiently trained for the workplace and adult responsibilities. "Mental tests threaten just now to become a sort of educational fad," wrote one skeptic in the *Atlantic Educational Journal* in 1914. "It has been presumed in certain quarters that the matter of classifying and grading individuals according to their mentality can be made as easy as simple addition through use of Simon-Binet tests." Some zealots even said that mental tests promised to solve "about one-half of the present-day problems in education."

The benefits of intelligence tests, achievement tests, and other standardized measures seemed obvious to countless educational leaders and administrators. Every complaint about the "mania of testing" generated counterclaims that standardized tests, however imperfect, were here to stay. Educators smitten by visions of social efficiency greeted the tests as a godsend. Certainly administrative reformers such as Cubberley and Strayer saw nothing but promise in scientific measurement. "We are all conscious of the fact that children are not alike," wrote a small-town superintendent in 1917 who had absorbed the message. "It is all too apparent that original endowment, or human nature, is extremely variable, and that it accounts for many of the important differences that we find among school children. Possibly no phase of educational psychology is more significant, today, than the changing conception of the relation of the individual to the school group." Tests and measurement and better classification were the answer.

Every child needed an appropriate curriculum, wrote Percival M. Symonds, an educational psychologist and true believer in human differences, in 1934. Otherwise, how could society know who should become a teacher and who should be a truck driver? Symonds believed that critics of the testing movement stood in the way of progress. The basic facts of each individual's "mental life" had to be determined and recorded. By knowing everyone's intellectual and emotional strengths and weaknesses, experts could ensure efficiency and harmony in school and society. After all, he wrote, "there is no more reason to hide one's talents, aptitudes, and capacities, acquired dispositions, or personal problems than to conceal the character of one's haircut or the style of one's clothing." With the proper tests, questionnaires, and rating scales, school officials could discover who was dishonest and incorrigible and on the road to a life of crime, and who was hard working and intelligent and (even in the depths of economic despair) destined to succeed.

Long before the widespread use of intelligence tests in America's schools, teachers had recognized the limitations of age-graded instruction. Grades conveniently grouped children of roughly the same age but hardly eliminated their varied range of intellectual maturity, language skills, and other personal traits. Elementary classes in the cities often had forty to fifty children per room. Overcrowding was common. As early as the 1870s, superintendent William T. Harris of St. Louis, who had taught in the local schools, established semiannual promotions to move more talented pupils more quickly to the next grade. Quite a few cities followed this example and tried other experiments to address the problem of individual differences. In a celebrated but not much imitated experiment in Batavia, New York, two teachers taught in each elementary classroom, where one of them coached the slower pupils. Still other communities experimented with different ways to individualize instruction and determine promotion.

Teachers in St. Louis and many cities more typically created what became known as ability groups. Test scores later helped identify who belonged in which group within a self-contained classroom. Before the turn of the century, however, teachers and principals everywhere based their decisions on grades and their own best judgment. Unlike well-known intelligence and achievement tests, ability groups did not have a single inventor. They emerged from everyday urban teaching practices. They did not reduce dependency upon textbooks, which were essential in organizing instruction given the many young and inexperienced teachers and large class sizes. Nor did ability groups necessarily imply dissimilar standards for promotion for different groups of children. In theory, improved methods of teaching pupils in the slower groups would enable them to catch up with the higher achieving scholars. Failure rates, especially in the earliest grades, were often high in the first two decades of the twentieth century, allowing efficiency reformers to accuse the schools of squandering economic resources and wasting everyone's time. By the 1920s and 1930s, child-centered educators and some psychologists increasingly emphasized the discouragement and hurt feelings of those who failed.

Often based on a teacher's assessment of the child's reading ability as well as overall performance, ability groups became a way to manage pupils as well as to instruct them. In 1898 superintendent Louis Soldan of St. Louis wrote that the city's elementary schools had two or three groups within each elementary class. For nearly three decades, he said, St. Louis tried to individualize instruction through rapid promotions for the most talented children and then through the creation of these subgroups. "The defects of the graded system and its inability to consider each child's individuality," Soldan admitted, "are chiefly found in the necessity of assigning a uniform daily lesson to each class, when it is evident that the few slow children should take a shorter, the brighter and abler ones, a longer lesson." Invariably, "the bright and the slow combined in the same class form a problem which the teacher is constantly required to solve."

William Bagley, who himself had worked in the St. Louis system, joined the legion of educators who pointed to the shortcomings of the graded classroom. As Bagley wrote in *Classroom Management* (1907), graded classes were generally beneficial but had serious shortcomings. "The unique problem of class instruction," he said, "is to secure the attention of *all* pupils to the matter in hand, and to keep all of the pupils up to practically the same level of attainment in spite of individual differences in previous attainment and capacity for further growth." Aiming at the golden mean, teachers and administrators set standards for an imagined middle range of achievement, which left the brighter students bored and the slower pupils trailing behind. Graded classrooms, snorted one educator from Pittsburgh, were created for the "average" child, a "mythical unit." In most cities, Bagley noted, the typical classroom had two or three ability groups taught by a single teacher. Textbooks remained the teacher's main means of instruction, which enabled pupils to learn progressively more difficult material and constituted a ready-made curriculum.

A number of factors converged in urban areas in the early 1900s to make new ideas about classroom organization, pupil classification and promotion, teaching, and curricular innovation very appealing. Researchers in New York City issued ominous reports on the multitudes of over-age children (then called "retarded") in many classrooms. Equally alarming studies soon multiplied on the high dropout and failure rates in numerous urban systems. In an age enamored with efficiency and the notion of individual differences, this was especially horrifying. Costs were rising, urban classrooms bulging, and perceived inefficiency rampant. After 1910, quantitative studies of school systems proliferated that demonstrated that many children simply could not master existing classroom standards. Eager to apply the latest methods of business efficiency and scientific management (which promised to revolutionize industry), school superintendents and school boards saw an opportunity to modernize their systems. The aura of science that surrounded the exploding number of research studies on city systems nurtured heady expectations that expertise could make the schools more cost effective and educationally relevant for a more intellectually diverse student body. The widespread lament that individuals floundered in the system only deepened as scientific tests exposed the range of intelligence found in most classrooms.

All of these concerns came together in the work of Edward L. Thorndike. Born in 1874 in Williamsburg, Massachusetts, Thorndike became a founder of the field of educational psychology. After earning bachelor's degrees from both Wesleyan and Harvard, he received a Ph.D. in psychology from Columbia, earning an appointment in 1899 at its Teachers College, where he taught for four decades. Thorndike brought the insights of experimental science and the study of animals to bear on human learning, and he popularized behavioral and quantitative approaches to educational research. In a landmark study published in 1901 with his student, Robert S. Woodworth, he claimed to disprove the hallowed idea of "transfer of training," the belief that the mastery of difficult subjects such as classical languages and mathematics literally helped in learning other academic subjects. Though their research was not universally accepted, their claims were manna from heaven to reformers intent on weakening the academic curriculum and addressing human differences.

On the origins of these differences, Thorndike was very clear. An avid researcher and prolific author, he underscored the decisive role of heredity in shaping human intelligence. In *Individuality* (1911), he explained that the "variations from the ordinary, common, or typical man range continuously to such extreme conditions as appear in the idiot and the genius, or Nero and Lincoln." Sentimental ideals about democracy and human potential held little place in Thorndike's social philosophy. While most people clustered around the average, "the differences that characterize men of the same time, country, and social status are largely original, determined directly by the germs from which the individual develops, and so indirectly by the ancestry from which he springs." The schools needed more vocational training programs to serve the least academically talented. Similarly, ability groups were absolutely essential in the elementary grades, precursors to more elaborate tracking in high schools. Since learning was the sum total of all one's stimulus and response experiences, curricula gauged to one's native endowment and likely social destination constituted the only rational policy. It was economically wasteful and socially inefficient to provide everyone with the same education, given pupils' unequal capacity to learn.

Thorndike was actively involved in the origins of mass intelligence testing, earned a fortune constructing various achievement tests, and shared the overall world view of the administrative reformers. Scholars such as Strayer and Cubberley usually cited him uncritically in their best-selling textbooks on education, teaching, history, and school administration. And they all contributed to what Counts had called an "orgy" of testing, as reformers attempted to apply the insights of science and business to the expanding public school system. Intelligence tests, achievement tests, and a variety of measurements and scales were their greatest legacy. These reformers decisively shaped new ideas about academic standards, promotion, and curriculum but would not shape the world of schools exactly as they hoped.

"The most striking development within recent years in the field of education is undoubtedly the movement known as mental tests and measurements," wrote Boyd Bode in 1927. "It had long been known that pupils differed widely in capacity. But these differences were based on impressions or haphazard evidence, not on objective and relatively simple tests." Now phrases such as "mental age" and "IQ" were part of the nation's vocabulary. Thomas Carlyle had once groused that "England has a population of twenty-six million, mostly fools." Now scientists apparently had the hard evidence. The headlines in America's newspapers and popular magazines similarly blared out disconcerting news for anyone who believed in human potential and egalitarian democracy. Around 25 percent of the population was reportedly "subnormal," only 40 percent had the mental capacity for high school, and only 15 percent for college. While Bode dismissed these claims as exaggerated and elitist, they reinforced conservative beliefs that most children could only be trained, not educated, and would become the "hewers of wood and the drawers of water."

The upsurge of interest in mental testing by World War I led to far-reaching claims about children's individual differences and school performance. Even before mental testers became influential, alarming data appeared on urban school performance. In 1908, already convinced that heredity largely determined intelligence, Edward Thorndike documented the large numbers of children who flunked classes, repeated grades, and left elementary school without mastering the basics. Attacking the waste and inefficiency of business as usual, he believed that high failure rates resulted from an "incapacity for and lack of interest in the sort of intellectual work demanded by present courses of study." The varied mental capacity of students precluded widespread access to an academic curriculum, either in the elementary grades or in the high schools.

In 1909, Leonard P. Ayres published *Laggards in Our Schools,* one of the most talked about books of its generation. New England born and college bred, Ayres taught in Puerto Rico at the turn of the century and quickly climbed the administrative ladder, becoming superintendent of the San Juan schools and then the island's chief superintendent and head of its bureau of statistics. Returning to the mainland, he published studies on medical inspection of the schools and earned his master's and Ph.D. degrees. In 1908, he joined the staff of the Russell Sage Foundation in New York, administering a "Backward Children Investigation." Like the best muckraking literature of the day, *Laggards* made the newspaper headlines and shocked many readers, inspiring a proliferation of studies on the failures of city systems. It was not a study of the feebleminded, a group which then preoccupied researchers, and this gave *Laggards* added punch. Ayres studied "retarded" children, "varying with local conditions from 5 to 75 percent of all children in our schools, who are older than they should be for the grades they are in."

Towns and cities varied in their promotion rates, but about one-third of all children fell into the "retarded" category. The facts about these "misfits," Ayres believed, were appalling. While most urban children stayed in school through fifth grade, only half survived to eighth grade, and only about one of every ten ninth graders went on to receive a high school diploma. Along the way a significant percentage of pupils failed a grade, sometimes two or three. Contrary to popular belief, the curriculum was geared to the brighter, not to the average, child. This helped explain why relatively few children progressed smoothly from grade to grade. Moreover, at a time of heightened concerns about efficiency, the nation spent an estimated $27 million just on the repeaters. Ayres discovered that boys were 13 percent more "retarded" than girls, whose gender advantage subsequent studies confirmed. The nation's immigrant groups on the whole generally fared well compared to the native born, even though promotion rates overall were the worst in the largest cities. Ayres believed that children left school prematurely for various reasons: poor health and medical care, social distractions, an irrelevant and difficult curriculum, boredom, embarrassment with failure, and the desire and necessity to work to help their family. Unfortunately, in his view, the typical school measured its quality by the percentage of children it failed. Without failures, there were no successes. And when children failed, they themselves were largely blamed. "If the function of the common school is, as the author believes, to furnish an elementary education to the maximum number of children, then *other things being equal* that school is best which regularly promotes and finally graduates the largest percentage of its pupils." In other words, educators had yet to fit the school to the child.

Numerous surveys of urban systems during the next decade revealed similar patterns of failure and nonpromotion. Intelligence tests became more widely marketed after 1908, when the Simon-Binet tests from France were dramatically revised and test results reinforced the idea that the elementary schools were too academic, irrelevant, and difficult for most children. Many of those who shaped the new field of educational psychology, including Thorndike, embraced *eugenics,* a word coined by the English statistician Francis Galton in the early 1880s to describe the genetic basis of human differences. In the 1920s, when lay critics such as Walter Lippmann and educators such as William Bagley and John Dewey attacked the hereditarian assumptions and undemocratic biases of the testing movement, anthropologists, sociologists, and a new generation of psychologists underscored the environmental basis of intelligence. Before the war, however, those engaged in mental measurement believed deeply in ineradicable human differences and in the futility of teaching academic subjects to everyone.

Of central importance to the mental testing movement was Lewis Terman. Terman was a farm boy from Indiana who ultimately joined Cubberley's faculty at Stanford, where he became the leading proponent of intelligence testing. A graduate of Indiana University, he earned his Ph.D. at Clark University, where he studied with G. Stanley Hall, whose child-study methods helped inspire the testing movement. Hall's scholarship was widely regarded as romantic, impressionistic, and idiosyncratic, despite his reputation as a scientific researcher. In contrast, Terman and his closest colleagues based their research on systematic, quantitative explorations of large-scale empirical data, utilizing the latest statistical techniques. Their surveys of schools and publications bulged with curves and charts, tables and frequency distributions. Terman helped revise the Binet scales, later known as Stanford-Binet, which were widely administered during his lifetime. Convinced that intelligence was largely inherited and unchanging, he emphasized the importance of individual differences and curricular differentiation. "Instead of a single curriculum for all, merely divided into eight successive levels [in the elementary grades]," he wrote in 1919, "it would be better to arrange parallel courses of study for children of different grades of ability."

These words appeared in Terman's widely cited book, *The Intelligence of School Children*, in which he summarized research inspired by *Laggards* that confirmed innate human differences. Terman wrote that schools ignored these findings at their peril. It was now common knowledge, he said, "that more than ten percent of the cost of tuition is for repeated instruction, that about a fourth of the pupils leave school with not more than a sixth-grade education, and that the ranks of the vocationally incompetent are recruited largely from children who in school were over-age for their grade." George Strayer's numerous studies of urban systems confirmed that about one-third of their pupils were retarded, and inefficiencies were especially blatant in rural schools. One particularly difficult group of children to teach were labeled "feeble minded," though definitions of the condition varied. Terman shared the common professional view that they were prone to crime and a "burden rather than an asset" to society. Those who seemed educable needed special, segregated classes, now found in hundreds of towns and cities. The most hopeless cases required placement in residential facilities.

After the Civil War, urban school systems had created some segregated "ungraded" classes for children whose severe learning or behavioral problems or poor English-language skills severely hindered their scholastic progress. But "special education" received a major boost during the early twentieth century from the testing movement. Many people at the time complained about the lack of attention to the individual child and argued that the "average" child did not exist. In 1906, a northern urban superintendent called for greater efforts on behalf of the "submerged tenth," those unable to profit from academic instruction. Contemporaries referred to children with varied learning problems as "weak minded," "defective," "feeble-minded," and "born-short," among the more flattering descriptions. They were often viewed with pity and as often with scorn for distracting children in regular classes, where they were a "drag" on school efficiency. Mental testers documented their low range of intelligence, and medical inspectors searched for the physical cause.

These children frequently repeated courses and helped inflate the high failure rates. The solution, said Edward Thorndike in 1907, was additional special classes and more vocational education and trade training. Like countless periodicals, the *Atlantic Educational Monthly* in 1912 claimed that millions of dollars were wasted trying to teach the weak-minded serious subjects. A year later a Harvard professor who completed a survey of the New York City schools identified 15,000 "mentally defective" children who, unless segregated into special classes, would clog the school machinery. Most researchers who studied these children stressed the power of heredity and eugenics, frequently advocating sterilization. Special classes, though enrolling a small percentage of students, became common in graded school systems in the early twentieth century. They often contained pupils with a diversity of learning impediments and with below-average test scores, which only confirmed existing impressions of them. Intelligence tests had not led to the establishment of special classes, which existed prior to the rise of mental testing. Grades and teachers' judgments of pupil progress primarily determined classroom placement, but IQ scores and other scientific assessments certainly helped place pupils in special settings, which grew in number.

Special education classes usually set lower academic goals than regular classrooms. Whether in New Orleans or Indianapolis, they often offered large doses of manual training and domestic science to keep the children occupied and presumably to teach habits and skills of lifelong value. These subjects hardly rose in status once they became the core of the special education curriculum. In contrast, the authors of *Fitting the School to the Child* explained in 1924 that there was no shame in having a low IQ or in attending a segregated class. And "there are numberless occupations on which civilization depends which may readily be performed by a person with a 50 to 75 IQ." Advocates of special classes persistently argued that, if properly trained, these children could become self-supporting even if limited to low-level, low-paid jobs.

Intelligence and achievement tests certainly provided abundant data that helped determine classroom placement, grade standards, and promotion policies. Any child attending a graded school after 1910 had an excellent chance of encountering various forms of scientific measurement. By 1920, educational researchers constructed various scales and norms to measure academic achievement in school subjects. Professional literature proliferated that extolled the benefits of scientific evaluations. By 1917, nearly fifty thousand children in various states had taken the Courtis arithmetic tests, named for a prominent research specialist in the Detroit schools. Courtis, Ayres, and Thorndike had competing scales to measure handwriting. Every administrator in the know adopted the Thorndike-McCall or Gray scales in reading or the alternatives by Starch and the ubiquitous Courtis.

Soon every subject attracted scientific researchers eager to measure and evaluate pupil performance. As two scholars remarked during World War I, these tests took the guesswork out of evaluation. "The adoption of these objective scales for the measurement of school products," they wrote, "is bound to establish a scientific attitude in the schools, which will energize and direct the work of the teachers and raise the administrator's task from the realm of mere opinion to the level of scientific judgement." Furthermore, school administrators used student achievement to infer teacher competence, and test scores could be compared not only within but also across districts. What a wonderful check, they said, on "inefficiency." The tests largely confirmed what everyone already knew: "the great individual differences in ability that exist even in the same class."

Textbooks for future teachers and budding administrators underscored the value of standardized testing. However, many districts could not afford unlimited numbers of tests, many administrators struggled to interpret the results, and teachers, frequently criticized for their lack of scientific acumen, often taught and organized classrooms in traditional ways. Moreover, local systems never seemed to hire enough psychologists, guidance counselors, or other specialists skilled in the ways of testing. Some urban systems had established their own research bureaus by the 1920s to help them place more children under the pedagogical microscope. But many administrators lacked the economic and human resources to dramatically alter classroom practices. Moreover, while ability groups were increasingly the norm in graded systems, they never provided the new and improved teaching methods that educational science and the testers promised.

Henry J. Otto, who taught at Northwestern University, shared the era's professional infatuation with "individual differences" and became a leading scholar of elementary school organization and teaching practices. Like other researchers, he knew that ability grouping was common in most towns and cities. In 1934, however, he concluded that ability grouping was mostly an "administrative device," not an opportunity to teach children with varying methods and distinctive curricula. All the children in a classroom typically had the same assignments; some advanced more quickly, others more slowly. Not much had changed since the turn of the century. Other researchers confirmed that the slower groups simply received more drill and dull instruction than the more advanced pupils.

Homogeneous grouping of children dominated graded systems. Administrators and teachers often examined standardized test scores to help place students. Otto nevertheless discovered that "very few districts, however, formulated class groups solely on the basis of standardized mental and achievement tests." As in earlier periods, teachers considered children's past achievement and whether they worked to their capacity. Decision making was thus a mixture of objective and subjective assessments. Otto and other researchers adamantly believed that children's measured "ability" (and not grades or teacher estimates) should determine classroom placement. They discovered a wide range of ability even within supposedly homogeneous groups. Somehow the news had not seemed to matter to administrators and teachers. When Otto studied promotion policies, he found a variety of practices, including schools that still failed many students despite the scientific evidence that this was counterproductive and economically wasteful.

Growing attacks on eugenics, part of a backlash against fascism and Nazi Germany, where eugenics was used to justify genocide, further undermined the idea that science was going to provide many educational panaceas. By the 1930s, more educational writers recognized the role of environment and culture in shaping intelligence. They found testing helpful if not taken to zealous extremes. "The intelligence test has won a place in education," wrote one educator from West Virginia in 1937. But the hereditarian biases of the early testing movement, he said, had fostered "undemocratic, reactionary theories and practices" inimical to American democracy. Despite Terman's claims, the tests hardly measured "innate capacity." Bagley and others had persuasively demonstrated the influence of environment in explaining the differential scores of recruits tested by the Army during World War I. African Americans living in the

North scored higher than those in the South, who lacked as much access to schools; and they also surpassed many native white Southerners, who supposedly had the purest racial stock. Standardized measures made sense if people lived standard lives. But, asked the West Virginian, "how can a New England boy be expected to have the same environmental background that a Southern boy has? Does the child in a factory district have an environment comparable to that of a fashionable boulevard?" Since children lacked "equality of opportunity" in life, the grandiose claims of the early mental testers hardly stood up to logic, never mind to the needs of a democratic society.

By the 1930s and 1940s, graded school systems in particular had gathered large amounts of empirical data on their students. There were achievement scores, Stanford-Binet scores, classroom grades, and statistics on everything from children's heights to incidence of chicken pox. Experts at universities nevertheless discovered that educators rarely relied exclusively on standardized tests to make decisions. Sometimes the results were simply ignored. One urban researcher studied record keeping in thirty-five districts in the early 1940s and found that records abounded, frequently gathering dust. "Elaborate record systems used as show pieces are of no credit to any school organization," he wrote in frustration in a state education journal. "How ridiculous it is to boast of filing cabinet after filing cabinet of significant information about children, carefully recorded but seldom used. There is no lack of cumulative record systems," he continued, "but there is an insufficient understanding of how these records and the information contained therein can be of use in the education of children, according to their needs and capacity." To the champions of a science of education, which would yield incontrovertible facts about individual differences, this was frustrating indeed.

In addition to various intelligence, achievement, personality, and vocational aptitude tests, students faced newly created "objective" tests for everyday use. By the early 1920s, students encountered true-false and multiple choice tests, in combination with the familiar oral recitations, surprise quizzes, monthly written exams, and comprehensive tests at the end of the term. Even if they were not all-powerful, tests had grown in variety and had become a more visible part of schooling. Appearances were sometimes deceiving, however, since these innovations actually reinforced traditional pedagogy and textbook instruction. The pedantic "ten questions on a blackboard" teacher hardly disappeared from children's lives.

Tests nevertheless became so pervasive that they were easily parodied. A

small-town teacher in 1942 told a joke about a colleague standing at the pearly
gates. St. Peter remarks:

> I'm getting so I shame to let a teacher in;
> They're *so* progressive down below;
> Our grading has been the same for years and years;
> No wonder pedagogues think we're mighty slow.
> But I'll surprise this fellow with some up-to-date technique.
> And he pulled a quill from out of his snowy wing,
> Tore a sheet from out of his register and gleefully called out,
> "Your I.Q., sir, and what quartile are you in?
> And have you any aptitude for fingering the harp,
> Or does a shovel better fit your hands;
> Are you fitted for a choir, or does tending to a fire
> Better meet the type of work your mind demands?"

The teacher has been so busy giving tests that he has not taken any and is too
nervous to take one now. St. Peter replies, "In that case, go down below," to
the "Plutonian shore. . . . They've no testing program there, I'm very sure of
that / It matters little what you are 'cut out for.'"

Here on earth, local districts often used tests and scores to help place children in special education classes, to justify more flexible means of promotion,
or to add more manual training, domestic science, and vocationally oriented
courses to the curriculum. Tests provided hard evidence on individual differences. As administrators tried to fit the school to the child, new courses and
programs helped expand the social roles of the elementary school in the first
half of the twentieth century. But most classrooms retained a very familiar face,
and progressives who wanted a more child-centered school and efficiency reformers enamored with quantitative measurements often despaired at what
they saw.

Since the time of Rousseau and the European romantics, educational reformers had often dreamed of perfecting the education of young children. The
elementary school, which the masses of pupils eventually attended, was the
logical site for pedagogical experimentation. Although they, too, would have
to face the music, high schools in the early twentieth century were widely re-

garded as stodgy institutions, everywhere bound by tradition and controlled by teachers and administrators who looked down their noses at the grades below. Few people would have argued with Harold Rugg and Ann Shumaker, who observed in 1928 in *The Child-Centered School* that "it appears to be impossible to find a school in America in which the child-centered philosophy is applied beyond the eighth grade." Even in the elementary grades, where test scores could be consigned to the basement, many observers before World War II were perplexed at the powerful hold of tradition.

Reformers of every stripe—from the advocates of social efficiency to those favoring freedom for the child—recognized that the best-laid plans would evaporate without the support of willing and enthusiastic teachers, the vast majority of whom by the early 1900s were women. Attacks on the old education were rife, and many primers on teaching condemned the power of textbooks and teacher authority. Teachers had to change, and quickly. "Drill for drill's sake is a positive fetish for many, especially in mathematics and the languages, including the mother tongue," wrote an experienced urban administrator in 1906. "Such drill is worse than waste." Almost a decade later, another educator, however, lamented that many teachers still emphasized memorization and confused children with "*walking encyclopedias*."

In the 1920s, normal school primers still questioned the ubiquity of textbook instruction in the lower schools, claiming it deadened children's curiosity. "One of the greatest sources of dissatisfaction with the curriculum of today is this very tendency, still so deep-rooted, of considering mere learning as the sole objective of education." It was better to do things than know things, said exasperated critics. Teachers forced children to memorize the names of the teeth but forgot to explain how to brush them. Experts who studied ability groups and teaching methods reached the same conclusion: textbooks and subject matter, not children and their interests, often ruled the roost. Textbooks on how to teach (ironically enough) often brimmed with photos of children playing in the fields, working on class projects, and making teepees, dolls, and model farms. They gave a false impression about change and obscured the great continuities in classroom practices.

According to most child-centered education enthusiasts, schools stayed stubbornly traditional, reinforced by the rising fascination with test scores. Despite the celebrated battles between the old and new education, drill, memorization, and tests of an increasing variety were very common. Only a few nationally prominent educators consistently defended the teachers. William

Bagley, openly critical of child-centered extremists and out of step with most professors of education, argued that studying basic subjects and memorization, though hardly in the tradition of Gradgrind, were essential to learning. Facts, rules, and definitions, he wrote in 1907, were essential to understanding larger principles and concepts, whether in history, mathematics, or English. Reading and studying could be irksome, but books opened up worlds beyond children's experience and background. The aged William T. Harris would have smiled.

After World War I, both social efficiency and child-centered advocates lamented the slowness of change. "Unless the rank and file of teachers learn to use tests the universal grading of children according to mental ability will remain largely a Utopian dream," feared Lewis Terman in 1919. His colleague, Ellwood Cubberley, also found city systems dragging their feet. In the revised version of his textbook, *Public School Administration,* Cubberley repeated the well-worn claim among the educational establishment that the best teachers worked in the city. Still, he noted that in many city systems hundreds of boys and girls flunked academic classes and repeated grades, confronting again and again "the puzzles of arithmetic and the technicalities of English grammar, when they ought to be in the high school or in a vocational school, studying something better suited to their needs and more likely to awaken their interest and enthusiasm." But there they sat, annoying the teacher and their classmates, wasting their time and the taxpayer's dollars, "usually accomplishing little" before joining "the ranks of the inefficient and the unsuccessful."

Those who struck a less officious and fatalistic pose similarly wondered why the great promise of the new education was unfulfilled. In 1927, Martin J. Stormzand, a professor of education at Occidental College, published *Progressive Methods of Teaching.* The first line of his textbook made his point clear: "Most teachers are text-book teachers." No other Western nation used textbooks so religiously as the main means of instruction, which produced cramming, student passivity, and dull instruction. Textbooks enabled inexperienced teachers to offer uniform subject matter to everyone, and Stormzand believed that nothing was likely to supplant them any time soon, except perhaps motion pictures. Regurgitating material for tests was the stuff of education. "The public," Stormzand added, also insisted on evaluations of the "abilities and achievements of the pupils." "Standings, marks, grades, estimates and letters of recommendation are demanded by the world from administrators and teachers. The further a child advances in school the more importance we find attached to such estimates of ability, work, and attitudes. Parents, employers, and each advancing step of the educational system itself, demand accurate grading." The lockstep remained unbroken.

When scholars investigated what children studied and how teachers taught, they were sometimes amazed at the iron grip of the past. Consider, for example, the elementary school curriculum. In 1905, Bruce Ryburn Payne published his much-cited dissertation, completed at Columbia University, that examined the elementary curriculum in several nations. After studying the records of fifty American cities, he concluded that "even after all the talk about the new education, the 'three R's' are in the ascendancy." The average time spent on basic subjects varied from city to city but was overall extensive. Students spent an average of 20.7 percent of their time on reading and literature, 4.7 percent on writing and an identical amount on spelling, plus 14.4 percent on grammar and composition and 17.3 percent on arithmetic. Well over half of the school day was spent on the three Rs, even more in the earliest grades. Most of the remaining time after third grade was occupied with content subjects such as geography, history, and science, in addition to drawing and music. While nature study and manual training appeared in many curricula, the author wryly noted that "getting a subject introduced into a curriculum, and getting it taught after it has been introduced, are entirely different matters."

In 1927, authors of a volume titled *Curriculum Problems* noted that textbooks remained pervasive: "More than anything else they are the courses of study for the vast majority of teachers." And the curriculum remained academic, even though student performance varied. A major study of elementary classrooms in 444 cities a year later again found that the basics were widely taught. On average, the percentage of time spent on reading (17.1%), phonics (1.6%), literature (1.7%), language and grammar (9.1%), penmanship (5.3%), spelling (5.3%), and arithmetic (11.6%) was fairly high. Content subjects such as history/citizenship/civics (4.4%), geography (5.8%), and science (1.3%) along with art and music (a combined 9.8%) rounded out the curriculum. Showing a higher rate than uncovered in the 1905 study, health and physical education grew to 8 percent of teaching time. However, manual training and the household arts registered under 1 percent.

Certainly debates about how to teach reading and whether social studies and civics were replacing history and geography received considerable publicity, and these controversies still wax and wane. But the testing movement helped administrators and teachers determine how well basic subjects were taught, not to eliminate them. The two most studied subjects, according to scientific surveys, were reading and arithmetic. The reasons are clear. They were long the bedrock of the curriculum. Most children who failed first or second grade usually had poor reading skills; the biggest stumbling block after third grade was often arithmetic. As one educator noted in 1935, reading—so important to overall school success—had "a halo of importance . . . cast over this subject as if it were the most important pursuit in the world."

Given the wide-ranging attacks upon convention, the survival of traditional teaching practices was remarkable. Various cities experimented with new classification and promotion schemes and other innovations. Most classrooms nevertheless remained teacher dominated, textbook driven, and subject-matter based. In the 1920s and 1930s, a variety of private progressive schools (from anarchistic schools to more structured schools that were often heavily academic despite their reputation) flourished that dispensed with the formalities of the typical public school. Model public schools that wore the progressive label (lab schools near college campuses or those found in a few affluent suburbs) also attracted considerable publicity. Some teachers in the public schools also promoted learning through school projects, made popular by William Kilpatrick and reminiscent of the activities at Dewey's Lab School, or related curricular innovations that emphasized the importance of children's experience and active learning in the classroom.

Innumerable books and articles featured field trips, group activities, civic projects, butterfly collecting, the building of model airplanes, and editing of school newspapers. They tapped the interests of children, making school fun and interesting for the pupils, and they received attention because they challenged everyday practice. The best expressions of the project method, said one observer in 1934, were nevertheless in "privileged schools." Scholars who studied progressive teaching methods in rural North Carolina documented stiff resistance to anything that veered too far from familiar subjects or questioned teacher authority. Contrary to the truth of the matter, said one child-centered educator, "many people feel that activity work consists of having the child do nothing except what he wishes to do and that the usual result is a great deal of noisy nailing, hammering, and sawing."

In a thoughtful appraisal of elementary school practices in the late 1930s, one educator noted that many teachers were simply uncomfortable in child-centered classrooms. That was not how they had been taught, and most parents shared their conservative views about unconventional classrooms and preferred arithmetic to leathercraft. Another observer lamented in 1938 that "the majority of schools in this country . . . have been content to follow the conventional school practices with only piecemeal or partial reform." In truth, only a handful, he said, actually tried to implement anything radical; few valued "the so-called progressive, experimental, or newer-type school." A few notable public school experiments won national acclaim. They were usually atypical schools in wealthy districts such as Winnetka, Illinois. Many child-centered innovations were short-lived and depended on charismatic leaders and teachers, always in short supply.

Most children did not spend their school days hammering and sawing, as conservatives feared and some progressives desired. Traditional pedagogy could even creep into courses on basket weaving, said exasperated child-centered educators who found manual training teachers lecturing from textbooks. By the 1940s, the average size of urban elementary classrooms dropped from an average of fifty or sixty students to under forty, but classes obviously were still fairly large, sustaining many traditional practices. Children spent considerable time reading textbooks, listening to teachers, taking tests, and filling in "work books" (also called "self-directed instructional materials"). At least, that is what researchers discovered after observing classrooms. In a volume entitled *Theory and Practice in the Elementary School* (1941), one perceptive educator, Weems Aurelius Saucier, said that most teaching "consisted quite largely of formal drill on bits of prescribed subject matter." "It is true that activities, projects, or realistic experiences are being incorporated into this school program," the author admitted. "Yet it seems that often they are included chiefly to break the monotony of meaningless routine instruction and to show that the teacher or the school is to some degree 'progressive.'"

One notable change in elementary schools that reflected its expanding social nature in the 1920s and 1930s appeared in the form of new report cards. Instead of simply registering marks in the various subjects, the new cards reportedly showed that "mere learning," the great bugaboo of many reformers, had been supplanted by loftier social ideals. Hoping to banish failure from children's lives, one small-town educator in 1935 offered the well-worn complaint that academics had an exaggerated place in most schools. "It may be more useful in later life," she said, "for a boy to know that he should remove his hat in an elevator or for a girl to know that she offers her hand to the boys if there's any handshaking to be done, than for either of them to know the capital of Venezuela or that a preposition is a poor thing to end a sentence with."

Discussions about report cards usually included slurs on the hidebound nature of schools: their preoccupation with marks and grades, standards and pro-motion, success and failure. Schools were social institutions, everyone seemed to agree, so teachers should provide parents with information on children's neatness, initiative, sense of cooperation, willingness to follow directions, and other character and citizenship traits. Innovative report cards grew so popular that the U.S. Office of Education collected dozens of new examples and pre-pared stereoptican slides of them to loan to local districts. Even parents of kindergarten pupils in Raton, New Mexico, received a report card four times a year in the early 1930s. Under the category of "Citizenship" appeared entries such as "Keeps Off Lawns," "Goes Directly Home," "Attends to Own Affairs," and "Neatness in Building and Playground." This was not exactly what Froebel had in mind but typified the widespread interest in all aspects of children's de-velopment.

Advocates of social efficiency believed that ratings of social virtues were more important than grades in penmanship or history. Child-centered educa-tors in turn criticized the traditional report card as divisive, pitting one child against another, making grades rather than the intrinsic love of learning the chief motivation for study. Madison, Wisconsin, a liberal college town, at one point banished homework. In the early 1930s it stopped marking children in subjects and simply reported on the pupil's "ability, effort, and problems." An anonymous writer claimed that the "new report is intended to do away with any sense of inferiority a child may feel from a low grade in some subject, when in reality he has accomplished as much as he could." Another Midwesterner, a county superintendent of schools, added that "real education" is determined "not by grades on report cards, but by usefulness and contributions during 50 to 60 years of living after school days are ended." If the child left school with-out a passion for learning, the system had failed. "Too often," he added, "the person who stood at the head of his classes in the elementary school, the high school, and the college will be found wasting his talents on some routine job fifteen years later because he has not learned the art of getting along with oth-ers." But many parents still wanted to know how children fared in their course work. In 1938, a cartoon in a state magazine showed a father's displeasure with his son's report card. The boy responded: "Don't take it so hard, Pop—condi-tions are bad everywhere!"

For decades efficiency experts declared that few children could profit from serious academics, and they berated teachers for not understanding modern testing techniques and methods of evaluation. Professors who trained and certified the nation's urban administrators regularly complained that teachers did not know the difference between the mean and the mode. Teachers were too tough, or too easy, or too oblivious to the great breakthroughs made by standardized testing. They often were very subjective in their assessments of written tests, graded inconsistently, and did not understand the science of test construction or validity and reliability. Why such flawed human beings suddenly had the skills to judge subjective matters such as initiative, attitude, and civic spirit was unclear.

Various school systems changed their grading scales, substituted letters for numerical grades, and occasionally dispensed with report cards altogether until parents revolted and the reports and scores again appeared every month or term. And report cards usually included grades, either letters or percentages, since principals and teachers knew parents expected it. That did not halt the spread of the new-style reports, which now included checklists of performance on character traits and citizenship. While these additional assessments added to the statistical profile of children and pleased many reformers—whether efficiency minded or child centered—this development actually reinforced tradition. Most educators in the nineteenth century expected children to be industrious, punctual, cooperative, neat, and socially responsible. This emphasis on citizenship and civic virtue hardly contradicted the values of the old-time school. The new report cards were more intrusive since they recorded children's assessments beyond academic achievement. But they were fully compatible with traditional mainstream education.

Had they been able to visit America's graded elementary schools at mid-century, Horace Mann, William T. Harris, and other nineteenth-century educators would have encountered many familiar practices. Moreover, local educators by the score, wherever they stood on social efficiency and child-centered education, still embraced many of the well-known goals of the common school: a sound education in the basics, the Americanization of immigrants, education for social stability, rewards for talent and punishments for failure, and the inculcation of moral values (still explicitly Christian). Many schools still began the day with a school prayer and, after the 1890s, with a salute to the American flag and recital of the Pledge of Allegiance. As in the past, children were expected to respect adults, obey the rules and regulations, and arrive at school ready to learn. At the same time, school administrators now had more powerful tools to measure student performance and teacher efficiency. They had scientific evidence to document individual differences. More data than ever before were gathered on every child, especially in the graded systems in the nation's burgeoning towns and cities. Report cards took account of a wide range of personal behaviors and civic values in addition to the traditional assessments of the various school subjects. If the center of gravity in the classroom had not shifted from the subject matter to the child, as many reformers desired, there was still no denying the powerful ways in which the language of human differences had entered the schools.

CHAPTER SIX

The People's College

"Education is said to be the ruling passion of the American people," wrote the editor of *School Life,* a publication of the U.S. Office of Education, in the spring of 1929. "No sacrifice is too great, and no expenditure is too heavy when the proper training of America's children is involved." Hyperbole aside, the editor proudly announced congressional approval of a $225,000 appropriation to fund a major survey of the nation's secondary schools. Ever since the first free high school opened in Boston in 1821, public secondary schools had been a controversial and contested part of the American school system. Debates over their nature and purpose had never disappeared, and ballooning enrollments after the 1890s only intensified them. Increasingly, high schools were drawn into the nation's dominant educational debates: about the meaning of democracy and social efficiency, equal opportunity and individual differences, and curriculum and pedagogy. By 1950, going to high school, once a fairly unusual experience, was a familiar one for the majority of American youth.

In the early 1900s, visitors from Europe commonly remarked that the American high school already taught an unprecedented number of pupils. This was, they believed, American democracy in action, though many predicted an inevitable lowering of standards. In 1903 a professor from Sheffield, England, marveled at the tax dollars spent on American high schools, especially in the cities. "In the United States," he claimed, "secondary education has reached a high state of efficiency, and it has become as really and actually a part of the American system of education as the primary school. . . . The city high schools are prominent everywhere. They are architecturally fine structures, and internally well fitted and equipped with all modern school requirements." For example, Central High School in Scranton, in the heart of Pennsylvania's anthracite region, was a beautiful facility with a gymnasium and an assembly hall that held over a thousand pupils. Another Englishman noted that the newest urban high schools reflected the nation's fascination with inventions and gadgetry. Many had already installed electric clocks, bells, and telephones.

With evident pride, the editor of *School Life* further remarked in 1929 that "in other lands, the outstanding structures are monumental churches and royal palaces; Americans build monumental colleges and palatial high schools." Already three-fourths of the survivors of eighth grade entered high school, even if most never graduated. "New York has more secondary schools than all of France, Los Angeles more than all of Austria, and Detroit more than London, though its population is only one-tenth as great," the editor boasted. Expanding enrollments had nevertheless brought unexpected problems. "We were not prepared for it in any particular. Neither physical equipment nor fully prepared teachers nor improved methods of instruction nor matured curricula could be provided rapidly enough to meet the new and unprecedented demands." One word best described the situation: "chaotic."

Those who remembered high schools before the 1890s searched for the right metaphors to describe their dramatic expansion. Analogies to troop movements proliferated. Perhaps their authors remembered G. Stanley Hall's notorious warning that a "great army of incapables" was descending upon the classroom. Educational leaders routinely complained that high schools were too academic, rigidly traditional, and out of step with the needs of youth, but battalions of new recruits still appeared at their door. If local secondary students marched abreast in military formation, said one writer during the Progressive Era, they would extend far beyond the horizon. Americans built an average of one new high school per day between 1890 and 1920, not all of them palaces, but an indication of impressive demand. By the mid-twentieth century, nearly every community—whether Ashland, Oregon, or Jacksboro, Texas—had proudly issued postcards showing off their new secondary school.

New professional magazines such as the *High School Journal,* which first appeared in 1917, reflected this growing interest in the secondary schools. "The rapid development of secondary education in the United States since 1890," wrote the editor, N. W. Walker of North Carolina, "is one of the arresting facts of our recent educational history." While many people worried about the quality of the students, curriculum, and teachers, the educational train raced along on an upward course. "The youth of the land," Walker explained in 1929, "are flocking into the secondary schools from every social and economic group of the community with the widest sort of differences in abilities, interests, and probable future careers. And the high school is maintained to serve them all." The swelling enrollments of the high school simply amazed many citizens. In 1890, high schools enrolled approximately 7 percent of all 14- to 17-year-olds; this jumped to nearly 38 percent in 1920 and 65 percent by 1936. From 1890 to 1930, the high school population doubled every decade due to several causes. Technological innovations displaced teen laborers. Child labor laws were strengthened. Parents had rising aspirations for the new generation, who during the Depression found jobs scarce. In the early 1930s, an estimated one hundred thousand students returned to their alma mater high schools for postgraduate training. Youth seemed to have nowhere else to go, and some secondary teachers feared that their schools were becoming custodial institutions, holding tanks for the unemployed.

One widely shared belief among many reformers after the 1890s was that the intellectual orientation of the high school was inappropriate for its changing clientele. Champions of vocational education and social efficiency, as well as child-centered education enthusiasts, viewed the curriculum as obsolete and the typical classroom as lifeless and sterile. The failure to meet the needs of the majority predictably led to high dropout and low graduation rates. No wonder students seemed more excited about Friday-night football games, dating, and 4-H meetings! Many critics said colleges controlled the curriculum and subverted the high school's proper role: to educate youth for work and for life. College domination had to end, the sooner the better.

As high schools became mass institutions in the first half of the twentieth century, jeremiads abounded about their presumed decline from a previous golden age. Various intellectuals and conservative educators pointed to the popularity of school sports, extracurricular activities, and vocational classes for the non–college bound as a sign of the times. These critics disagreed about what caused the alleged degradation of academic standards: the weak-minded students, the nostrums of efficiency or child-centered reform, or some combination of these factors. By the 1930s and 1940s, however, the academic character of many secondary schools had actually survived—without question, somewhat battered and bruised—despite the enormous expansion of social activities and a furious, semisuccessful assault on the traditional curriculum. The more that elite reformers across the pedagogical spectrum debunked academic instruction, the more many parents and teachers, if not all students, embraced it.

✎

Nineteenth-century Americans often called the high school the "people's college," but the phrase, which lingered in the early 1900s, always had an ambiguous ring. Certainly Whigs and Republicans had enthusiastically championed free secondary schools for ambitious, academically talented white youth, the epitome of republicanism and reward based on talent. Largely serving a minority of middle-class white students, the high school arose in the 1820s as an alternative to the Latin grammar school, the traditional public secondary school in New England that prepared boys for college. By the 1880s in the North, it had also helped eliminate thousands of tuition academies and seminaries that taught secondary subjects. While high schools in the nineteenth century prepared a small number of boys for college, the curriculum was largely nonclassical and dominated by the modern or English subjects, including English, history, mathematics, science, geography, and a foreign language, often but not always Latin. Only a handful of atypical urban high schools had a majority of students in the classical, college preparatory course. Most high school students everywhere were women, who had little access to further education until after the Civil War, and they often became common school teachers.

College preparation was a small part of the social function of high schools in the nineteenth century. But critics of academic instruction by the 1890s increasingly thought otherwise. Only a few educators in the early twentieth century realized that the high school was not originally a college preparatory institution. Indeed, critics who favored practical courses and weaker academics blamed colleges for the ills of the high school. Because high schools enrolled only a small percentage of adolescents before the early 1900s, critics often associated them with the elite branches of higher learning, whether the earlier

Latin grammar schools or contemporary colleges. The driving demand of reformers in the early twentieth century was to make high school more practical and less academic. That invariably conjured up the bogeyman of "college
domination."

The view that the high schools were too academic for an expanding student
population, and that colleges were largely to blame had many sources. Beginning in the 1870s, the University of Michigan, followed by other states, certified public high schools, which enabled graduates of approved high schools to
matriculate without further examination. In some states, including Indiana,
the state department of public instruction rated the schools. Whatever the
arrangement, more students (including women) now attended college, adding
to the image of the high school as a college preparatory school. Since college
admission depended upon the mastery of academic and increasingly modern
subjects, complaints accelerated about the supposedly elitist nature of the high
school. It mattered not that the high schools were mostly teaching the same
nonclassical subjects in the 1890s as they had a half-century before. Academic
courses and college entrance requirements were impossible to disentangle, and
the curriculum allegedly favored the few over the many. Since most pupils did
not go to college, why should it have any power over them?

Regional accrediting associations also worked with high schools to create a
more standard curriculum, forcing them to offer minimum credits in particular academic courses to qualify pupils for college admission. Comprised of college and high school administrators and teachers, these associations gathered
quantitative information about factors such as enrollment, courses taken by
students, and teacher credentials. As colleges and universities grew, the high
school became a more important source of students, and accrediting agencies
expanded their authority to better connect secondary and higher education.
According to the *High School Journal,* by 1921 about eight thousand of the nation's fourteen thousand secondary schools were accredited or approved by
state departments of public instruction, individual colleges or universities, or
regional accrediting groups. Most high schools were very small institutions,
with a few teachers and a few dozen students, and they were unable to offer
many electives or vocational classes. Since a small but often socially influential number of pupils aspired to college, accreditation requirements meant that
the academic course of study had to be maintained, and it was the core curriculum for the college and non–college bound alike.

For those educators and reformers who wanted to replace or weaken the academic curriculum, college interference, as they saw it, made it impossible to establish a more practical education for the masses of secondary pupils. High schools could not abandon the academic course of study, or they would risk losing certification. In addition to the accrediting associations, other developments also seemed to demonstrate the special attention accorded to the college bound. The College Entrance Examination Board, founded in 1900, largely served private, elite New England colleges, and critics saw it as another example of outside meddling, since high schools were under pressure to make sure that their pupils could pass the examination, which meant preserving the academic curriculum. Carnegie units, which assigned points for courses based on how many hours they met each week, arrived on the scene in the early twentieth century, and a full high school course became equated with a specified number of units. The appearance of the Scholastic Aptitude Test in the 1920s was further evidence of external interference and the undue attention accorded to future collegians. Academics for the few, not practical education for the many, seemed to be in the driver's seat.

To the majority of critics, the most egregious example of outside pressure occurred in 1892, when the National Education Association published an infamous report written by the Committee of Ten. Nothing raised more pedagogical hackles in the following decades than this publication. Charles W. Eliot, the president of Harvard, headed the committee, which studied the high school and made recommendations on its curriculum. Although several of its members had public school teaching and administrative experience, as historian Edward A. Krug has demonstrated, the committee was soon attacked for the fact that many of its members worked at the college level. Charges of college domination echoed for the next half century. What the Committee of Ten basically argued was that the high school, which was likely to continue to enroll relatively few students, should not differentiate between pupils preparing for college and the majority preparing "for life." Since few secondary students would attend college, college preparation was "incidental" to the high school's main purpose, intellectual and cultural training.

Eliot's committee believed that "every subject which is taught at all in a secondary school should be taught in the same way and to the same extent to every pupil so long as he pursues it, no matter what the probable destination of the pupil may be, or at what point his education is to cease." Critics then and later were furious, accusing the committee of saying in effect that what was good for the college bound was good for everyone. They were also angry that the report ignored the place of manual training in the secondary curriculum. Eliot and his colleagues believed that the high schools primarily existed to prepare pupils for the broad "duties of life," and not for college, but their sins of omission were also never forgiven.

Indeed, many prominent educators accused the Committee of Ten of imposing high intellectual demands on pupils for a selfish motive: to ensure an efficient flow of students to the nation's expanding network of colleges and universities. Edward Thorndike and his colleagues had presumably exposed transfer of training and mental discipline as bogus science, yet the academic orientation and collegiate imprint on the high school remained powerful, according to the critics. Only 5 percent of students went to college, but the needs of the other 95 percent were ignored, the editor of the *Wisconsin Journal of Education* declared in 1902. In 1909 his counterpart in Ohio accused high school "professors" of academic pretensions inherited from the early Latin schools. The U.S. Office of Education regularly published bulletins and reports that condemned the smothering hold of the colleges and universities. In 1932, *School Life* stated that progress could only occur if "the slipping grip which colleges and universities have on our high schools will be further loosened."

The charge of college domination was one of the sharpest arrows in the reformer's quill, essential to slay the dragon of high academic expectations. Myths emerged about the origins of the American high school, and educators could not say enough about the evils of college influence. Advocates of social efficiency such as William Bagley, who later denounced the weakening of academic standards, assailed "college domination" as early as 1906 in *The Educative Process*. State school superintendents, teachers' associations, and professors of education routinely attacked the undemocratic influences of colleges and universities upon mass education. It was imperative that the high school respond quickly and decisively.

Many revised the past and said that the high school had always been an elite place for the college bound. Paul Hanus of Harvard, for example, argued in 1926 that college preparatory work characterized the earliest high schools and that Latin, Greek, and mathematics (in reality closer to the Latin school curriculum) had always dominated. Doing right by the majority, the non–college bound, meant severing the aristocratic roots of the institution. Similarly, a contributor to the *Encyclopedia of Educational Research* in 1941 repeated the conventional wisdom: "During the latter portion of the nineteenth century preparation for college was regarded as the primary purpose of secondary education. Preparation for life activities was a subordinate objective. . . . The curriculum offering was narrow, classical in nature, with strong emphasis upon acquiring subject matter." Other writers in the volume said that "social efficiency" required practical education for the majority of students.

Throughout the early decades of the twentieth century, numerous educators and reformers wanted the high school to soften its academic character. Ideas about the pronounced individual differences between children were now increasingly applied to secondary school pupils. In 1900, Hanus criticized the many "uncultivated parents" who pressured schools to retain the conventional academic curriculum. He believed that parents seemed oblivious to "the practical concerns of life" and to their children's probable futures. Most ninth graders, Hanus explained, never even received a diploma, and one could only pray that parents and educators soon recognized "that individuals differ in their tastes and capacities." Hanus believed that the dry teaching and sterile textbooks in the typical high school would bore the new student population. Unless pupil interest was tapped by engagement with more practical subjects, good teaching and social efficiency seemed impossible.

Slurs on the academic aspirations of the "uncultivated" and of the "army of incapables" proliferated but were buried in euphemisms, due to the avoidance of candid discussions of social class. More visible was the general attack on the overly intellectual purposes of the high school. Ellwood Cubberley, emphasizing the importance of social efficiency, observed in 1914 that high schools from Maine to California unfortunately shared many things in common. "This is due," he said, "to the fact that this institution has been, and is to-day, fundamentally a preparatory school to the colleges and universities, which by association and concerted action have set a more or less definite standard of requirement for entrance, and thus to a large degree have dictated a common curriculum for these schools." Growing support for vocational education and job training, however, offered "renewed promise" for that unrealized "dream of a people's college." In 1917, a manual arts teacher from Poplarville, Mississippi, emphasized that "the modern school for the masses must give up its initiative of the scholasticism of the middle ages, cease the solving of school born conundrums and formal grammar and quit hiding behind the justification for this by calling it mental discipline." He wrote that gasoline was more important to young people than Greek, and electricity more vital than Latin prose composition. Encouraging students to belong to corn clubs, pig clubs, and other extracurricular organizations was a much more sensible approach to education.

The radical historian Charles Beard launched an attack in 1917 on academics and classical education (which were usually conflated), in a lecture titled "Efficient Democracy" given at a technical high school in Pennsylvania. Beard called for the liberation of high schools from colleges and celebrated hard work, application, and physical labor. He supported the elimination of all foreign-language teaching, as did many xenophobes during World War I, but also wanted to get rid of most mathematics and science courses, except for those with practical applications. Beard said, "A great deal of the historical and higher literature instruction should go, on the same principle. Anyone may live a useful and happy life in the United States and cultivate a love for the true, the beautiful, and the good without ever having heard of Plato, Julius Caesar, Louis XIV, or the battle of Waterloo." There was nothing wrong with knowing these things, but "what nine-tenths of our high school graduates know about them two years after graduation is not worth knowing, and . . . the cost of producing real results is too great to be considered."

Whether left wing or economically conservative, reformers were furious that colleges retained their stranglehold on the high schools. Like Beard, Charles Prosser, a major advocate of vocational education, advocated the elimination of most academic subjects in high schools, believing they stood in the way of really preparing for life. Becoming famous for his advocacy of "life adjustment education," Prosser announced in 1939 that "business arithmetic is superior to plane or solid geometry; learning ways of keeping physically fit, to the study of French; learning the technique of selecting an occupation, to the study of algebra; simple science of everyday life, to geology; simple business English, to Elizabethan classics." The combined weight of history and college influence, Prosser feared, allowed the academic needs of the few to supersede the practical needs of the many.

By the early 1900s, as secondary enrollments expanded, the doctrine of individual differences among pupils became popular in diverse intellectual and pedagogical circles. The new students were often viewed as mentally inferior compared with their predecessors, who had to pass an entrance examination for admission. Now anyone interested seemed to attend. Experts reported that many pupils were incapable of serious academic study and that high intellectual achievement and open door policies were incompatible. The traditional curriculum, they agreed, was inappropriate for the majority of students, did not prepare them for their likely place in the social order, and stood in the way of progress.

By 1912, Michael Vincent O'Shea, a prominent professor of education at the

University of Wisconsin, among others sensed a sea change in attitudes about the high school. "Fifteen years ago," he said, speakers at educational conventions emphasized "'the discipline of the intellectual faculties,' and the 'training of character.'" Now "the dominant note everywhere was efficiency." Educators at professional conferences focused on the need for a practical education, and school officials printed innumerable reports and speeches on the subject. High schools were once a paradise for youth who loved to read, said one New England educator, but practical knowledge more likely came not from textbooks but from field trips and manual training. Only a handful of students really needed traditional academic instruction.

Criticisms of the intellectual aims and formalism of the high school were loud and insistent throughout the first half of the twentieth century. This produced some strange bedfellows, including those who held sentimental views of the child and those who wanted schools to prepare more docile but reliable workers. Those on the left as well as the right side of the political aisle often assaulted the academic elitism of secondary schools. Efficiency advocates said a common curriculum was a waste of time and money. Child-centered reformers called textbooks and rote teaching an abomination. On one issue, however, everyone agreed: the social functions of the modern high school had to expand to weaken the iron grip of traditional academics. Schools had to better prepare adolescents for life, not for college, and the social side of going to school needed to grow, like student enrollments already had, exponentially.

By World War I, a consensus emerged among leading educators that high schools could be both efficient and democratic. That is, schools should open their doors as widely as possible but also offer a more practical curriculum to address the diverse needs and abilities of pupils. George W. Gerwig, the secretary of the Pittsburgh school board, blended images of the machine and the garden, democracy and efficiency, in his appraisal of contemporary education. The title of his book, *Schools with a Perfect Score* (1918) reflected his passion for industrial management; and its subtitle, *Democracy's Hope and Safeguard,* his faith that weakening the intellectual basis of the high school best promoted the common good. Living in a city that epitomized the Industrial Revolution, Gerwig nevertheless drew upon Pestalozzi and the romantics and titled his chapters "The Head," "The Heart," and "The Hand." Like the romantics, he wanted to educate the whole person, which ultimately came to mean favoring the training of the hand over that of the mind.

"The old scholastic education was thought of by many as a thing apart from the actualities of life—something almost sacred," Gerwig explained. "Its goal was culture." A person was not regarded as educated or "cultured if his Latin accent proved defective." Industrial education and an anticipated reduction in academic subjects, however, portended a better future: "The old idea that the only road to culture or efficiency lay through the Latin dictionary is forever gone." In a perfect democratic society, "every one works, rendering service according to his ability." The Germans used trade training to build a strong (though militaristic) state, and America's working classes needed an industrial rather than effete education. For "while the pen is mightier than the sword, the trowel, or the compass, or the lathe is sometimes mightier than either." For too long the high school had favored the academically talented, but farsighted educators now realized that "equality of educational opportunity" did not mean access to a common curriculum but to nonacademic alternatives, especially for those "who happen to be industrially, commercially, or otherwise inclined."

If the modern high school did not exist primarily to train the mind, then what was its purpose? Gerwig and his contemporaries pondered this question. One familiar response was the establishment of the separate secondary manual training and trade schools for the working classes, often sponsored by business associations and other civic groups, that first appeared in the mid- to late 1880s in a number of cities. But battles frequently broke out on the local and national levels over whether these schools were too European, class based, and undemocratic. Labor unions suspected that privately run trade schools were "scab factories," and John Dewey and other liberals often opposed the creation of separate vocational high schools. Some districts still established them, but most American secondary schools after 1900, especially in urban areas, increasingly became "cosmopolitan" or "comprehensive" high schools. In these schools new courses or curricula in industrial and commercial education coexisted under the same roof with the standard academic course (the nonclassical modern or English course that now became synonymous with the college preparatory track). Many citizens viewed this as a reasonable compromise between extreme differentiation and doing nothing for those labeled "motor minded" or "hand minded." Others asked whether the high school had any clear purpose or rationale.

By 1910, according to O'Shea, the high school had become "the storm-center of educational unrest." He wrote, "Wherever one goes throughout the country, he is told, alike by teachers and by laymen, that the high school does not adequately meet the needs of a majority of its pupils." Citizens complained that secondary students put on airs, employers said graduates were poor workers, and the colleges said entering students lacked basic knowledge. "It has been said that the years between fourteen and sixteen are generally spent in forgetting everything learned in school instead of applying it," one of O'Shea's contemporaries in Pennsylvania later remarked. "We must take into account the fact that children differ in ability, temperament, and special aptitudes. This means that at twelve or thirteen years of age courses must be planned to meet these differences." Across the nation, secondary schools did not prepare adolescents well for life or ensure the greatest good to the greatest number, said one North Carolinian in 1916. Such complaints remained common even in the 1930s, when the Depression made vocational training sound a bit odd given the absence of jobs, which swelled already overflowing high school rosters.

Despite fears that high schools were chaotic, undemocratic, and adrift, a professional consensus was nevertheless emerging about their main purposes. It was unexpectedly bolstered by a National Education Association report in 1918 that was widely circulated by the U.S. Bureau of Education. Entitled *Cardinal Principles of Secondary Education,* the report became the era's most-cited statement on the nature of the high school. School administrators and educational leaders generally regarded the *Cardinal Principles* as the best guide to the social purposes of secondary education. Its main author, Clarence Kingsley, was a former high school teacher who skillfully blended themes of social efficiency and democracy into a coherent worldview. Issued during World War I, Kingsley's report received enormous publicity and became the measure by which leading professional educators judged the success and efficiency of their schools.

A creative synthesis of educational theories then current, *Cardinal Principles* succinctly summarized the main problems of secondary education. Like so many contemporary writings, the report stated that the goal of the high school was twofold: to serve society as well as the individual. But its authors noted that the high school, "like any other established agency of society, is conservative and tends to resist modification." The rise of cities, industrialization, the division of labor, and immigration nevertheless made change essential. Everyone knew that in the past quarter century high schools enrolled a student pop- ulation "of widely varying capacities, aptitudes, social heredity, and destinies in life." Most pupils still did not graduate from high school; about one-third of all ninth graders in four-year high schools ultimately received a diploma. Clearly, the report stated, the high schools had to adjust curricula and intel- lectual expectations in line with scientific evidence on youth's "*individual dif- ferences in capacities and aptitudes.*" Economic efficiency and democracy alike demanded that schools cease regarding knowledge as "an end in itself" and promote broader social goals and practical outcomes.

In a few pages, the report thus presented the leading criticisms of high schools: their isolation from life, bookish nature, failure to recognize human differences, and resistance to change. In an age when lists, goals, and state- ments of creeds (such as those of the contemporary Boy Scouts) were common, the *Cardinal Principles* enumerated seven main objectives for the American high school: students' health, their "command of fundamental processes" (i.e., basic literacy), "worthy home membership," vocational training, civic educa- tion, "worthy use of leisure time," and moral training. Only one of the goals spoke directly to academic concerns, and even it was shrouded in jargon and given the least space. The *Cardinal Principles* went on to discourage traditional teaching methods; it favored group projects and problem solving over memo- rization and recitation and endorsed more practical and vocational subjects. It also criticized the schools for emphasizing "intellectual discipline" for the stu- dents, who often failed to enjoy what they studied. Sprinkled throughout the report were references to popular buzzwords, including growth, efficiency, and democracy. Suffused with antiacademic rhetoric, *Cardinal Principles* cleverly paid its respect to the contending ideals that shaped the high school during the Progressive Era. As historian Herbert M. Kliebard has deftly observed, the famous report "reflected with reasonable accuracy the winds of change that had swept the educational world in the previous quarter-century."

While clearly favoring more nonacademic instruction, Kingsley highlighted the high school's responsibility to teach "common ideas, common ideals, and common modes of thought, feeling, and action, whereby America, through a rich, unified, common life, may render her truest service to a world seeking for democracy among men and nations." Thus, he implied, Woodrow Wilson's current "war for democracy" would also be fought on the home front in the comprehensive high school. The modern secondary school would address in- dividual capacities and needs while uniting the student body through ex-

tracurricular activities such as "arts and crafts clubs, literary and debating societies, and musical organizations." Teachers would enhance the social development of students, ending the tyranny of subject matter.

Educators invoked the *Cardinal Principles* to justify nearly any position,
whether the expansion of athletics, slurs on colleges and academics, or assaults
on pedagogical convention. In 1929, in *Secondary Education and Industrialism,*
the radical educator George S. Counts called the seven objectives of the *Cardinal Principles* mere platitudes. Exactly what does it mean, he asked, to use one's
leisure time well? What is a proper vocation: joining a union or running a factory? What is the individual's role in a democratic society and what constitutes
"worthy home membership"? Some conservatives also assailed the report for
its preoccupation with social aims and neglect of academic goals. Typically,
however, most educational leaders worried that the schools had not sufficiently implemented its broad recommendations.

Nearly three decades after the appearance of *Cardinal Principles,* Hollis
Caswell, a renowned reformer who specialized in curriculum revision, wondered why high schools stubbornly resisted change. Caswell believed that
Kingsley and his committee had written an excellent statement and "efforts
have been made to relate the high school program directly to the life young
people have to live in our society—to the conditions and problems of home-
making, citizenship, and personal relations. Yet no basic program of general
education has been developed, and surveys reveal that, in general, high school
work is of little use to youth in meeting their common problems of living. How
many years of verbal acceptance will be necessary before bold steps are taken
to make practice conform to demonstrated need?" Especially galling was that
within most high schools "the overwhelming percentage of courses taken
and content studied is in academic areas dominated by college entrance requirements." Pupils continued to take subjects, the professor feared, not for
practical use but "in terms of prestige value and outworn theories of mental
training."

Throughout the first half of the twentieth century, critics of public education asserted that high schools were isolated from life, taught an irrelevant
curriculum, and failed to adopt the latest pedagogical methods. At the turn
of the century, Mr. Dooley, the creation of humorist Peter Finley Dunne, had

quipped, "if you can find anything that the boy doesn't like, put it into the curriculum." The dead hand of the past hovered over the nation's secondary schools, and social-efficiency advocates as well as child-centered progressives bemoaned the power of tradition in the people's college. It was not that high schools had not changed at all during their boom years. Educators added more vocational courses, modified some aspects of the curriculum, and pressured teachers to consider new teaching practices. But secondary teachers and parents were routinely accused of favoring academics instead of making classrooms more student friendly or socially efficient. Complaints about "college domination" and resistance to reform continued in the 1940s, when the high school became a mass institution in many communities. Only in one place— the extracurriculum—was change seemingly dramatic, though no less contested.

After the Civil War, urban high schools frequently had a lively student culture of organizations and associations ranging from astronomy clubs and French clubs to athletic teams, literary organizations, and secret societies. Young men and women edited school newspapers and magazines, under the watchful eye of the principal and staff. Many of the initiatives such as athletics were student run and operated, until scandals and corruption led to greater institutional oversight. The mass culture of student life that was later encouraged by the *Cardinal Principles* was well underway by the turn of the twentieth century. According to many educators and social reformers, especially in larger towns and cities, high schools had to counter the appeal of commercial amusements, gangs, pool halls, and street corner society. Champions of the extracurriculum welcomed its expansion as relief from the intellectual orientation of the high school and a realistic response to the gregarious nature of youth. More nonacademic activities would help integrate the new army of students into the system.

Numerous commentators insisted that the expanding social role of the schools had special importance in the lives of adolescents. In his rambling and quirky contribution to the debate, G. Stanley Hall argued in *Adolescence* (1904) that the teen years were characterized by "storm and stress." He had caustically denounced the Committee of Ten and was a reliable foe of college domination. While contemporary educational literature highlighted individual differences, Hall and others detected common patterns that boys and girls, in their different ways, experienced while coming of age. Nearly every expert on adolescence in the Progressive Era underscored the difficulties of growing up, including the physical, mental, and emotional strains. The idea of "storm and stress" echoed in many writings. Irving King, a professor at the State University of Iowa, wrote in *The High-School Age* (1914) that young people were a "powder magazine of emotions." But, like many writers, King also believed that adolescence was less a distinct stage of life than part of the human continuum. Nearly everyone nevertheless agreed that youth needed active engagement with the world. If rightly conceived and managed, the extracurriculum promised to enliven school and undermine tradition.

The most worrisome aspect of student sociability included secret societies such as fraternities and sororities, which were banned in many high schools and various states during the early 1900s. Regarded as socially exclusive and undemocratic, a prime example of college influence, secret societies frequently thrived underground despite official condemnation. Competitive team sports, especially men's football and basketball, ultimately prospered as sanctioned school activities but also were endless sources of complaint. Football in Pennsylvania and Texas and basketball in Indiana and Utah stoked the indignation of some citizens horrified by the number of schools caught cheating and by injuries and even deaths on the gridiron. A 1929 Carnegie study of college sports described how commercialism and corruption had moved down to the high school level. Several towns in Indiana had "high schools built around basketball courts." Flora High enrolled 90 students; its gymnasium held 1,200. Martinsville's gym seated 5,000, larger than the town's population. Similarly, in this age of mass entertainment and mass sports, football stadia across the nation welcomed fans with their Friday night lights.

The prevalence of secret societies and sometimes rabid community endorsement of athletics often embarrassed those who wanted to enhance the social side of schooling. Ineligible players, rule breaking, and non-student "ringers" on local teams did not exactly reflect what the *Cardinal Principles* report called "the worthy use of leisure time." Small-town as well as big-city newspapers nevertheless followed sports teams with a fanaticism missing when covering the debate squad. In 1916, Michael Vincent O'Shea editorialized in the *Wisconsin Journal of Education* that "everything possible should be done to exalt the intellectual work of secondary schools, and subdue the importance which is attached to athletic prowess. We need to celebrate individual achievements by every form of public demonstration in order to impress upon students the importance of brain as contrasted with brawn." State after state formed athletic organizations to regulate competitive sports, which included girl's basketball leagues in some states by the 1930s. Yet educators often believed that sports enthusiasts had won the day.

In 1924, the *Alabama School Journal* observed that "there are more scouts traveling out of the colleges these days in search of football players than ever went forth to bring in great students." Star athletes were "pestered to death" by recruiters and sometimes bribed to select the right college. This was another example of college domination, of course, and some teachers were pressured to pass undeserving athletes. Others noted that social activities were supposed to invigorate the lethargic student body; most students, however, were fans on the sidelines. "Are you going to be team backers or school slackers?" asked Eva Kilpatrick, editor of the *High School Flyer* in Presque Isle, Maine. "Let's cooperate with the cheerleaders and 'raise the roof.'" "High school folk, we've got to boost," said her counterpart in Mount Airy, North Carolina, in 1925. A state high school supervisor in the Midwest found the overall situation fairly grim. "The commercialization of basketball and football, in particular," he wrote in 1927, "has advanced to the point where the school administration is no longer able to control the situation in the interest of educational purpose. In one or more states the basketball situation is clearly out of hand, and school men are forced to yield to the demands of enthusiastic alumni and prominent businessmen of the community that every means be used to develop a championship team." George Counts smirked that for all the talk about the "social functions" of sports programs, Americans cared most about individual stars besting their opponents as the buzzer sounded.

In addition to the usual array of sports teams, institutions such as Muncie Central High School in Indiana in 1919 typically had a range of student clubs, including the Uke Club for devotees of the ukulele. While secret societies and especially athletics exemplified the popularity of the extracurriculum, pupils joined an amazing assortment of groups. In the 1930s, Japanese American students at Roosevelt High School in Los Angeles not only often excelled in the classroom but also were active in student government, athletics, and in the Japan Club. School clubs met both during and after regular class hours, frequently with a faculty advisor to ensure adult guidance and propriety. Some of the activities were similar to the past: joining the Spanish club or Latin club and working on the school paper, "annual," or yearbook (usually aided by the English teachers). Hobby enthusiasts also met after school. Clubs did not attract mobs of fans but nevertheless proliferated.

Tens of thousands of rural youth belonged to corn clubs, pig clubs, and affiliates of the national 4-H. Students proudly competed for prizes—for producing superior canned goods, well-tended calves and pigs, and apple pies—at the county or state fair. In addition, secondary teachers chaperoned dances and mixers, alternatives to dance halls in the age of ragtime and jazz. It seemed impossible to attend high school after 1900 and avoid the extracurriculum. Surveys of student activities, however, indicated that some pupils were only passively connected to the otherwise flourishing extracurriculum. Others had trouble keeping track of their busy social calendar. Two educators in Wyoming said in 1936 that "there is a tendency for some pupils to take part in too many activities and for other pupils to take part in too few. Some receive practically all the benefits while others take little or no part and consequently receive practically no benefits. Some have so many duties to perform that they neglect almost all of them."

High schools greatly expanded the youth culture as they embraced youth from a wider range of social backgrounds and peers spent more time together. High school newspapers, as in the previous century, called for more school spirit, but the social lives of many adolescents had often already expanded considerably. In *Babbitt* (1922), Sinclair Lewis introduces the character Theodore Roosevelt Babbitt, a junior at East Side High School in the mythical town of Zenith. Ted borrows the keys to the family car to drive some female friends to a rehearsal of the school chorus, among his many activities. His father, a realtor, tells his son, "Well, upon my word! You and your social engagements! In high school!" Ted also belongs to Gamma Digamma, an exclusive fraternity. His stylish clothes include a vest adorned with "a high-school button, a class-button, and a fraternity pin." Ted, who epitomizes the bourgeois still dominant in high schools in the 1920s, clearly has school spirit. He might not play on the football team but he has an intense social life and knows the school cheer.

Teachers frequently stated that academics suffered in this atmosphere. Membership in the National Honor Society was restricted to 10 percent of the senior class and was reportedly far down the list of student interests. Ted Babbitt regarded manual training, "typewriting," basketball, and dancing as the only worthwhile activities at East Side High, where the college bound still studied geometry, Cicero, and "old-fashioned junk by Milton and Shakespeare and Wordsworth and all these has-beens." As the president of the University of Minnesota remarked about real students in the early 1930s, "the fads and frills have become the fundamentals of education." The phrase "fads and frills" insulted many educators who continued to see great pedagogical promise in the extracurriculum. They were no happier when Isaac Kandel of Columbia University's Teachers College argued in 1934 that, now that the high school was trying to be all things to all people, only the extracurriculum glued it together. Athletic competitions alone, he thought, consistently honored talent and merit. "If only the spirit which dominates the side shows could be transferred to the main tent, education would vibrate with a new life!"

To progressive educators who yearned to place the student at the heart of the educational experience, the extracurriculum was vital to counter the staid ways of the schools. It tapped student interest, engaged pupils, and offered informal ways of learning that had a distinct social dimension; attending a field trip to study rocks, plants, and streams, or joining the school orchestra or Spanish club was more enjoyable than the typical textbook-driven class. Social-efficiency activists, in turn, believed that student clubs might nurture vocational interests better than the regular course of study. In the radio club or Future Farmers of America one might meet one's destiny. While the child-centered progressives were distressed that the regular high school classroom was more impervious to change than the lower grades, the efficiency lobby repeatedly wrote in the 1930s and 1940s that the extracurriculum had not expanded sufficiently. While others might sneer that fads and frills were undermining academics, efficiency activists dreamed of the day when they would completely undermine the traditional curriculum.

Across the ideological spectrum, Progressive Era reformers demanded that schools become better connected with life. Some had utopian dreams that schools, armed with quantitative information on a pupil's IQ scores and ability and the job market could devise just the right curriculum to fit the child into the social order with clinical precision. Others simply wanted to make the schools more inviting and less removed from the everyday world. Too much knowledge, said a chorus of critics, was stored in stuffy books, and many students dropped out of schools that were too academically demanding. This charge, first leveled most strenuously against the elementary schools, intensified in the early 1900s.

The extracurriculum was supposed to be different, tied to student-initiated projects, tangible rewards, and individual interests. Many citizens, however, thought it had already gone too far by the 1920s. Ted Babbitt already lived in many communities. In *It Can't Happen Here* (1936), Sinclair Lewis continued to rake the schools for their conformity and anti-intellectualism. Set in a New

England community that succumbed to fascism, Lewis's anti-utopia is filled with citizens unable to distinguish Patrick Henry's speech on liberty or death from "a high-school yell or a cigarette slogan." Some educators, in contrast, regarded the social dimension of secondary education as an unfulfilled democratic promise. They actually wanted the sideshow to become the main event.

Some early theorists of the extracurriculum believed that ideally it should emerge out of the regular course of study. The best sports programs, said one educator in 1931, would grow out of a wider program of health and physical education. Similarly, an innovative Latin Club was unlikely if the regular Latin class was "all syntax and translation." Other theorists saw the extracurriculum, so often tied to the immediate life experiences of students, as superior to the regular curriculum, which had been inherited from the past and was dry as dust. In 1931, David Snedden, one of the nation's leading proponents of social efficiency and vocational education, wrote a fantasy about the American high school of 1960. By then, he dreamed, stigmas had disappeared for students with lower IQs who were enrolled in nonacademic tracks. Moreover, the extracurriculum, which addressed immediate needs and interests, had finally undermined the academic curriculum. "Not infrequently indeed these 'side shows' claimed a much more spirited interest than did the shows in the 'main tent,'" Snedden explained, describing the early twentieth century. Happily, Americans had awakened to this reality, and half of the American curriculum by 1960 responded to current needs. This included "shop arts, household arts, gardening arts, general science, current events, amateur performance of music" as well as scouting, dramatics, and photography.

Those less given to fantasy also hoped that the extracurriculum would guide the destiny of the modern high school. In 1940, Harold Spears, director of research and secondary education in Evansville, Indiana, similarly questioned the overly academic nature of high school. Generally, Spears said, teachers stubbornly believed that the curriculum was "synonymous with the course of study." "Extra-curricular activities were originally bootlegged through the back door of the school by the pupils themselves, as an important part of their everyday life which they refused to leave outside, and the school administration found it easier to supervise the program than to suppress it." Educators, however, too often saw the extracurriculum as something outside the regular order of business. Spears's experience was that teachers occasionally used the extracurriculum to stir pupil interest in academic course work, "to bolster a tottering subject curriculum." If building a wooden ship or taking a trip to city hall stimulated students to study their textbooks more, all the better, said the teachers. But it meant that the schools and the curriculum stayed centered on subjects and not on the pupils. And it was another example of how teachers, who after all are an essential ingredient in instructing the young, were again a disappointment to those who wanted to reform the schools.

As in every generation, America's teachers remained the focus of recurrent criticism and complaint. They conveniently served as the great hope for the schools and a major cause of disappointment when reformers failed to reach the promised land. Despite their profound differences, the authors of the Committee of Ten report and of the *Cardinal Principles,* over a quarter of a century later, agreed that better secondary schools required a higher quality teaching staff. As the high school population expanded and grew more diverse, pressure intensified after 1900 to require secondary teachers to take more courses in teaching methods, as was already required of the normal school graduates who increasingly taught in the elementary grades. Social-efficiency and child-centered education enthusiasts alike complained that high school teachers cared too much about subject matter and too little about individual students and their needs. Whether in the classroom or on field trips, teachers had to make the people's college more relevant in the so-called real world. The old education had emphasized textbooks, memorization, and teacher authority. The new education demanded greater pupil engagement, which the extracurriculum could foster. But teachers—and many parents, too—often seemed unwilling to abandon so easily basic academic values, an attitude which proved enormously frustrating to a wide range of reformers.

As secondary enrollments swelled, many commentators assumed that academic standards inevitably declined. They were unaware that educators had said similar things in the 1870s, when memories of early high schools recalled a golden age of academic excellence and student propriety. In 1900, Paul Hanus of Harvard had already declared that high schools suffered from "intellectual flabbiness," among the gentler criticisms of the era. In 1911, William Bagley, a savvy observer of contemporary trends, agreed that it was impossible to maintain the standards of European secondary schools, which screened their clientele and excluded the masses. Greater access for less privileged pupils, however, honored democratic traditions. "It may be true that some of our brightest pupils suffer from the lack of competition from their equals in mental capacity," he wrote in *Educational Values,* "but it is also true that others equally bright, but less favored by the conditions of birth, are receiving a much more effective stimulus than would be possible under European conditions."

Bagley and numerous critics later offered more searing commentary on the erosion of academic standards. In too many districts, Bagley wrote in 1930, electives had squeezed out more demanding requirements, and the growing elementary school practice of passing children from grade to grade for seat time rather than for academic achievement (often called social promotion) had crept into some high schools. In addition, comprehensive end-of-year examinations had disappeared, and the only hope was a "stiffening of standards," which seemed unlikely. He equally scorned the child-centered education enthusiasts, who he said favored passing children undeserving of promotion, and certain educational psychologists, who undermined the doctrine of mental training despite what he saw as the flimsy evidence against it. Embracing the idea of equal access to academic subjects and refusing to condone relaxed standards, Bagley strengthened his reputation as a conservative.

As high schools boomed in the 1920s and 1930s, critics assailed their loss of intellectual purpose. Abraham Flexner, an internationally prominent educational researcher employed by major philanthropic foundations, said the public valued credentials over intellectual attainment. Both he and Charles Judd, a social-efficiency educator at the University of Chicago, found classrooms filled with lazy students, who marked time and avoided serious study. Districts struggled to find competent teachers to serve the swelling numbers of pupils. Isaac Kandel, among others, said that, while meeting accreditation standards, many high schools had divided learning into units and credits and served pabulum to the masses instead of hearty academic fare. Compiling credits and counting Carnegie units had become synonymous with becoming educated. In 1929, a Carnegie Foundation study on the low achievement of secondary students in Pennsylvania received considerable publicity, deepening the view that modern high schools were mediocre. Subsequent reports by the foundation criticized high schools for cramming students with a mass of "undigested information" they barely recalled for exams and promptly forgot. The foundation put forth that learning how to think, reason, and express oneself well orally and in writing was not the norm in the American high school.

In 1932, literary critic Albert Jay Nock claimed in invited lectures at the University of Virginia that pedagogy had become "the hunting-ground of quackery." Educators had debunked mental discipline in the name of science, and vocationalism, he believed, now best defined the higher learning. High schools and colleges alike had also confused equality of access with equality of results, and they promoted the bright pupils but also the dullards, ignoring Jefferson's idea that schools should separate the "jewels from the rubbish." The burden of success, Nock said, had shifted "from the student to the instructor," now pressured to lower standards and pass everyone. Horrified at what was happening, an assistant superintendent in the New York City schools said in 1936 that high schools (like the New Deal, he believed) were teaching youth that they could get along fine without working. High schools now had numerous "misfits," the product of a "two trials, on you go" philosophy on promotion in some elementary schools.

Concern over declining standards was ubiquitous in the 1920s and 1930s. Leading professional educators frequently commented on how students with a range of IQs sat in the same classroom and administrators and teachers simply adjusted to that reality. Many educators were nevertheless very proud of the expansion of the high school. This was reflected in the *Cardinal Principles* report, which encouraged admitting anyone to high school who was old enough and unable to benefit from further instruction in the grades below. Doing so nevertheless proved unsettling to those who believed high schools reaped a whirlwind of problems from this policy. Trying to raise faltering standards at Walla Walla High in Washington State, the local superintendent in 1929 recommended charging students $30 to repeat a class. A few educators recommended restricting admission to children from the highest ability groups, an untenable position as jobs for young people vanished.

An increasing number of secondary schools took their cues from the lower grades and established their own ability groups. In the larger urban high schools, administrators and teachers placed students into separate classrooms, and even specific vocational tracks, based on ability. Students in smaller high schools were sometimes placed in ability groups within classrooms. As in the elementary schools, administrators and teachers determined student placement through IQ and achievement scores, grades, and recommendations from parents and even the pupils. In addition, urban areas by the 1920s and 1930s also built separate junior high schools, usually consisting of the seventh and eighth grades. Here pupils were streamed into quasi-vocational or separate academic tracks in preparation for high school. Rural areas and small communities often could not afford separate buildings and lacked the population density to separate children so dramatically, which intensified pressure to consolidate with neighboring districts. Most administrators and teachers had thus reorganized their classrooms or facilities to address the new stream of secondary students, which became a flood once the economy collapsed. School officials were often skeptical of New Deal programs, such as the Civilian Conservation Corps, that provided government-funded jobs for youth during the Great Depression, threatening the schools' monopoly on students. School administrators viewed expanding enrollments as an opportunity to provide wider service during hard times.

What especially annoyed a variety of critics of high schools in the 1930s and 1940s, however, was their essential conservatism, not their abandonment of standards. That is, both social-efficiency advocates and child-centered reformers found the schools too academically rigid and parents and secondary teachers too resistant to change. Despite the many controversies surrounding the extracurriculum, traditional course taking and pedagogy remained common in most high schools. Pupils enrolled in many academic courses, whether or not they planned to graduate or to attend college. Parents and teachers, said many, were conservative about education and naive about their children's ability and potential. As Charles Prosser, a leading advocate of nonacademic education for the masses, recognized in 1939, when he lamented the continued appeal of traditional courses, the high schools had boomed when they were known for their academic (even allegedly college preparatory) orientation. Bad habits died hard. This was especially true in the smaller high schools (which were the most numerous) and those in rural areas, particularly in African American communities in the Jim Crow South.

Many educators had confidently asserted at the turn of the century that the academic curriculum was doomed and that college domination was drawing its last breath. However, the typical high school in America before World War II was small, with a handful of teachers, and enrolled under 120 students. The undermining of academics seemed to occur most dramatically in larger urban areas, where students could become more easily sorted into separate curricula. In the 1950s, critics of the high schools often studied the course-taking patterns of earlier generations of students and reached fairly grim conclusions. According to one study, while 45 percent of all high school pupils took algebra in 1890, only 39 percent did so in 1950, and the percentage of students taking geometry dropped from 21 to 13 percent, while enrollments for trigonometry (often taught in the senior year) held steady. The trend, especially in the larger districts, was to stream weaker students into basic and remedial math. Similarly, the xenophobia of World War I, when wed to traditional anti-intellectual sentiments, decimated foreign-language instruction (especially Latin and German): the percentage of pupils studying any foreign language dropped from 54 percent in 1890 to 22 percent by 1950. The number of students taking courses in science actually increased, but in the softer subjects. Physics enrollments dramatically declined. That social studies edged its way into the domain once dominated by history did not make academic critics of the schools happy.

Until more rural and village schools consolidated, however, full-fledged vocational tracks were unlikely there, and adding multiple courses of study was easier to do on paper than in reality. Finding first-rate vocational teachers even in the cities was often impossible, according to many principals. Moreover, high school teachers were largely innocent of child-centered pedagogy; most were college graduates, not normal school alumni, and they often taught as they had been taught, emphasizing the mastery of subject matter. And while the typical elementary school teacher was a young woman, men were more prominent in high school teaching, adding to its conservative cast. Despite some exceptions to the rule, male teachers were usually seen as the key disciplinarians on the high school staff and less likely to embrace flexible teaching methods. The new education, of course, had traditionally been associated with female teachers, long concentrated in the elementary grades. High school teachers also taught smaller classes and were paid more than elementary teachers, until that gap started to close in the 1930s. And secondary teachers enjoyed higher status than those who taught young children.

Small high schools, the most common ones in America, often had a relatively strong academic orientation, though their teachers were often accused of lowering their standards if they accommodated a wider array of pupils, or, alternatively, were criticized for not offering a general, less academic, course for these particular pupils. Like earlier critics of the elementary schools, many "experts" attacked high schools for their excessively *high* standards, given the allegedly poor intellectual makeup of the new student body. They predictably blamed unrealistic standards and an irrelevant curriculum for the high dropout rates, which were easing in the 1930s, though the majority enrolled still did not graduate. Despite the booming enrollments, a professor in Michigan complained in 1928 that high schools tried "to teach pupils things which they cannot learn, and do not wish to learn." Similarly, Milo Stuart, the principal of Arsenal Technical High School in Indianapolis, a large comprehensive institu-

tion, said the smaller schools desperately needed a more "differentiated curriculum." "It is the small school with one course," he wrote in 1929, "which
is the chief offender in mechanizing education." Stuart saw large urban high
schools as the model in an industrial society and the place where the doctrine
of individual differences should reign. Yet his own institution, like many earlier manual training high schools, had ample academic courses due to student
demand. Arsenal Tech was not Shortridge High, the leading academic high
school in Indianapolis, but it was still strongly academic (despite its name) and
sent many pupils to college.

As Stuart and other educators realized, student enrollment in Latin classes
for a time had actually increased nationally after the turn of the century, despite proliferating rhetoric on the benefits of nonacademic, vocational instruction. In a national survey of course taking in 1925, North Carolina's white high
schools had the highest percentage of secondary students enrolled in Latin, and
the lowest percentage enrolled in bookkeeping. "Times have changed," wrote
the editor of the *High School Journal,* who was saddened by the popularity of
Cicero and Caesar and academic subjects in general in "the average North
Carolina classroom." When, he asked, would people come to their senses? Despite such protests, the typical small school lacked guidance counselors and
expensive vocational programs, which were of doubtful benefit anyway, given
the obsolete pre-industrial skills often taught and the growing absence of jobs.
Small schools also had many conservative teachers who, like many parents,
favored academic courses. Dropping these classes risked the loss of accreditation, not a happy thought for a local principal, even if most pupils never received a diploma. As one educator noted in 1940, the typical American high
school was small and mostly offered a "straight academic course," whatever
its quality and despite decades of advice by many professionals to the contrary.

Parents who were convinced of the benefits of academic instruction were a
major stumbling block to reformers. School administrators and professors who
had themselves received an academic education and used school credentials
for professional mobility too often mocked those from the lower reaches of society who had high aspirations for their children, whom experts did not think
were especially bright. Isaac Kandel marveled at how intellectuals whose own
children were well educated placed a "halo" around humdrum "manual activities" that common people regarded as "chores" and "drudgery." It was no secret that pupils enrolled in academic courses had higher status than those in

commercial, industrial, or vocational classes. In 1915 an educational researcher in New Orleans, Mary L. Railey, explained: "The choice of the college course by many who do not intend to enter college can in some measure be explained by the belief happily current among laboring classes that cultural education is the first essential for social elevation. In this strata of society, high school graduates are accorded great prestige if their course has been cultural rather than commercial." And so the "future manicurist and milliner, hat importer and code marker" studied academic subjects instead of more practical ones. Washerwomen thought their sons and daughters might one day use their brains, not brawn, when in reality most were destined for menial labor.

As Thomas Briggs, a prominent advocate of vocational education, wrote in 1930, the "differently gifted" did not belong in academic courses, where they only lowered standards before emerging ill-prepared for the workplace. But the working classes, like everyone else, had made a fetish of the academic curriculum, Briggs believed. Parents with unrealistic views of their children's intelligence, ability, and potential asked teachers to perform the "impossible task of putting a tremendous amount of heterogeneous ore through a process that was devised to refine only a limited kind." Briggs acknowledged that many high schools, especially the small ones, had done a credible job of teaching pupils academic subjects. "Probably never before have so many boys and girls actually learned foreign languages, mastered the elements of mathematics, developed abiding interests in the best literature, and acquired skill in both oral and written expression." Briggs still regarded this as economically wasteful and socially inefficient. Most pupils did not graduate, were not college bound, and inevitably worked with their hands. "Abstract academic education" only made sense for those who could "assimilate it for the social good."

Despite the inroads made by vocational courses and the extracurriculum, teachers and parents were a hindrance to the reconstruction of the high school. Both advocates of social efficiency and of student-oriented instruction had few good words to say about them. The editor of the *High School Journal* spoke for many in 1931 when he called secondary teachers deeply conservative. Science had conclusively demonstrated that youth "differ greatly" in their "abilities, interests, aptitudes, character traits . . . economic status, vocational outlook, and in whatsoever trait or aspect . . . far greater than was once assumed." And yet teachers too often believed that going to high school meant "the relative mastery of a few traditional subjects." Most still taught groups of students, critics said, and did not treat pupils as individuals. In 1940, William Kilpatrick, champion of child-centered education and the project method, typically described the high school as very "subject matter oriented." On the opposite end of the pedagogical spectrum, Charles Prosser thought that "like Mark Twain's weather, there has been a great deal of talk about the curriculum of the secondary school but nothing much done about it."

Educational leaders frequently criticized high school teachers. They were accused of the worst pedagogical practices, akin to those adhered to by Thomas Gradgrind in *Hard Times*. They heard lessons and did not teach, they treated pupils like parrots who repeated definitions and facts on command, and they marked and graded and brought the antiquated methods of the past (and from the college) to the high school. Drill, lifeless instruction, and dependence upon textbooks were common. In small schools, teachers taught a variety of subjects they knew little about, reinforcing these tendencies. "If the emphasis were shifted to teaching the *student* rather than the *subject,* the High School would become a place of greater attractiveness and strength," said the associate superintendent of Philadelphia's schools in 1910. A decade later little progress had been made: many teachers were still "ten questions on the blackboard" pedants, lectured and talked excessively, and were veritable "marking machines." The rise of true/false tests, multiple choice examinations, and worksheets keyed to textbooks meant even more student passivity. Yet everyone knew some inspiring teachers, the exceptions to the rule.

John Dewey concluded in 1931 that the old education lived on. Many high school teachers regarded the student as a "recording phonograph, or one who stands at the end of a pipe line receiving material conducted from a distant reservoir of learning." Though field trips, group activities, and the extracurriculum had enlivened many schools, the authors of a textbook entitled *High School Administration* in 1936 claimed that "the majority of teachers would be hopelessly lost without a textbook." A contemporary simply added that the high school resisted progressive pedagogy far more than elementary schools: "It has inherited a point of view which conceives learning in terms of subjects, and it has been unable to break effectively with the past." In villages, small towns, and rural America especially, tradition powerfully shaped teaching and the curriculum. The reformers had an urban vision and believed that rural America had to adjust to modernity through consolidation and greater investment in buildings, salaries, high schools, and expensive vocational programs. In the heavily rural South, as well as other agricultural and nonurban areas, however, tradition stood as a bulwark against rapid change. Project methods and activity-oriented curricula were certainly found in progressive rural schools, but they competed against textbooks, teacher authority, and parental resistance to consolidation and many aspects of the new education.

"Too long have we had an educational hold-up by the scholastics for the benefit of the few," claimed the Berks County, Pennsylvania, superintendent of schools in 1909 in a stirring endorsement of vocational education for rural youth. "Classics and calculus are no more divine than machines and potatoes. . . . Let the mountain, the plain, the shop, the mill, the forge, the foundry, the field, the brook, the farm and the mine, *supplement* the text and the school. The environment of the American boy and girl is the greatest university ever set up in the world." In the wake of the Country Life movement in the early 1900s, reformers from all walks of life claimed that the modernization of rural schools, including the creation of industrial and agricultural high schools, would stem the flow of migration out of the countryside. The flow was indeed reversed temporarily during the Great Depression, but it had little to do with school reform and everything to do with high unemployment rates in cities.

Professional educators and a host of commentators in the first half of the twentieth century found rural schools especially resistant to change. Books and professional journals routinely assailed the textbook-oriented curriculum, outmoded teaching methods, and stubborn adherence to academics among those being driven off the land and forced into the urban industrial economy. Corn clubs, said *The Educational Exchange* in Alabama in 1912, would keep youth down on the farm. Pupils did indeed join pig clubs, corn clubs, and the Future Farmers of America in impressive numbers, but still left the farms. Optimistic Mississippians had thought agricultural high schools would bring scientific farming to the region, yet they failed to halt the rush to the cities. Perhaps more nature study and field trips would reveal life's possibilities on the prairie, plains, or plantation, thought many reformers who sought solutions to America's "rural school problem."

Before World War I, social efficiency advocates such as Ellwood Cubberley emphasized the hidebound nature of the rural school curriculum. Book instruction predominated, he wrote in *Rural Life and Education* in 1914. Something needed to be done, he and other educators believed, to connect rural schools to life, to end their isolation from the local environment and the practical needs of the people. In an article in the *School Journal* in 1917, E. M. Rapp, president of the state teachers' association in Pennsylvania, called the rural exodus a national funeral procession, claiming it sapped the nation's strength and reflected the antirural biases of country schools, still oriented, like too many of their urban cousins, around academics. In 1927, an expert on rural schools condemned their "monkish" orientation and adherence to the discredited ideal of mental training; he was shocked to discover that in Texas algebra was the most frequently studied course among rural secondary students. He stated that while individual and social efficiency was the proper function of rural education, textbook instruction in old-fashioned subjects remained common.

As late as 1942, half of America's children lived in nonurban areas. A concerted movement toward consolidation had yielded considerable success in different regions, but America still had 130,000 one-room schools. Many village and county high schools had the outward appearance of modernity when little had otherwise changed. Some rural schools (especially consolidated ones) had expanded their extracurriculum, including clubs, assemblies, and competitive athletics, but that only dented the armor of traditional learning. While it was unsuitable for the majority of pupils, the traditional academic curriculum had survived, said the authors of *Rural America Today* during World War II. Rural schools needed more vocational programs, guidance departments, and scientific management. But rural folk, often mired in poverty, working as tenant farmers, or struggling to save the family farm, realized that jobs nearby were scarce. Countless reformers spun their wheels in the countryside.

When the new education did arrive in rural America, it had to adapt to survive. For example, reformers in many states pressed legislators to fund vocational education, including agricultural high schools. Some utopians dreamed of consolidated rural schools with departments of horticulture, beekeeping, and blacksmithing. In 1921, the *Mississippi Educational Advance* explained that forty-nine agricultural high schools (for whites) existed in the Magnolia State but that many of their graduates went on to college. As in many technical high schools in the North, students flocked to the academic courses, even if citizens sometimes quipped that these secondary schools were "neither agricultural nor high." Wherever one looked, rural secondary schools had a traditional curriculum. An anthropologist studying a rural community in Missouri in the late 1930s discovered that the local high school "was less 'modern' than it seems." By state law, it dutifully taught some classes in vocational agriculture, and "it is the only subject which a large portion of the community opposes and ridicules." In sparsely settled Montana, the state financed consolidated high schools and even built dormitories, and academics similarly reigned.

"There is yet too great regard for 'liberal education,'" said the principal of the Candler, North Carolina, high school in 1934. "School officials must realize that the rural schools should abandon traditional ideals" and teach more courses to put pupils into "sympathetic touch with rural life about them, in which the great majority of them ought to find their rural homes." That the traditional course of study in the country schools was largely responsible for the flight to the cities was a common refrain. William Bagley, who early in life tried scientific farming, nevertheless thought the idea that poor schools emptied the countryside was absurd. Rural schools, he agreed, were often terribly funded and had atrocious teaching. Given the collapse of the farm economy by the 1920s, however, access to an academic curriculum appealed to parents, who saw better opportunities for their children in the cities. Rural schools were indeed conservative, textbook oriented, and not very efficient or child centered and thus were barriers to those who literally wanted to keep farm children in their place.

One poignant and telling example of support for academics came from one of the most oppressed social groups: African Americans in the rural South. Efforts to bring industrial, nonacademic instruction to the masses of rural blacks had made Booker T. Washington the great hero of some white southern conservatives and many northern philanthropists at the turn of the century. His rival, W. E. B. Du Bois, while demanding provisions for higher studies for what he called the "talented tenth" of African Americans, vehemently attacked any attempts to water down academic instruction for the masses. Southern whites continued to seriously restrict educational opportunities for African American children during the Progressive Era. State governments spent far less money on black schools despite the "separate but equal" doctrine enshrined in *Plessy v. Ferguson* (1896). "The alarming neglect of and discrimination against the Negro schools are plainly evident to any one who reads the reports of educational officers in the southern states," wrote Du Bois and a colleague in the *Common School and the Negro American* in 1911. "Moreover, strong outside pressure is being applied to improve the industrial work while very little and in many places practically nothing is said about learning to read and write and cipher."

The southern movement for free white high schools lagged behind the North but gained considerable steam in the early 1900s, which only made blacks, the majority of whom still lived in rural areas, more disadvantaged. While there were relatively few southern black high schools before World War I, they increased in number afterwards. Despite poverty and job discrimination, African Americans usually favored academic instruction. A small army of white philanthropists, officials in the U.S. Bureau of Education, and some southern whites were sympathetic toward investment in industrial education for African Americans, which likely contributed to black enthusiasm for academic subjects. Privileged whites had a habit of downplaying academics in other people's lives.

Despite increased access to high schools, fewer African American than white southern youths attended secondary schools after World War I, as poverty and racism conspired against them. In 1929, Mississippi had forty-nine agricultural high schools for whites and only one for blacks. That same year, a congressionally funded study of the nation's secondary schools estimated that about 10 percent of African Americans between the ages of fifteen and eighteen attended high school, compared to 34 percent of whites. In 1933, when white attendance rates boomed during the Depression, 230 counties in the former Confederate states did not have a single black high school. Heavily dependent on private donations from churches, northern philanthropies, and their own financial resources, southern blacks labored mightily to educate their children and often resisted efforts to convert their schools into vocational institutions. Birmingham's black Industrial High School became the largest of its kind and added courses in haircare, chair caning, leathercraft, and shoe repair; but it was otherwise strongly academic.

Very few occupations except teaching and nursing (in segregated settings) were open to black high school graduates, as A. M. Jordan explained in an essay in the *High School Journal* in 1935. Drawing upon a state-wide study of North Carolina high schools, Jordan said that "domestic service, the factory, hotel work, the barber shop, the filling station, drug store, absorb many of the graduates. The vast majority . . . go into unskilled and semi-skilled occupations." But African Americans seemed wedded to academic study, which he found puzzling. Why should a student study the "mathematics of Euclid, the literature of Shakespeare, the hexameters of Virgil or the oratory of Cicero only to have him wait on a table, shine shoes, sweep and dust buildings or carry packages?" At the same time, he agreed that janitors and cooks might be more useful if they mastered the laws of hygiene and chemistry. In his landmark study *Caste and Class in a Southern Town* (1937), John Dollard highlighted the plight of well-educated blacks: "Education dresses them all up and they have no, or little, professional place to go."

Whites and some black leaders condemned the tradition-bound curriculum of black secondary schools, which were often ridiculed and caricatured. Ambrose Caliver, an African American and specialist in "Negro education" at the U.S. Office of Education, knew that blacks were treated shamefully everywhere but especially in the segregated South. There African Americans, he wrote in 1934, had shorter school terms, higher retardation and dropout rates, less money spent on their schools, poorer buildings, and lower salaries for teachers. What also annoyed Caliver, however, was that blacks engaged in a "slavish imitation of others" by embracing "outworn" beliefs. While he had a greater appreciation of racial injustice than white social-efficiency educators, he too believed that more vocational education and guidance would ameliorate the plight of African Americans.

In 1941, Horace Mann Bond, the prominent black educator, remarked that African Americans typically came "from homes in the lower economic brackets to a high school dominated by tradition and the prestige of the college-preparatory tradition." Poverty and white opposition, he said, made the creation of vocational programs for African Americans unlikely, and the relatively meager funds available for Negro high schools stayed focused on academic subjects. "Negro education has mostly remained 'academic,' and differs only in its level of expenditure and effectiveness," wrote Gunnar Myrdal, the Swedish social democrat and social scientist, in 1942. Through the power of the church, school, and self-help, southern black illiteracy rates plummeted by 1950. Moreover, in Birmingham, Washington, D.C., St. Louis, Indianapolis, Little Rock, and other cities, African American communities were very proud of their segregated high schools, their prestige heightened by their academic atmosphere.

Urban-oriented reformers frequently criticized the academic pretensions of rural high schools, white and black, during the first half of the twentieth century. Those who hoped to connect education to life, whether they admired the fields or the factories, were optimistic about the potential of large consolidated high schools. Efficiency experts in particular believed that the ideal high school would restrict academic instruction to those likely to profit from serious study. They believed that, in a perfect situation, experts would scientifically determine students' IQs, abilities, and aptitudes and find the right curriculum to fit everyone into the proper social niche, determining whether they should be, for example, homemakers or workers. College domination, which had led to an antiquated curriculum, would also disappear. The extracurriculum helped tap the real-life interests of pupils and ultimately might replace the course of study entirely, or at least seriously alter its direction. In rural America, of course, with farms failing after World War I and a steady exodus to the cities, these ideas seemed unrealistic and were widely ignored.

Rural whites and African Americans alike wondered why children needed nature study, manual training, and domestic science when these lessons were easily absorbed in their home environment. They felt schools should be places where teachers taught familiar subjects from books that exposed the young to the knowledge, symbols, and skills that the better classes regarded as the marks of civilization, culture, and status. African Americans, accused of worrying too much about what whites studied, recognized that even if discrimination was woven into the fabric of their social existence, education should not aim to keep youth in their place. As late as 1940, Ambrose Caliver's complaints that African Americans were foolish to reject vocational education often fell on deaf ears.

By the 1940s, American secondary schools had faced enormous pressures to change. The comprehensive high school served as an imperfect compromise in many urban areas, where ability groups, vocational classes, and a thriving extracurriculum first entered the people's college. Tradition and college domination were condemned, but reformers discovered considerable public support for a time-honored curriculum and conventional pedagogy. Students were tested and graded and parents received report cards that tallied the scores. The most visible parts of the extracurriculum, football and basketball, proved enduring in this age of mass culture, sometimes embarrassing the schools when corruption triumphed over fair play. An administrator in Evansville, Indiana, a small city on the Ohio River, reminded people in 1940 that many modest communities, not just big-city neighborhoods, took pride in their high schools: "Take the high school out of the average community of a few hundred souls— such as Goose Corners, Kansas, or Swayzee, Indiana—and you have just about eliminated any concerted spark of culture that was there." The local high school might not be a palace, but it was a symbol of high aspirations, even if those found greatest expression in the gym or stadium.

By the end of the 1940s, high schools had become a more familiar part of the public school system. In the bigger high schools especially, vocational courses reached more students than ever, and in many places more electives and social promotion took an academic toll. Approximately one-third of all high schools utilized some form of ability grouping, as secondary schools adapted to perceived individual differences. But manual training, industrial, and agricultural high schools frequently became comprehensive institutions that offered many academic subjects. Working-class parents often rejected narrow vocationalism as dysfunctional for their children; they preferred something more intellectually and socially respectable. Parents and youth also knew that much that was deemed practical—whether agricultural education in the county high school or leathercraft and wood shop in the cities—lacked economic utility. Most jobs required few specialized skills, which were quickly learned in the fields, in the office, or on the shop floor. Courses in typing, shorthand, and bookkeeping had practical value, but many high schools, especially the smaller ones, retained their academic character. Field trips, group projects, sports, and club activities added new activities to the school day, but at midcentury the typical high school teacher still taught familiar subjects in familiar ways.

The people's college had grown remarkably in the first half of the twentieth century as it became an essential part of the public school system. Shifts in labor markets and growing aspirations among less privileged classes led masses of adolescents into institutions that had taught a tiny fraction of youth in the nineteenth century. And the high schools labored, never fully successfully, to please the diverse demands, academic and otherwise, that local communities placed upon them. Going to high school became less special, which ultimately weakened the status of secondary teachers, whose profession became more common as throngs of pupils filled the nation's classrooms. A legion of reformers, who often yearned for more efficient or child-centered institutions, had found the high schools wanting. In the postwar era, the expectations of Americans rose even higher, and schools were again placed in the center of contentious debates about the good life and the efficacy of public education. Schools faced another torrent of criticism, both from outside and inside the system, as economic and social transformations once again led reform-minded Americans to focus on education as a lever for individual and social improvement. Schools that had often disappointed more than a few citizens in the past were again asked to play a central role in building a better and more stable social order.

CHAPTER SEVEN

Rising Expectations and Raising Standards

Between the end of World War II and the ascendancy of Ronald Reagan as president, no institution bore a heavier burden for improving society than America's public schools. When asked in a 1980 Gallup poll to assess the importance of schools to one's "future success," a whopping 82 percent of respondents replied that they were "extremely important" and another 15 percent said they were "fairly important." Only 2 percent thought schools were "not too important" to one's future and only 1 percent lacked an opinion. In some ways, the centrality of schools in social and economic life after World War II simply reflected enduring trends. After all, earlier generations had underscored the transcendent importance of schools, long entrusted with grave responsibilities including the survival of the republic, the preservation of a fluid social order, and the melting pot ideal. But a not-so-subtle change had occurred by the 1950s that forever altered the nation's perspective on its schools.

Postwar America was an age of rising expectations for academic performance and declining deference to educational leaders. As a result, public schools were the focus of almost ceaseless attention and constant criticism. This criticism reached its apogee in 1983 when the Reagan administration issued *A Nation at Risk,* which blamed schools for America's failure to compete well with Japan and other industrial powers. Linking scholastic performance with the health of the economy, the report emphatically demanded higher academic standards in the public school system. Criticisms of the schools had been fairly ubiquitous throughout the 1970s: parents widely believed that discipline was the number one problem facing the schools, followed by the policies associated with desegregation. A steady drop in Scholastic Aptitude Test (SAT) scores also fueled the tinder box of political agitation. Faced with the unsavory consequences of the oil embargo, stagflation, and the Iranian hostage crisis, the Carter administration lost the confidence of the American people. A former B-movie actor and governor of California became president and the Republican Party swept into power.

Anxieties about the economy and dissatisfaction with the schools formed the immediate backdrop to educational reform during the Reagan era. But the linkage of schools and economic success and concern over standards revealed in public opinion polls reflected historical developments that had profoundly changed America after World War II. Rising expectations forced countless political leaders and the courts to involve themselves in school reform. No one urged the schools to do less. Eisenhower Republicans told them to shape up or the Soviets, as Khrushchev later said, would bury us. As a result, raising the academic performance of the talented few attracted considerable national attention by the late 1950s. Far more concerned with advancing civil rights and egalitarian ends, Johnsonian liberals in the 1960s enlisted the schools in a war on poverty, aiming to give the poor some hope in the race for success. Elected to his first term as president in 1968, Richard Nixon remarked that, thanks to Lyndon Johnson, "we will all have to be education presidents now." Reacting to the perceived excesses of modern liberalism, critics of overall low standards in the schools dominated educational discourse in the 1970s and 1980s, as conservatism regained its momentum. Throughout the entire postwar period, every crisis had seemingly become an educational crisis.

Speaking to the National Association of Secondary School Principals in 1969, Edward W. Brooke, an African American senator and liberal Republican from Massachusetts, announced that "education has moved front and center in the ranks of American institutions. Interest in every level and facet of the educational process has soared to unknown heights." Citizens wanted their children to have more than competence in the three Rs. Young people now required better vocational and moral training to secure their niche in the social order. Brooke warned that the schools, especially in the cities, were failing abysmally, as urban economies weakened and classrooms filled with poor minority groups. Few people now looked to the cities for examples of academic excellence. A few years later, governor Ronald Reagan spoke to the same organization. "In many respects," he told his listeners, "we expect more than we reasonably should from our schools. Every year, new and complex demands are made on education. Schools are expected not only to educate our young people, but to lead the way in solving social and racial tensions, even the nutritional problems of the poor." The public, however, was losing its patience—particularly with unruly pupils and teacher strikes—and voters began to reject bond measures to increase school spending, especially during the recession of the 1970s. Reagan believed educators had allowed academics to slip and needed to restore the work ethic. "Schools," he sniffed, "are not playgrounds."

The postwar phenomenon of rising expectations and demand for educational improvement came from two broad sources: the white middle classes and the champions of the civil rights movement. Both were responding to dramatic economic and political changes that were altering American society. By the 1950s, many people believed that the schools' role in the economy had increased and would only continue to escalate. Increasingly ensconced in relatively affluent suburbs, the middle classes feared that public schools had lowered their standards, especially high schools. On this score, numerous college professors, popular writers, and assorted pundits regularly lambasted the schools in the national press, proclaiming that something needed to be done about mediocrity in the classroom. Going to college was now the indisputable road to the expanding world of white-collar work and the professions. Employers used high school and college credentials to screen applicants, yet the secondary schools, which were passing more and more students, were getting lower and lower grades from the public. No school board could ignore the anxieties or demands of (largely) white parents of future collegians, given their power over the public purse and importance to public opinion.

Representing other social and racial interests, the civil rights movement also contributed to the phenomenon of rising expectations and the need for more effective schools. These activists, for the moment, worried less about academically weak secondary schools or about who went to college. Instead, they insisted that schools fulfill their democratic promise and include those who historically had been excluded from the system. Building upon an older struggle against Jim Crow, African Americans and their white liberal allies first had to defeat segregation through the courts. Then they waged a long, bitter, and often frustrating struggle first to equalize and then to integrate the schools. Inspired by this civil rights movement, other parents and reformers soon argued with equal moral passion for the inclusion of other outcasts, including children with a range of special needs and disabilities, into the schools. A rights revolution was in the making.

This embrace of hopefulness reinforced the old assumption that schools were fundamental to individual and social betterment. And it received a major boost in the 1960s. More than ever before, the federal government dedicated resources to address the educational aspirations of the poor, often minority, families whose children were fast becoming the majority in the nation's urban schools. Lyndon Johnson's Great Society initiative, which made historic strides on behalf of civil rights, promised results, not simply rhetoric, and it expanded federal expenditures for education through innovative programs, including Head Start and the Elementary and Secondary Education Act of 1965. They aimed to raise the academic achievement of disadvantaged pupils as part of a larger war on poverty. By requiring evaluations of the effectiveness of these programs, the Johnson administration also tried to ensure that unless the performance gap between the achieving classes and the poor shrank noticeably, someone would be held responsible. But when the schools could not deliver on utopian promises, the ranks of the angry and disillusioned swelled.

Criticisms of the schools—focusing on their permissiveness, flabby curriculum, and preoccupation with fads and frills—had been loud enough in the immediate postwar decade. But the cacophony of complaints became deafening as attacks on institutions and authority generally accelerated in the 1960s. It was an age of practical experiments in social improvement as well as wishful thinking, of heightened aspirations that almost inevitably led to discouragement. This helped spawn the racial and social divisiveness that shattered the Great Society and in part fueled Republican resurgence. Challenged by conservatives on the right and romantic radicals and cultural critics on the left, Great Society liberalism withered on the vine of ethnic, racial, and gender conflict and in the poisoned soil of economic decline in the 1970s. The Republicans reaped a political windfall as soaring expectations clashed with cultural malaise and faltering schools.

The great challenge for the schools in postwar America was how to satisfy the middle and lower classes simultaneously. As the schools became more socially inclusive, many people assumed, without saying it so bluntly, that more equality meant more mediocrity. Those who left the city for the suburbs usually believed in equality of opportunity, if that meant superior schools for their own children. Most people felt that more democracy led to less efficiency, and lower standards were unacceptable when credentials held elevated importance. Yet the civil rights movement simultaneously pressured the courts, politicians, and school officials to break down the barriers separating marginalized groups from the American dream, which depended on quality education, and did not accept the argument that equality led straight to mediocrity. Everyone agreed that schools were essential to individual and social progress. As the educational stakes rose, so did the social tensions.

✏️

By the 1950s, vast social changes had begun to transform American life, forming the backdrop to rising educational demands. Between 1946 and 1964, the stork delivered seventy-six million babies in America. The famous "baby boom" was a demographic phenomenon destined to reshape fundamental aspects of American society. By the early 1950s, some sort of educational crisis— not enough elementary schools, not enough qualified teachers, low standards—was constantly in the news, locally and nationally. With wartime allies as well as enemies still economically prostrate, America enjoyed an economic expansion unmatched in history. Approximately 85 percent of the boomers would graduate from high school or receive a General Educational Development (GED) equivalent, an incredible figure, unimaginable in most nations. On average, the gross national product rose 3.9 percent annually between 1950 and 1970. Until the bloom came off the economic rose, Americans enjoyed prosperity and rising living standards that were the envy of the world. As historian David Farber has explained, a community like Harlem, desperately poor by American standards, was still richer than many nations.

Confidence in the material promise of America abounded. Countless magazine writers, social commentators, and politicians reveled in the nation's affluence, despite the anxieties caused by the cold war and its threat of nuclear annihilation, and nervousness among many white people, initially in the South, regarding the civil rights movement. Ideas about the power and potential of schools accelerated. The Great Depression slowly retreated from public consciousness as an expanding and vibrant economy absorbed the returning veterans, who helped build the world's largest consumer society. America was now a military and economic titan, even if rivalry with the Soviet Union, the success of the Chinese Revolution, and the war in Korea directly challenged American hegemony and self-confidence. Unlike in the previous generation, economic and social progress was palpable and seemingly irreversible. In his bestseller of 1958, *The Affluent Society,* Harvard economist John Kenneth Galbraith caught and advanced the spirit of the age by calling for more aggressive federal action to address chronic social ills. Investment in jobs, health care, education, and social services could help eliminate poverty, a happy prospect as more poor people moved to the cities. "Educational deficiencies," Galbraith concluded, "can be overcome. Mental deficiencies can be treated. Physical handicaps can be remedied. The limiting factor is not knowledge of what can be done." The best and the brightest had the expertise, and America had the money, if not yet the will, to conquer human woe.

Politically, the Republican 1950s seemed an unlikely time to expect much federal intervention in local affairs, especially in sensitive areas such as public education. The success of free enterprise seemed self-evident to many citizens, who retained a traditional suspicion of Washington. The auto and chemical industries, for example, had few serious international competitors. Unionized workers, while a minority of the labor force, secured wages and benefits that allowed millions of people, whites especially, to enjoy more material comfort, including the purchase of a home, a car, kitchen appliances, a television, and other accouterments of the good life. Historian James T. Patterson and other scholars have reminded us that no other nation had ever produced and bought more consumer goods. No other nation then had as many young people in secondary school or spent as much money on education. The GI Bill, a major piece of legislation passed in 1944 during Franklin Delano Roosevelt's waning years, helped millions of veterans (many of whose parents never went to high school) attend college. Material abundance and federal housing loans allowed many white urban dwellers to retreat to the expanding suburbs, bastions of middle class prosperity far from their old poverty-stricken neighborhoods. In 1940, one-fifth of Americans lived in suburbs; by 1960, the figure had increased to one-third of the population.

The flip side of rising expectations was round-the-clock anxiety. Affluence brought disquiet, not tranquility, and many people focused their hopes and fears on the schools. Multinational corporations and their interlocking financial units now dominated the economy and were beyond any individual's control. Antimonopoly movements had disappeared. But the schools were still locally controlled and of growing significance. Whatever was wrong in society might be corrected. As in the antebellum period and Progressive Era, citizens turned to the schools as an essential means of social improvement. Frank P. Whitney, a veteran urban school principal, typically remarked in 1955 that most Americans still regarded the schools as a panacea. "The school is looked upon as the great palliative. It is the Castoria magnificent of a society afflicted with boils. It is the hope of every reformer." Educators faced demands high and low: to raise standards, teach morals, discipline, and patriotism, and even to ensure (as in Wisconsin) that children consumed enough dairy products. The principal said that "using the schools to avoid the hard work of putting over your own bright ideas about saving the community or the state has become a great game."

"Attacking the schools is assuming the proportion of cross-word puzzles, bridge, and golf as a favorite sport, indoor and out," said one contributor to the *High School Journal* in 1953. Two years later, the superintendent of the Richmond, Virginia, schools wrote in the more highbrow *Atlantic Monthly* that Americans had an unshakeable, sometimes blind faith in schools, but at the same time always found them wanting. Throughout the decade, parents and critics frequently accused public schools of being godless, of contributing to delinquency, of being subservient to John Dewey and his minions, of not teaching the three Rs, or of only teaching the three Rs. In several notable instances, school board members and superintendents were turned out of office for allowing progressive education to creep into the classroom. Best-selling books explained why Ivan and Natasha but not Johnny and Mary could read, how teacher education programs had ruined the people's schools, and what it would take to restore the basics.

Even before the Soviet Union launched the unmanned satellite Sputnik in 1957, generating a national uproar in the U.S. over what was seen as the comparatively poor academic quality of American schools, a broad range of professors, social critics, and popular writers complained incessantly about their many shortcomings. In 1956 H. L. Mencken's magazine *American Mercury* reprinted an article first published in 1938: Albert L. Bell's "Are High Schools for Morons?" More bilious than most authors, Bell argued that "morons and nitwits" and "subnormals and delinquents" filled the nation's "multi-million dollar high schools." Anti-intellectual to the core, these schools used workbooks, audio-visual aids, and "brass bands, field trips, athletic contests and variety shows" to entertain the "seat warmers" and "loafers." Bell wrote that, to "keep the misfits happy," progressive educators simply lowered standards. Visitors to a study hall would notice enough "coughing, humming, and stamping of feet" to think they were in a "schizophrenic ward in a mental hospital."

Some people said that things had only worsened. During the war many people praised the schools for sponsoring bond drives and victory gardens and for preaching toleration and national unity as the allies battled Nazism and totalitarianism. Books soon appeared, however, with titles such as *Quackery in the Schools* (1950), *Educational Wastelands* (1953), and *The Diminished Mind* (1954) that were unlikely to inspire confidence in anyone with high hopes for their children. Mass circulation magazines such as *Time,* the *Ladies' Home Journal, Cosmopolitan,* and *Life*—found in the waiting room at the doctor's office and on countless coffee tables in the suburbs—told the familiar tale of public schools, especially high schools, in trouble. Articles had titles such as "The Educational Malaise," "Oceans of Piffle," and "Is Your School a Clambake?" In 1958, *Time* interviewed a teacher who quit in disgust from the storied Boston Latin School. He complained that public schools had become "The Big Kindergarten," thanks to John Dewey and lax college admission standards.

By the early 1950s, educators faced a rising tide of criticism, which they usually dismissed as the work of zealots, the uninformed, and the enemies of free public schools. There were certainly enough hare-brained tales about communist and godless influences in the schools that lacked any credibility and harmed the innocent. Often defensive of their labors, educational leaders frequently dismissed the negative press, citing their superior knowledge about pedagogy and insights into children's welfare. In 1951 a contributor to the *High School Journal* claimed that the public confused more relaxed classrooms with less respect for standards. Perhaps he had a point, but the journal frequently published articles by professors of education who in the name of democracy demeaned academic achievement and favored student-oriented over subject-oriented teaching. In 1952 the director of public relations for the National Education Association (NEA) asserted without any evidence that, contrary to popular opinion, "students today read more, they read faster, they understand better what they read, and remember it longer than their grand parents did." In response to "widespread" criticisms of the schools, James Earl McGrath, the U.S. commissioner of education, replied that the champions of back-to-the-basics probably also favored the elimination of "school busses" and longed for "the days of the long hike to the little red school house."

The most searching and thoughtful criticism of the decade was Arthur Bestor's *Educational Wastelands*. To the educational establishment, Bestor, a professor of history at the University of Illinois, was a major nuisance. But the timing of the appearance of his book was excellent. Professors in the academic disciplines had long attacked progressive education, but now the public paid additional attention since students attended school longer and academic credentials mattered more. The nation was still on edge about whether the booming economy might collapse, and the cold war, like many previous crises, also caused people to search for any breach in the dam of educational tradition. Mainstream periodicals in the 1950s freely sounded the old alarm about the pernicious influence of child-centered, content-free education. This, too, created a wider market for Bestor's ideas, which were widely reported in the mass media.

Bestor understood how the educational establishment functioned and had not only a scholarly but also an insider's perspective on progressive education. He had attended the Lincoln School at Teachers College, Columbia University, which conservatives routinely demonized as the birthplace of progressive education. Bestor had also taught at Teachers College. Despite his criticisms of the excesses of progressive education, John Dewey remained everyone's favorite whipping boy, though he had retired from the philosophy department at Columbia in 1930. His lasting influence was due in part to William Kilpatrick, who had been strongly influenced by Dewey, popularized the project method, and taught at Teachers College. In addition, more than a few of Kilpatrick's colleagues in the 1930s shared his child-centered ethos or were outspoken political radicals, which helped give progressivism a socialist tint. Bestor was a liberal, not a conservative, despite what numerous critics in schools of education then and later assumed. He praised the Lincoln School but believed that Dewey's misguided followers led progressive education into unfortunate directions in the 1920s. "Progressive education became regressive education, because, instead of advancing, it began to undermine the great traditions of liberal education and to substitute for them lesser aims, confused aims, or no aims at all." Educators had ignored the democratic advice offered by the Committee of Ten, which had not confused high standards and academic training for everyone with elitism. Instead, progressives had embraced the undemocratic ideals of the *Cardinal Principles of Secondary Education,* which endorsed academic instruction only for the few in the emerging comprehensive high school.

In various writings Bestor argued that academic course taking in the liberal arts had precipitously declined in the high schools since the early twentieth century. In its place had come watered-down subjects and the addition of classes in "life adjustment" (e.g., dating, human relations, how to bake a cherry pie). For Bestor, life adjustment was the prime example of the anti-intellectual tendencies of the modern educational establishment, and it had little to do with the philosophical views of John Dewey, as many critics alleged. Devised by Charles Prosser, a vocational educator who thought only a minority of students could handle academic courses, life adjustment was sanctioned by the U.S. Office of Education and endorsed by many state departments of education, including in Illinois. It was praised to high heaven in most professional journals until Bestor and other critics, including William H. Whyte Jr., in his best-selling book about suburban life, *The Organization Man* (1956), brought it to the attention of a wider lay audience. Contributors to *Time* and other mass magazines soon called life adjustment classes drivel.

As far as Bestor was concerned, the great scandal of the age was how youth were shortchanged intellectually in the contemporary high school. When high schools earlier in the century expanded to include more lower-class students, he pointed out, educators quickly assumed that few of them could master academic subjects. Once the high schools became large enough and "comprehensive," poorer students dominated in the newly formed vocational and general tracks, isolated from the higher-status college preparatory students except for a few classes in common and in the extracurriculum. Bestor read deeply in the professional literature on individual differences, the educational mantra of the twentieth century. He agreed with the many experts who said that pupils with a wide range of talents now attended high school. But he was furious that educators streamed many of the slower students (who clearly needed more time and help with their work) into nonacademic courses and passed them regardless of their achievement. Even the college preparatory curriculum had weakened thanks to the spread of elective (rather than required) courses, which he likened to a cafeteria style of learning. As Bestor later wrote in *The Restoration of Learning* (1956), "terror-stricken policy-makers have done a grave disservice to democracy by arguing that their programs are necessary because of the supposed intellectual inferiority of the student body of a modern public high school when compared with the student body of an aristocratic school of the past. This is an outrageous—and factually unsupported—slander upon the intellectual ability of children from lower-income groups."

Basically, Bestor was a Jeffersonian democrat, believing that talent was found in all social classes. He backed the Supreme Court's rulings on school desegregation and avidly supported public education, insisting upon society's obligation to provide everyone with a quality academic education. He was no utopian. He realized that individuals with extremely low IQs could not learn difficult subjects, but nevertheless thought educationists wildly exaggerated the size of that group. Bestor asserted that denying the great majority of pupils access to academic study was insidious. Now that high schools had begun imitating the elementary schools, however, they were essentially promoting everyone. As many citizens knew, a diploma represented time served, not academic competence. But Bestor believed that the poorer and slower students could do academic work if provided with extra help, remedial classes, tutorials, and other programs. Unfortunately, change would not be easy. Part of an "interlocking directorate of professional educationists," schools of education certified teachers, principals, and superintendents and would not easily relinquish their power. Professors in the arts and sciences as well as an aroused public had to help restore the liberal arts to their central place in the schools.

Bestor stood out among critics of the high schools because he favored a high-quality education for every student. Contemporaries such as Admiral Hyman Rickover, who linked education and national defense, and James B. Conant, the most important defender of the comprehensive high school and its differentiated curricula, typically wanted quality academic education reserved for the few most talented pupils. The aspiring but anxious middle classes probably missed such distinctions, since they were primarily interested in shoring up quality instruction for their own children. In his brilliant parody, *The Rise of the Meritocracy* (1958), British sociologist Michael Young said it best: "They desire equal opportunity for everyone else's children, extra for their own."

Various factors ensured that the suburban and richer schools provided "extra for their own." Throughout the 1950s, other arts and sciences professors besides Bestor also became interested in school reform, and their research and influence, such as it was, mostly left a mark on suburban and not inner-city schools. Curriculum reform projects in math and physics were already underway before the launching of Sputnik made academic quality a larger national concern. Funded by private philanthropy and the National Science Foundation, which had been created during the early years of the cold war, these professors developed new, intellectually challenging curricula that often confused parents and students but tried to promote inquiry, problem solving, and high-level thinking skills. When in 1958 the Eisenhower administration passed the

had centered their energies on the destruction of legalized segregation, including the schools. Nothing, they believed, was more likely to affect the future of black children. These activists knew that the crusade for desegregated schools would not be easy, either in the Jim Crow South, where laws had mandated segregation, or in the urban North, where housing patterns, school board gerrymandering, and other administrative maneuvers often placed blacks in largely segregated and poorly equipped and staffed schools. But immense social changes were at work in the postwar economy that, along with the *Brown* decision, could not help but raise expectations among African Americans.

While the movement for integration was slow and contested, there is no denying that the legal victory of 1954 and the civil rights movement heavily shaped the larger history of postwar school reform. The black movement for equality and justice ultimately encouraged other marginalized groups to demand their rights. It blazed the trail for the advocates of children with special educational needs, gender equity, and ethnic group consciousness, which accelerated after black power became more influential within the civil rights movement in the mid-1960s. The *Brown* case also had influence beyond the world of education, since it was a major legal precedent that helped undermine segregation in other areas of public life.

One cannot stress enough the symbolic importance of the moral underpinnings of the movement for integrated schools. World War II had officially been a war between democracy and totalitarianism, with the allies victorious against a Nazi regime committed to genocide. African American veterans were in no mood to return to the *status quo ante*. They had fought in segregated units abroad against racism and for freedom. Now they had to fight for freedom at home. Famous civil rights leaders made the news and entered the history books, but the struggle occurred at the grass-roots level, community by community, where most of the activists led modest lives and thus had much to lose. The white South mightily resisted the Supreme Court order to end legal segregation. Ministers might have been right in saying that moral conviction could move mountains, but conviction could not shield peaceful protestors from violence and bloodshed. The pain and suffering they endured was increasingly seen on television and reported in the press, giving the early civil rights movement dignity and spiritual force in the eyes of a growing number of sympathetic citizens, including liberal whites, essential to the passage of major civil rights legislation in the coming years.

The often desperate situation of African Americans in the South made the

1954 court ruling all the more incredible. Consider the situation in Mississippi. When Medgar Evers, a black veteran of World War II who was later murdered for his activism, returned home from overseas, he and other activists faced entrenched forms of discrimination that mocked basic ideals of opportunity and common decency. As historian John Dittmer has explained, most blacks in Mississippi labored in dead-end jobs in agriculture or domestic service, surviving poverty notable even in the South, America's most impoverished region. Southern black schools everywhere had shorter terms, lower teacher pay, and hand-me-down textbooks discarded from the white schools. In 1949, a white newspaper editor in Jackson admitted that "in the matter of education we have for many years been treating Negroes most outrageously. The type of education we have been providing for them is nothing short of a disgrace." Black schools were "poorly equipped, shabby, dilapidated, and unsightly," mostly one-room schools with "rickety stoves" and horrific sanitation. In 1950, approximately 2 percent of all black Mississippians had earned a high school diploma. Mississippi spent $122 per capita annually on the education of each white child but only $32 for each black student. Even before the *Brown* decision, white southern leaders sensed that the courts would overturn Jim Crow, so the states of the former Confederacy began to invest more money in black schools. Although they fell short of the amount needed to make real changes, they improved teacher salaries and made other financial concessions to help maintain the fiction of "separate but equal."

But the *Brown* case was another matter entirely. Building upon important lower court victories, including some in higher education, the Legal Defense Fund of the National Association for the Advancement of Colored People (NAACP) successfully presented its case that separate educational facilities were inherently unequal and unconstitutional, a violation of the equal rights provisions of the Fourteenth Amendment. Its lead counsel Thurgood Marshall, who would become the first African American member of the Supreme Court, intimately understood the importance of education. His mother was a teacher in Baltimore, which had segregated schools. Unable to attend the all-white law school at the University of Maryland, he studied at the highly regarded but segregated Howard University, whose law school dean was a legendary champion of civil rights. Using controversial social science evidence that claimed that segregation irreparably harmed blacks psychologically, the NAACP victory greased the wheels of progress.

The white southern response to the court ruling ranged from disbelief to caution to outrage. African Americans were concerned about what the decision actually meant. As John Dittmer documents in his history of the freedom struggle, black teachers and administrators in Mississippi actually remained cool toward the dismantling of Jim Crow. Like their counterparts in other states, they rightly feared losing their jobs if segregation disappeared. While civil rights leaders were energized by the *Brown* decision, in public opinion polls only a bare majority of black Southerners said they approved of the ruling. Their schools, after all, had received more funding in recent years, and white teachers, they assumed, would not welcome black children into their classrooms. Moreover, Jim Crow had been a way of life for decades, enforced by law, custom, and violence.

The white South responded defiantly and often violently to the *Brown* decision. While some cities such as Baltimore and Louisville in the border states began to desegregate, elected officials throughout the South resisted. President Dwight D. Eisenhower only encouraged more resistance when he made it clear that he was unhappy with the Supreme Court, saying that laws could not change men's hearts. Southern governors and legislators doubted that he would use federal authority to enforce desegregation, and they announced that black and white children would never attend school together while they were in office. State proclamations and legislation stated that public schools would close down rather than integrate. In 1955, the U.S. Supreme Court issued *Brown II*, ruling that schools must desegregate "with all deliberate speed." Without any definite timetable for desegregation or agreed-upon definition of integration, decisions now fell on the shoulders of federal district courts, whose judges mostly supported Jim Crow.

By 1957, southern resistance kept most schools totally segregated. A quarter-million whites had joined local branches of the Citizens' Council, whose members intimidated and harassed civil rights workers. Civil rights leaders and sympathizers had their mortgages recalled, their credit withheld, their homes burned. A revived Ku Klux Klan engaged in terror and violence. When governor Orville Faubus of Arkansas, in a tight race for reelection, interfered with the integration of Central High School in Little Rock, television cameras brought the ugliness of racism home to everyone's living rooms. Faubus sent in the National Guard, ostensibly to prevent impending violence, but really to keep African American students out of the building. The nine well-dressed and well-mannered African Americans who tried to attend Central High were taunted, ridiculed, and threatened by unruly white mobs. When a judge ordered Faubus to relent, he withdrew the troops and violence greeted black bystanders. Camera crews caught southern whites on their worst behavior. Unable to force a compromise with Faubus, Eisenhower reluctantly nationalized the Arkansas National Guard and sent in the army to protect the black students and enforce compliance. As during Reconstruction, it seemed as if only fixed bayonets could guarantee the peace and rule of law, which made cold war rhetoric about democracy and education vacuous and hypocritical, as the contrast between America's high ideals and grim southern realities made international news. At Faubus's insistence, Little Rock's four high schools closed the following year except for one school-sponsored activity: football.

Eisenhower's initial failure to provide firm leadership reflected his overall reluctance to face difficult social problems or utilize federal power for race reform. His stance on the *Brown* decision played well in the South, since he neither championed the cause of civil rights nor supported other liberal causes such as federal aid to education. It is unlikely that he would have approved the landmark National Defense Education Act (1958), a cold war measure, absent a national outcry for some federal response to Sputnik. With the economy robust, affluence growing, and consumerism widespread, Eisenhower and his supporters preferred a limited federal role in most domestic policies. Ike did not roll back Social Security, farm subsidies, or other popular New Deal programs. As Roy Wilkins of the NAACP aptly noted, if Eisenhower "had fought World War II the way he fought for civil rights, we would all be speaking German today."

While hardly recognized by white racists, North or South, as a moral campaign for equality and freedom and for a rightful share of the American dream, the civil rights movement under the leadership of the Reverend Martin Luther King Jr. pressed forward and assumed the high moral ground. Born into a family of prominent ministers in Atlanta in 1929, King was a legendary orator who linked his campaign for racial integration and social harmony to timeless symbols of freedom, justice, and the American dream. Long before his famous "I Have A Dream" speech at the 1963 March on Washington, in which he imagined a world that judged children by "the content of their character" and not their skin color, King stressed the moral values that undergirded the larger civil rights movement. He preached love and compassion for bigots as well as for friends to the end of his life, prematurely ended in 1968 by an assassin's bullet. By then his campaign for exclusively nonviolent resistance and integration had already lost support among some younger African American activists.

King and other urban ministers organized the Southern Christian Leadership Council (SCLC) in 1957 after his rise to prominence during the Montgomery bus boycott. SCLC wanted to see "all schools integrated—north and south." Nothing short of equal access to the schools and other institutions, which allowed greater individual and group mobility, was acceptable. Speaking in 1959 at a rally on behalf of school integration with Daisy Bates, A. Philip Randolph, Jackie Robinson, and other black activists, King characteristically emphasized something that Richard Nixon and so many cold warriors in both major parties ignored when they spoke of "democracy in education." King told his listeners—twenty-six thousand high school and college students—that they had "discovered the central fact of American life—that the extension of democracy for all Americans depends upon complete integration of Negro Americans." In 1963, sensing that some of the southern walls of oppression were crumbling, King reiterated a familiar theme in his speeches and writings: that all people were created in God's image and that integration was not only a Judeo-Christian ideal but also a social and political imperative. But the walls of segregation did not in fact blow down easily. At the time, nearly all black children in the South still attended all-black schools. Some southern districts had shut down their schools and ignored court orders to desegregate. Prince Edward County in Virginia, for example, closed all public schools but ran private academies for whites only that received tax support until 1964, when the U.S. Supreme Court ruled against the policy and required the establishment of a desegregated system.

Demographic and economic changes also rapidly altered the lives of Southerners in the postwar era and led to the expansion of the civil rights movement to the North and to the rise of the Great Society. According to historian Allen J. Matusow, the population of the rural South declined from 16.2 to 5.9 million people between 1930 and 1960, and many of the displaced workers, white and black, sought work in southern or, more often, in northern cities. Feudal working conditions reminiscent of slavery—sharecropping and tenant farming—had been the foundation of political authority during the age of Jim Crow. But then the poor were increasingly displaced from the southern economy, as New Deal agricultural policies, agribusiness, and technology made their farm labor redundant. As Pete Daniel demonstrated in his history of civil rights in the 1950s, once the agricultural order unraveled, the material foundations of Jim Crow crumbled.

Removed from the land and beckoned by the promise of industrial jobs,

African Americans as well as poor whites increasingly headed north. The trickle of black migrants that had begun during World War I became a mighty current in the 1950s. White Appalachians and southern blacks left by the millions. Kentucky lost a little over a third of its population, West Virginia about a quarter. In 1940, most blacks lived in the rural South, and nationally an incredible 87 percent of black families, compared with 48 percent of whites, lived below the poverty line. In less than a generation, African Americans increasingly lived in the North and in cities, and the percentage living in poverty had dropped dramatically to 29 percent by 1980, compared to 8 percent for whites. Even though the booming economy lifted white boats higher, the gaps had narrowed. For African Americans, the North brought hardship and discrimination but also more freedom, the right to vote, and a higher standard of living. The black middle class grew, but segregation and declining urban schools tarnished this story of progress. Poor rural Southerners, white and black alike, arrived in the North just when success at school mattered more than ever. Given these demographic and political realities, it did not take long for the civil rights movement to shift its energy from the South to the North. Beginning in the mid-1960s, it did just that.

Urban schools had long been the bellwether of educational progress. Nineteenth-century reformers praised them as the center of innovation, home to the first graded classrooms, high schools, and standardized curricula. Reformers routinely contrasted the excellence of city schools with the one-room schools of the countryside, which could not match their urban cousins in quality of architecture, richness of curricula, or variety of extracurricular programs. Education officials who made these comparisons ignored all the impoverished, overcrowded, underperforming urban schools and all the exemplary country schools that taught the basics well and enjoyed strong community support. After World War II, more and more rural schools disappeared as farm populations dramatically declined and school consolidation rapidly accelerated. Soon the new symbols of academic excellence were found not in the cities but in the suburbs.

Just as rural migrants, black and white, arrived in the cities, several major developments occurred that placed their schools in desperate straits. Suburbs exploded as returning white veterans used their economic and racial advantages to find homes there. While fewer blacks relative to whites entered the ranks of skilled labor and the professions, many prospered, buying homes in the city and aspiring to a better future. In the 1960s, however, decent jobs in the cities increasingly became scarce. Earlier shifts from blue-collar to white-collar work accelerated, hurting those without educational credentials, who often found themselves trapped in the low pay service economy. Such was the competitive world facing southern transplants to Indianapolis, Chicago, or New York City.

How about the prospects for the coming generation? The service economy did not provide security, benefits, or a ladder upward, and this was even before many golden arches appeared on the skyline. Unions protected the existing blue-collar jobs and frequently discriminated against African Americans, further laying the foundations for black protests and riots in the 1960s. The exit of the white middle classes to the suburbs, population decline, and weakened manufacturing meant declining tax revenues. Cities that once boasted of high teacher salaries and fancy schools now had trouble raising sufficient money to deal with the masses of children, increasingly black, sometimes Hispanic, and usually poor, who now entered many urban schools. Precisely when educational credentials counted for more, these children's needs were greater, and their schools faltered.

City schools had never enjoyed a golden age when everyone had attained a uniformly high standard of achievement. As the saying went, those who dropped out of school could drop into some job. Countless children, whether immigrant or native poor, had flunked their share of classes, repeated grades, and not enjoyed school. These "laggards" had filled many urban classrooms during the Progressive Era. Poor children then as later had trouble mastering the basics. They disproportionally ended up in lower ability groups in the elementary grades and less-academic tracks if they progressed to junior high school. While some ethnic groups generally did extremely well at school, poor children often struggled and dropped out to work. Ability grouping and the growing use of social promotion by the 1930s allowed many of them to stay in school as long as they or their parents wanted, but their school performance, by most accounts, was frequently low. They were among those who Arthur Bestor believed were still being shortchanged in the 1950s. Over the next thirty years, urban schools everywhere had a growing percentage of poor and minority children, and school failure was a common problem without easy or clear solutions.

Numerous educators after the war worried about how to educate the grow-ing concentration of poor children, whose often poorly educated parents did not typically join the PTA. The poor often struggled to pay the rent, to keep their children in the same schools, and to hold their families intact. Experts lamented the low reading scores in impoverished urban neighborhoods. More students passed from grade to grade, but achievement gaps progressively widened. High schools in Chicago and Los Angeles enrolled many children who were reading at the fourth grade level. Mainstream magazines sympa-thized with high school teachers, who once taught the cream of the crop, but now had some students better fit for reform school. Many educators and writ-ers in mass magazines said that delinquents stayed in school because they could not find jobs. In 1955, a principal from Brooklyn confessed that no one knew how to deal with the surfeit of "non readers." That year's hit movie *Black-board Jungle* set in a New York vocational high school, includes a memorable scene in which a teacher uses an animated cartoon of "Jack and the Beanstalk" to reach his unruly brood.

The situation in many northern industrial cities further deteriorated. James B. Conant, the former president of Harvard and a major figure in policy de-bates on the high school, famously stated in *Slums and Suburbs* (1961) that so-ciety had planted "social dynamite" in the inner cities. He predicted a nasty explosion unless the prospects of the poor improved and citizens invested heavily in their education. Though an extreme example, Detroit lost tens of thousands of jobs almost overnight, leaving black residents economically dec-imated. The principal of Detroit's Central High School wrote in 1963 that the situation was already desperate, and that without much hope for employment, students lacked incentives to study. White flight left many cities increasingly black and poor. Minority groups soon dominated in urban systems as white parents (as well as some black middle-class parents) either left for the suburbs or sent their children to parochial or private schools.

Liberal professors and some elites in tony neighborhoods often endorsed any variety of school reforms—from busing to black community control—but usually sent their children to private schools. Thurgood Marshall, practicing law in New York, sent his children to private schools in Harlem; like other pro-fessionals he chose the best he could afford. In his 2002 case study of New York City, Jerald A. Podair explains that African Americans increased from 17 to 33 percent of New York City's total school enrollment between 1957 and 1967, as white flight from the system accelerated. The city had a handful of prestigious academic high schools with strict scholastic admission criteria, and the system awarded different kinds of high school diplomas, from academic through vocational. Comprising almost a third of the student population, African Americans received under 3 percent of the "academic" sheepskins.

Explanations for school failure among the poor in general and African Americans in particular proliferated. The city systems seemed to be changing topsy-turvy overnight. Southern journalists and politicians enjoyed tweaking northern liberals after the *Brown* decision, asking them why so few black teachers were on the payroll in Chicago, New York City, and other northern centers, and why the North, with very segregated housing and neighborhood schools, could so smugly call Southerners racist. Studies consistently identified how the slum schools failed to hire and retain the best teachers. New and inexperienced teachers were often assigned to the ghetto schools; if they survived or even better, thrived, they were promoted with a transfer to a "better" post. Teacher turnover was high, and absenteeism among teachers in the most troubled schools rivaled that of the students. Podair also discovered that in New York City, administrators furloughed the worst teachers in the better schools to the slums, one way to flush the weak-but-tenured out of the system.

To slow down the exodus of whites from urban systems, school boards and superintendents often redrew district lines to create all-white and all-black districts, applying the brakes to racial integration. Some white schools had empty classrooms while segregated black schools nearby were bursting at the seams. This produced anger and discouragement among black parents and certainly did not counter low achievement or high dropout rates. Prize-winning books such as Jonathan Kozol's *Death at an Early Age* (1967) chronicled the racism of white teachers in the Boston system, and numerous exposés poured from the presses on the failures of teachers, principals, school boards, and politicians to correct the problems engulfing the cities.

As urban schools in the North deteriorated, psychologists and social scientists tried to uncover the sources of educational failure. Many experts in the 1950s and early 1960s subscribed to the idea of a "culture of poverty" or "cultural deprivation." Though their definitions and emphases varied, these writers argued that children born to poor and minority families had personality traits that made them unlikely candidates for academic success. Most schools, they said, valued middle-class norms such as time discipline, obedience to authority, and delayed gratification. This cultural explanation for school failure among poor and minority children was a liberal invention. As historian Alice

O'Connor has demonstrated, anthropologists and social scientists in the 1920s and 1930s explored the cultural determinants of human behavior and attacked the genetic theories underlying scientific racism that had undergirded, for example, the early testing movement. Stated simply, the culture of poverty argument claimed that a number of mutually reinforcing factors—harsh child rearing, lack of intellectual stimulation at home, and poor health care, diet, and housing—all contributed to school failure. Breaking the links in the chain of failure, to invoke the common metaphor, might lead to success at school. Whether to focus on the ills of the school or of children and their families was the great dilemma for contemporary reformers.

Psychologist Frank Riessman's *The Culturally Deprived Child* (1962) was one of the genre's best known works, widely quoted in the popular press and in the professional literature. He estimated that in 1950 about 10 percent of all school children in America's leading cities were "culturally deprived," but that within a decade the figure had more than tripled. In a footnote, Riessman explained that he used "the terms 'culturally deprived,' 'educationally deprived,' 'deprived,' 'underprivileged,' 'disadvantaged,' 'lower class,' 'lower socio-economic group'" synonymously. Just about anyone not from the comfortable classes who did poorly at school was labeled "culturally deprived." The book described the culturally deprived as anti-intellectual, pragmatic, impulsive, and more oriented toward physical feats than mental tests, which accounted for their athletic prowess. The culturally deprived recognized the growing importance of school credentials but too often lacked either the ability to delay gratification or an intrinsic love of learning. Riessman apparently assumed that the middle classes, who were the best at acquiring credentials, studied because of its intrinsic appeal. They were not motivated by crass (or "extrinsic") motives like the pleasure of getting the most As, attending the best colleges, or enjoying the finer things of life.

According to Riessman, in this dichotomous world of competing social groups, the culture of the lower-class child and the middle-class values rewarded at school—sitting quietly, doing homework, performing well on tests—inevitably collided. Riessman argued, in fact, that since teachers could not do anything about family life, they should focus on adapting the school to the child, an old progressive assumption. But when it came to how to do this, he was more than a little vague. While the above descriptions of lower-class families seem like popular stereotypes, he accused urban teachers of being condescending. They lacked empathy for the deprived child, whose earthy ways Riessman admired. Blind to the virtues of the impulsive and streetwise, middle-class teachers simply wanted to control, manage, and socialize the poor. Throughout the 1960s, liberal and radical critics increasingly blamed teachers (and their repressed bourgeois values) if children did poorly.

Then as now, some liberal and radical professionals found glamour, excitement, and appeal in the lives of the poor, seeing in them a modern version of Locke's man living in a state of nature or Rousseau's noble savage. Writing in the *High School Journal* in 1964, a professor of education and youth studies from Tufts University critiqued public schools and their irrelevant curricula. Admiring the "hipster" language of the inner city, he scolded the schools for trying to make the poor absorb middle-class values. Like many a progressive, he said the schools emphasized abstract thinking instead of offering real life problem solving. *Compensatory Education for Cultural Deprivation* (1965), coauthored by some high-status education professors at the University of Chicago, similarly described the socially disadvantaged as accustomed to "things and activities which are concrete and which have immediate and tangible rewards." Lower-class black children, they said, often came from homes without books and other reading materials, but they had a "wonderful zest and expressiveness" soon crushed in the middle-class school.

Teachers who corrected children's grammar or pronunciation increasingly found themselves attacked as racists or compared with Professor Henry Higgins and his patronizing attempt to uplift Eliza Doolittle (in Bernard Shaw's play *Pygmalion*). "Let's Dump the Uptight Model in English," read the title of an essay in the *Elementary School Journal* in 1969: "Uptight ain't right." Soon some teachers urged more "rapping" with and less teaching of pupils. As Charles A. Reich, a law professor at Yale, observed in his bestseller *The Greening of America* (1970), "hip" blacks exemplified "the sensual, the earthy, and the rebellious elements of man," while the schools were like prisons without bars that destroyed the soul.

Throughout the 1960s, policy debates about school failure frequently deteriorated into shouting matches whose participants blamed one side or the other, the teacher or the child, the family or the school. In 1965, radicals and liberals alike heaped a firestorm of criticism on Daniel Patrick Moynihan, then working for the Johnson administration, when he argued that the black family was in trouble, pointing to the dramatic increase in out-of-wedlock births and families with single mothers, mired in poverty. Had he said the same thing a few years earlier, few people would have noticed. Sociologist James Coleman's study of school achievement appeared in 1966 and argued, in the sober and less flamboyant language of social science, that family background, not school resources, decisively shaped educational achievement; this was also unwelcome news to many liberals. Conservatives, however, took comfort because this confirmed what they already believed, that spending more money on the lower classes would not make an appreciable scholastic difference. Few of them suggested that suburbanites should stop passing bond measures for their already well-heeled schools, cut out Advanced Placement courses, or, later, to cancel the Kaplan and Princeton Review SAT-preparation lessons.

Many people realized, however, that the low achievement of the urban poor was a scandal, and looked for someone or something to blame. By the end of the decade, black critics and left-leaning liberals dismissed the views of Riessman and other "culture of poverty" theorists as white paternalism, which had demeaned the culture of the child and let the school and its institutionalized racism off the hook. Psychologist William Ryan called it "blaming the victim," a phrase that soon became a cliché. Critics also attacked compensatory education, saying it was based on the idea that poor and minority families, and not "the system," were responsible for high dropout rates and low school performance. Despite this verbal commotion, school achievement for the urban poor did not improve. Nearly every prominent school periodical published during the 1960s had something to say about the ills of city schools, the low achievement, and the myriad programs, curricula, and workshops that were created to address the problem. Because expectations for the schools had risen dramatically, urban policy making was a lush landscape of ideas littered with many ideological land mines.

In the mid-1960s the civil rights movement was fragmenting into competing factions, and the Great Society of the Johnson administration initiated major federal programs of compensatory education for "the disadvantaged," based on "culture of poverty" assumptions. No one could tell with certainty whose innovative proposals offered much concrete advantage for the nation's poorest children. The battles among liberals and civil rights activists working outside and inside the federal government were nevertheless among the most heated and politically charged expressions of contemporary school reform. As criticisms of urban schools mounted during the 1960s, a new, younger generation of civil rights activists also appeared on the national scene. Impatient with the strategies of their elders and the glacial pace of racial progress, they believed in direct action and red-hot rhetoric. Seeing the necessity for more direct, even violent, confrontations with the white establishment, they had bravely risked their lives by the early 1960s at sit-ins, freedom rides, and marches throughout the South. They were much less interested, however, in integrated schools, and they rejected the nonviolent approach of Martin Luther King Jr. as well as the legalistic strategy of the NAACP, which continued to pursue racial justice through the courts and other branches of government.

Although he died before he was forty years old, King represented an older generation. Like his critics within the movement, he was frustrated with the dragging speed of social improvement. But he also worried that slogans such as "black power," made famous by Stokely Carmichael of the Student Non-violent Coordinating Committee (SNCC) in 1966, would alienate otherwise sympathetic whites and embolden the silent majority of moderates and conservatives. On moral grounds King could not condone appeals to racial hatred or violence. Rejecting the notion of a culture of poverty that so many white liberals had embraced, the younger members of the civil rights movement advocated black pride, black power, the teaching of black history and culture, and community control. They purged whites from membership in the SNCC and called integration a form of racial genocide. By rejecting the idea of assimilation—a message heard by various ethnic groups—they questioned the old notion of the school as a melting pot.

The ethnic revival, which always had some separatist overtones, received more fuel in 1968 with the passage of the Bilingual Education Act. Originally conceived by Democrats seeking favor with Spanish-speaking voters, it largely aimed to help disadvantaged children better learn English to improve their school performance. Without any clear definition, but soon appealing to more groups and professionals who saw a growth area, bilingual education became ever more controversial as some educators and administrators used the program not to assimilate children into the academic mainstream but to maintain languages other than English. The lack of convincing evidence that bilingual education in its various forms improved school achievement ultimately led Congress to place some restrictions on the use of federal funds for it in the late 1970s. By then, however, a landmark U.S. Supreme Court decision in 1974 and local practices had already led to more bilingual instruction in hundreds of school districts. Whether schools existed to assimilate children became hotly debated for the rest of the century. In congressional hearings in 1977, Gary Orfield, an eloquent champion of racial integration, argued that there was little evidence that bilingual education would lift academic achievement and warned against its segregationist character.

Since advocates of black power, Chicano power, and Italian and Polish power were in the headlines, it is easy to confuse the statements of self-proclaimed leaders with the sentiments of the masses, whose beliefs are often difficult to gauge. In the 1960s, however, the popularity of black power radicals at least did not appear to rest among the black masses, as historian Stephen Thernstrom and policy analyst Abigail Thernstrom have revealed through the study of public opinion polls. The black rank-and-file typically endorsed the mainstream black leaders whom the radicals called Uncle Toms. For example, Malcolm X, Stokely Carmichael, and H. Rap Brown, leading champions of black power, had very low approval and high disapproval ratings among African Americans in public opinion polls. In contrast, Martin Luther King Jr. was regarded as the leading champion of civil rights and enjoyed very high approval and very low disapproval ratings. The younger radicals attained iconic status thanks to their courage, bold rhetoric, and support from black students, liberal academics, artists, public intellectuals, and left-wing movie stars. Author Tom Wolfe called this "radical chic."

Fissures within the civil rights movement existed within a larger social and political context. Even before black power grabbed the headlines and conservatives returned to political power in Washington in 1968, civil rights activists, both liberal and radical, were shaping but also being shaped by events in the nation's capital. Activists in the mid-1960s had to share the national stage with a Southerner they really never trusted.

As the civil rights movement underwent its metamorphosis, the role of the federal government in American life also changed dramatically. At the dawn of Lyndon Baines Johnson's presidency, there was a brief calm before the storm. Though John F. Kennedy's assassination weighed heavily on the nation, the economy seemed vibrant, Vietnam some distant land, integration the major goal of social justice, and the social dynamite inert. The cause of civil rights was stalled, if only temporarily. A moderate Southerner distrusted by most northern liberals, Johnson was an old New Dealer who had done a remarkable job as head of the Texas branch of the National Youth Administration during the Depression. The youngest Senate majority leader in history, he was largely responsible for the Civil Rights Act of 1957, which while weak by later standards was then praised by black leaders. In the 1950s, he not only responded favorably to the *Brown* decision but was also one of only three senators from the region who did not sign the 1956 "Southern Manifesto," which denounced the ruling and defended Jim Crow.

An internationalist and a hawk, Johnson had a Texas-sized sense of destiny. Historian Robert Dallek has emphasized that Johnson passionately wanted to pull the South into the modern world, integrate it into the national economy, and end its legacy of slavery and racial oppression. As president he planned to reshape the nation, including its public schools. Though it seemed puzzling, the more civil rights legislation he passed, the angrier the ostensible beneficiaries became. In 1964, Johnson signed the momentous Civil Rights Act. The following year he signed the Voting Rights Act, and riots broke out a few days later in Watts, a largely black ghetto in Los Angeles. Some participants in the riots said they had tired of waiting for improvements in their lives. It would have provided LBJ little comfort to know that Alexis de Tocqueville once wrote that revolutions occur when life is improving, not when it is getting worse. Johnson was shepherding more social welfare legislation through Congress than anyone had seen in a generation and responding to the demands of the civil rights movement to extend and guarantee protection for African Americans. By fueling the wider trend of rising expectations, Johnson advanced social justice but ensured his own political demise. Expectations had soared that no one could quickly satisfy. After years of summer riots and growing divisiveness over Vietnam, he shocked a divided nation in 1968 by announcing that he would not accept his party's nomination for a second term.

Johnson's enthusiastic embrace of using federal power in domestic affairs broke ranks with tradition and with important segments of his own party. While there was bipartisan agreement on the need for a strong military, especially during the cold war, such consensus had always evaporated when anyone proposed federal protection for civil rights or aid to the schools. Southern Democrats, states' rights die-hards when it suited their purposes, had ultimately turned on FDR. Though an essential part of the New Deal coalition, they remained suspicious of centralized federal authority that might challenge Jim Crow. Moreover, many Americans in the 1950s opposed federal aid for the schools, and that included not only southern Democrats but most Republicans. About 1 percent of local school budgets came from the federal government, earmarked for vocational education, reimbursements to local districts that educated children from nearby military bases, and an assortment of smaller programs.

The NEA had long lobbied for federal aid with no strings attached. Federal aid gained the support of Roosevelt's successor, Harry S. Truman, and a handful of liberal northern Democrats. Most people, however, feared that this would mean support for Catholic schools, then unthinkable because it would weaken the public schools and aid the so-called immigrant church. The majority of state constitutions also prohibited tax support for parochial schools, so gathering the votes for a general aid bill was not easy. Others opposed the idea as government paternalism, if not creeping socialism and communism, that would lead to a national curriculum and the abridgement of local control. But the rising expectations that citizens had about schools, and the growing frustrations of civil rights activists after the *Brown* decision, soon provided ambitious leaders such as Johnson with the opportunity to expand Washington's reach into everyday life—in education, nutrition, health care, voting rights, and so forth—in ways that seemed unimaginable only a few years earlier. Certainly John F. Kennedy, the first Catholic president, had no such mandate from the voters. As a presidential candidate he assured voters that no tax dollars would flow into parochial schools. Elected by a razor-thin margin, he was not going to hitch his star to civil rights and risk losing his southern constituency.

Seizing the moment and packaging the early Great Society as a tribute to a martyred president, Johnson signed impressive civil rights and social welfare legislation, causing many people to compare it to the early New Deal. Like most mainstream liberals, Johnson did not seek to redistribute wealth or income but favored a growing economy and expansive programs of training and development. The former teacher may have mythologized the role of schooling in his own social mobility, but he had a bedrock faith in the salutary influence of education. Gauging the attitude of a people is difficult, but Johnson seemed more in tune with the spirit of the times than Barry Goldwater, his Republican opponent in 1964, who dismissed the assumption that education was of great importance. "The child has no right to an education," Goldwater asserted. "In most cases he will get along very well without it."

The Supreme Court had underscored the significance of education when it ruled against Jim Crow. Economists stressed the role of education in human capital development and explored its varying rates of return for different social groups. Many people called for enhanced spending on those students designated gifted and talented. While many social scientists and educators believed that the value of a high school degree was weakening, education seemed vital to the economy, though in what precise ways was a matter of dispute. The Johnson administration left no part of the educational system untouched. In addition to programs for preschool and elementary education and smaller ones for high school, it expanded grants and scholarships for college through the Higher Education Act of 1965, which helped many working-class and middle-class students further their education. Nothing, however, matched the importance of the Elementary and Secondary Education Act (ESEA) of 1965 and the less costly innovation enacted in 1964, Head Start, both of which were integral to Johnson's celebrated War on Poverty.

Johnson bet his money on the power of education to promote social mobility. Head Start is a preschool program of compensatory education for underprivileged children that tries to address the nutritional and health needs and enhance the educational and social skills of the underprivileged. Even in the 1960s, critics believed that Head Start should place more emphasis on reading, given its importance in school success. ESEA was more significant politically than Head Start, because it undermined time-tested objections against federal aid. Francis Keppel, the U.S. commissioner of education, and his colleagues proposed that ESEA money would aid the impoverished child and not the school. Including parochial school children broadened its appeal to Catholics and their representatives in Washington. In terms of precedent, the GI Bill, a very popular piece of legislation, had provided financial aid to veterans but skirted church-and-state entanglement by providing aid to students, not to the institutions of higher education they attended (ESEA dollars, in contrast, were sent to local school districts, not to pupils or their parents or guardians). After Johnson lobbied the NEA, which was traditionally opposed to any bill that helped Catholic schools, it too signed on. Title I, the heart of ESEA, provided federal aid to improve the scholastic achievement of poor children, which seemed fundamental to their success in the modern world.

The still buoyant economy of the mid-1960s helped fill government coffers and tapped a traditional American optimism about the value of education and schooling. As Johnson's vice president, Hubert H. Humphrey, the talkative liberal from Minnesota, recalled, LBJ was "a nut on education. . . . He felt that education was the greatest thing he could give to the people; he just believed in it, just like some people believe in miracle cures." In 1965, in a major speech at Howard University that trumpeted his War on Poverty, in which education and training figured centrally, Johnson explained that he sought "not just freedom but opportunity—not just equality as a right and a theory but equality as a fact and as a result." Without providing any specifics, Johnson's speech also called for more aggressive steps to overcome historic patterns of racial discrimination, anticipating what became known as affirmative action. High-flying rhetoric about equality as a result perfectly suited the tenor of the moment but would surely spell disappointment if inequality, whether measured by test results or income, persisted. In an age when social scientists produced impressive quantitative evidence of every facet of social life, rhetoric might prove no match for evidence. The Civil Rights Act, for example, mandated the social science research that culminated in the Coleman report, which questioned whether spending more money on schools would lift achievement. This contradicted liberal assumptions about the relationship between investment and performance. To try to minimize press coverage, the Johnson administration released the report on the Fourth of July.

The initial fascination with measuring the effects of school programs came from various liberal quarters. Robert F. Kennedy, who grilled commissioner Keppel at the congressional hearings on ESEA, firmly believed in what conservatives later called accountability. Knowing how machine politics functioned in many cities, he was skeptical about whether local school officials would actually spend the allocated money on poor children. Keppel shared similar fears and actually supported the development of national achievement tests, despite the furor he anticipated arousing among teachers. And so a provision was added to ESEA that mandated evaluations, the earliest of which failed to show noticeable improvement in the achievement of the poor. Early evaluations of Head Start were also discouraging. Whatever advantages children in Head Start enjoyed when they entered school seemed to fade out in a few years. In contrast to ESEA and Title I, later evaluations of Head Start were more positive, claiming that former pupils graduated at a higher rate, encountered less trouble with the law, and had fewer teen pregnancies.

Rhetoric about equality of results notwithstanding, the circumstances surrounding the passage and implementation of ESEA undermined its potential to help the poor. To secure congressional support, the vast majority of America's school districts gained access to Title I funding. State departments of education, notoriously weak and often poorly staffed, could not easily monitor local spending. Chicago's school superintendent, for example, openly spent federal money in his system any way he pleased, and not necessarily on the poor. Suburban schools, which usually had a small percentage of poor children, also leveraged ESEA monies to help finance, among other things, "remedial" reading classes to help middle-class children. While LBJ thought his educational innovations would help fight poverty, their impact on improving the achievement of the poor was modest. Urban school performance languished.

But history is full of unintended consequences. There is more to a school than test scores, and Johnson's civil rights legislation and programs actually helped move the South along the path of desegregation. Given the numerous strategies that the South pursued to block desegregation after 1954, this was both unexpected and remarkable. Some southern parents, like their northern cousins, dealt with the prospect of racial integration by simply leaving the system: they moved to the suburbs or sent their children to private schools or openly segregationist academies. In addition, school boards in various places evaded court orders, tied up the NAACP and civil rights activists in legal battles, and devised freedom-of-choice plans, later struck down as illegal, that made integration depend on the willingness of individual black students to transfer to all-white schools. Administrators sometimes leisurely submitted time tables for integration, some promising decisive action in the next millennium.

Among its many sweeping provisions, the Civil Rights Act of 1964 forbade racial discrimination in public schools and empowered the Justice Department to sue districts that failed to comply more rapidly and effectively with court orders to integrate. It also gave authority to the Department of Health, Education, and Welfare (HEW) to press for more compliance, which led its administrators to set numerical quotas to measure whether a school was integrated. Critics said this seemed to contradict the Civil Rights Act, which forbade discrimination based on race. By the late 1960s, however, southern districts realized that they were going to lose costly court battles as well as the monies flowing from various federal spigots. The incentives to desegregate had escalated. Still the poorest region in the country, the South talked confidently about the virtues of self-reliance and states' rights but depended heavily on federal spending, most visibly with its many military bases and NASA space centers. The schools could scarcely afford to do with less money while also paying mounting legal bills. Poor states such as Mississippi especially relied upon federal funds—from Title I to school lunch subsidies—to keep some semblance of a modern school system intact. Ironically, just as black power activists attacked the idea of school integration, the federal government had actually pressed hard enough to make it become more of a reality. Especially unpopular with whites, court-ordered busing was the common means by which southern schools integrated. Different communities experienced varying degrees of racial tension, violence, and unhappiness with court-approved plans for integrating the system. Black students were typically forced to travel longer on buses and for more years of their schooling. Numerous black teachers and administrators lost their jobs once formally segregated schools disappeared, but the number of black elementary and secondary teachers increased dramatically between 1940 and 1970, from 67,580 to over 227,000. Raising the achievement of African Americans, whose families remained disproportionally poor, was still very difficult. In many "integrated" schools, black students were streamed more often than whites into lower-level ability groups, remedial classes, special education, and vocational tracks. Self-segregation by race at the cafeteria, on sports teams, and in extracurricular activities remained all too common. Equality of results remained elusive.

Despite these serious examples of racial inequality, the civil rights movement and Great Society delivered some fatal blows to Jim Crow. By the early 1970s, southern schools were actually more integrated than those in the North. Who in 1954 would have predicted this? In a single generation after *Brown,* black attendance in high schools across the nation soared. On average, blacks may have earned lower grades, had higher rates of suspension and expulsion and lower graduation rates (especially for males), and had an overall tougher road to adult achievement, but a beginning had been made. The sheer presence of African Americans in high school and at college, compared with in the age of Eisenhower, was impressive. A British journalist could not believe how effectively the federal government and the courts had pressed for integrated schools. By 1972, he wrote, "for the first time, the South, with roughly half of the nation's black population, had both a smaller absolute number and smaller proportion of black children in segregated schools than the rest of the country."

Much of this had occurred after 1968, when the winds of change otherwise seemed to blow cold on the civil rights movement. By then, the Democratic Party was seriously divided over Vietnam, rising crime, the growing welfare state, and a worsening economy. Richard Nixon beat Hubert Humphrey in a tight election, even though George Wallace siphoned off millions of conservative votes. Appealing to the moderate to conservative "silent majority" of voters, Nixon pursued a "southern strategy" that called for less federal intervention in domestic affairs and more respect for "law and order." Sensing the unpopularity of court-ordered busing, which later led to violence in places such as Pontiac, Michigan, and Boston, he reined in the Justice Department and HEW and benefited from the divisive effects of busing and affirmative action on the Democrats, who were losing their lock on the white working classes. Nixon favored more vocational education and, anticipating Reagan, preferred block grants to the states over the categorical grant programs of the Johnson era. He deepened the growing appeal of the Republican Party in the South and among working-class members of white ethnic groups in the North.

By the late 1960s and early 1970s, the nation had turned to the right for numerous reasons, including a changing mood about the schools. The morning newspapers as well as *U.S. News & World Report, Time,* and *Newsweek* routinely reported on mounting violence in classrooms and worsening levels of achievement. The problems of large urban systems dominated the headlines: "Schools Hit By New Violence," "More Breakdowns in Public Schools," "Crisis in the City Schools," "Detroit's Schools Head Toward Disaster." Some prominent liberals flip-flopped on the use of schools as a means of social reform, as neoconservative intellectuals emphasized "benign neglect" and warned of the dangers of big government. Genetic theories of human development enjoyed a revival, leading some scholars to question the logic of Head Start and social intervention in the lives of the poor.

At the same time, conservatives and middle-of-the-road commentators approvingly cited and affirmed the Coleman report's findings of a lack of a positive connection between school spending and academic achievement. Later they praised Coleman for arguing in another study that forced busing accelerated white flight and for endorsing more school choice and private schools. In the North, concentrated residential segregation undermined the prospect of integrated schools, which often led to foot-dragging by white-controlled school boards. This forced the lower courts to monitor a process of integration that depended largely upon mandatory busing. That many of the judges were suburbanites whose own children went to private schools did not lessen the anger of white working-class citizens, who often furiously resisted racial integration, through word and deed. All of this contributed to Nixon's mauling of Democratic candidate George McGovern, and with him northern liberalism, in the presidential election of 1972.

The prospects of racial integration in the urban North became ever more difficult as whites exited the city, where deepening economic woes exacerbated racial tensions. In a major decision in 1973, the U.S. Supreme Court denied that there was a constitutional right to equally funded schools. It had earlier upheld the constitutionality of busing, but then ruled against busing between suburb and city in the *Milliken* decision in 1974. Increasingly there were very few whites left in cities to integrate. Many urban systems thus administered their schools—including Indianapolis, Dayton, and Cleveland, to name just a few in the Midwest—under complicated and often contentious desegregation plans, often monitored by federal district courts. The Indianapolis public school system, whose jurisdiction was in the heart of the city proper, was linked for the purposes of integration with some adjacent white townships in Marion County, which otherwise had a merged government with the city. Despite township resistance to their inclusion in court-ordered busing, approximately seven thousand African American students from the city were bused in the early 1980s to the suburban districts. None of the white township students were bused the other way. Over the next decade, enrollments in the city system declined precipitously as the economy unraveled. As in other urban areas undergoing massive demographic changes, racial integration in Indianapolis often seemed elusive.

As white student numbers declined but black, Hispanic, and, in some cases, Asian populations increased in numerous cities, the courts allowed districts to experiment with different ways to integrate their systems. Some established magnet schools, similar to the specialized high schools that had long existed in New York and some other big cities. These schools emphasized the performing arts, math or science, or other curricular themes or approaches in an attempt to attract students voluntarily, without coercion from school boards or court edicts. Sometimes officials paired schools from different neighborhoods and bused children in ways that guaranteed a more diverse racial mix. Most districts used a combination of approaches, from voluntary transfers to quotas, to seek the often elusive goal of integrated schools. But the public mood and federal power had shifted decisively away from the heady years of the Great Society.

Demographic changes, which had led to the deepening divide between suburb and city after World War II, continued to alter the American landscape. The poverty of mostly non-white inner cities and relative affluence of largely all-white suburbs stood out as the major impediments to a more racially integrated society and school system. The period after 1973 witnessed rising inflation and unemployment, the oil embargo, and negative attitudes toward government, which only deepened after Richard Nixon's abuse of power finally forced his resignation. Throughout the decade, public opinion polls revealed that most people believed that the schools were in trouble. A solid majority of citizens supported back-to-basics curricula, higher standards, and better discipline. By 1980, the majority of state legislatures had passed laws requiring students to pass minimum competency tests, sometimes for grade-to-grade promotion, sometimes to receive a diploma. The road had been paved for the ascendancy of Ronald Reagan and a new era in American education.

Like Eisenhower, who favored a limited role for the federal government in domestic affairs but had preserved the New Deal, Reagan elevated the importance of markets over government but did not eliminate the Great Society. Title I of ESEA, the most expansive and expensive of all federal education programs, became Chapter I in 1981 under new legislation that emphasized block grants and more devolution to the states, but the program did not undergo substantial changes. Head Start did not disappear. During the 1980 campaign, Reagan had vowed to abolish the newly created Department of Education, established by Jimmy Carter in part as a reward to the NEA for its political support. In the end, however, Reagan simply cut its budget. Ironically, it became an effective tool of public relations and school reform, first through its 1983 report *A Nation at Risk,* and later through the prominence of William Bennett as secretary of education. During his tenure, states slightly increased academic course taking in public schools, and Bennett became an unofficial minister of morals, calling for more personal responsibility, higher standards, and improved test scores.

By demanding a more academic curriculum and tougher standards for all pupils to beat the Japanese and other foreign competitors, *A Nation at Risk* spoke to fears generated by the ongoing cold war and realities of economic decline. It also suited the conservatism of the age, which had been reacting against Johnsonian liberalism since the mid-1960s. Without question, postwar Americans had placed a tremendous amount of money and faith in the power of schools to improve the lives of individuals and reform society. Expectations generally rode on the coattails of postwar affluence, found most dramatically in the suburbs. Once it had ended legalized Jim Crow, the civil rights movement pressed for integration and then for more effective schools for the children of minorities and the poor. Having inclusive and high-quality schools was the great impossible dream of the postwar era.

While *A Nation at Risk* became the most talked about educational document of the time, some prominent policy makers and educators pointed out that promising too much, common among reformers of every political persuasion, had stirred a whirlwind of trouble. In his prominent book *High School* (1983), Ernest Boyer, the head of the Carnegie Foundation, criticized the lax teaching, "smorgasbord curriculum," and "decline of academic standards" in the nation's secondary schools. Arthur Bestor, he recalled, had once warned that it

CHAPTER EIGHT

Guardians of Tradition

Between the end of World War II and Ronald Reagan's ascendance to the presidency, progressives and traditionalists renewed their old battles for supremacy in the public schools. Once again, as in the antebellum period and the Progressive Era, both sides were on a collision course concerning curriculum, pedagogy, and academic standards. In the 1950s, people who had never read a word written by John Dewey heard his name shouted in angry school board meetings or learned secondhand about his ideas and supposed influence, for good or ill, in magazines and newspapers. To most professors of education and leaders of the profession, Dewey was something of a savior. His inspiration, they said, led to most of the great advances in the schools: the broadening of the curriculum, child-centered pedagogy, and practices ranging from team teaching to field trips. To many critics of the schools, the devilish work of the progressives had caused the nation's elementary and secondary schools to deteriorate. It was time to restore the basics, discipline, and order to the schools. These sentiments, uttered so passionately and so often by citizens in the 1950s, would never lose their appeal among moderates and conservatives in the coming decades.

Given the flurry of popular books and mass circulation articles that attacked the schools, progressive education was constantly in the news after the war. As the school superintendent of Richmond, Virginia, wrote in the *Atlantic Monthly* in 1954, the public generally regarded it as a dirty word. That same year, an author in *Commentary* discussed the current "Hot War Over Our Schools" and said that Dewey and his followers were at the epicenter of the latest strife between traditionalists and progressives. Even president Dwight D. Eisenhower blamed Dewey and the progressives for lax standards and growing permissiveness. Seeking security in a world of uncertainty, when the cold war generated fears of survival and the civil rights movement demanded justice for the oppressed, Americans in the postwar era again turned to the schools as a source of stability and a fulcrum for change.

As a result of rising expectations about education, school policy making remained tense from the age of Eisenhower to the Reagan era. As schools became more inclusive institutions and more closely linked in the public mind with adult success, they became more intimately associated with children's, and thus the nation's, future. Every postwar reform movement—whether championed by cold warriors or civil rights advocates, suburbanites or urban leaders, Johnsonian liberals or Reaganites—included far-reaching proposals for school improvement. Radicals and libertarians who endorsed "deschooling," which called for the weakening of compulsory education laws and the creation of innovative networks of learning outside of schools, caused a stir in some academic circles in the 1970s, but such views were disconnected from the mainstream of American life. For better or worse, whether during the long run of postwar affluence or the gloomy economy of the 1970s, the public generally heaped more obligations and expectations onto schools.

The more schools did, the more people complained, but that was inevitable because public schools had so many different responsibilities. Nineteenth-century reformers wanted schools to strengthen citizenship, assimilate immigrants, and enhance literacy and learning. Progressive Era activists in the cities promoted the teaching of more subjects as well as the use of public schools as agencies of reform, from feeding hungry children to helping a new wave of immigrants learn standard English and the pledge to the flag. Teaching children to read well, write well, and do their sums, and then instructing them in rudimentary knowledge about other basic subjects, was always easier said than effectively done. Moreover, large segments of the population—African Americans in the South, and children with special needs nearly everywhere—were marginalized or excluded from the system. Now, however, the schools were supposed to integrate society, teach everyone for more years of their lives, and increasingly attend to their emotional, vocational, custodial, and even academic needs. For teachers, it made for a long and very complicated workday.

The national debates that often echoed on the local level between traditionalists and a new generation of progressives had the potential to transform every intimate aspect of going to school. What should children study? How should they be taught? What standards should be applied for promotion and graduation? According to conservatives as well as liberal critics such as Arthur Bestor, child-centered zealots had their most powerful influence upon elementary schools, which anticipated a wider drift toward mediocrity as progressivism crept into the secondary schools. The education of young children had historically been the prime hunting ground of child-centered activists. From the time of Rousseau through the era of Pestalozzi, Froebel, and beyond, children were the great hope of these reformers. They believed that, unlike adolescents and adults, the little ones were malleable and when cultivated with love and care became well adjusted, informed, and happy individuals. That progressivism had made America's schools soft and destroyed teacher authority and classroom discipline had been heard before. Now the cold war, middle-class striving, and the civil rights movement elevated the place of schools in society. It added to the overall level of anxiety among the citizenry. Schools were already a common part of everyday life, but the further expansion of the system—the advent of the boomers and rise of previously excluded groups—brought even more scrutiny to the system.

Generalizing about the elementary schools of postwar America is complicated by their size, diversity, and complexity. In the 1949–50 school year, America had 83,718 school districts, enrolling over nineteen million students below high school in tens of thousands of buildings. Though they were rapidly disappearing, there were still nearly sixty thousand one-teacher schools in the countryside. Thirty years later, Jim Crow was legally dead and the enrollment figure was over twenty-eight million pupils; one-room schools numbered less than a thousand. Children with various learning disabilities were newly enrolled in the schools, sometimes mainstreamed in regular classrooms. As in the past, foreign visitors were impressed by the sheer magnitude of the American school system. They remained puzzled that so many schools across a vast land had so many things in common. After all, compared to Europe, where central ministries of education were often powerful, America's schools were under state and local control. While the federal role in education grew in some dramatic ways after World War II, Americans remained ambivalent about weakening state and local power. As a result, a separate, cabinet-level Department of Education was not established until 1979.

Throughout the postwar period, citizens worried a lot about education, and many believed that the schools were in a perpetual state of decline. Were they right, or had citizens confused change with decline, or not noticed anything familiar about schools? Had the latest waves of reform actually transformed curriculum, pedagogy, and the basic character of elementary schools?

In 1977, the *Elementary School Journal* published a coauthored article that dismissed hyperbolic claims about a revolution in the schools. The existence of some open classrooms, team teaching, and other innovations notwithstanding, it was an illusion, they claimed, to think that traditional school practices had disappeared. Reformers were still squared off in opposing camps, the traditional and the progressive. The former wanted the three Rs, drill, better discipline, accountability, tests, and more tests; the progressives talked endlessly about the growth, development, and welfare of the child. But schools were still pretty old-fashioned, as one observer noted: "Most classes still move on the bell; the majority of classrooms are closed; the division of students is still made largely on the basis of age or grade; the school year and the school day are still rigorously defined; conformity and discipline are still overly stressed; the teacher is still the dominant figure in the classroom; and the teaching-and-learning situation remains very much routinized." Had tradition triumphed in this age of reform?

There was a certain familiarity about elementary schools in postwar America that brought some comfort and predictability if not joy and excitement to the lives of many children. The era's students could expect a classroom with a teacher (almost always a woman) standing behind her desk in front of the blackboard, textbooks and workbooks galore, lines to stand in, wooden (later plastic) seats in a row, the joy of morning and afternoon recess, milk breaks (chocolate milk a plus), and the bolt for the door at the end of the day. Garrison Keillor's *Lake Wobegon Days* (1985) recalls memories of classrooms with faded portraits of Washington and Lincoln displayed like "an old married couple on the wall." Report cards had another coupling: letter grades in school subjects with comments on work habits, conduct, and citizenship. Teachers often began the morning with a short, nondenominational prayer (legal before the early 1960s) and the pledge to the flag (to which the Eisenhower administration added the words "under God"). By 1950, the school year averaged just under 180 days, which stayed relatively constant during the coming decades. It seemed like school never ended and that summer always slipped away.

For children in one-room schools, life was still an endless stream of recitations, of moving through textbooks as quickly as talents and ambitions allowed, of spelling bees (the popularity of which spread to urban schools as well), and of community school suppers with all the fixings. Life on the prairie, high plains, desert, or Appalachian hillside seemed a universe away from the worlds depicted in the movie houses showing *Blackboard Jungle* or *Rebel without a Cause*. No single image can capture the diversity of America's elementary schools in the 1950s: Mexican Americans in Texas and the Southwest striving in underfunded and sweltering schools, African Americans in the Jim Crow South in the remaining log-hewn shacks that whistled on windy days, the white middle classes in suburban temples of concrete and glass equipped with good libraries and film strips, movie projectors, and even black-and-white televisions.

How children experienced or remembered going to school differed from how the adults in authority understood its mission. The aims of elementary education had long been expansive, and professors of education and leading school administrators since the early twentieth century compiled an expanding catalogue of educational "objectives." The influential advocates of testing drawn from educational psychology usually emphasized anything that could be measured quantitatively. But the objectives were often so broad as to be meaningless and defied easy measurement. In 1953, the Russell Sage Foundation published a committee report that enumerated suitable aims for the modern elementary school. They included emotional development, ethical training, "social relations," aesthetics, and literacy. Training the mind had always taken a back seat to character training, and few school leaders ranked it as the prime function of education.

In 1956, Benjamin Bloom, a psychologist in the education department at the University of Chicago, published a famous taxonomy of objectives in various "domains," including the cognitive, affective, and psychomotor. He then devised categories of learning within these domains that students should master step by step as they climbed the ladder of accomplishment from the simple to the more complex. A generation of future teachers memorized the names of these domains for term papers and exams. Like many modern educationists, Bloom reduced learning into its innumerable parts and criticized age-graded instruction and student competition. Individuals, he said, should master material at their own pace and not be compared with others. He was neither the first nor last theorist to say such things, but the words of the experts were not always heard or heeded. As a national authority on elementary schools wrote in 1960 in the *Encyclopedia of Educational Research,* teachers often had tin ears about advice from learned educators, who seemed far removed from the classroom. "Unfortunately, many if not most teachers and staffs in the elementary school find great difficulty in translating overall statements of objectives defined in terms of the qualities of 'the educated adult,' the 'good democratic citizen,' or 'areas of competency,' into the activities of educational programs organized traditionally around bodies of subject matter." That is, teachers thought in terms of teaching reading, or geography, or science, thereby affirming traditional practices. Even a concrete reform—the end of age-graded instruction—contradicted common practice and was rarely pursued. Neither was the elimination of in-grade competition for the teacher's favor, gold stars, prizes, and the best report card.

Teachers politely nodded in agreement or quietly rolled their eyes when reminded of the noble goals of the elementary schools, whose mission included pupil "adjustment," the cultivation of good manners, character education, community pride, and patriotism. A contributor to an updated edition of the *Encyclopedia of Educational Research* in 1969 noted that the objectives were often phrased in "global, if not glorious terms—such as how to prepare the learner to become a constructive, participating member of his society." Who could disagree? In his national study of elementary education *A Place Called School* (1984), John Goodlad argued that as expectations grew in the postwar era, schools lost their clarity about their academic purposes. In 1980, California's rules and regulations for bilingual education filled forty-two pages, while the list of general elementary and secondary subjects took only two. National commissions, state departments of public instruction, professional organizations, and most districts had a growing list of goals and "behavioral objectives" (a favorite in the 1970s) for the elementary grades. They ranged from social, civic, and global awareness to self-realization.

The swelling expectations for new teachers in postwar America were reflected in their professional preparation. Leaders of the educational establishment—whose voices were heard in the major professional organizations and magazines and in the colleges and universities that trained teachers—had a reasonably clear consensus about what constituted an ideal teacher and school. Their voluble pronouncements about the nature of the child, the classroom, learning, and pedagogy made them relatively easy targets for anyone who thought schools should primarily train the mind and raise standards, at least for some children. The public schools, leading educators never tired of saying, were for everyone. This was not aristocratic Europe, which maintained the highest standards for the few, but democratic America, where a place and an appropriate curriculum should exist for everyone. When their rhetoric soared, educators piously claimed that teachers taught children, not subjects.

Who were these teachers? The great majority of elementary school teachers at midcentury were women, and most had not majored in an academic subject in college. According to a 1957 study by the National Education Association, about a third of all elementary teachers had not graduated from college. Most who had graduated had a degree in education, and they were lampooned in *Time* and other national magazines as the weakest students on campus. After roughly two years of liberal arts courses, future teachers took various classes in education, student-taught, and applied for a state license. What their professors of education taught them about schools, as older normal school alumni could have told them, often seemed impractical or unduly critical of institutions in which as students they had felt successful. Few were likely to live up to the ideals set before them. But the degree was increasingly a requirement, a necessary hurdle on the path to future employment.

A composite portrait of an ideal elementary teacher emerges from the professional literature and readings in pedagogy courses in the postwar era. Budding teachers were taught that IQ scores, achievement tests, and experience proved that children were different; individual differences necessitated ability groups and tracks to address these differences through appropriate curricula and diverse pedagogical methods. They learned that, though they were a clever innovation of the nineteenth century and remained the basic form of classroom organization, age-graded classrooms defied everything psychologists and experts knew about individual differences. Also standard in teacher education was the idea that children learned best when teachers tapped their natural interest in learning, not through fear, grades, or other forms of extrinsic motivation, because unless they were interested in the material, pupils found learning boring, irrelevant, and meaningless. Finally, textbooks and the teacher, not experience and the student, too often occupied the center of most classrooms; teachers lectured and talked too much and did not listen to what children said or wanted to learn. More diverse teaching methods would stimulate student interest and end the stifling pattern of memorization and drill found in most elementary classrooms.

These assumptions suffused mainstream thinking and scholarship about elementary education. Some examples from a book that presented state-of-the-art thinking illuminate the point. In 1953, Harold G. Shane published an edited volume entitled *The American Elementary School*. Shane later became a chaired professor of education at Indiana University and was a prolific writer and theorist of "futures education." In this volume, John Childs, a philosophy of education professor at Teachers College, waxed enthusiastic about John Dewey and the new education, which "marks a great advance over the older 'listening' schools with their authoritarian methods of discipline, and their strict emphasis on memoriter processes and their endless reciting of lessons" that lacked any meaning for the students. One author from Northwestern University attacked age-graded instruction and common standards of achievement: "To attempt to make pupils reach such norms is to deny their uniqueness in ability, their growth stages and cycles of development, and their personal goals." In a coauthored essay, Henry J. Otto of the University of Texas and William M. Hadley, the superintendent of schools in Alice, Texas, resurrected and then buried the ghost of William T. Harris, who they felt had wrongly emphasized academic instruction for everyone. Instead, modern educators now shared a common faith in the goals of instruction: to teach pupils how to learn, solve problems, and engage in inquiry. Edgar Dale of Ohio State University, a national figure in the promotion of audio-visual instruction, said teachers had a naive faith in textbook knowledge. No one in Shane's book said that the principal goal of the school was training the mind, as Arthur Bestor asserted that very year in *Educational Wastelands*.

In sum, leading teacher educators in the postwar era preached the virtues of child-centered, not subject-centered, classrooms, and continued to emphasize individual differences. As in previous eras of reform, most researchers within the progressive fold believed that elementary schools more than high schools had been receptive to their ideas. Like John Dewey decades earlier, a few did worry about the excesses of child-centered rhetoric and behavior. Writing in the *Elementary School Journal* in 1956, Benjamin Brickman, a professor from Brooklyn College, explained that public schools had reached "a critical juncture in the history of elementary education . . . where some decision needs

to be made relative to the 'old' (traditionalism) and the 'new' (progressivism)."
Certain progressive notions seemed appealing, such as teachers who encouraged pupils to share in constructing the curriculum and guiding classroom
activities. To turn classrooms into laboratories of learning, reminiscent of
Dewey's school in Chicago, was also worth pursuing. So was experimenting
with new instructional methods. For example, "making school posters relevant
to a water shortage not only would further the development of artistic talent
but would also quicken the sense of civic duty." Given the current flood of criticisms of the schools, Brickman urged a rapprochement between the old and
the new. Even if some progressive ideas were exciting, they could lead to anarchy and permissiveness. More informality in the classroom, while welcome,
encouraged some teachers to pretend that the children were their equals in
power and authority. It was therefore unwise and impolitic, he wrote, for a
teacher to greet children on the first day of school with the invitation: "You
can call me Caroline."

Public opinion polls in the postwar period consistently showed that many
adults wanted schools to focus more on the basics and discipline, and critics
easily cited examples of the silly side of progressivism. Primers on elementary
education and articles in professional journals frequently highlighted the benefits of field trips, the importance of children's nonintellectual needs, and
vague goals such as personal fulfillment. According to the *Oklahoma Teacher,*
in 1956 the Garfield School in Lawton already sped down the road of life adjustment: it had a class in driver's education. "For the very young children, pie
plates are used for steering wheels, and classroom aisles are traffic lanes." This
sounded like fun but fed the notion that play, not work, had become the stuff
of modern education. Over the next generation, educationists continued to
disparage textbooks, uniform standards, and the typical practices of ordinary
schools.

In 1973, Arthur W. Foshay of Teachers College voiced a common complaint
that public schools and teachers were far too conservative. Everywhere "teacher-
centered instruction" based on textbooks prevailed despite contemporary demands for change. Schools were stubbornly attached to books, middle-class
norms, and old-fashioned reward structures and punishments for the students. Foshay questioned the value of homework, saying it was "in large part
a placebo for parents." He said that some suburban children studied more
hours than their fathers worked, a line that deserved an editor's red pen. Homework, he believed, "grows from no learning theory, except as the particular assignment may reflect some theory of memory, response, and reward." In other

words, teachers—usually, but not always, with considerable support from parents—wanted students to learn basic knowledge about a subject (and even those dreaded things called facts), so they traditionally assigned homework; children, in turn, completed assignments or took tests that documented if and how well they learned the material. Those who scored higher received higher grades.

Actually, Foshay was not against homework per se but traditional assignments: "There is a vast difference, both practically and theoretically, between the kind of homework assignment that consists of 'do page 33 in the textbook' and the kind that asks the child to 'interview his parents and his neighbors how the furnace works.'" Life adjustment was obviously alive and well at Columbia University. Knowing about a furnace may be useful, but why it trumped page 33 was unclear. Professional educators had long ridiculed textbooks and tradition, and they had a romantic view of practical skills and trades that were nowhere in evidence in the halls of academe, except among the janitorial staff.

That professors in schools of education expounded upon their beliefs through lectures, published scholarship, or assigned readings in their courses added no small irony to the situation. But this was also nothing new. Recall that Pestalozzi's disciples could not clone the charisma of the great master (who confused even some of them), so they wrote primers on object teaching. Froebel's acolytes, too, often tried to follow the great teacher's step-by-step progression of "gifts" and "occupations," producing numerous sectarian squabbles. Most college classrooms remained teacher centered, whether in the arts and sciences or in the education schools. Professors dominated group discussions, even when everyone began sitting in a circle (an arrangement reminiscent of old photographs of kindergartens). By the early 1960s, mainstream progressive thinkers in teacher education nevertheless urged teachers to promote inquiry and discovery in the classroom, usually linking this to the philosophy of John Dewey, whose name was invoked to support just about anything except an academic curriculum. Anyone familiar with the origins of progressivism recognized this as old wine in new bottles, a fresh draft of the view that the child and the learning process took precedence over everything else. Inquiry and discovery received a further boost from the national curriculum projects of the 1950s and 1960s and especially from cognitive psychology.

The revival of the progressive notion that inquiry, discovery, and "higher order" thinking skills should guide instruction emerged from many sources in the 1950s and 1960s. Bestor's call for the restoration of the liberal arts and higher standards for everyone had horrified most professors of education. The attacks on progressive education and loud complaints about public schools after Sputnik were also alarming. But the new curriculum projects, while centered in the arts and science departments in major universities, were more palatable. The academic researchers devising the new curricula were primarily interested in subject matter content, which led them to write and sponsor new textbooks, initially in such areas as mathematics, physics, and biology, to replace outmoded approaches. Given the heavy reliance of most teaching on textbooks, replacing the old ones was necessary if the researchers were to have any impact on schools.

The reform-minded professors from the academic departments were less threatening to professional teacher educators for one basic reason: they shared a progressive ethos about teaching. As John Goodlad perceptively explained in 1966, "the current curriculum reform movement is marked by an updating of content, a reorganization of subject matter, and some fresh approaches to methodology in fields traditionally taught in the schools. It is not simply a return to the Three R's. Nor is it a rejection of John Dewey and progressive education." But it was discipline centered, not child centered. The physicists, biologists, and mathematicians were more interested in subject matter than teacher educators, but their mutual fascination with the process of learning made them very appealing to each other. The "new physics," "new math," and later innovations in the social sciences and humanities did not sanction old-fashioned memorization and drill but discovery, inquiry, problem solving, and complex thinking skills. Moreover, the curriculum reformers brought status to the study of education, helping to elevate its national importance after Sputnik. They shared the wider mood of rising expectations, promising students the intellectual tools to understand the very structure of the academic disciplines.

The pivotal book in cognitive psychology that promised such remarkable results appeared in 1960, Jerome Bruner's *The Process of Education*. It became all the rage in schools of education. Born in New York City in 1915, Bruner was educated at Duke and Harvard, where he received his Ph.D. in psychology. Joining the psychology department at Harvard, he and a colleague opened the Center for Cognitive Studies. Bruner's scholarship challenged the dominant behaviorist trends of twentieth-century psychology, whose greatest legacy was testing and measurement. In contrast, his research focused on understanding how people construct meaning and understand themselves, their culture, and the world. Like the new curriculum planners, Bruner held views that were compatible with older progressive notions. Battered on all sides by critics who blamed them for Sputnik and low standards of achievement, educational leaders and scholars welcomed his rejection of conventional norms about how children learned. Traditional education was based on a fixed curriculum, on a sequential and hierarchical ordering of subject matter, and on memorization and recall. Like progressives of the past, Bruner and other cognitive psychologists rejected these notions as timeworn and dysfunctional.

"In September 1959," Bruner explained, "there gathered at Woods Hole on Cape Cod some thirty-five scientists, scholars, and educators to discuss how education in science might be improved in our primary and secondary schools." Bruner had chaired the conference, sponsored by the prestigious National Academy of Sciences and National Science Foundation, and it provided the inspiration for *The Process of Education*. Ten of the participants at Woods Hole—the largest single group—were from the field of psychology, five each from mathematics and biology, four from physics, the rest from a sprinkling of other fields. There were two experts on cinematography and only three on education. Seen as the key to a thriving economy and a strong national defense, science was the focus of the conference, but the cross-fertilization of ideas from the various disciplines and areas of study enabled Bruner to reflect more broadly on a theory of learning.

The opening lines of Bruner's influential volume evoke optimism and high hopes. "Each generation gives new form to the aspirations that shape education in its time. What may be the emerging mark of our own generation is a widespread renewal of concern for the quality and intellectual aims of education—but without abandonment of the ideal that education should serve as a means of training well-balanced citizens for a democracy." Honoring democracy and high achievement in practice required a conjurer's art. Bruner, however, quickly showed his hand. Like James B. Conant, Bruner emphasized the education of the gifted and talented, specifically of the "top quarter of public school students" who he believed provided the basis for the "intellectual leadership" of the coming generation. Whether studying science or any other subject, however, the best and brightest pupils should not simply memorize facts and store away knowledge for later use; rather, they needed to understand the structures of academic disciplines. Like professors on campus, whether working in laboratories or libraries, students needed to think like professionals. Anyone studying history, for example, needed to learn the ways of an historian.

Bruner said many things in his slim volume that appealed to the educationists. Cognitive psychology emphasized that children were a dynamic part of the learning process, and this was also a guiding belief of progressive education. Bruner also criticized age-graded instruction for undermining respect for individual differences and praised intrinsic motives for study over extrinsic ones, affirming mainstream pedagogical thinking. Politically, Bruner's book reflected cold war concerns. Like Conant and innumerable political leaders and educators, he underscored education's contribution to national security and the centrality of public schools in preserving a meritocratic social order. The late bloomers and bright but poor children would not be left behind. But Bruner did not rock the social class boat too hard. "Questions about the enrichment and the special handling of gifted students," Bruner assumed, "will doubtless persuade the more enlightened and wealthier schools to modify current practices." Since most children identified as gifted were not from poor families, this would hardly rattle the most comfortable classes. Bruner also soothed the consciences of readers by immediately adding that "we can certainly ill afford as a nation to allow local inadequacies to inhibit the development of children born into relatively poor towns or regions." Written at a time when proposals for national aid to the schools promised more opportunity for everyone, appeals to fair play hardly offended anyone.

Bruner and other cognitive psychologists helped nurture a generation of teacher educators who shared the hopefulness of the era, providing them with a theory at odds with traditional notions about learning. It was inspiring to read his famous, much-quoted claim that "any subject can be taught effectively in some intellectually honest form to any child at any stage of development." While as vague as the idea of teaching about the "structure" of a discipline, it sounded more glamorous than being associated with schools that taught the humdrum basics. Nothing so prosaic here. Most importantly, Bruner and the curriculum reformers helped educators salvage progressive ideals from the assaults of outspoken critics such as Arthur Bestor. What remained less certain was whether the public and its schools would ride this new wave of progressivism. Would teachers stop asking children to address the subject matter on page 33?

If a stranger without any personal knowledge about education arrived in America in the early 1970s and began reading the latest proposals for reform, she could easily see that a pedagogical revolution was both imminent and inevitable. Future teachers were reading John Holt's *How Children Fail* (1964), Herbert Kohl's *The Open Classroom* (1968), A. S. Neill's *Summerhill* (1970), Charles Silberman's *Crisis in the Classroom* (1970), and any number of stirring and often angry personal accounts of the urban school crisis. Reform-minded professors taught their students about the progressive infant (primary) schools of Britain, where the child was king, and about the cognitive revolution in how children learn, the death rattle of the old system of "drills and skills." Not far from campus, future teachers might visit an open classroom where informality reigned, or the local alternative high school, the choice for disgruntled or failing students. The cultural revolution emanating from the civil rights and antiwar movements was being felt everywhere. These were the educational expressions of political radicalism and community activism.

Two bestsellers in 1970, Alvin Toffler's *Future Shock* and Charles Reich's *The Greening of America*, painted a future of constant change, where the old order was rapidly fading, as Bob Dylan sang in "The Times They Are A Changin'." Nothing familiar seemed likely to survive. "We have to cut ourselves off from the old ways of thinking, of feeling, of adapting," said Toffler, a former editor of *Fortune Magazine*. "We have set the stage for a completely new society and we are now racing toward it." The signs of change were ubiquitous. Geographic mobility was a nationwide trend; a third of the members of the National Society for Programmed Instruction changed their addresses in one year. Parents anticipated a world of test tube babies, with the right IQs genetically guaranteed. As currently organized, public schools, based on corporate models, were out of sync with the consumer culture. If the schools did not provide more educational choice and curricular freedom, the market would do so. Adapt or disappear. According to Reich, America was entering a new stage of consciousness. Thus the traditional regime of the schools—tests, memorization, competition—was an anachronism. The meritocracy only produced compliant recruits for "the industrial army" while teachers destroyed children's imagination, joy, and natural eagerness to learn. Yet Reich did not call for a socialist revolution. Like most reformers, he concluded that the "central American problem might be defined as a failure of education." America needed "education for consciousness" to promote "transcendence, or personal liberation."

This age-of-Aquarius rhetoric should not be confused with the realities of most schools. Without question, schools in 1950 and 1980 were hardly the same: the civil rights movement had ultimately broken the back of Jim Crow, leading to many integrated classrooms; open classrooms were not unknown;

the idea of school choice gained in popularity (especially among conservatives hostile to the public schools); and special education became more significant than anyone could have predicted. And yet many essential aspects of schools remained unchanged. As the French historian Fernand Braudel once wrote, the hurricane that roils the ships at sea masks the more stable calm near the ocean floor.

Educational researchers who lived in the postwar era and had spent years visiting and studying schools were frequently surprised by the remarkable continuity in their organizational structure and classroom practices. Throughout the period, most elementary classrooms were self-contained, taught by a single teacher, usually a woman, sometimes helped by a part-time volunteer. The teacher taught most subjects, though there were sometimes specialists who taught music or physical education or worked with children with identified learning problems, such as in speech and hearing. Average class size dropped from 29 students in 1961 to 25 twenty years later. Other changes came from the Great Society, including pull out (ESEA, Title I) compensatory reading programs in which poor children were taught outside of regular classrooms by special teachers. Additional federal legislation in the 1970s guaranteed the rights of disabled children to gain entry to and additional services in local schools.

Elementary school teachers usually organized most classes into three ability groups, from high to low, based on reading proficiency and other factors. In theory, children in each group would have different reading assignments and receive a different kind of instruction; in reality, children in the slower groups read the same material, had more didactic instruction, and often mastered less, frequently falling behind higher achieving peers. Moving from lower to higher ability groups was uncommon. For schools with sufficient numbers of students (more common as one-room schools declined and more districts consolidated), there were multiple classes of the same grade, as the brightest and slowest separated into different rooms. The low ability groups typically formed the basis for the general and vocational tracks in high school; the higher ability groups, which had the most middle- and upper-class children, merged into the college preparatory or academic stream. That poor and non-white children were overrepresented in the lowest ability groups and tracks led to frequent criticisms, occasional lawsuits by the 1960s, and some movement toward more heterogeneous grouping in some schools. But age-graded instruction and ability grouping were mainstays of most elementary schools.

John Goodlad, a prolific author who began writing about elementary schools in the 1950s, frequently commented on the power of tradition. In 1959, he and Robert Anderson coauthored *The Non-Graded Elementary School*, with the following dedication: "To our children, in the hope that *their* children will come to know graded schools only through their history books." The authors explained that age-graded classes were only justified on administrative, not pedagogical grounds—they were a convenient and efficient way to manage children. They said this arrangement harmed many children who could not meet common academic standards. Even by first grade, children's measured abilities in various subjects differed enormously; the gap only widened the longer children stayed in school. It was a myth that a fifth grade teacher taught fifth grade students: in particular subjects, some pupils performed like average first graders, others like ninth graders. Goodlad and Anderson concluded that "American public education is essentially a conservative enterprise," and "the citizenry seems to react more nervously to changes in school practices than to many other kinds of social change." In the coming decades, some districts organized multi-aged or nongraded alternatives, but the age-graded classroom proved fairly impregnable.

Since the 1920s, schools had increasingly promoted a higher percentage of children, though the practice varied enormously from district to district and even within schools in the same district. Goodlad and Anderson discovered that some schools passed every pupil, while others in extreme cases (probably in classes with more poor students) held back a third of the class, especially in the earliest grades. The trend, however, was toward more promotion across the board. One of the nation's leading experts on the subject, Henry Otto, and Dwain M. Estes claimed that in 1950, 74 percent of public school children were in their "expected grades." About 11.5 percent were one year behind and 7.6 percent were two years behind. By 1960, Otto and others believed that "the present trend is away from the practice of failing students."

Studies of Chicago in the early 1960s by developmental psychologist Robert Havighurst found that high school teachers were particularly annoyed by the growth of social promotion, a practice that varied from school to school. Even without stated policies, subtle pressures from principals to pass more and more pupils were increasing. Havighurst quoted one teacher who said, "If students are alive at the end of the semester, they pass. Our principal comes around and tells teachers with few or no failures, 'You're doing a fine job.'" By 1960, most professors of education favored almost universal promotion. For decades, their research claimed that those held behind did not benefit much academically or socially but frequently developed a syndrome of failure. Once relatively common, repeating a grade became a stigma. The overall trend seemed to be, when in doubt, pass the children. Even in 1960, however, an estimated one to three million elementary school children had to repeat a grade. Failure rates shot up again for minority students especially after 1980, when standardized testing grew more influential. A U.S. Department of Education study showed that in 1988 about 30 percent of minority students in eighth grade "had repeated at least one grade."

Whether they passed or failed, students born after World War II lived through a tumultuous age. Yet scholars found remarkable continuity in many school practices. In 1970, for example, Goodlad and a team of researchers published a study based on observations of 150 classrooms in 67 schools, which included a mix of institutions, though more were urban than not. The researchers wrote that, at the time, "magazines of national scope, the daily press, and many books have proclaimed a revolution in the schools." What he and his colleagues found was something less than a new world in the making. Schools in different places seemed to follow almost identical practices. Age grading had not disappeared. In the classroom, teachers talked, children listened. "Rather than probing, seeking, inquiring, children were predominantly responding and covering. Even when using the material of curriculum projects presumably emphasizing 'discovery' methods, pupils appeared bent on covering the content of textbooks, workbooks, and supplementary reading material."

If the education revolution simply needed a bit more time, the 1970s proved inhospitable. The economy deteriorated after 1970, public opinion polls said that the number one problem in the schools was discipline, minimum competency tests caught the approving eyes of most state legislatures, and back-to-the-basics lost none of its sheen. The U.S. Supreme Court had banned state-sponsored prayer in the schools in the early 1960s, a decision that proved extremely unpopular and was widely ignored in many schools, especially in rural areas and in the South, which was becoming increasingly conservative and Republican. A large majority of adults consistently favored a constitutional amendment allowing school prayer, which Ronald Reagan endorsed in his campaign speeches.

Traditional school practices proved difficult to alter, especially in conservative times. After observing over a thousand classrooms and studying many facets of elementary education, Goodlad published his magnum opus, *A Place*

Called School (1984). While noting, like other scholars, that elementary school teachers used more varied teaching methods than their counterparts in high schools, he found that conformity ruled. Despite some exceptions, there was an "extraordinary sameness of instructional practices" in most classrooms. "Inside the classrooms we observed, teachers lectured and questioned, students listened, textbooks were the most common medium for teaching and learning—there was much pedagogical conformity." A closer look at the elementary school curriculum and pedagogy in the postwar era reveals that traditional practices endured in the typical classroom.

From the 1950s through the 1970s, public opinion polls showed that teaching the basics enjoyed widespread support among adults, including parents. When Gallup asked them in 1955 whether the schools paid "enough attention" to the teaching of reading, 48 percent said no and 39 percent said yes, the remainder lacking an opinion. When asked if reading was taught not as well as or better than in the past, the margin was smaller, but 41 percent still said "not as well" while 36 percent said "better." In 1980, after a decade of public clamor for the basics, 61 percent of parents (and 72 percent of non-parents) claimed that "not enough" attention was being placed on the three Rs. The public also believed (without the benefit of "learning theory") that children should work diligently on their lessons. Questioned in 1975 about whether elementary school children "work too hard in school and on homework, or not hard enough," only 5 percent said pupils worked "too hard," and 28 percent thought they worked about "the right amount." But 49 percent answered "not hard enough." When asked a year later to rank what would most "improve the quality of public school education overall," "basic skills" (51 percent) topped the list, followed by "stricter discipline" (50 percent).

Polls have their limitations: the phrasing of a question can skew responses, and many pertinent questions of historical interest were never asked. They still help reveal what citizens valued and expected of schools, regardless of whether their opinions were based on solid knowledge, hearsay, or ignorance. Whether parents favored discovery, inquiry, and problem solving is unknown. But the mastery of fundamental subjects, especially the language arts and mathematics, had strong and long-running public sanction. While leading educationists spoke out loudly against drill and competition and focused on loftier aims than the basics, taxpayers and parents, while never of one mind on anything, frequently disagreed with the experts. This helps explain why dislodging familiar, everyday practices from the schools proved difficult.

How school days were organized also remained remarkably constant during the postwar period, which is fascinating given America's system of decentralized control. The school day was typically divided into blocks of time, often 45- to 60-minute segments, and the sequence of subjects often followed predictable patterns from district to district. For example, reading and arithmetic, the most difficult foundational subjects, were typically taught first thing in the morning. While Arthur Foshay of Teachers College disliked the heavy hand of tradition, he provided a succinct description of a typical classroom in 1973. The elementary school day, he wrote, "is often arranged on a declining plane: first language, then a recess; next, mathematics, followed by another long recess; then, the social studies, followed by lunch and a long rest." The afternoon brought more social studies and then art, recess, and some science. Textbooks predominated as well as teacher talk. Countless observers of elementary schools in the postwar era discovered very similar routines.

Despite the occasional lapse into courses in life adjustment—as in the example of driver's education in Oklahoma—most schools, like any institution, had a schedule, even if not followed perfectly. Studies showed that the language arts and arithmetic consumed considerable time. Poor reading and math skills, of course, had traditionally been the stumbling blocks to promotion in the elementary grades. A 1963 study of sixty-four metropolitan school districts explored how much time was spent daily in elementary schools (all grades below junior high school) on different subjects. The averages were: 60 minutes for reading; 45 minutes for arithmetic; 45 for social studies; 40 for English; 30 minutes each for science, physical education, and music; and 20 minutes for spelling. Art averaged under an hour per week, as did a few subjects such as health and handwriting. Other rituals—homeroom, announcements, collecting milk money, the occasional school assembly—surely detracted from formal instruction. Such a crowded schedule left little time for too many fads and frills or life adjustment.

The minutes spent on "basics" such as reading, arithmetic, English, and spelling constituted about 53 percent of the total instructional time. Since more time is spent on reading in the lowest grades, the figure would be higher there than the average for all of the elementary grades. Comparing time spent on teaching certain subjects with that in earlier historical eras is difficult. The names of subjects changed, the content certainly changed, and some subjects later regarded as essential (e.g., social studies) did not always exist, or, like science, were once novelties and not seen as fundamental to elementary school.

In addition, the persistence of public support for the basics highlights the power of tradition, but it is not self-evident what the phrase means or how society's expectations evolved over time. In the 1970s, pollsters regularly pointed out that citizens did not define "the basics" narrowly: it meant instruction in certain subjects but also behaving and respecting authority. After World War II, being poorly educated doomed many people to dead-end jobs, so attention to academic competence in the basic subjects was never far from public consciousness, even if most schools never strayed very far from emphasizing them. John Goodlad's study of over one thousand classrooms in the early 1980s concluded that about 54 percent of teachers' time was spent on reading, the language arts, and math, similar to what other researchers had earlier found.

What is taught is not always taught well, or learned. Certainly the growth of grade inflation beginning in the 1960s and widespread social promotion did not produce a satisfied public. The explanation for why the public often believes that schools are doing a poor job lies deeper. Any failure in young adults—the inability to fill out a form properly, sloppy handwriting, poor diction, poor work habits, a lack of common courtesies—often reflects poorly on schools. Whether that is fair, given all the influences that shape a person, is beside the point. Expecting more from schools leaves people perpetually unhappy, but also provides an outlet for the anger. It also allows citizens to not think about alternative explanations for school failure or reconsider their high hopes for what schools can reasonably accomplish.

Professional educators who wrote ad nauseam in the postwar years about the conservatism of schools found their own reasons to complain. They were not simply imagining that didactic teaching practices, schoolroom competition, report cards, and other time-tested features of the schools seemed impervious to nationally prominent movements to reform the schools, from the labors of academic reformers to those engaging in countercultural revolt. In more ways than one, elementary schools were the guardians of tradition.

The traditional curriculum, conventional methods of instruction, heavy reliance upon textbooks, and competitive pupils were all major challenges for reformers and campus-based professionals in the postwar era. In the very same issue of the periodical that called attention to the driver's education class for small children, a professor from Duke University complained that teachers everywhere failed to grasp new approaches to pedagogy. While he acknowledged that schools could not solve every social problem, from malnutrition to bad driving habits, he wrote that "the tradition and training of many elementary-school teachers are so deeply rooted that they find themselves drawn to subject-matter orientation. They teach spelling as if skill in spelling were important of itself, a kind of parlor trick, instead of teaching it as a means of communication. . . . They teach science as a kind of cookbook activity instead of seeing it as one of many ways of solving life's problems." Social studies and the other subjects also taught trivia, disconnected from children's lives.

Professional complaints from outside public schools were ubiquitous. In the official *Encyclopedia of Educational Research* published by the American Educational Research Association (AERA) in 1960, experts on the elementary schools could not find many pleasant things to say about them. One Wisconsin educationist said that classes were still divided into fixed time periods, the sequence of studies monotonously familiar, and home economics and manual training classes rare. Moreover, "in terms of time and emphasis, the reading school of yesteryear is still the reading school of today." Most of what the children learned, he said, was "meaningless," disconnected from their immediate lives and likely forgotten by the time they became adults. Another scholar reported that "teacher-centric" methods were universal. "Although research has failed to make a favorable case for the efficacy of the recitation, it is still widely used in schools." A study based on observations of two hundred classrooms concluded that "memorizing of subject matter in textbooks was the common method employed." Lecturing, which lacked any "research" to justify its value, remained more common than discussions with the children.

The new edition of the AERA encyclopedia in 1969 included articles that showed that despite innovative practices in some schools, they were much less common than one might expect in an era of tumultuous social change. Arno Bellack and other scholars found that the typical method of instruction was for the teacher to ask a question, leading to a student reply, and then a reaction by the teacher. Lectures, an efficient way to teach, prevailed, and so did pupil passivity, especially if teachers enforced a code of pupil decorum. As in past decades, pupils filled in workbooks, often sat quietly at their desks, and spent considerable time listening to other people, especially the teacher. Ironically, wrote one contributor to the *Encyclopedia*, "even the severest critics of the lecture method often find themselves lecturing." The lower ability groups, frequently dominated by poor and minority pupils, received the worst of this drill, drill, drill. Children in the higher ability groups, in contrast, had their share of this treatment but more often worked on projects to cultivate creativity and higher order thinking. Having better mastered the basics, they seemed more receptive to more advanced instruction.

These findings, based on extensive research, contradicted the assumptions of Bestor and kindred spirits in the 1950s and 1960s who believed that child-centered progressivism had actually transformed the typical elementary school classroom. Some observers thought it unlikely that child-centered progressivism was as all-powerful as many popular critics assumed. "Those who have written recently about the perils of progressivism," wrote one perceptive writer in *Look* magazine in 1957, "have had to go out of their way to find the beast. In visits to well over 100 classrooms, I did not find one where, for example, the pupils decided what they should study and how they should study it." Following Sputnik, the historian Oscar Handlin stood out among the crowd by defending John Dewey, blamed by many as having "destroyed the good old system and left American children illiterate basket weavers unprepared for the microscope and the cyclotron." Public schools, Handlin thought, simply had too many "mediocre and incompetent teachers," some of whom tried to behave like progressive teachers but lacked the intelligence or pedagogical skills. Inadequate teachers later became the common explanation when innovations such as the "new math" ran into trouble.

In the 1950s, many people had an opinion about progressive education and its influence, but few teacher educators or educational researchers believed that it had actually transformed the schools as much as it shaped pedagogical rhetoric. Professional education journals assailed the tyranny of textbooks, the dominance of the lecture, and the conservatism of the teaching staff who like the public were wed to the basics, social order, and routine. Various innovations, however, promised to improve instruction, from better audio-visual (AV) teaching aids to actual teaching machines and programmed instruction. Indeed, Bestor called the audio-visual movement the latest fetish in public education. School districts spent an estimated $20 million on new teaching aids by 1960, and AV equipment filled up closets and storage rooms. Visibly prominent in wealthy suburban districts, they hardly altered the main characteristics of the typical classroom. More tape recorders, record players, overhead projectors, movie projectors, and film strips—like maps, globes, and older teaching devices—helped break the monotony of the school day, but they never replaced the ubiquitous textbook. Moreover, many observers of classrooms soon noticed that extensive use of AV actually reinforced student passivity, notwithstanding the *Blackboard Jungle* scene in which hoodlums who move to the beat of rock and roll destroy one teacher's favorite jazz records.

In the 1950s and early 1960s, a new generation of teaching machines, a behaviorist's dream, also promised more individualized instruction. The baby boom had led to serious teacher shortages in many parts of the nation, fueling greater interest in the development of these machines. Major corporations and their subsidiaries as well as start-up companies invested millions of dollars in the new educational technology. The machines, which never became very popular with teachers, appealed to the lowest common denominator in instruction, teaching rote skills and basic facts in the various school subjects. Typically, pupils would sit in front of a machine, which dispensed basic questions about a subject as well as the correct answers. The questions and answers were stored on paper, cassette tapes, or sometimes electronically. To reply to a question, pupils pressed a button, pulled a lever, or wrote or typed an answer. Pupils received a quick response from the machine telling them if they had answered correctly; if so, they could proceed to the next question. Children could work at their own pace, receive regular positive reinforcement, and not have to take common exams with their peers, which critics of traditional schools said led to much discouragement and failure for the slower pupils.

The machines varied in terms of their design, cost, and practicality. The "Visitutor," available from Hamilton Research Associates in New Hartford, New York, weighed thirty pounds, fit on a standard school desk and, depending on the model, could cost anywhere from two hundred to five hundred dollars. To begin instruction, a pupil pressed a button to receive the first question, then pressed another button to select an answer among various choices, as in a multiple choice test. If the choice was correct, the pupil could proceed to the next question; if incorrect, the answer was revealed, and the pupil was supposed to write the correct answer on paper. The pupil thus corrected his or her own work and through repetition reinforced learning the right answer. Then, as an advertisement for the Visitutor explained in 1962, the student "begins the cycle anew by pressing the question button again." Another machine, the "Sakoda Sortcard Automated Tutor," in the same price range, taught basic skills such as the multiplication table. To determine if one knew the right answer to seven times eight, a student selected one of four levers. Answers were stored in the machine on decks of cards. If the correct lever was pulled, the card was "ejected from the deck," and the student could then work on the next problem. But the card did not move if the student chose incorrectly and she could not proceed until the correct answer was chosen.

An expert on the history of experimental psychology, Arthur I. Gates, emphasized the great potential of teaching machines in 1961. Ironically, he did so after explaining that most past attempts at using them had failed! Teaching aids were nothing new; neither was American fascination with machines and the prospect of greater efficiency. Blackboards, maps, and globes were already common in many schools by the mid-nineteenth century. In the early 1900s, "projection lanterns, tachistoscopes and other quick-exposure apparatus, phonics wheels and word ladders, flash cards and display racks were hoary with age when the motion picture, the flash meter, and a variety of other mechanical devices appeared." Then behavioral psychologist B. F. Skinner built his famous teaching machine to advance individualized instruction in the late 1950s. It all sounded great, but group instruction in graded classrooms reigned.

Teachers usually adapted ideas about individualized instruction and technology to their own traditional practices. For example, elementary school workbooks rose in popularity by the 1930s, allowing students to work alone, at their own pace. They fit well into a classroom environment in which the memorization of facts and rote material was the norm, and they also drew upon the example of the earliest teaching machines. Sidney Pressey, an educational psychologist at the Ohio State University who was heavily influenced by Edward L. Thorndike, invented rudimentary teaching machines in the early 1920s. However, these machines were cumbersome and expensive compared with pencils and paper and rarely used by teachers. Workbooks were another story. They were a simpler, cheaper, and more convenient way to drill pupils in facts and reinforce basic subject matter through a process of filling in the blanks. Progressive educators naturally attacked them for reinforcing pupil passivity and ignoring higher order skills. The new generation of teaching machines in the 1950s promised to make the child a less passive part of the educational process, but they were in fact another example of mechanical, lifeless instruction in the basics. As children pushed buttons or pulled levers on the machines in classroom demonstrations, they resembled chickens pecking at seed in the barnyard. The analogy is not frivolous. Edward L. Thorndike, a father of behaviorism, used chickens in his early experimental research on learning. Beyond their other limitations, teaching machines could not dislodge age-graded classes, which could repel nearly any instructional interloper.

Throughout the 1960s, behaviorism was challenged directly by cognitive psychology and the shared theories of learning underlying the new curriculum reforms emanating from arts and science departments. The countercultural movement that arose during the decade was also light years from behaviorism and promised to revolutionize education through open classrooms in alternative education. But the long-range impact of these various reforms was never as dramatic as some people believed. Many innovations proved either short-lived or were absorbed into the system without fundamentally altering the curriculum, classroom instruction, or the basic character of public schools. Although they had different historical origins, both the curriculum reformers and the advocates of alternative education faced similar difficulties related to social class bias and the perennial problem of finding enough suitable teachers.

Many of the new curriculum reformers had initially focused on secondary schools, which had more status in the eyes of professors than the education of young children, and the best-known projects were classic top-down innovations, for, but not by, classroom teachers. The innovations were largely conceived on university campuses. Tens of thousands of teachers attended workshops to help implement these curricular improvements, which promised to bring out the creative, inquiring impulses buried within students. As early as 1964, John Goodlad, in a book entitled *School Curriculum Reform in the United States,* saw trouble on the horizon. In math and science education, for example, there were unrealistic expectations of elementary school teachers. Recall that most teachers had not majored in an academic subject but usually taught all of them. "In elementary schools," Goodlad wrote, "teachers with backgrounds in science and mathematics constitute a species that is about as rare as the American buffalo." He also noticed that the pilot programs using innovative materials usually appeared in wealthier districts, in the suburbs more than in rural areas or inner cities. Coming from prestigious universities, curriculum reform, he concluded, was *"essentially a middle- and upper-middle class movement."*

Other critics were less gentle as they described the poor preparation of teachers, quickly seen as unlikely candidates to pull off major reforms. In a 1966 *Esquire* article entitled "Could You Pass the Third Grade?" Martin Mayer correctly explained that the aim of the curriculum reforms was to teach pupils how to think. Here was the problem: "Miss Smathers (you remember Miss Smathers) is still there, standing at the front of the classroom, trying too hard and talking too much." The administrators at her school had advanced degrees in education, another bad omen. Understandably, Mayer said, the university-based reformers tried an end run around the problem. "Increasingly, the reformers have been turning to films, both for the teacher-training and in some cases as a substitute for activities hard to introduce to the classroom." With money now flowing freely in the form of grants and publishing contracts, Mayer predicted a deluge of second-rate scholars ready to climb aboard the bandwagon, helping the young understand the joy of discovery and the "structure" of the disciplines. And Miss Smathers probably had tenure.

Whole swaths of the school population were untouched by the curriculum reformers, whose labors centered in better-off districts. Reformers everywhere still faced those mere mortals called teachers and the usual tug of war with tradition. More than a few scholars studying the implementation of the new curricular reforms noticed that teachers relied on textbooks, printed materials, and films and that they and their students often searched for the right answer in class, not for the mysterious "process" of education. Jerome Bruner's involvement in social studies reform, through the controversial "Man: A Course of Study" (MACOS) curriculum, was also not an altogether happy one, since its materials were removed from many schools after critics said they promoted cultural relativism, not time-tested American and moral values. In the end, progressive educators, cognitive psychologists, and curriculum reformers left no more than a toeprint on the landscape of learning.

The fate of the curriculum reformers was shared by the devotees of another celebrated innovation, the open classroom. Open classrooms gained national acclaim in the late 1960s and early 1970s, the high tide of cultural radicalism. They made the news more than they remade American education. Forming the larger context for reform, the peace movement, black power, and the New Left as well as flower power and a new romanticism all sought to reshape American society wholesale. Part of this larger countercultural impulse, open classrooms sought an old progressive goal—more freedom for the child—but should not be confused with other alternative experiments. Civil rights activists had created a small number of street academies and alternative private schools for the inner city poor throughout the 1960s. Separate from the public system, these schools were privately funded, sometimes attracting some foundation or small government grants, and they tried to establish strong political ties to parents and the local community. By the early 1970s, a tiny number of the white middle and upper classes also opted out of the system, retreating to the hills from Vermont to California and placing their children in schools that embraced arts and crafts and "doing your own thing." The parents sought personal fulfillment and inner peace and were often less engaged in civil rights and overt political struggle. By 1972, enough alternatives to regular public schools existed that two prominent books documented the phenomenon: Jonathan Kozol's *Free Schools* and Allen Graubard's *Free the Children*. Both traced the origins of various alternative forms of education and emphasized their enormous diversity in terms of intent, clientele, and working nature. Whether they dreamed of consciousness raising, political struggle, revolution, or an escape from bourgeois conformity, the counterculture set its sights on new forms of freedom.

Open classrooms, a tame expression of alternative education, focused on change within the public schools and suffered from the problems endemic both to overpromising and to child-centered education. The reform owed its popularity to the times generally, and specifically to the British infant schools, so celebrated in important articles by Joseph Featherstone in the *New Republic* in 1967. The journalist Charles Silberman, a longtime editorial staff member at *Fortune* magazine, notably publicized their virtues in his 1970 bestseller *Crisis in the Classroom*. Recounting the child-centered, flexible, humane, informal teaching practices in Britain, Silberman condemned the regular American public schools for their boring, lifeless, "mindless" character. But a new reforming impulse was emerging that offered real prospects for change. Vito Perrone, for example, ran an innovative teacher education program in North Dakota that promoted pedagogical methods reminiscent of Pestalozzi and the pantheon of progressive theorists. Like pilgrims who once visited Pestalozzi's model schools or Froebelian kindergartens, many reform-minded educators traveled to England to see the future. By the early 1970s, numerous magazines had feature stories on infant schools, open classrooms, and similar educational innovations.

Open classrooms were yet another effort to transform the schools through progressive teaching practices. Though the Coleman report, early evaluations of Head Start and ESEA, and the nation's political turn to the right discouraged liberals and radicals, they managed a final burst of energy for reform before the doldrums of the 1970s set in. Starting with elementary schools, the usual site for pedagogical experimentation, open classrooms appeared in a number of school systems across the United States. While theories and practices varied, they all emphasized more child-centered instructional practices, flexible learning environments, and less overt authority, either in the office of the teacher or in traditional curricular materials. A number of new schools were built and old ones remodeled to usher in the new age. No more seats lined up in a row or teachers (now sometimes called facilitators) standing in the front of the room. To enhance the child's freedom, these classrooms had learning centers, pods, moveable partitions between rooms, more openness in floor plans, and greater freedom of movement for the child. Newsletters, books, and formal and informal networks emerged to educate novice teachers and share innovative ideas.

A funny thing happened on the way to this revolution. Complaints soon arose about chaos and anarchy in the classroom. While some members of the educational counterculture openly praised John Dewey, many seemed unaware of his warnings about the permissiveness and aimlessness of many child-centered schools of his day. They ignored Herbert Kohl's similar concerns in *The Open Classroom* (1968). A number of factors contributed to the decline of open classrooms and return to tradition. Back-to-the-basics was in vogue, the testing movement accelerated, and school budgets were in trouble as the economy stagnated. At the outset, some radicals predicted failure for anyone who tried to fix the public schools. For over a decade a host of romantic, radical, and left-wing writers had relentlessly attacked the schools as a tool of social order that credentialed people for an unequal, racist state. How could freedom exist in a system whose raison d'être was social control?

Jonathan Kozol, for example, who had opened a private alternative school with minority parents in Boston, wrote a searing indictment of the flower children in the countryside and the liberal-minded suburbanites who favored alternative classrooms within the existing school system. In *Free Schools* he questioned the purpose of creating "alternatives within the system" when the system itself oppressed the poor and perpetuated capitalism. Kozol criticized those who escaped to rural retreats or stayed in the city but dropped out of the political struggle. Regarding alternative curricula, he doubted that Harlem really needed "a new generation of radical basket weavers." He called the British infant approach and its imitators within America's schools "antiseptic little opiates," a fake radicalism that shielded privileged elites from confronting their own complicity in the existence of poverty. These reformers were not rebels, as they might think, but allies of a corrupt system.

With the countercultural movement that produced alternative schools and open classrooms came a revival of many themes associated with child-centered education and progressivism: the evils of textbooks, tests, competition, grades, and report cards, and the failure of the schools to nurture the individual. Reformers had been trying to undermine traditional practices since the days of Pestalozzi and Froebel, and open classrooms ran into familiar difficulties. Finding enough suitable teachers and sympathetic administrators was a problem. While some campuses began small training programs to prepare teachers, running a classroom in a fundamentally new way was also not easy. Many teachers and children had difficulty living with too much freedom. The open classroom movement was barely off the ground in 1972 when a contributor to the *Elementary School Journal* concluded: "We must face the reality of having at least some rather unexceptional leaders working with many rather unexceptional teachers in most rather unexceptional schools."

The *Elementary School Journal* occasionally published articles on open classrooms over the course of the decade, but interest in them faded in a climate of rising concerns over test scores, discipline, and the basics. Reports also circulated of open classroom teachers reverting to question-and-answer pedagogy, chalk and talk (if a blackboard was available), and drill. In 1973, two contributors to the journal—a teacher and community college professor—tried to provide some guidance on how to convert traditional classrooms. They wrote that in the typical school "every child has the same assignment; every child sits at his desk; every child's desk faces the front of the room." Open classrooms could change that. But in the same issue of the journal another article described four open classrooms for African American children in Kansas City that were noisy, chaotic, and without the right instructional materials. And, of course, there was the matter of the teachers. "Teachers," the authors of this essay emphasized, "have their own hang-ups with open education because of their past training in closed education. Often teachers simply do not know how to capitalize on the students' interests. Teachers are stymied by narrow, rigid conceptions of the learning process. They have not been sufficiently freed from their past."

The *Architectural Record* that same year published a lengthy article on Columbus, Indiana's new Mt. Healthy School, built on the open classroom plan. The local school board had long resisted anything but traditional education, but finally relented and approved the construction of this particular elementary school. Classroom photos revealed open space, not eggcrate rooms, and tables with chairs, not seats lined up facing the front. Locating the front of the room, in fact, was not simple. Oddly enough, however, a huge clock was the most imposing feature in one classroom, (though the room was missing that famous pair, Washington and Lincoln). While some photos showed the children stretched out on the floor doing their lessons, one showed them, incongruously, standing in line. Even though this was definitely not a regular classroom, in practice many open classrooms had to conform to some degree if they hoped to survive; largely attended by white middle-class and upper-middle-class children, they were often much less subversive than early proponents imagined.

Open classrooms were more mouse than lion. While attracting considerable attention in the press, they reached relatively few children. Efforts to open them in working-class schools typically failed. Pestalozzi decried the stubborn peasants who preferred catechisms over object lessons, and the modern working classes also seemed to prefer the basics over inquiry and order over freedom. Open classrooms served a small but socially important slice of the student body, but that hardly popularized the cause. In 1975, Gallup asked citizens whether they knew "what is meant by the 'open' school concept or idea." Only 30 percent of parents of public school children answered yes, and 56 percent said they didn't know. Of those who said yes, only 14 percent approved of open education. They were not asked if they would expose their children to it. By the end of the decade, architectural firms that had built some new-style buildings watched their business slow as elementary enrollments overall declined with the end of the baby boom, budgets tightened, and the new progressives receded from view. Open classrooms were often very noisy, annoying teachers in adjacent rooms, so in came the carpenters to replace thin partitions with solid walls. Teachers could lecture on well-worn carpeting as well as on the old hardwoods.

By the time Ronald Reagan was elected president in 1980, the countercultural revolution already seemed like a distant dream. Many of the alternative schools outside of the system had closed their doors, and open classrooms became one in a long history of reforms that promised much more than they could deliver. Most children had never experienced child-centered education, wherever they went to school. While open classrooms had been making news, a quiet but more significant revolution mostly went unnoticed in comparison to the counterculture of the 1970s. It had begun inauspiciously enough but was the final important development to shape elementary education in the postwar era.

✎

Addressing the education of children with identifiable physical, mental, learning, and other disabilities became one of the most explosive issues in public schools after World War II. Riding on the wave of the civil rights movement, which promised more educational access and inclusion for African Americans, enrollments exploded in "special education," a catchall phrase whose imprecision contributed to its controversial status. The first special education classes began in the late nineteenth century in northern cities, which opened segregated classes for previously excluded blind, deaf, and physically disabled children, who traditionally stayed home or were sent to state institutions. A handful of cities also had segregated classes for children who were truant or otherwise unmanageable in the regular classroom. With the rise of IQ testing, however, a new, genetics-based explanation for school failure emerged as more children were scientifically measured in relationship to each other. Those who struggled in school, either behaviorally or academically, were often given psychological and achievement tests, the results of which could lead to their isolation into separate classes.

Taught at first by teachers without much specialized training, these classes generally emphasized drill in basic skills. Arts and crafts, long a favorite of progressive educators, became a staple in special education, often on the dubious assumption that the mentally slow were more physically adept. Arthur Bestor wrote in 1955 that the education of the "slower" pupils (some of whom would be assigned to special education) was a scandal and reprimanded the schools for providing them with a watered-down curriculum; while he agreed that some children had such low IQs that they could not master a high-quality academic curriculum, 90 percent of all children could do so, he believed, if given enough time and enough support. Few people listened to him. Professional educators had long endorsed a differentiated curricula, reflected in ability groups and tracks, and the loudest voices in educational policy wanted more money spent on the talented few, the truly gifted. The curriculum of special education remained oriented around basic skills and reflected turn-of-the-century views. As a special educator from New Jersey wrote in 1956, these children really benefited from "learning by doing. Paints, crayons, wool and raffia, wood, clay, cardboard," looms, and workbenches were the essential ingredients.

Not everyone was convinced in the 1950s about spending more money on special education. Some experts said that these children, many of whom were still excluded from school, would drain precious money from normal children and the gifted. Many articles and books emphasized that the most neglected children in America were not the mentally retarded but the gifted, America's hope during the cold war. The best and the brightest—academics and other public intellectuals—were entering the highest corridors of power in Washington. Many of the curriculum reformers, experts on the high school such as Conant and cognitive psychologists such as Bruner, also pointed to the failures of the graded classroom, which forced teachers to teach to the average student, shortchanging the gifted. Hardly novel complaints, they took on special resonance after the public reaction to Sputnik. But higher achievement in math and science, considered necessary for national security, was not really secured, while special education programs for the lowest achievers enjoyed a generation of expansion.

Bruno Bettelheim, a psychologist and educator at the University of Chicago, wrote one of the most perceptive articles about education in the aftermath of Sputnik. He observed that while liberal policymakers urged racial integration they simultaneously favored intellectual segregation. Writing in *Commentary* in 1958, he said that northern white liberals wanted to obliterate the color line while replacing it with a hierarchical caste system based on intelligence. The movement to the suburbs was one way to ensure that their own children had a leg up on everyone. But gifted programs (and the new Advanced Placement programs in high school) promised middle- and upper-class whites (and some blacks who made it out of poverty) greater access to the highest-quality education. Despite all the Jeffersonian talk about how talent inhered in all classes, the poor were unlikely to benefit from gifted programs or the new curriculum projects. A new caste system was in the making, parodied so brilliantly in Michael Young's 1958 fantasy, *The Rise of the Meritocracy*. Bettelheim sarcastically asked why elite liberals were so worried: "Have these so-called gifted been winding up in the coal mines, have so few of them managed to enter Harvard, Yale, City College, or the University of Chicago?"

Complaints about the paucity of strong gifted programs for the talented few, usually from better-off families, never disappeared, and regular special education programs boomed after the war. Estimates varied about how many children had which disabilities or learning problems. A 1958 study of "special" students by the U.S. Office of Education estimated that 55 percent were speech impaired, 25 percent mentally retarded, and 6 percent gifted. Other categories included the blind, deaf, and "socially and emotionally maladjusted." Imprecise labels did not hurt the rise of special education programs; more experts yielded more categories, shifting diagnoses, and proposed solutions. Children with the same characteristics received one label in 1960 and a different one in 1980. Clearly, some children had a complex of problems not easily reduced to a single category.

Special programs grew rapidly after World War II. Advocates made emotional as well as logical appeals, and absorbing the language of the black civil rights movement, often took the high moral ground, trying to shame any opponents. Special education constituted under 1 percent of total public school enrollment in 1930, 2.5 percent by the time of Sputnik, and over 10 percent in 1980. This expansion came from the growth of programs outside of urban areas, the inclusion of previously excluded students, and the reclassification of those who earlier might have been streamed into the lowest ability groups, not into special education. Originally dependent on local funding, programs received state aid as legislatures routinely passed laws by the 1950s that required greater inclusion of children with special needs. Federal aid for children with disabilities and related conditions also grew in the 1960s and received a major boost from Public Law 94-142, signed reluctantly in 1975 by president Gerald R. Ford, who worried about more federal spending during a recession. Caps were placed on the federal share of its funding, which never proved sufficient, and the law required the admission of a wider range of children with special needs to the schools, mandating their education in "the least restrictive environment."

Defining such an environment, which required a formal agreement between parents or guardians and a child's school, often became a thorny issue. The perennial problem of determining who belonged in special education was also controversial. For example, the concept of learning disabilities first grew popular in the 1960s and later came to embrace ever larger numbers of children within the special education population. An essay published in 1992 explained that in the decade following the 1976–77 school year, the number of students labeled emotionally disturbed had increased by 36 percent and the number labeled learning disabled a whopping 142 percent. The label "mentally retarded" was seen as pejorative and the percentage of students with that description dropped by almost one-third. At a time when schools were still dealing with the prospects of racial integration, mainstreaming special education students into classes with students without disabilities further complicated the lives of teachers and administrators. Local practices varied, but children in special education were usually poorly integrated into the academic curriculum.

Special education was a perfect example of the rising expectations of society, as activists and parents lobbied for more opportunities for those often previously denied educational access or services. While it rode on the broad coattails of the civil rights movement, special education had long served as a "dumping ground" (a commonly used phrase in the literature) for poor and minority students. Poor children traditionally filled the lowest ability groups and tracks, but the rights revolution led more people to speak out on their behalf. In the 1960s, lawsuits were initiated against ability grouping and tracking programs, famously so in Washington, D.C., in the 1967 *Hobson v. Hansen* case, which forbade the practice locally. The placement of poor and minority children into lower ability groups and special classrooms hardly disappeared. In *Blaming the Victim* (1971), which includes an unsparing attack on liberalism and compensatory education, William Ryan notes how the labeling process perpetuated racial and class privileges. In New Haven, Connecticut, hardly the only example, the city integrated its schools in a common way. "'Culturally deprived' children were, of course, put in the low tracks" while the white professionals and middle classes generally dominated in the academic streams.

Not surprisingly, those who were labeled culturally deprived and suitable for compensatory education were also prime candidates for special education. Activists noticed that poor and minority children were overrepresented in the expanding special education programs, a phenomenon reinforced by the rise of state mandated standardized tests in the 1970s. Since special education students were usually exempt from such tests, reclassifying low-achieving pupils into special education helped raise a district's average test scores. It also served its older function of isolating children who were difficult to manage and teach. Boys generally have more difficulties with reading and language and misbehave more; historically, they had worse grades, failed more, and graduated at lower rates than girls. Poor minority boys became disproportionally labeled learning disabled at the very time that the courts required racial integration. The South, with its history of separate but unequal schools, had the nation's most racially integrated schools by the early 1970s, but also the highest percentage of children streamed into special education. Adding to local complaints everywhere was the hard truth that the federal government did not come close to covering the costs of the additional health, social, and instructional services it now required by law.

Educating children with special needs became an important additional responsibility of the nation's schools in postwar America. Every social group—suburban parents worried about academic excellence, civil rights activists championing the rights of African Americans, curriculum reformers revising basic subject matter, cognitive psychologists offering innovative theories of learning, and the medley of activists enamored with child-centered and progressive teaching—had pressured schools to improve the lives of various groups of children and guarantee the progress and stability of the larger society.

Despite the complex and often contradictory demands made upon public schools, there was still considerable continuity in everyday school practices. Particular classrooms may have become more racially integrated or inclusive of special students. Yet there was a remarkable familiarity about most classrooms that went beyond surface impressions. They were still largely teacher centered and textbook dominated. They were still mostly taught by a solitary, female teacher who taught virtually every subject in a self-contained room. Desks—even moveable ones—were often lined up in a row; and, by the 1970s, state-mandated tests reinforced didactic teaching methods. Despite many-sided efforts to promote inquiry, problem solving, and child-centered methods, students memorized facts and fundamental knowledge and competed for approval, gold stars, and high grades. High schools, too, faced enormous pressures for change in the postwar era, as the winds of reform battered the sturdy pillars of tradition.

CHAPTER NINE

The Fate of the High School

"High school is closer to the core of the American experience than anything else I can think of," wrote the novelist Kurt Vonnegut Jr., in a 1970 *Esquire* article. "We have all been there. While there, we saw nearly every sign of justice and injustice, kindness and meanness, intelligence and stupidity, which we are likely to encounter later in life." An old friend had recently reminded him that even after graduation, the cheerleaders and other high status classmates refused to relinquish power. The wife of secretary of defense Melvin Laird was a former classmate, and it was easy to recall those students who once made life miserable for everyone else. And now these people ran the country. "Richard Nixon," Vonnegut noted, "is a familiar type from high school. So is Melvin Laird. So is J. Edgar Hoover. So is General Lewis Hershey. So is everybody."

The acclaimed author of *Slaughterhouse-Five* and other contemporary classics had not attended just any high school. A native of Indianapolis, Vonnegut graduated in 1940 from prestigious Shortridge High, located in a fashionable downtown neighborhood in the American heartland. Shortridge traced its lineage to the original Indianapolis High School. Like many an affluent central high, it had a history of academic distinction not seen in many working-class neighborhood schools. It had a daily—not weekly or monthly—newspaper since the 1890s, a notable example of the extracurriculum that reformers had touted since the Progressive Era. Vonnegut himself had worked on the paper. He left Indianapolis after graduation but told local college students in 1983 that "every joke I've ever told, every attitude I've ever struck, came from School 43 and Shortridge."

Shortridge was more elite than most urban schools, but Vonnegut had underscored an essential truth about modern secondary education. There was more to the high school than football stars and prom queens, future warmongers and establishment figures, since virtually all types were represented there. Its greatest achievement, enrolling nearly everyone, fulfilled the old republican promise that America was a land of opportunity where merit alone conferred distinction in a fluid social order. The democratization of the high school was also its Achilles' heel. As teenagers streamed into the classrooms in the 1950s, warnings accelerated of declining standards. The cold war, civil rights movement, and economic changes had led to rising expectations and renewed demands for educational reform to ensure personal mobility and social improvement. The fear that America was dividing into two nations, slums and suburbs, with rural America in steady decline, also deepened public anxieties about the capacity of schools to prepare young people well for the modern world.

As secondary schools expanded, numerous social reformers, concerned parents, politicians, and pundits freely offered prescriptions to cure their many ills. As more students than ever attended and also graduated, high schools lost whatever mystery they once had among ordinary people. Familiarity did not always breed contempt. In many places, the local high school, or at least successful sports teams, shaped community identity and sustained local pride. But the belief that the high school was mostly a troubled institution was ubiquitous in the postwar decades. With more and more, principally middle-class, students attending college by the early 1960s, many people characterized the institution as insufficiently academic, dominated by an inscrutable teenage peer culture, and in a kind of academic free fall. Such complaints, loudly registered in the 1950s, resurfaced in the 1970s, and still recur. Whether any secondary school could enroll everyone yet honor excellence was uncertain. Ultimately, most educational leaders concluded that a diverse student body required a differentiated curriculum, complete with ability groups and formal tracks. That students who could barely read or write sometimes had high school diplomas enabled critics to say that social promotion, soft standards, and a creeping progressivism had likely ruined the people's college forever. Vocational, nonacademic education—mostly for other people's children—also retained its place in the schools despite its often doubtful economic or pedagogical value.

Critics of the schools, whose numbers expanded as the economy declined in the 1970s, despaired at the spread of electives and rise of a drug culture, mounting classroom violence, and a more casual atmosphere in many high schools, which many blamed on liberalism and permissiveness. Despite occasional campaigns among teachers to make classrooms more student centered, high schools frequently remained inhospitable to progressive pedagogy. Even though critics said that the curriculum was watered down and insipid, high school teachers, unlike their peers in the lower grades, were specialists in particular subjects, especially outside the smaller institutions. Latter-day progressives reminded everyone that teaching remained mostly textbook oriented and didactic. Traditional practices, while challenged by more relaxed classroom environments by the 1970s, were reinforced by public opinion, which favored discipline, adult authority, and more standardized tests for promotion and graduation and as a way to document equity in educational opportunity.

Like the lower rungs of the system, high schools were enormously diverse in the postwar era. Enrollments grew dramatically until the 1970s, when the last of the baby boomers entered secondary schools. There were 5.7 million pupils in grades 9 through 12 in 1950, 8.4 million in 1960, 13 million in 1970, and slightly more a decade later. Students with special needs increasingly attended, their inclusion ultimately mandated by federal law. Many high schools, throughout the South initially but also increasingly in the urban North by the early 1970s, took center stage in the movement for desegregation. High schools thus faced America's most pressing, difficult concerns: creating a dependable workforce, instilling loyalty to free enterprise, and giving more attention to college preparation, racial justice, and previously excluded pupils. Rising expectations reflected an optimistic but naive faith that schools could address these complex problems, sometimes simultaneously, and to everyone's satisfaction.

Reconstructing the history of America's high schools is complicated by their incredible variety and expansiveness. In 1960, when educational experts still called for closing small schools, America had over twenty-five thousand public high schools, the majority of them in villages, towns, and rural areas. The extremes represented by slums and suburbs attracted the most media atten-tion, but high schools existed everywhere: in the sparsely settled countryside, affluent bedroom communities, ghettos and barrios, and numerous places served by a single secondary school. Some institutions had a thriving academic culture and solid parental support; others languished in declining neighbor-hoods that denied ethnic minorities and the poor much opportunity and hope. On the eve of the publication of *A Nation at Risk* (1983), which attacked the system for low achievement and blamed it for the nation's economic woes, the U.S. Department of Education could still identify over twenty-three thou-sand schools "with secondary grades."

Such diversity masked the common challenges high schools faced after World War II. As Vonnegut explained, nearly everyone attended. Teenagers might work in the evening in the growing service industry, but on weekdays they were usually in school. Since not everyone received a quality academic education, raising standards was a common refrain, especially in the 1950s and 1970s, and it was easier to propose than to define or do. Other reform-minded citizens worried more about how to make high schools more accessible and egalitarian, to help the previously excluded or groups that traditionally did poorly. Relatively few students attended a high-powered academic institution such as Shortridge, which slipped into history in 1981 when the demography changed and it became a junior high. But teenagers everywhere went to high school, whether reluctantly, infrequently, or inattentively. Equality and excel-lence, democracy and efficiency, progress and tradition again battled for the soul of one of America's most inclusive and controversial institutions.

✎

Throughout the 1950s, many adults across the nation engaged in divisive debates about the nature and future of the American high school. They argued about the aims of secondary education, the curriculum, the teaching staff, the peer culture and consequences of universal attendance, and who to blame when the schools failed to produce enough angels and scholars. The contro-versies would hardly recede in the coming decades. In the late 1960s and af-terward, *Time, Newsweek,* and *U.S. News & World Report* routinely called the high school beleaguered and said it was in a state of crisis. Falling standardized test scores and other indicators of decline led many people to conclude that market competition—either indirectly through tuition tax credits for parents who preferred private schools, directly through vouchers, or through some form of choice within the public system—was the only remedy for a deteriorating system. Providing everyone with access to a high school education had been achieved, to no one's particular satisfaction. To understand the modern high school in its many complexities requires seeing it from the perspective of many interested parties, beginning with the public school establishment, whose policies generated ubiquitous criticisms and affected the lives of teachers and students.

At midcentury, the educational leaders who shaped the professional ethos and common practices of the high school shared a distinctive worldview. They devoted themselves to the preservation and extension of public education and to the principles of scientific management, institution building, and providing every child with an appropriate education. At most schools of education and teacher training colleges, professors ridiculed society's rising concern with academic achievement, dismissed the idea of a common curriculum, and repeated old pieties about the evils of college domination and lifeless instruction. They still embraced the comforting ideals of the *Cardinal Principles of Secondary Education* report of 1918, which de-emphasized academics, championed the extracurriculum, and endorsed the comprehensive high school, with several curricular streams housed under a single roof. Recall that Arthur Bestor's *Educational Wastelands* (1953) blamed the "interlocking directorate of professional educationists" for weakening the curriculum and fostering "life adjustment." However, until Bestor's overall criticisms gained greater public recognition and more people condemned the schools following Sputnik, high school administrators and teachers in many districts lived in something of a cocoon, shielded from many assaults on their professional autonomy. In a few famous incidents, school superintendents had been attacked as subversives for endorsing progressive education, which conservatives equated with godless communism and humanism, but more criticism and complaint were imminent.

Throughout the 1950s, many administrators, teachers, and professors of education applauded the growing reach of the system. They usually viewed rising enrollments as a sign of public favor and downplayed issues of quality instruction or wavering achievement. While citizens grew skeptical about many aspects of the high school, they proclaimed their commitment to democracy, best expressed through a differentiated curriculum in the larger institutions, to meet the needs of a diverse student body. In 1950, the secondary curriculum coordinator for the Los Angeles County public schools emphasized that more slow learners were now in attendance, thanks to social promotion and the disappearance of many full-time jobs for teenagers. He estimated that 20 percent of the students had IQs in the 70 to 90 range and recommended letting them work at their own pace on jigsaw puzzles, crafts, and hobbies instead of academics. A professor of education at Penn State sang the usual refrain: "Pupils are different and widely different. Since the case for individual differences has been established through research and experience, there is no solace in denying the facts."

Writing in the *High School Journal* in 1953, a University of Wisconsin professor explained that many high schools taught pupils with IQs from 60 to 160. Moreover, students ranged "from the delinquent to the highly cultured," the lazy to the ambitious. "Our 'Omnibus' public high school has a great variety of passengers," he concluded. "Yet each is an individual, in his own right. No two are alike, were alike, or will ever be alike. As the percentage of children in attendance increases, the range of individual differences increases in all its facets." A few years later, Max W. Barrows, deputy commissioner of education in Vermont, urged the high school to shed its college preparatory shell, since today's students "possess a wide range of native ability and a greater variety in the level of accomplishment." Like most school officials, Barrows emphasized that the high school was for everybody and had to "serve the needs of all its pupils." Professional journals regularly endorsed more differentiated curricula, ability groups, tracks, and counseling and guidance to channel the bright and the dull to an appropriate curriculum. Until Bestor published his blockbuster, most openly praised life adjustment as a democratic response to an elite curriculum and less intelligent student body.

Experts on secondary education often seemed woefully out of step with rising public expectations that high schools strengthen their curriculum, if not for everyone as Bestor desired, then at least for the influential and growing cohort preparing for college. Textbooks assigned to future secondary teachers usually emphasized watering down the curriculum overall and protecting average or weak minds from difficult subjects. In a revised edition of *Secondary Education* (1950), Thomas Briggs, in the winter of a long career at Teachers College, and his colleagues emphasized not higher or more uniform standards but "more appropriate programs of study and methods of instruction" for the less talented. High standards would only lead to higher dropout rates. Harold Spears, former head of secondary instruction in Evansville, Indiana, and then the assistant superintendent of the San Francisco schools, ridiculed academics for the masses, who he felt should understand carburetors, not *Ivanhoe*. Was it more important, he asked, "to be able to date the Battle of Hastings, or to be able to date the captain of the football team? To recognize a split infinitive, or to recognize a split personality?" Down at Palo Alto, a professor in Stanford's School of Education chastised high school teachers in 1957 for failing to accommodate diverse learning styles. He made the usual attacks on rote instruction, textbooks, and common standards and then endorsed hiring more guidance counselors and a teaching staff that would have better rapport with students and give more group assignments. And, he added, rather than a test, why couldn't a cleverly designed bulletin board demonstrate mastery of an academic subject?

As the storm of complaints about the high schools reached gale force, school administrators joined with professors of education to protect themselves, as Bestor predicted when he called their alliance an "interlocking directorate" of self-interested professionals. But they received even better cover when psychologists such as Jerome Bruner and the new curriculum reformers called for more progressive teaching practices, from inquiry to problem solving. (School officials tended to ignore the interest of many of these scholars in subject matter.) Equally unexpected, yet another person from Harvard appeared who became, at least for a time, helpful in warding off dangerous critics. James B. Conant was almost a godsend. Born in Dorchester, Massachusetts, in 1893, Conant was a bright student with family advantages, who earned a Ph.D. in chemistry from Harvard in 1916. Involved in poison gas experiments during the Great War, he became a professor at Harvard in 1919 and its president in 1933. A member of the NEA's prestigious Educational Policies Commission, he had little respect for Harvard's School of Education but allowed it to survive. An advisor to the Manhattan Project, he became the ambassador to West Germany but was popularly known for his many books on education, particularly on the high school.

Given education's low status in the professional world, educationists were no doubt flattered that a learned, high-status, former Ivy League president dedicated decades of his life to studying the schools. Not since the days of another Harvard president, Charles Eliot of Committee of Ten fame, had someone so esteemed taken the enterprise so seriously. But it was what Conant said that really made the difference, since his views were really not very radical; indeed, his writings actually blunted the harshest contemporary criticisms of the schools. He favored just about every position popular among educational leaders in the 1950s. Cautious about civil rights and integration, he preached tolerance for ethnic minorities and favored the meritocratic ideal. He also supported federal aid to education, school consolidation and the elimination of small high schools, the differentiated curriculum, and the comprehensive high school. He scoffed at the idea of a strong academic curriculum for everyone, writing in 1959 that "it is impossible to have one standard academic curriculum for all pupils. That is, it is impossible if high standards in mathematics, science, and foreign languages are to be maintained." In harmony with most educational leaders, Conant believed that separate curricular streams simply reflected the varying abilities of pupils. Certainly the top 15 to 20 percent of the student body, the college bound, needed a stronger academic curriculum. At a time when civil rights for blacks and inclusion of children with special needs vied for attention, he emphasized that the neglect of the talented had weakened the national defense and the economy.

In every way, then, Conant, a mild critic of the high schools, was much more palatable to the public school administrators than those who complained about educational wastelands, the evils of progressivism, juvenile delinquency, and potentially disloyal teachers. Conant was so famous that Michael Young included him in his satire *The Rise of the Meritocracy*. Linking Conant's name with the hallowed notion of a world governed by the best and the brightest was hardly accidental. Throughout his many writings, Conant hammered home the idea that providing everyone an "equal chance," or equality of educational opportunity, was the genius of America and the goal of its school system. In an early major work, *Education in a Divided World* (1948), he pointed to the emerging ideological clash between the U.S. and the Soviet Union, which would be waged in part in the classroom. The schools, he argued, played a fundamental role in ensuring that poor children, if they were bright and ambitious, could rise to respectability and even prominence. "That the country would be a great deal better off if careers were freely open to all the talented seems hardly a matter for debate. That our belief in a society with a minimum of class distinction is contradicted every time we segregate Negroes or discriminate against those of Mexican, Japanese, or Jewish ancestry is as obvious."

Like mainstream educators since the Progressive Era, Conant insisted that equal opportunity did not mean the same education for everyone. Calling the early identification and separation of pupils into different secondary schools in Europe patently undemocratic, he favored more comprehensive high schools, which tracked students into separate curricula but offered common activities and some courses for everyone to bind them together. Without question, he wrote, America currently denied equal chances to poorer children, and this was reflected in unequal funding for different school systems and dramatically revealed in the widening gap between city and suburb. Some suburban high schools were already "the pride of our public school system," islands of excellence in a sea of urban mediocrity. This was unfortunate, since the "boys and girls . . . are all entitled to a fair chance." Compounding the problem, he realized, was an intractable issue at which Michael Young later took direct aim: "But a moment's consideration makes it plain that there is a fundamental conflict between a general desire to give all the children in a community an equal chance and the special desire of each parent to do the best he can for his own offspring." Only state-funded schools could keep the social system fluid by providing opportunity for poor-but-talented youth, which he believed would help strengthen the social order and defeat communism.

Throughout the 1950s and 1960s, Conant's name was present in nearly every prominent discussion about the American high school. Like many Yankee theorists of education since the antebellum period, he applauded the Jeffersonian notion of a merit-based school system and greater educational access to the nation's secondary schools. In a series of lectures at the University of Virginia in 1952, while sidestepping the issue of Jim Crow, Conant again emphasized the centrality of public education in the survival of free enterprise and an open social system. "If the battle of Waterloo was won on the playing fields of Eton, it may well be that the ideological struggle with Communism in the next fifty years will be won on the playing fields of the public high schools of the United States." Revising his lectures as a 1953 book entitled *Education and Liberty*, he reaffirmed the importance of free public schooling in general and the comprehensive high school in particular. High schools, he pointed out, varied greatly across the nation. Most were small and could not offer many curricular choices. Some big cities such as New York, on the other hand, had dozens of larger high schools, including a handful that were very academic, with strict admission standards. Neither model, he thought, was superior to socially inclusive comprehensive high schools.

In his many speeches, articles, and books, Conant never wavered from his claim that small high schools had to give way to larger comprehensive ones. The earliest generation of urban school administrators and corporate-oriented reformers afterwards had all favored school consolidation: dreams of bigger and bigger schools, administered by wise and cosmopolitan professionals, taught by well-trained teachers in a growing system danced in their heads like sugar plum fairies in children's tales. Conant thus hit upon another time-tested, popular reform among educational leaders, who pressed for the consolidation of school districts and closing of small high schools whenever possible throughout the postwar era.

As Conant told his listeners in Virginia, variety still characterized America's public school system. "Anyone attempting to describe the secondary schools of the United States in a few pages," he insisted, "has an impossible task. The variations are so great from state to state because we do not have a national system; even within a single state they are as great as they are because strictly speaking we do not have a *system* of free schools anywhere in the Union." In saying this he was hardly mistaken. Just as principals and teachers commonly remarked on the incredible diversity of the growing student body, so too were they concerned about the enormous differences among the nation's secondary schools. The small size of most high schools was their most obvious feature, which had long agitated the school administrators. In 1950, a contributor to the main journal of the National Association of Secondary School Principals estimated that 40 percent of all secondary students were in schools with less than one hundred pupils, 64 percent in schools with fewer than two hundred pupils, and 80 percent with less than four hundred. In an article in the *High School Journal* in 1958, William Marshall French, later a professor at Teachers College, estimated that the average enrollment in the American high school was about 200 students.

Writing in the wake of Sputnik, French outspokenly attacked what he viewed as the lax standards of the modern high school, which embraced social promotion and undermined the status of a diploma. But he too saw the small high school as an impediment to quality education and only called for upgrading academics for the middle and upper tiers of students. Secondary teachers, he believed, often had insufficient content knowledge and little training in teaching methods. "Some schools are so small," French added, "that they can offer only a small number of standard, traditional courses. . . . At the other end of the scale is the large, cosmopolitan high school with nearly as many subjects offered as the five-and-ten has variety of merchandise." Numerous educational writers argued that small schools offered too few electives, had a weak curriculum, and could never be comprehensive. Conant avidly supported more school consolidation, even though some professionals, including French, presciently said that excessively large institutions would breed student alienation and anomie.

Conant's 1959 book *American High School Today* appeared with exquisite timing given the hullabaloo over Sputnik. The Carnegie Corporation had generously funded his research, and the book, which echoed themes from his earlier writings, became a bestseller. As historians David L. Angus and Jeffrey E. Mirel have concluded, Conant provided "a ringing endorsement" of America's secondary schools. He stressed the importance of meritocratic values, counseling and guidance, testing to identify talent, and the upgrading of academics for the best and the brightest. Better vocational education for the less talented, stronger math and science and foreign-language training for the brighter students, and special attention to the gifted (the top 3 percent of all students) were among his other basic recommendations, none of them particularly original or controversial. Small high schools—those graduating less than one hundred students—would have to be eliminated, since they could not attract the best teachers or offer diverse curricula or extracurricular programs. Their elimination was something administrators and educational officials over the decades had championed thousands of times. What especially calmed the nerves of many educators, after a decade of strident attacks upon them, was Conant's assurance that they needed to strengthen education for the talented but did not require any "radical alteration in the basic pattern of American education . . . in order to improve our public schools." Reducing the number of high schools—from twenty-one thousand to nine thousand—promised to yield the greatest benefits and seemed the best way to convert most of them into comprehensive institutions.

Conant's recommendations reinforced the movement to close smaller schools, as a new wave of consolidation engulfed many states after World War II. More educators and parents by the early 1960s questioned whether large schools were necessarily good ones, but many administrators in particular, still emulating the corporate model, remained under the spell of the "edifice complex." Late in the decade, Sidney P. Marland, superintendent of the Pittsburgh schools and later commissioner of education in the Nixon administration, proposed closing neighborhood high schools in favor of massive "educational parks," a reform that the Steel City rejected. By 1970, Conant conceded that high schools with a graduating class of two hundred were acceptable.

The slowing of the big school movement came from different sources. The

streams, particularly in urban areas where one found the largest and most of the comprehensive high schools. Everywhere the traditional English or modern course evolved into the main academic, or college preparatory, curriculum. The non–college bound were often funneled into a diluted version of the academic curriculum (often called the "general" track by the 1930s) or into a purely vocational one. Even in the 1950s, as Conant and less prominent reformers criticized small high schools, everyone admitted that they were the most academic. The reformers, however, came to bury, not to praise them.

At midcentury, a state commission exploring Indiana's educational system concluded that the smaller secondary schools shortchanged their pupils. These schools, it reported, lacked well-trained teachers, had few extracurricular activities save basketball, minimal electives, and almost no alternatives to an academic course of study. "Teachers in many of the smaller schools which provided limited curricular offerings," said the commission, "were attempting to teach the traditional academic subjects to all pupils regardless of their aptitudes and vocational plans." Similar complaints suffused educational literature in the 1950s, appearing both in professional journals and in college textbooks assigned to future teachers. As a contributor from North Carolina noted in the *High School Journal* in 1950, the typical high school was usually small and taught five basic academic subjects and little more, which most educational leaders found appalling. Leslie L. Chisholm, a professor of education at the University of Nebraska, in a state with thousands of small country schools, wrote in *The Work of the Modern High School* (1953) that "the struggle to break the ultra-academic tradition and the ultra-exclusiveness that settled over the high schools of America, and thereby transform the school into schools of the people dedicated to the welfare of *all* youth, has not been an easy task."

A few education professors allowed that small schools were often the source of community pride. Two teacher educators from Michigan even broke ranks and wrote in the *High School Journal* that the modest little secondary schools benefited their students, who could be encouraged by their teachers and not get lost in the crowd. But community pride, said the superintendent of Wyoming's schools in 1958, stood in the way of evolution, that is, school consolidation. In the 1950s, one rarely read anything positive in the professional literature about small high schools, given their common emphasis on academics. Even in largely rural states, educational leaders still favored consolidation, efficiency, and economies of scale. Urban-oriented, they often ridiculed small secondary schools. When studies regularly showed that small schools offered more academic training to more pupils than the comprehensive high school, they saw this as a strike against the little places. Since the majority of pupils did not go to college, why educate everyone in academic (i.e., elite) subjects? The experts said it only led to school failure and high dropout rates.

Small was not beautiful in the 1950s. In the coming decades, teachers and students would periodically seek the intimacy of small places in their big impersonal buildings by establishing "schools within schools." But that had to await another day. In the 1950s, bigger was better. Academics for the many, said the leading educational theorists, ignored the individual needs, talents, and ambitions of an ever more diverse student body. Little wonder, then, that many citizens concerned about raising standards, at least for their own children, concluded that educationists were ruining the schools. Professors of education and many administrators seemed to revel in their own antiacademic, if not anti-intellectual, rhetoric. The experts knew that the small schools were the most academic, but the rising demand to build more schools, thanks to the baby boom, reinforced the old movement to construct large ones that were comprehensive and multitrack. Historically, comprehensive high schools were never built to advance high standards for everyone. Understandably, few educators warmed to Bestor's proposal that, if given the appropriate tutoring, time, and support, the vast majority of pupils could master academic subjects.

Another major stumbling block to raising standards in the immediate postwar era was the character of elementary schools, which had undergone some profound changes in recent decades. This had enormous effects on how academic standards were defined and implemented throughout the system. Recall that before the 1890s, the high school served many purposes: reformers used it to pull more middle-class pupils out of private schools and into the public system, it trained many urban elementary teachers, and it also helped standardize the curriculum and upgrade standards in the lower grades. But an unexpected reverse flow of influence occurred in the twentieth century. The top of the system became increasingly shaped by its base, a transformation decades in the making.

Except for some special, atypical secondary schools in a few cities, entrance exams to high school had disappeared in many northern communities by the late nineteenth century. The age-graded classroom, an urban invention, existed more in theory than practice, given the high failure rates in the first and second grades. But high rates of failure in lower grades actually gave high school teachers and principals some confidence that, after decades of use, the entrance tests had sufficiently raised standards and standardized the curriculum to make the exams superfluous. To graduate from eighth grade meant you deserved admission to high school. Regional accrediting organizations, formed roughly when entrance tests disappeared, did not measure school quality per se but various quantitative measures—size of institution, number of teachers, and courses that met Carnegie units for graduation. In an unpredictable confluence of events, rising interest in going to high school and changes in elementary school practices occurred at about the same time, with momentous consequences for the higher learning. The growing use of ability groups in the lower grades in the early 1900s and spread of social promotion after the 1920s meant that high schools, whose enrollments were booming, now taught a widening stream of pupils unlikely to excel academically. Many were now simply passed along. Going to high school became less a privilege and more a right. While it never fully lost its status relative to the elementary grades, the stature of the high school was clearly diminished.

As educational researchers David Cohen and Barbara Neufeld once argued, Americans theoretically embrace equality but usually are repelled by its realization. Democratic appeals to human equality clash with the imperatives of an economic system that inevitably generates inequalities. Public school rhetoric, too, traditionally emphasized that talent resides in all classes but that sameness is not a common attribute among students. Educators had long assumed that intelligence and ambition, like worldly goods and family fortune, were distributed unequally, and IQ and achievement tests and classroom performance only confirmed these assumptions. And, by midcentury, the practices of the elementary school were increasingly applied to secondary pupils. That children varied enormously was a hardy professional dictum that resonated among those dealing with booming secondary schools. Moreover, ability grouping and tracking became easier to implement as secondary schools consolidated. What remained complicated and politically controversial was how to balance the demands of the college bound with those of racial minorities and youth with special needs, groups once largely excluded from the system but increasingly demanding more access and fairer treatment.

Ability grouping and tracking were already common in larger high schools by the end of World War II, and the closing of smaller institutions only accelerated their spread. In 1960, one national authority, drawing upon a recent report from the U.S. Office of Education, wrote in the *Encyclopedia of Educational Research* that about half of all junior and senior high schools arranged classes by ability. Smaller institutions had some ability groups within each class, while separate classes based on ability and achievement routinely appeared in larger consolidated buildings. Abundant research on lower- and higher-achieving ability groups consistently demonstrated that the former had a watered-down or otherwise modified curriculum and more didactic instruction; these groups formed the basis of placement into separate (academic, general, or vocational) curricular streams in high school.

Michael Young, Bruno Bettelheim, and other critics in the 1950s incisively commented on the intellectual differentiation occurring in the schools precisely when the civil rights movement preached more equality and better access for the excluded and underprivileged. The spread of ability grouping and tracking, along with honors courses, which had been in some urban high schools for decades, led to more differentiation. In addition, Advanced Placement courses, begun by the joint efforts of elite East Coast private universities and feeder schools in the early 1950s, quickly proliferated, especially in suburban and middle-class high schools, providing another way to separate students. The aspiring middle classes, whose children were most likely to attend college, resisted any attempt to tamper too much with courses linked with Carnegie units and college preparation. Assistant superintendent Harold Spears in San Francisco accused high school teachers of believing in the doctrine of mental discipline and teaching classes where an "aristocracy of aptitude" reigned. In 1955, Lowell High School, San Francisco's premier secondary school, tried to add some vocational courses, leading to massive protests by alumni and parents who threatened to send their children to private schools, a public school superintendent's worst nightmare.

Teacher educators throughout the postwar era blamed the parents of the college bound for ignoring the benefits of life adjustment classes (necessary for effective, democratic living, they said) and fewer academic courses. They believed parents inexplicably saw enduring value in college preparatory classes and wrongly measured school quality by the number of graduates heading to college. The professional literature abounded with complaints about the conservatism of these parents. As one school administrator aptly wrote in 1971, to attempt to reorganize the curriculum by lessening college preparatory courses always led to trouble. Whatever college admissions required, parents of future collegians demanded. In 1995, several scholars concluded that making dramatic changes in the curriculum was an exercise in futility. In most comprehensive high schools, "curricula are organized around college-level preparation, out-of-date vocational education, and basic skills remediation in the form of general education courses." In words that could have been written in 1950, they concluded: "What is more, many college-bound youth and their parents resist any reform that eliminates traditional college preparatory course work."

Various schemes emerged in the postwar decades—such as mastery learning of low-level basics or minimum competency tests—to try to ensure that low achievers could complete an application form and read a map, goals reminiscent of the life adjustment movement. Ironically, studies showed that the pupils widely lacking these skills never took the state-mandated tests, since they had often already dropped out. Generally, mainstream policy makers persisted in their belief that a diverse student body required the availability of different subjects and the absence of common standards. They thought it undemocratic that college preparatory students garnered most of the public's attention and respect. They criticized teachers who aspired to teach only the most talented students. They knew that parents believed in equal opportunity for all, special privileges for their own. While they saw themselves, whatever their political affiliation, as Jeffersonian democrats, many educational leaders believed so fervently in human differences that they accepted a stratified social and intellectual order. They doubted the intellectual potential of many of the poor, working-class, and minority students disproportionally trapped in the least prestigious ability groups and tracks from which transfers were unusual. The professional consensus was that if high schools were for everyone, ability groups, tracks, and differing standards allowed each individual to taste some success, remain in school, and perhaps graduate. In the 1950s, numerous cities, including Washington, D.C., Indianapolis, and Topeka, Kansas, codified the process by awarding different diplomas to pupils from the various tracks.

Even though college admission requirements and vitriolic attacks on life adjustment shielded many academic subjects from the executioner's block, course taking in the most advanced academic subjects did not increase noticeably following Sputnik. Certainly only a handful of individuals wanted to upgrade academics for everyone anyway. Numerous citizens, including many educators, earlier concluded that most secondary students lacked the intelligence to study anything serious. The headmaster of the private Phillips Andover Academy bluntly wrote in the *Saturday Review* that "it is foolish to try to pound Latin into the head of a youngster whose ambition is to run a garage." Too much was being spent on "retarded children," he said, rather than on the talented. The principal of the Hornell, New York, junior-senior high school, located in a small industrial city, proudly announced in 1952 that the weaker pupils were spared difficult academic courses. "We do not segregate these pupils in anything except their classes. In sports, home room, social activities—the things which the students count important—there is no segregation." The Port Neches Independent School District in Texas boasted of "minimum essentials" for the slower pupils and more academics for the talented. Everyone seemed to say that it was undemocratic and unkind to foist academics upon every student. At the national convention of secondary school principals in 1959, an administrator from Great Neck, New York, presented his vision of an imaginary Dream Junior High School where, faced with pupils with a range of IQs, grouping practices guaranteed fair treatment for everyone. The name of that school's principal? Dr. Weaim T. Helpthemall.

Those writing such patronizing statements about democracy in action via ability groups and tracks generally kept their own children out of the low-status streams. Theirs was a paternalism with a smiling face, since anything could be justified by saying it helped the student. Some approvingly quoted E. W. Butterfield, Connecticut's commissioner of education in the 1930s, who had written that already half of the secondary population could not meet basic standards for graduation. Standards had to be lowered, at least for them. The typical American, after all, only read the morning paper, skipping the headlines and heading right for the comics and sports page. "He never reads Macauley, or Thackeray, or the *Atlantic Monthly*. He never writes an essay, but he reads the essays of Brisbane and Will Rogers," Butterfield wrote. To raise standards even for the academically capable, Butterfield thought, was "intellectual sadism." By the late 1950s, as William French observed, the dumbing down of the curriculum already had accelerated for many pupils (probably more so in the larger schools). A weak student now swapped algebra and plane geometry for "the simple computations of arithmetic that are related to his present and future life needs. Rather than trying to fathom the plays of Shakespeare or the poems of Tennyson, he is taught to read the local newspapers and certain popular magazines such as *Reader's Digest*."

As more poor and minority students remained in school, high schools struggled to educate those who read at an elementary level. Throughout the postwar era, *Time* and *Newsweek* reported on the "non readers," delinquents, and rough characters now in attendance who read at the comic-book level, a problem both in rural hollows and blighted urban neighborhoods. Professional journals for secondary teachers published special issues on reading, a skill most high school teachers thought should have been mastered in the elementary grades. In 1954, the principal of the Coosa County secondary school in Cottage Grove, Alabama, simply said: "Give them all a diploma." He initiated a five-year experiment that completely abdicated responsibility for academic standards, since "we contend that a high-school diploma generally is proof of just one thing: namely, that its possessor has studied for some period of time at or under the direction of some high school." The school eliminated all required academic requirements and tests. Anyone who showed up and behaved received a diploma. Since "the great majority of people will never be more than just ordinary citizens," trying to teach them serious subjects was a waste of "time, money, and energy." Simple folk "can live a complete and successful life without having heard of either Shakespeare, Euclid, or Galileo."

While this principal had an unusually virulent strain of antiacademic fever, the link between achievement and the diploma weakened as social promotion spread throughout school systems. Reminiscent of the famous footrace in *Alice in Wonderland* in which every runner wins—Dodo explains that "*all* must have prizes"—educators increasingly said that everyone needed to feel successful. In the lowest-ability English classes in the cities, students were not subjected to *Silas Marner* or *The Tempest* but read driver training manuals and spellbinders such as "Pat the Pilot." National figures such as Conant and many teacher educators concluded that everyone should be promoted and receive a diploma if they attended school faithfully, applied themselves, and behaved. By the 1950s, educators concocted various euphemisms to describe the policy. They had not abandoned standards, only adopted new ones that were varied, diverse, relaxed, and flexible. There were also "sympathetic promotions." While practices varied in different high schools, the trend was toward more promotion and graduation regardless of achievement.

Politicians including the aged Herbert Hoover and vice president Richard Nixon attacked soft standards and automatic promotion, and a handful of professors in schools of education, including William French, lamented the cheapening of the diploma. French worried about the growing claim that if a child was not promoted, the teacher had actually failed. "In one system," he noted in 1957, "the heading on the final report to the superintendent was changed from the traditional 'pupils who have failed' to 'pupils whom I was unable to prepare to complete the grade successfully.'" In some places, "a high school diploma may be regarded as a certificate of reasonably satisfactory attendance and nothing else," a statement that would have won a prize in Coosa County. In the coming decades, however, citizens with contrasting political beliefs worried about the low achievement of many graduates, especially the poor, though no one had a magic solution to society's contradictory expectation that schools with a very diverse student body raise graduation rates without lowering overall quality. In his moving portrayal of Appalachian poverty, *Night Comes to the Cumberlands* (1962), Harry M. Caudill lamented that high school graduates from that depressed region were "scarcely literate," leaving them especially vulnerable in a competitive economy. Districts elsewhere with "zero reject" policies, or universal promotion, later faced lawsuits when functional illiterates with high school diplomas sued, claiming a violation of their civil rights.

By the 1970s, citizens expressed their disdain for low standards in many ways. In a Gallup poll in 1974, only 7 percent of those surveyed favored universal promotion, and 90 percent wanted students to repeat the year if they could not meet basic standards. That 87 percent of the juniors and seniors polled agreed with their elders on this latter point said something about the disconnect between school policy and public opinion. Those who were the poorest and thus most vulnerable seemed especially ill served by public schools, thanks to a general loosening of standards for weaker students. In 1983, when *A Nation at Risk* attacked the schools as mediocre, Gary D. Fenstermacher and John Goodlad wrote that "curricular variation," based on the hoary idea of children's individual differences, helped deny millions of children access to a common, quality academic curriculum, or what John Dewey had called the "funded capital of civilization." This was precisely what earlier concerned William T. Harris, William Bagley, and Arthur Bestor, all of whom remain vilified by many educational scholars. An expert on elementary education, Goodlad had also studied secondary schools. In his major study on teaching practices, he found that pupils "were predominantly tracked in the four basic subjects usually required for college admission: mathematics, English, social studies, and science." Many students did not have access to high quality, higher status academic subjects. In 1983, statistics from the U.S. Department of Education revealed that, despite regional and local variations, across the nation an average of 38 percent of the pupils enrolled in the college preparatory course, 37 percent in vocational track, and 25 percent in the general stream.

This retreat from any pretense of common standards, many decades in the making, accelerated as more small high schools closed. It also led to the proliferation of new courses, either electives or watered-down alternatives to traditional subjects. The U.S. Office of Education reported in 1950 that the nation's high schools taught 274 different courses; 172 pupils studied Norse. An article in *Life* magazine in 1953 featured the Davenport, Iowa, high school, a comprehensive institution that enrolled two thousand pupils and already had 137 courses. One expert in 1965 counted about five hundred different courses in the nation's high schools. Ernest Boyer reported about 2,100 courses in the 741 high schools in Illinois in 1977. Curricular chaos seemed evident by the time Arthur G. Powell, Eleanor Farrar, and David Cohen published their insightful study, *The Shopping Mall High School* (1985). Academic coherence and excellence seemed incompatible with mass education.

The spread of ability groups, tracks, social promotion, electives, remedial classes, grade inflation, and pass/fail courses—not to mention rising levels of classroom violence and teacher strikes—seemed to characterize a high school careening out of control. And, when Scholastic Aptitude Test scores plummeted in the 1970s, more than a few citizens concluded that standards had fallen abysmally, even though the test was designed to measure fitness for college, not overall school standards. By then, however, more working-class as well as most middle-class youth advanced to some post-secondary school, so test score decline, which occurred even among the top tier of test takers, caused many people to question the efficacy and efficiency of the system. The demand for back-to-the-basics and accountability enjoyed another revival. Civil rights advocates and conservative Republicans alike, despite their different political philosophies and ideas for reform, said that the school system was in trouble.

As ability groups, tracks, and social promotion became more universal, more youth were systematically expected to learn less. This made the elimination of high school tracks fairly difficult despite lawsuits and ongoing criticisms of the practice. Educators proudly wrote in the 1950s and 1960s that grouping practices protected the least talented from competing with the brighter students and that social promotion allowed everyone to feel successful. In addition, public pressure on secondary schools to increase their retention rates, given the disappearance of decent jobs for dropouts, undoubtedly meant that more pupils passed without meeting basic requirements. The dropout rate remained relatively high for poor and minority pupils throughout the postwar era, though graduation rates tended to rise for all groups. Jobs became tied to educational credentials, if not achievement per se. Some educators insisted that schools labored to meet everyone's needs, and not only in the dream world where Dr. Weaim T. Helpthemall presided. But the public was not persuaded. By the 1970s, Americans from various backgrounds wanted a tightening of standards, even as they continued to expect the schools to reform and uplift society.

✎

The demand for more effective, high achieving schools that coalesced by the 1970s and 1980s came from opposite ends of the political spectrum. Conservatives routinely blamed liberalism and the sixties for an eroding economy, political defeat in Vietnam, and poor school instruction in the basics. They pointed to the collapse of dress codes and more drug use and open sexuality among students as signs of cultural decline. Civil rights advocates were critical of the schools for different reasons. They attacked the white backlash against busing in the urban North in the early 1970s and the deepening segregation of poor blacks and Spanish-speaking youth in nonacademic high schools. Poorer pupils were usually overrepresented in the lowest ability groups, special education, and vocational tracks. Everyone seemed to agree that overall achievement levels were too low, especially for minority youth, fueling the movement for more testing programs that ultimately attracted bipartisan support.

Testing and measurement, long mainstays in the schools, rose to new heights in the postwar era, as poor and minority children and those with special learning needs and disabilities increasingly attended secondary schools. In addition to the usual array of IQ and achievement tests, interest in statewide and national testing programs grew in the 1950s and 1960s. When asked in 1958 and 1965 whether diplomas should be awarded on the basis of national test scores, about half of those polled agreed. The percentage rose to 65 percent in 1970 and 82 percent a decade later. In fact, without the family resources to fall back upon if their children faltered, the less educated actually favored the tests the most! Asked by Gallup in 1971 whether such tests should be used to compare schools, over 75 percent of the respondents said yes. Citizens disagreed whether local, state, or national tests were preferable, but they showed fairly wide support for competitive exams to measure school performance. Riding the rising tide, most state legislatures required minimum competency tests years before *A Nation at Risk* elevated complaints about school achievement even higher.

Fascination with testing emanated from various sources. The liberal architects of the Great Society's educational reforms required evaluations of federal programs to see if they produced "equality of results." To disillusioned liberals, James Coleman's famous report cast doubt on whether schools could overcome negative family influences upon achievement, but the trend toward more quantitative studies continued unabated. To secure federal money for local programs, state departments of public instruction also devised more tests to measure educational outcomes. Francis Keppel, the commissioner of education in the Kennedy and early Johnson administrations, endorsed a national achievement test in the late 1960s but predicted strong opposition from teachers and their unions. Albert Shanker, venerable head of the American Federation of Teachers, firmly defended union prerogatives but ultimately supported testing programs to show that teachers were not necessarily opposed to the new wave of accountability.

The new testing movement assumed many guises. With initial Carnegie Foundation funding and then Congressional appropriations, the National Assessment of Educational Progress (NAEP) began in 1969. Soon called "the nation's report card," it periodically tested student achievement in various academic subjects and was much less controversial among educators than minimum competency or other achievement tests, since it did not report scores on individual students or schools. NAEP owed much to the labors of Ralph Tyler, a seasoned educational researcher who had chaired the research team of the famous Eight-Year Study (1933–41), sponsored by the Progressive Education Association decades earlier. (Professional journals cited the study approvingly and said it proved that the traditional curriculum, like the concept of mental discipline, lacked any scientific basis.) In addition, by the late 1960s veteran civil rights activists such as Kenneth Clark, whose controversial research undergirded the *Brown* decision, lamented the low achievement scores of minority students in the nation's urban ghettos. Testing, evaluation, and accountability, therefore, had deep roots within liberal circles and were not simply hatched *de novo* by Republicans, who led the movement with gusto after the 1970s, with New Democrats in tow. Led by rising political stars such as Bill Clinton from Arkansas, the New Democrats arose as reformers within the party in the mid-1980s who sometimes stole the thunder of their opponents by praising the free market, teacher testing, and traditional Republican policies.

Romantics and countercultural critics attacked this emerging bipartisan movement to measure school effects. They wanted more community schools,

"schools without walls," open classrooms, alternative high schools, and more learning pods, electives, and student freedom. Some of these ideas bore fruit, though student-centered classrooms were already struggling in the lower grades. A few radicals endorsed deschooling society, but most leftist critics were less extreme, realizing that schools were now deeply embedded in society. Much dark talk about schools could be heard. In 1970, Charles Silberman said that most high schools, like the rest of the system, had a "repressive, prison-like atmosphere," pretty far removed from infant school pedagogy. He attacked the idea of a common curriculum, repeated the old child-centered maxim that the schools should fit the student, not the other way around, and said students should explore what interested them. That same year, Alvin Toffler's *Future Shock* called schools "a hopeless anachronism" and a common curriculum absurd. He suggested eliminating every subject, from French to algebra, unless it met one's future needs. A curriculum based on tradition was dysfunctional in a world of constant change. Charles Reich, author of *The Greening of America,* called for the end to competitive exams and rankings. Other writers favored "progress reports" over report cards as well as "rap sessions" with students, perhaps to reduce rising levels of classroom violence.

By the mid-1970s, such proposals seemed alien as back-to-the-basics, accountability, and innumerable schemes of evaluation (performance contracting, behavioral objectives, and others) competed for attention, light years away from countercultural concerns. Eliminating all failure in the classroom, especially in the cities, was a pipe dream. Beginning in the 1950s, when stories of blackboard jungles abounded in the media, the widening gap between suburban and urban school performance was frequently in the news. The low reading and achievement levels among the poor, particularly African Americans, reflected the grim quality of many urban systems, which had difficulty hiring enough certified teachers and retaining the best of them. While expensive new buildings went up in many suburbs, city schools often resembled gothic fortresses, many in a state of disrepair. In 1963, one-third of New York City's schools were at least fifty years old and were used as target practice by students, who that year alone set 122 fires and broke 181,000 windows. Urban dropout rates in the 1960s were abysmal, vandalism increased, and the infrastructure crumbled. Policemen became a fixture in many urban schools, patrolling the halls first with night sticks and then with guns. By 1973, "Fort Crenshaw" was the nickname for one high school in Los Angeles. At the time, New York City was training 1,200 additional school security guards, and Detroit, in desperate economic shape, counted numerous assaults on teachers every month. A national study of secondary education sponsored by the Charles F. Kettering Foundation thus concluded that city systems "were on the verge of complete collapse."

James Conant and others worried about the yawning gap in achievement between white and black youth in the immediate postwar era, but schools used ability groups, tracking, and vocational courses to hold poorer youth in school, pass them along, and keep them off the labor market as long as possible. Once jobs became scarce in the inner cities, the low achievement so common among poor children of all backgrounds, but especially poor minority children, had increasingly dire consequences. In 1964 Ovid F. Parody, the head of secondary school programs in the U.S. Office of Education, recognized that school and society worked at cross-purposes: the cities filled up with poor, non-white children, and society funded their schools poorly yet demanded academic excellence. Parody concluded that "thousands of boys and girls from minority cultures are educationally disadvantaged in our big cities, and their problems continue to mount at an alarming rate."

The rhetoric and substance of various urban school reforms also seemed to come up short. Calling the schools bourgeois and the poor culturally deprived did not translate into obvious ways to raise achievement. The idea of compensatory education proved insulting to many radicals, who called it racist and demeaning of poor and minority families. A Great Society that promised to end poverty financed urban school initiatives but also aided the already advantaged suburban districts. Cognitive psychologists advanced new learning theories that praised inquiry and discovery, but this seemed far removed from the daily labors of teachers trying to teach the basics in impoverished neighborhoods. The new math and science projects also usually avoided poor urban and rural districts. Some researchers studied the "learning styles" of the poor, always a mysterious notion, and one that seemed unscientific and led to pedagogical dead ends. When achievement lagged, some commentators cynically concluded that many youth were simply "dropouts in residence."

By the early 1970s, liberals and conservatives quarreled over how to lift achievement among the urban poor. Conant's warning about "social dynamite" had come to pass, and fear of urban riots, a rising crime rate, and expanding welfare state produced a Republican Party that stressed the importance of discipline, the basics, and accountability. The courts ruled against busing between suburb and city and denied that equal per capita spending on education was a constitutional right. Once the economy unraveled, even the shame of Watergate could not hold back a revitalized Republican Party that more often praised private than public schools, the marketplace than the public space.

As demands for higher achievement became commonplace, the federal government also pressed for more gender equity in the schools, another important expression of the modern civil rights movement. In 1972, Title IX advanced the cause of women's equality, from graduate school admissions to sports program funding; even without the legislation and despite discrimination on many levels of school and society historically, girls on average had higher grades, fewer expulsions, and better high school graduation rates than boys. Early NAEP scores, noted the Kettering Commission, indicated that except in science, girls outpaced boys in academics. Public Law 94-142 (1975) required more access for students with disabilities and other special populations, a classic underfunded federal mandate, and the previously excluded sought appropriate educational environments and sometimes mainstreaming, which was usually better achieved in the extracurriculum than in the academic arena. As white parents resisted mandatory busing and abandoned the cities for the suburbs or private education, magnet high schools opened to try to stem the white exodus by attracting pupils to quality, specialized programs in areas such as the performing arts or math and science, a mission made more difficult as cities became more racially and ethnically segregated. And the public in innumerable polls called for more standardized tests and higher achievement yet continued its love affair with the view that education, at least for quite a few students, should be practical. This ensured that over one-third of all secondary students in 1983 were in vocational tracks, the least academic curricula.

High schools were thus expected to perform sometimes mutually contradictory tasks. School administrators frequently muddled along while trying to meet everyone's needs and respond to the constant complaints registered by politicians and the media. As urban systems were attacked for low achievement in the 1970s and 1980s, many poor and minority children in the lower ability groups found themselves labeled special learners and remained disproportionally represented in vocational courses. The once culturally and socially disadvantaged were called "slow learners," then "at risk," and then part of the "underclass." By placing these children in special education or vocational classes, school systems in the South as elsewhere made academic classes the preserve of white children.

Special education and vocational education had many things in common.

Both had an academically weak, low-status curriculum and served youth who had various behavioral and hard-to-diagnose learning problems. When the number of special education pupils—students with IQs below the 70 to 90 range, depending on the school system—began to boom in the early 1950s, educators worried about what to teach them. Educators explained that those likely to become waiters, domestics, janitors, and workers at the car wash needed some sort of useful education. Parents complained of the stigmas placed upon their children enrolled in what insensitive people called "dumbbell" classes. Following tradition, these classes emphasized manual training, domestic science, and simple literacy, plus skills such as following directions and making the correct change. While youth labeled gifted were generally from the highest socio-economic strata, special education students were more often poor and minority ethnic groups. Called the "dumping grounds" of the secondary schools, such classes were also a place to send troublemakers, as the *Nation* reported in a study of New York City's schools in 1958. Those who acted out elsewhere were also "reclassified" and sent to special education, a theme John Waters spoofed in his satirical look at early 1960s Baltimore, *Hairspray* (1988): one obstreperous student is platooned to a special education class filled with poor black youth and "retards."

As demands for higher achievement rose, urban administrators naturally worried about how to respond. The superintendent of the Gary, Indiana, schools warned in 1977 that "it is important that the standards of performance and expectation be realistic. Just as one would not ask a physically crippled child to run the dash, so no one of sound mind would expect mentally retarded children to read Chaucer." And no one thought that those in vocational education, who usually but not always had higher IQs than pupils in special education, should be reading the great books or studying difficult subjects. Few of the small high schools that dotted the land in 1950 had vocational education programs to any great extent, but they multiplied as schools consolidated and added more expansive course offerings. Educational leaders often publicly applauded vocational education, but everyone knew that most programs were low status, second rate, and frequently of doubtful utility. Calling it "career education" in the 1970s or "tech prep" later hardly mattered. Educators' faith in vocationalism was nevertheless widespread, and this probably reflected wider public sentiment. A prevailing principle in the Kennedy and Johnson administrations was manpower training, not income or wealth distribution, to solve the problems of poverty and to buttress a growing economy that could support a generous welfare state. Federal vocational education bills in 1963 and later reflected this faith in human capital investment in those unlikely, unwilling, or unable to handle academic subjects. Between 80 and 90 percent of adults polled at different times in the 1970s endorsed more "career education."

The realities of vocational education programs were sobering. Conant noted that, since vocationalism was always for "other people's children," suburban parents made sure that their schools focused on academics. Being assigned to vocational or special classes reduced one's chances of going to college, and examples of vocational programs in the city systems were hardly appealing. After all, *Blackboard Jungle* was based on the story of violence and social tensions at Bronx Vocational High School. By 1961, twenty-nine of the eighty-six high schools in New York City were vocational, as opposed to a handful that were strictly academic. Throughout the 1950s, urban administrators around the country reported, either in a matter-of-fact or despairing way, that vocational programs or schools were at the bottom of the status hierarchy. Herman Shibler, the superintendent in Indianapolis, was proud of his city's comprehensive high schools. Harry E. Wood Vocational School, founded in 1952, had a different focus. It offered classes in "barbering, shoe repair, commercial food preparation, dental assistant, beauty culture, and automobile body-and-fender bumping and painting. It also provide[d] curriculums for normal, mentally retarded, and socially maladjusted children." Little wonder, then, that when Franklin Keller, principal of the Metropolitan Vocational High School in New York City, traveled across the country in the early 1950s studying comprehensive secondary schools, numerous administrators shared the open secret that vocational education was for students considered dullards. Vocational classes were "too often the repositories for the dull and troublesome youngsters in academic classes," their "discards and rejects."

Champions of learning by doing such as Keller linked vocationalism to the progressive traditions of Rousseau, Pestalozzi, Froebel, and Dewey. He regretted that in the typical comprehensive high school the academic curriculum was still oriented around English, American and modern history, science, mathematics, a foreign language, health and physical education, music and fine arts, and some home economics for girls and shop for boys. The vocational tracks, however, were filled with poorer youth, were low status, and were largely nonacademic. Throughout the postwar era, critics complained about the shortage of topnotch teachers with good craft skills, of instruction in obsolete skills such as leathercraft and wood carving, of antiquated equipment, and of disruptive students with low IQs. Vocational classes were supposed to lower the dropout rates and raise the self-esteem of the pupils. Compared with those in the academic tracks, however, studies showed that in both categories students in vocational tracks fared worse. Providing vocational students with higher literacy and strong marketable skills—given the prevalence of ability groups, tracks, and the doctrine of human difference undergirding the modern graded school—seemed impossible. Vocationalism and special education thus shared much in common, as both were prime examples of the response to rising enrollments in the nation's high schools. These programs labored to keep youth in school, ensuring everyone had a place. They confirmed that Americans believed in equality of educational opportunity for all and extra for their own.

Almost everyone who attended high school in the 1950s and 1960s has similar recollections of it, whether serious or mundane or comical. The sights and sounds, the looks and phrases, soon became memories. Football, prom queens, fast cars, rock and roll. Student government, Spanish Club, yearbooks, teachers talking. Cheerleaders, majorettes, band practice, cutting class. Blue jeans, class clowns, report cards, dean's lists. Yellow buses, faded carpets, boring classes, driver's ed. Shop class, home economics, surprise quizzes, final exams. "Raise your hand!" "Quiet in the back!" "Where's your homework?" Notebooks, library passes, dusty blackboards, dropping out. Homeroom, the right clothes, dirty looks, clocks and bells. Ducktails, moptops, Afros, sideburns. Poodle skirts, dress codes, the wrong crowd, bathroom smoke.

National Lampoon's spoof of a 1964 high school yearbook—complete with its inane greetings from the principal, profiles of the seniors, in-jokes and put downs—became a minor cult classic because enough people recognized the social conventions it parodied. As Kurt Vonnegut observed, high school had become part of "the core of the American experience." The subject of countless movies (filled with juvenile delinquents and sometimes heroic teachers) and learned studies of curriculum and teaching (read by a handful of other experts), it occasionally became the central villain in tales of moral and educational decline. Since everyone now knew something about the high school experience, Hollywood and the media multiplied images of youth: teenage hoods in countless movies, sullen suburbanites in *Rebel without a Cause* (1955), and any number of tales of teenage love. A Presbyterian youth minister, speaking at the annual meeting of the National Association of Secondary School Principals in 1957, warned against creating stereotypes, given the diversity of the pupils now in school. Yet the students had obviously created their own slang, value systems, and cultural reference points within an expansive and intense peer culture. The minister said, "We call them hot-rod maniacs, crazy mixed-up kids, the rock-and-roll generation, the juvenile-delinquent generation," as if everyone smoked cigarettes, disrupted class, or engaged in teenage rumbles.

Administrators, school board members, self-appointed experts, teachers, taxpayers, and media figures always had suggestions about how to uplift youth and reform their schools. But adult concerns—including raising academic achievement and improving pedagogy—were hardly at the center of the student world, which revolved around other planets. Depending on time and place, students could be involved in gangs, ongoing efforts to integrate schools, petitions to add more electives, protests against petty rules and regulations, and all sorts of activities large and small, including doing homework and sitting quietly in class. While violence and incivility, drug use, and weak scholastic performance became serious problems by the 1960s and 1970s, and not only in the inner cities, citizens had long worried about students disconnected from adult norms of propriety and success. School expansion, consolidation, and popular culture would only widen the apparent divide between youth and their elders. Few pupils cared a whit about the fine points of Life Adjustment or *Educational Wastelands*. Of greater immediate significance, they were becoming integrated into an expanding consumer culture where having a car and the latest clothes were more important than geometry class. While academic success was emphasized in striving families, for boys the highest status at school came from being an athlete, not a scholar. For girls, appearance, personality, and being a cheerleader made one popular. The worlds of adults and students often seemed very far apart, though high schools were actually miniature versions of society, concerned with money, appearance, status, and sports and firmly rooted in mainstream cultural norms.

In an important study at midcentury of Wabash High School, a pseudonym for a suburban Midwestern secondary school, sociologist C. Wayne Gordon affirmed that the "big wheel" among the boys was the star athlete. For girls, it was the "Yearbook Queen," usually chosen on the basis of popularity, appearance, school spirit, leadership qualities, and moral reputation. This particular high school, which enrolled 576 students, had fifty different student organizations, exemplifying the proliferation of the extracurriculum, which professional educators still applauded as a democratizing force even though study after study showed that it was dominated by middle-class and upper-class students. Despite the existence of dozens of student groups and activities, Gordon discovered that only a handful conveyed high status. Students rated everything, including prospective dates. When asked what really mattered at their school, the senior boys crowned athletics king, placing different sports in the four leading spots on an itemized list. Girls, on the other hand, listed student government, cheerleading, varsity basketball, and the National Honor Society. As in most high schools, girls studied harder, behaved better, and earned higher grades. The boys listed the National Honor Society eighth on their list, far down the status ladder.

In the 1950s, James Coleman also studied secondary schools in the Midwest, conducting a comparative analysis of adolescents in ten different communities in northern Illinois, ranging from the suburbs to rural areas. His 1961 book *The Adolescent Society* underscored a widespread public concern: the perceived separation of teenagers from adult culture. "The adolescent is dumped into a society of his peers, a society whose habitats are the halls and classrooms of the school, the teen-age canteens, the corner drugstore, the automobile, and numerous other gathering places." Boys dreamed of being star athletes, not rocket scientists, despite the national brouhaha about science achievement following Sputnik. As Gordon and others before him had emphasized, athletes and cheerleaders had the highest status. "Being a biology assistant," Coleman added, "counts far less in the adolescent culture than does making the basketball team for boys, or making the cheerleading squad for girls." Being attractive, having the right personality (something president Eisenhower said was a key to success), and finding the right date consumed much of the time and energy of students. Middle-class students above all might acquiesce and study to get decent grades to please their parents and prepare for college, but few adolescents thought academics central to their daily lives. As Coleman concluded, generally "academic achievement did not 'count' for as much as did the other activities." Asked whom in their high school they most admired, students never named a star pupil.

Changing the culture of high schools to nurture higher intellectual goals would not be easy. Coleman noted that a principal who stressed academics stood accused of favoring the college bound. As he later wrote, anyone who entered the main foyer of the typical American high school usually did not meet a reproduction of "The Thinker," but tall cases of athletic trophies. Students called the bookish overachievers "grinds" and "brown-nosers," relegating them to one of the less desirable of the innumerable student cliques, whose membership was determined by curricular track, athletics, social background, and other factors. Like consumerism, sports mania was a defining characteristic of American culture, almost guaranteeing an honored place at school. Citizens who thought teachers were overpaid and otherwise balked at raising taxes always seemed to find a way to build a new basketball gym or football stadium. Harry Caudill noted that high school teachers in Appalachia, where schools often lacked chemistry or language labs, received pitiful salaries compared to coaches.

The student body and local communities fervently rallied around sports teams, turning a few youth into heroes and many into spectators. There were noticeably few boosters for history or physics. Coleman and various commentators also noticed that when engaged in sports, whether as participants or even as fans, many pupils shrugged off the passivity that was the hallmark of most classrooms. Progressive educators had long attacked all levels of the schools for not making classrooms student centered, and the high schools remained the worst offenders in the postwar years. While students might cheer and endorse collective goals such as a league championship, no one proposed selling tickets to fill a stadium or auditorium to honor the highest-achieving scholars. That the thought itself is ludicrous says much about the value system operating in most high schools. Despite the preeminent role of athletics, the extracurriculum also involved many students in drama, music, and other areas of personal interest, a welcome release from regular classroom routines and the attention accorded to the few.

Citizens wanted the schools to educate their children well, which was always a vague goal. Tocqueville's early-nineteenth-century observation that Americans embraced the practical and useful and had a populist suspicion about speculative thought and theory aptly characterizes traits still powerful after World War II. Also prevalent was the time-honored view that schools could promote individual mobility and social reform. High schools were unrealistically expected to do just about anything and everything, and they correspondingly disappointed many people. Even when the public seemed to demand more academic excellence and solid instruction in the basics, it hardly limited the schools to those goals. When pollsters asked the public in 1957 whether extracurricular activities were taking up too much time in high school, 49 percent said no and 38 percent yes. Asked in 1978 to rate the importance of the extracurriculum, 47 percent of public school parents said it was "very important" and 40 percent answered that it was "fairly important." They were also asked what "subjects" or "experiences" from high school were the "most useful in later life." In order from most to least useful they ranked English, mathematics, commercial subjects (typing and bookkeeping), and "extracurricular activities." Given the competing goals of the high school—academics for some, practical subjects for others, and social experiences of some sort for everyone, with some students as leaders and most as followers—many people concluded that the institution lacked a clear focus. To close down male sports programs and emphasize academics, however, was unthinkable to communities that usually wanted it all.

Predictably, the high school also disappointed various waves of progressive critics who called its teachers mired in tradition. While students perked up when it came to sports, dates, nice clothes, and fast cars, they found classrooms dull, something to be endured but not enjoyed. Workbooks, textbooks, quizzes, exams, report cards and all the other familiar signs from the past had survived intact. Nearly everywhere the school day was divided into forty- to fifty-minute periods, students earned set numbers of credits, classes were dismissed by the bell, and the building opened and closed at predictable times. Many teachers were responsible for monitoring a homeroom and a study hall, advising student organizations, and teaching five classes, whose average size declined from 28 students in 1961 to 23 twenty years later. As the student body became more diverse, many educators said audio-visual aids, team teaching, film strips, movies, and other pedagogical innovations would diversify instruction. Even when these innovations entered the schools, however, they tended to reinforce pupil passivity.

Teachers could lecture in teams as well as alone. Those who observed the new science in practice sometimes found teachers showing films of star college professors lecturing on a subject. Science labs generally did not teach inquiry and discovery per se, since most experiments led pupils to preordained outcomes. Inquiry and higher-order thinking certainly infused some classrooms, but it was the exception, not the rule. Students often paid as much attention to film strips on amoebas and protozoa as to lectures. That high schools bored the students was a staple in teacher training books and professional journals. William French observed that "the formal classroom is a rather dull place in which an unenthusiastic teacher drills uninteresting facts into the minds of reluctant pupils." While walking down the hall of a typical school, the only voices heard coming from classrooms were teachers'. Based on their observations in Chicago's high schools in the early 1960s, Robert Havighurst's team of researchers found that many teachers struggled to teach those reading at the fourth-grade level. "Many merely read the textbook through line by line with the students and give only short-answer quizzes. Some do nothing at all; their students can be seen dozing or staring into space." Various studies later found that high school teachers talked even more than elementary teachers, usually well over 70 percent of the class time. The usual pattern? Teachers asked a question, students raised their hands, were called upon, answered, then were asked more questions.

While there were some tire-iron wielding adolescents in the 1950s and gun-toting pupils later, students were generally fairly passive throughout the school day. Compared to the lively rhythms of rock and roll, the flashing images on televisions and movie screens, and a consumer culture of changing styles, schools seemed tired and antiquated. Some critics, however, believed that youth were actually receiving a functional education: poorer students fated to labor in the burgeoning service industry were being prepped for the future. Many commentators also blamed teacher-centered instruction and pupil passivity on tradition, the strangle hold of Carnegie units, large class sizes, the example of college professors (who loved to lecture), and parental conservatism. To have a quiet and orderly classroom remained the sine qua non of good teaching. Prepackaged teacher-proof curricula, teaching machines, and other attempts at individualized instruction also reinforced student passivity, and the memories of millions of high school pupils recorded long days of boring classes dominated by rote instruction, memorization, questions and answers, and drill.

A senior from New Rochelle, New York, told *Newsweek* in 1970 that the physics teacher "goes down the attendance list asking questions in alphabetical order. If you don't know the answer, he works you over for twenty minutes. By then, he's told you the answer, you've told him the question, you've told him the answer, he's asked the question again—and there's always somebody in the class who didn't understand any of it." A senior from Atlanta, in a perennial complaint about history classes, wanted more on current events and less about wars, diplomacy, and details about long-dead presidents like Millard Fillmore. Student activists called for more "relevant" courses, which only led to the proliferation of more electives. "We get very little education about the Pill, abortion, planned parenthood," said a female student from wealthy Evanston, Illinois. Numerous writers argued that African American student activists wanted more black studies and political relevance, while white suburbanites more often sought group affirmation and feel-good classes.

Bob Greene, later a well-known journalist, kept a journal in 1964 when he was a junior at Bexley High, in a suburb of Columbus, Ohio. He edited it but tried to honor its original spirit when it appeared in 1987 as *Be True to Your School*. For students, Bexley High was a place where sports, dances, cars, friends, music, clothes, and dreams of sex were the constants. Teachers, in contrast, constructed a dull world of "tests and quizzes. Today we had a quiz in Algebra; we got a Chemistry quiz back; we took a French test; and we got an English paper back. It's like you're being judged three or four times a day, every day." Varsity sports, however, was exciting, since players represented "Bexley against another school." Otherwise, Greene wrote, it was the "usual boring day in school." Like many students, Greene carried books home from his locker, sometimes never opened them, and toted them back the next morning. "Even dad doesn't have to bring home work from the office," he noted. Greene was in the college track, where homework and academics mattered most, but even there hardly defined student life.

Many observers of the high school emphasized that academics was not at the heart of the student experience. In the early 1970s, professor of education Philip Cusick, for example, found the students mostly bored and passive. Teachers stood in the front of the room and mostly lectured to students, whose desks were lined up in familiar rows. Taking attendance, checking absentee slips and library passes, asking students questions and then asking more, teachers talked about 75 percent of the time. Cusick's book *Inside High School* (1973) described students engaged in "a great deal of yawning, looking about, playing with papers and pencils, doodling, sleeping, looking at pictures, wallets, and whatever. It is very difficult to be an active and attentive listener for five periods a day." Cusick also noted that schools had low academic expectations, a theme later reinforced in the work of Theodore Sizer and other scholars. As Sizer wrote in *Horace's Compromise* (1984), for a variety of reasons, including teachers' responsibility for so many students, teachers and pupils informally agreed to not expect too much from each other. To many experts on the high school, despite some great exceptions most teaching was uninspired and full of routine.

Historian Robert L. Hampel has convincingly written that high school classrooms had a far more relaxed environment in 1975 than had been true even a decade earlier, never mind thirty years before. Depending on the high school, students might also have peers with different skin colors, whose native languages were not English, or who had learning problems or physical disabilities. But few students sought or found the holy grail of high achievement. For a variety of reasons—economic background, family structure, parental expectations, aptitude and ambition, and degree of access to well-funded schools— the majority of pupils in the first twenty years of NAEP mastered math, science, and reading only at a basic level. Their lack of high achievement was not particularly sanguine given all the talk about raising standards. Relatively stagnant NAEP scores across these subject areas in the 1970s hardly met the high hopes of the postwar era. In addition, many studies showed that, on average, Asian Americans did the best on various standardized achievement tests, followed by whites, African Americans, and Spanish-speaking children. Within these broad categories, gender and social class also shaped the results. More assimilated Spanish-language pupils from middle-class families typically performed better than new arrivals living in poverty.

Even before World War II, students lived in a world where sports stars and beauty queens, not the honor society and the Future Farmers of America, enjoyed the most status. Throughout the postwar decades, some reformers still dreamed of restoring an imagined past when high schools had educated students well. But high school was now for everyone, and rising expectations clashed with the reality that not every pupil could be above average.

As the last quarter of a century recedes in time and the present becomes the past, scholars of American education will slowly gain some distance from the events that recently shaped our times. Issues that now seem vital may fade in significance, while others now only dimly perceived may prove more influential. While it is impossible to predict what historians will conclude about this generation of America's public schools, every credible conclusion will share one thing in common: a sense of the enormous passions of the age. Like any era of momentous change, these years were exciting as well as troubling, filled with bold plans for school innovation and, depending on one's perspective, far-reaching or tepid reforms. Americans witnessed the triumph of free market capitalism across the Western world, the collapse of communist alternatives, and a conservative turn on the national level that undercut the legitimacy of liberal assumptions about schools and the social order. At the dawn of the twenty-first century, Republicans and many Democrats joined forces in a major attempt to reform the schools, this time through federal legislation, the No Child Left Behind Act of 2002.

This legislation, a reauthorization of the Elementary and Secondary Education Act of 1965, was the latest incarnation of a fascination with standards, testing, and evaluation whose roots were old but well watered over the last generation. It represented not simply the triumph of Republican politics but a popular faith in using schools as a lever of social progress, a familiar theme in American history reinforced by the rising expectations of the post–World War II era. Although it is doubtful that schools will yield universal success, "No Child Left Behind" should be understood in its widest historical context. As John Dewey wrote over a century ago, education is the fundamental means by which Americans try to improve individuals and society. Since the 1980s, countless reform-minded citizens still placed the schools at the center of broad discussions of the good life and the future direction of the nation. That Republicans mostly led the campaigns for school reform and Democrats often followed hardly invalidates that claim.

Full-fledged assaults on the "public school monopoly" from the right and left in the postwar era evolved into competing schemes to make schools more competitive and private alternatives more tenable. That markets and private interests deserved more public support—whether expressed in direct or indirect aid to private schools—gained considerable political and legal sanction. Choice became a multi-faceted reform ideal, embracing everything from open enrollment plans within school systems to charter schools and even home schooling. Federal involvement in educational policy, particularly in the setting of national goals and achievement standards, also gained political authority in the waning decades of the twentieth century. And yet there was something very familiar about the wide-ranging expectations of society toward the public schools, which still enrolled around 90 percent of all school-age students. Demands for higher standards, better discipline, and the basics remained popular. Teachers and administrators were told not only to raise achievement scores but also to produce well-behaved, model citizens and a winning team on Friday night. In many poor communities, schools were a safe haven from dangerous streets, and countless schools provided basic health and social services to needy children.

When asked in a Gallup poll in 1999 whether they would rather reform the public schools or seek alternatives to them, 71 percent of respondents favored reform and 70 percent preferred that course of action to vouchers, which would allow parents to spend a specified amount of tax money on schools of their choice. These are somewhat remarkable figures given the bad press that schools generally received throughout the period. Since the time of *A Nation at Risk,* many critics routinely called the schools mediocre, crime-ridden, and uninspired places of learning. They pointed to the overall low achievement of the poor, particularly of African American and Hispanic students. At the same time, citizens in numerous surveys rated local schools as satisfactory, and as better than public education generally. Many reform-minded people also lobbied for various pedagogical and curriculum reforms, reflecting a time-honored impulse to use schools to enhance individual mobility, secure social harmony, and build a better society. Some critics assume that the days of the public schools are numbered once parents have more choices, but only time will tell.

Education's role in the economy dominated many political debates by the 1980s, when Japan seemed invincible and America's industrial belts rusted away. Schools became a scapegoat for these and other economic ills. Some people assumed that slovenly work habits among the workers, not decisions made in corporate boardrooms, were largely to blame and a result of faulty schooling. It helped fuel the growing belief that the federal government had to play a more important role in educational policy. By the 1980s, Republican leaders, like their forebears in the nineteenth century, principally shaped the reform agenda. After *A Nation at Risk,* business leaders, politicians, and many educators were also involved in hundreds of state-level task forces that promised to strengthen the curriculum, raise standards, and generally toughen the fiber of public schools. Professional organizations representing subject areas such as mathematics and English later labored to reframe content standards in their respective fields. Less interested in the dream of building racially integrated schools or in furthering Great Society initiatives such as bilingual education, the Reagan and Bush administrations kept education in the national spotlight, frequently assailing teacher unions and failing schools. With Republicans ever dominant, moderate Democrats such as governor Bill Clinton of Arkansas and Albert Shanker of the American Federation of Teachers accepted and advanced the cause of school accountability and more testing of teachers and students.

Throughout the 1980s and early 1990s, culture wars further enlivened educational debate. Multiculturalism—a catchall term without a uniform definition—became a favored ideal in teacher education programs, though proposals for Afrocentric curricula gained fewer professional endorsements but much public scrutiny. In 1987, two bestsellers rolled off the presses, Allan Bloom's *The Closing of the American Mind* and E. D. Hirsch's *Cultural Literacy.* Both added fuel to many rhetorical fires, Bloom arguing that sixties liberalism and cultural relativism had undermined the Western canon on college campuses, Hirsch contending that most students lacked any common core of knowledge or cultural referents thanks to the influence of Rousseau, Dewey, and modern progressive educators. In California and Texas in particular—huge markets for school textbooks—cultural battles resembling an educational Armageddon pitted liberals and moderates against conservative Protestants and patriots, who demanded the removal of passages deemed left wing, irreligious, and critical of America from reading materials. Conservative evangelicals simultaneously attacked public schools for teaching "secular humanism" and supported independent Christian schools that valued God, traditional discipline, and the basics. Liberal academics criticized the scholarship of James Coleman and others that praised, and encouraged public aid to, Catholic schools, which increasingly enrolled many urban minorities. Politicians were inevitably pulled onto these fields of pedagogical engagement, which intensified complaints about low school achievement and energized the call to arms for national standards and testing.

In 1989, having crowned himself the "education president," George H. W. Bush invited the nation's fifty governors to gather together in Charlottesville,

Virginia, the first such meeting since Franklin D. Roosevelt invited their predecessors to help him deal with the Depression. Republicans and key members of the Democratic Leadership Council such as Bill Clinton ultimately identified a number of targeted reforms that became known as America 2000. As governor, Clinton gained a national reputation by testing Arkansas teachers to ensure their competence, and America 2000 evolved during his first presidential administration into Goals 2000, which Congress approved in 1994. By the turn of the century, American educators were supposed to reach a kind of promised land: guaranteeing the readiness of children entering school, world leadership in math and science, better graduation rates, full adult literacy, and safe and drug-free schools.

How well these ideas were conceived or achieved will continue to be contested. They nevertheless reflected the growing belief that schools, traditionally a state and local matter (except for aid to vocational education and the Great Society reforms) were the province of national oversight and concern. For example, the No Child Left Behind Act, yet another classic underfunded mandate, required mandatory testing of children in grades three through eight in basic subjects, invoked penalties on schools with persistent low performance, and largely defined schools by their test scores. In his 2005 State of the Union address, president George W. Bush endorsed the expansion of the testing programs to include high schools. This enthusiasm for standardized testing built upon public support, widespread since the 1970s, for minimum competency tests, high stakes tests for graduation, and an end to social promotion. Outspoken defenders of public education saw the legislation as a ploy to discredit the lowest performing schools (mostly filled with the poor and racial and ethnic minorities) and to open the door to more private alternatives. "No Child" has its own utopian aim: the elimination of differential school performance based on race and ethnicity. Its sponsors wisely made the target date 2014, when few people will likely remember who passed the bill and whom to blame if the states fail.

The driving interest in national standards, national tests, and a toughening of the curriculum since the 1980s did not seem to produce appreciably higher levels of overall academic achievement. The "education governors" and "education presidents" in both major parties nevertheless reflected public concern with the importance of educational credentials (if not achievement per se) in a world of declining industries, more free trade, and low-wage service economies. As employers after World War II increasingly used school completion to screen applicants and high school attendance and graduation became more common, the competition for economic advantages and jobs correspondingly accelerated. Demands for access to quality education became more intense as the rights revolution encouraged disadvantaged people to seek further educational opportunities for their children, which threatened the more comfortable classes, who vote more often, pay more taxes, and cannot be ignored by politicians. Americans of all backgrounds recognized that decent school credentials yielded economic benefits, so it was difficult for anyone to deny the importance of schools for personal mobility and social progress. No politician revived Barry Goldwater's 1964 claim that a child could do fine without an education.

The defeat of communism and growth of free trade, another bipartisan project, also meant that market solutions to real or perceived educational ills gained political traction after the 1970s. "Choice" became a rallying cry for conservatives and then liberals, whether that meant choices outside of or within the public system. Some conservative economists since the 1950s had endorsed opening schools to market competition, presumably to produce educational excellence among the poor, ignoring how markets had eviscerated urban economies. Left-wing radicals by the early 1970s also liked alternatives to the public school monopoly, and some helped promote vouchers, which the rising movement of conservatism often found very appealing. Indeed, the Reagan revolution deepened the attraction of market solutions to educational mediocrity by fostering a more positive image for corporate business leaders, who regularly complained about the poor quality of high school graduates. Entrepreneurs such as Chris Whittle and his associates took over some faltering public schools, predicting a rise in test scores for the poor and a 15 percent return on investment. How many dollars can be made on educating the poor remains unclear. Whittle's Channel One initiative provided free televisions and other equipment to cash-strapped schools; the schools then had to require students to watch so many minutes of television commercials, as if they saw too few of them at home. Corporations similarly flooded many schools with reading materials and textbooks filled with product placement. As junk food and candy machines proliferated in the schools, choice even shaped student waistlines.

Historians may understandably conclude that markets and business values seemed invincible from the Reagan era into the next century. But even though schools were sometimes reduced to test score results and their economic benefits, they still performed a breadth of services in local communities, frequently with strong public sanction. Public opinion polls provide some sense of the wide ranging, sometimes contradictory expectations of citizens. In 1986, Gallup asked citizens why going to school was important. Above all, they replied, schools provided access to better jobs and opportunities (42 percent), better preparation for life (23 percent), and financial security (9 percent). A similar poll a few years later yielded similar results. During the same year that president George H. W. Bush and the governors agreed that America needed a world-class system, only 9 percent of those polled cited the acquisition of "more knowledge" as the reason "why they want their children to get an education." Getting a good job again topped the list. That more credentials, if not learning per se, often paid off in the marketplace was widely embraced by the public, whose high expectations seemed undiminished by recurrent complaints about the schools. While they usually complained if anyone suggested raising taxes, citizens consistently wanted much more than the basics.

In a 1990 Gallup poll, 90 percent of respondents favored *requiring* drug abuse education, 84 percent favored requiring alcohol abuse education, 77 percent education about AIDS, 72 percent sex education, 66 percent education about environmental issues, and over 57 percent more "character education." Nearly half wanted the schools to teach parenting skills. This was only part of the public's wish list. When provided in the early 1990s with a list of values and asked which should or should not be taught by public schools, 97 percent wanted the schools to teach honesty and over 90 percent also favored teaching democracy, tolerance, patriotism, "caring for friends and family members," "moral courage," and the "golden rule." Except for tolerance, a major concern in some schools by World War II, these were mostly longstanding educational aims, a page out of a McGuffey's Reader. Only a slight majority approved of teaching about homosexuality and abortion rights, but even that level of support is remarkable. Asking schools to even consider addressing social and political issues that divide the American people inevitably leads to conflict, as citizens conclude either that the schools have usurped the authority of parents and churches or that they have failed to keep up with the times. In one breath the public demands higher academic standards and the basics, in another attention to just about every divisive social problem. Teachers are rarely asked to do less, since so many citizens seem to think that every human problem falls under the school's purview.

According to the polls, the percentage of citizens who believed strongly in the importance of the extracurriculum in adult success also remained very high in the post-Reagan era. High school pupils, like the larger society, accorded higher status to athletics than to the life of the mind. When asked by Gallup in 1993 what social services should be available in local schools, 92 percent of adults wanted exams for vision and hearing, 87 percent favored free or cheap lunches, 84 percent inoculations against communicable diseases, 74 percent free or cheap breakfasts, 62 percent some provisions for after school care, and 58 percent endorsed provision for dental exams. In the wake of the AIDS crisis, 41 percent said yes to distributing condoms in high schools to any student who asked for them, while 19 percent said yes only if students had parental permission. But 38 percent opposed any distribution of condoms, ensuring that educators were again in the middle of an issue on which they could not please everyone.

The social services first provided by voluntary associations during the Progressive Era were now funded by the federal, state, or local government, but the plethora of activities found in many public schools was often astounding. Citizens still wanted the basics taught well—math and English in particular—plus all the familiar virtues of the old common school, plus all of the social and health services that later entered the schools, plus the extracurriculum. Strong majorities also endorsed prayer in the schools, even though the U.S. Supreme Court ruled state-sponsored prayer unconstitutional in the early 1960s, and reform-minded citizens and local districts kept lawyers employed as citizens clashed over prayer, moments of silence in the classroom, and other church-state conflicts. Many activists fought for equal time in biology class for "creation science," which was often mandated by law, as Darwin was again placed on trial. In early 2004, Georgia's state school superintendent, a Republican, suggested eliminating the word "evolution" (but not the teaching of evolutionary principles) from the state curriculum since it inflamed local passions. She preferred the phrase "biological changes over time." For this she was promptly criticized by moderates including former president Jimmy Carter, who said faith in a Christian god and modern science were compatible, and by a socially conservative Republican who wondered why one would teach the concept but avoid the word. The National Center for Science Education reported that "evolution" did not appear in state curriculum guidelines in at least five states.

Few people can do all things well, and neither can the public schools. So it is not surprising that the public remained dissatisfied with the schools. When asked to compare their own school experiences to those of their children, 41 percent in 1979 said the contemporary schools were better and 42 percent said they were worse. The figures hardly changed in 1998. By then, despite the failure of voucher initiatives on the ballots in several states, Milwaukee and Cleveland helped fund private (often religion-based) schools with public monies, a practice that was upheld by the courts. A wide variety of charter schools—public schools allowed to bypass various state regulations so they can be free to innovate—began to multiply. President Clinton, who spoke the language of accountability and standards once associated mostly with Republicans, heartily endorsed charter schools as preferable to more radical efforts to privatize the schools. Home schooling also grew more popular, though it was a tiny part of the expanding range of educational alternatives to the traditional public school. By 2001, 47 percent of all Republicans and 34 percent of all Democrats polled believed home schooling was overall a "good thing." This in a time when working mothers were ever common and few families could live well on a single adult salary.

Even with the triumph of consolidation, centralization of authority, and professional expertise in the schools over the course of the twentieth century, and the more recent appearance of national goals and testing programs, America still has the most decentralized school governance in the Western world. In the 1999–2000 school year, there were over fourteen thousand school districts legally responsible for over ninety-two thousand public schools. Only an average of 6 percent of school funding came from the federal government, but the testing requirements of the No Child Left Behind Act may prove to be a watershed in the history of education, a financial burden many impoverished districts already find unbearable. Long before the passage of the new federal law, most states had already established their own testing programs, which joined the multitude of IQ tests, assorted achievement tests, and other statistical measures already routinely employed in many districts. American pupils take more standardized tests than any other students in the world, and they are about to take even more.

Defenders of the "No Child" legislation believe that it will help the poor, since the law requires evidence of the academic performance of students identified by race and ethnic background. Critics see the law as a boondoggle for testing corporations that waste money better spent on tutors, better teachers, and school materials. Characteristically, when running against Al Gore for president, then-governor George W. Bush pointed to the Lone Star State's impressive educational achievements, including improved test scores in cities such as Houston (whose superintendent would later become the head of the federal Department of Education). The cheering was premature. In several cities across the country, the pressure to secure higher test scores led to some unscrupulous practices. For example, numerous secondary pupils in Houston who would have done poorly on standardized tests were not tested. Even when they passed their courses, these pupils spent extra years in-grade, stayed out of the testing pool, and ultimately dropped out without earning a diploma. Houston officials said dropout rates had dramatically fallen, a claim contradicted by the evidence. That principals received nice cash bonuses if their schools hit higher test targets added an unseemly chapter to Bush's "Texas educational miracle."

In various states where passing high stakes tests is required to earn a diploma, the poor and racial minorities have disproportionally failed. Districts have even sent poor testers into special education to remove them from the competition and thus inflate the scores. Ironically, states such as Michigan actually lowered their own state standards to ensure that they were not penalized for being tougher than the national minimum. Only a handful of affluent parents, concentrated in a few rich districts across the nation, have complained about this testing mania. They believe that it distorts the more creative teaching found in their schools and reinforces the familiar emphasis on chalk and talk, and drills for skills. And their children generally perform very well indeed on standardized tests. At the other end of the social scale, the urban poor have the most inexperienced teachers, who rely on workbooks and traditional teaching methods in their valiant efforts to maintain order and raise standards.

We stand too close to the most recent generation of school reform to know where the future lies. There was nothing inevitable about the creation of free public school systems in the nineteenth century, and there is nothing inevitable about their survival or transformation in the coming decades. No one could have guessed in the early twentieth century that urban schools, widely regarded by professional educators as the model for schools everywhere, would soon fall from grace. No one could have predicted that the civil rights movement and rights revolution would bring poor and disadvantaged youngsters into systems that once excluded or mistreated them. No one could have known that the old idea of the school as a melting pot would be discredited, especially in professional training programs. History can offer perspective but not identify the pathways to the future. Like the past, the future will be full of surprises.

In *America's Public Schools* I have emphasized the tensions between tradition and change in the evolution of the nation's educational system. I have tried to show how successive waves of reformers left their imprint on the schools, whether on the curriculum, the pedagogy, or the value systems underlying everyday practice. I have stressed that child-centered progressivism has triumphed rhetorically more often than in the classroom, and have described and tried to understand schools in their time and place, highlighting the continuity of many school practices, from emphasis on the basics to the competing social goals and diverse innovations favored by educators and reformers. Finally, I have underscored the reality that historically the public schools have never succeeded in making intellectual achievement, never mind high achievement for all, their central purpose. Only in the last half-century have most African Americans, Mexican Americans, and children of the working poor regularly attended and graduated from high schools or have children with special needs attended in large numbers, whether in special or mainstreamed classes.

Rhetoric about raising standards, ending social promotion, and increasing testing on basic subjects proved very popular to many citizens and their elected officials throughout the recent past. Ours is a competitive society that prizes individual striving and applauds personal achievement. That the test scores of poor and minority children remain relatively low is not particularly surprising, given the collapse of the urban infrastructure, rise of single-parent households and persistent poverty, and widespread faith of parents in equal educational opportunity for all and extra for their own. In the past, the poor generally dropped out of school and entered the workforce or perhaps joined the military. But the educational stakes rose after World War II, and so did the class, racial, and culture wars in the schools. Civil rights promised equality, but test scores guaranteed evidence of inequality. In the 1950s, upwardly mobile white parents moved their families to the suburbs, insisted on more Advanced Placement courses and honors programs, and positioned their children as best they could to compete and win. Families with disposable income later spent millions of dollars on personal tutoring services, Kaplan classes, and other means to help ensure success. In addition, despite ubiquitous complaints about the low cognitive achievement of American students generally, including scores on international tests, the public has long expected the schools to help address every imaginable social ill, while it admired athletes and cheerleaders more often than scholastic overachievers.

One should at least remember these realities as testing programs reach down to the youngest pupils. Even children in kindergarten, an institution born in an age of romance and revolution, are now increasingly tested. "I've got kids that have never held a pencil before," one kindergarten teacher from Mississippi tried to remind people in 1988. "And last year I had one that had never held silverware." After president Bill Clinton met in 1996 with dozens of business leaders and politicians in yet another "educational summit" that promised to raise standards, a senior officer of the National School Boards Association asked: "What about children coming to schools who aren't healthy, who are hungry, from crime-ridden neighborhoods, and who can't concentrate on learning because of all these other problems? How will standards fix those problems?" Schools cannot fix most of the problems they did not create, but, if historical precedent matters, that will not stop people from asking them to try.

Public schools remain the most intimate expression of governmental authority in most communities. Since more and more people have attended school for more years of their lives, the public is less deferential to teachers and administrators than it was decades ago, and freely offers advice on educational improvement. Few citizens believe that they can control the impersonal forces, from the global economy to environmental degradation, that shape our world. But the schools, ostensibly under local control despite rising federal mandates, are another matter. Yet the public never speaks with a single voice, and the aims of modern education, which focus on getting ahead, often remain muddled. Americans apparently expect schools to create a level playing field in a social order where inequality—in income, wealth, and consumer goods—mocks democratic values and ensures that children come to school unequally prepared to learn. Schools are expected to succeed at reconciling equality and excellence, standards and democracy, respect for tradition and commitment to progress. The public regularly pillories teachers and administrators for not teaching the basics well and for failing to produce enough high-achieving students, especially among the poor. At the same time, reformers from every side of the political spectrum periodically demand that teachers, accused of teaching their subjects so poorly, solve grave social ills that adults, not students, mostly created, such as racial segregation, sexism, and xenophobia, and also teach the young delayed gratification, honesty, the golden rule, and other values not always honored in practice by their elders.

Public opinion polls may indicate widespread support for national tests and higher standards, but few Americans want to strip schools of their many social obligations and have them concentrate on academics. For almost two centuries, nearly every campaign for social justice, human equality, and individual advancement has been waged in part in the public schools. So have popular movements for the preservation of traditional subjects, values, and morality. The humorist Will Rogers once wrote that "Russia is a country that no matter what you say about it, it's true." The same can be said about America's sprawling school system, whose fate remains in the hands of a citizenry that craves both continuity and change.

Essay on Sources

GENERAL WORKS

Except for textbooks, single-volume interpretations of the broad sweep of the history of American education are rare, a testimony to the difficulty of the subject and expansive nature of the public schools over the past century. Every student of educational history, however, must engage with the competing claims and themes presented in these landmark volumes: Merle Curti, *The Social Ideas of American Educators* (1935); Michael B. Katz, *The Irony of Early School Reform: Educational Innovation in Mid-Nineteenth Century Massachusetts* (1968); David B. Tyack, *The One Best System: A History of American Urban Education* (1974); Joel Spring, *The Sorting Machine: National Educational Policy since 1945* (1976); Joseph F. Kett, *Rites of Passage: Adolescence in America, 1790 to the Present* (1977); Diane Ravitch, *The Troubled Crusade: American Education, 1945–1980* (1983); Carl F. Kaestle, *Pillars of the Republic: Common Schools and American Society, 1780–1860* (1983); Herbert M. Kliebard, *The Struggle for the American Curriculum, 1893–1958* (3rd edition, 2004); and B. Edward McClellan, *Moral Education in America: Schools and the Shaping of Character from Colonial Times to the Present* (1999). Lawrence A. Cremin's *The Transformation of the School: Progressivism in American Education, 1876–1957* (1961) recognized the multi-faceted dimensions of reform and continues to teach and inspire students of progressive education. Less influential was his magisterial history in three volumes: *American Education: The Colonial Experience, 1607–1783* (1970), *American Education: The National Experience, 1783–1876* (1980), and *American Education: The Metropolitan Experience, 1876–1980* (1988), which emphasize the enormous range of institutions that educate, not just schools.

The *History of Education Quarterly* remains the authoritative guide to the latest trends in the field. In addition, important one-volume interpretations include Wayne J. Urban and Jennings L. Wagoner Jr., *American Education: A History* (1996) and John L. Rury, *Education and Social Change: Themes in the History of American Schooling* (2002). See, too, Richard J. Altenbaugh, ed., *Historical Dictionary of American Education* (1999). For debates on the historiography of the field, read Milton Gaither, *American Educational History Revisited: A Critique of Progress* (2003).

Nothing substitutes for research in the primary sources to understand how educators, lay people, and reformers of all persuasions understood their world and tried to shape educational policy at different moments in the past. Immersion in these sources was the foundation for this book. The following description of the essential primary and secondary sources drawn upon in this study reflects the chronological division of the book into three periods: the nineteenth century and both halves of the twentieth century.

THE NINETEENTH CENTURY

Understanding the evolution of education and schooling in their nineteenth-century settings requires a mastery of secondary sources too numerous to describe. So I must necessarily slight some otherwise excellent references because of the particular focus of my book and space limitations. No one can write broadly about many topics over long sweeps of time without depending on the labors of other scholars. I have been aided by numerous authoritative and masterful histories as well as extensive research in primary sources on the state and local level. To understand nineteenth-century political developments, which shaped the role of schools in society, read John A. Garraty, *The New Commonwealth, 1877–1890* (1968); Eric Foner, *Free Soil, Free Labor, Free Men: The Ideology of the Republican Party before the Civil War* (1970); Daniel Walker Howe, *The Political Culture of the American Whigs* (1979); Jean H. Baker, *Affairs of Party: The Political Culture of Northern Democrats in the Mid-Nineteenth Century* (1983); and Ronald P. Formisano, *The Transformation of Political Culture: Massachusetts Parties, 1790s–1830s* (1983). On social changes and reform movements, I drew heavily upon a range of important interpretations, especially Eric Hobsbawm, *The Age of Capital, 1848–1875* (1975); Mary P. Ryan, *Cradle of the Middle Class: The Family in Oneida County, New York* (1981); Alan Trachtenberg, *The Incorporation of America: Culture and Society in the Gilded Age* (1982); Lori D. Ginzberg, *Women and the Work of Benevolence: Morality, Politics, and Class in the Nineteenth-Century United States* (1990); John F. Kasson, *Rudeness and Civility: Manners in Nineteenth-Century America* (1990); Charles Sellers, *The Market Revolution: Jacksonian America, 1815–1846* (1991); David Montgomery, *Citizen Worker: The Experience of Workers in the United States with Democracy and the Free Market during the Nineteenth Century* (1993); Walter Licht, *Industrializing America: The Nineteenth Century* (1995); Daniel Feller, *The Jacksonian Promise: America, 1815–1840* (1995); Steven Mintz, *Moralists and Modernizers: America's Pre–Civil War Reformers* (1995); and Ronald G. Walters, *American Reformers, 1815–1860* (revised edition, 1997). The volumes by Garraty and Licht especially shaped my thinking because they so effectively identified the facts of economic change but also offered thoughtful interpretations of complex subjects. Similarly, Jon C. Teaford, *The Unheralded Triumph: City Government in America, 1870–1900* (1984), was indispensable in providing a persuasive analysis of urban developments and comparisons with Europe. Southern developments are richly documented and analyzed in Edward L. Ayers, *The Promise of the New South: Life after Reconstruction* (1992).

In addition to the influential books by Kaestle and Katz cited under "General Works," see especially Lawrence A. Cremin's insightful (and little-read) gem, *The American Common School, An Historic Conception* (1951) and the thoughtful volume by Maris A. Vinovskis, *Education, Society, and Economic Opportunity: A Historical Perspective on Persistent Issues* (1995). I have similarly drawn upon Carl F. Kaestle and Maris A. Vinovskis, *Education and Social Change in Nineteenth-Century Massachusetts* (1980) in describing northern patterns of school attendance and enrollment rates as well as the goals of common school reformers. Jonathan Messerli, *Horace Mann: A Biography* (1972) provides an incisive interpretation of Mann's psyche; and Kathryn Kish Sklar, *Catharine Beecher: A Study in American Domesticity* (1973), is similarly outstanding in recounting family influences upon her subject. Also read Edith Nye MacMullen, *In the Cause of True Education: Henry Barnard and Nineteenth-Century School Reform* (1991). For a broad understanding of how Americans thought about knowledge, literacy, and learning, see Lee Soltow and Edward Stevens, *The Rise of Literacy and the Common School in the United States: A Socioeconomic Analysis to 1870* (1981) as well as two outstanding volumes by Richard D. Brown, *Knowledge is Power: The Diffusion of Information in Early America, 1700–1865* (1989) and *The Strength of a People: The Idea of an Informed Citizenry in America, 1650–1870* (1996). On Benjamin Franklin, the collapse of the apprenticeship system, and its import for education, William J. Rorabaugh, *The Craft Apprentice: From Franklin to the Machine Age in America* (1986) is definitive.

On race relations, Eric Foner's *Reconstruction: America's Unfinished Revolution, 1863–1877* (1988) is the new standard; also read Leon F. Litwack, *Trouble in Mind: Black Southerners in the Age of Jim Crow* (1998). James D. Anderson's remarkable book, *The Education of Blacks in the South, 1860–1935* (1988) has only slowly been revised by a new generation of scholars. On immigrant struggles on the West Coast, Victor Low, *The Unimpressionable Race: A Century of Educational Struggle by the Chinese in San Francisco* (1982) is a principal source of my understanding of the subject for the nineteenth and twentieth centuries. On the Mexican Preparatory School in El Paso, see Mario T. Garcia, *Desert Immigrants: The Mexicans of El Paso, 1880–1920* (1981); on Tucson, read Thomas E. Sheridan, *Los Tusconenses: The Mexican Community in Tucson, 1854–1941* (1986). On rural schools and their ties to community, see Wayne E. Fuller, *The Old Country School: The Story of Rural Education in the Middle West* (1982), which is being challenged by scholars such as Paul Theobald, author of *Call School: Rural Education in the Midwest to 1918* (1995). On developments in the pre–Civil War South, see Joseph W. Newman, "Antebellum School Reform in the Port Cities of the Deep South," in David N. Plank and Rick Ginsberg, eds., *Southern Cities, Southern Schools: Public Education in the Urban South* (1990), 17–36. William A. Link provides an informative case study in *A Hard Country and a Lonely Place: Schooling, Society, and Reform in Rural Virginia, 1870–1920* (1986). An especially helpful overview of rural trends is David B. Danbom's, *Born in the Country: A History of Rural America* (1995), which I relied upon as an invaluable source of statistics and interpretations of various aspects of rural life, including education.

Seminal interpretations of individual school systems include Carl F. Kaestle, *The Evolution of an Urban School System: New York City, 1750–1850* (1973); Stanley K. Schultz, *The Culture Factory: Boston Public Schools, 1789–1860* (1973); and Selwyn K. Troen, *The Public and the Schools: Shaping the St. Louis System, 1838–1920* (1975). See Marvin Lazerson, *Origins of the Urban School: Public Education in Massachusetts, 1870–1915* (1971) on the history of early childhood programs and industrial education. Debates on the history of the origins and social significance of the high school intensified thanks to the innovative scholarship of Michael B. Katz in *The Irony of Early School Reform*, which led to the spirited response by Maris A. Vinovskis, *The Origins of Public High Schools: A Reexamination of the Beverly High School Controversy* (1985) and a probing forum entitled "The Origins of Public High Schools," in *History of Education Quarterly* 27 (Summer 1987): 241–58. In addition, my own volume, *The Origins of the American High School* (1995), offers a broad social analysis and lists many primary and secondary sources that also shaped *America's Public Schools*. Credentials and the marketplace are central in David F. Labaree, *The Making of an American High School: The Credentials Market and the Central High School of Philadelphia, 1838–1939* (1988).

Given the decentralized nature of the American public school system, scholars face the daunting task of trying to discern general educational patterns in a diverse society spread across a vast continent. Generalizations found in this book were largely based on research in primary sources, and I sometimes relied heavily on writings in professional school journals. These periodicals, usually published by teachers' associations, local districts, or private entrepreneurs, presented articles on every conceivable educational topic, providing a sense of the competing strains in educational reform. For national trends, I read Horace Mann's *Common School Journal* (1838–1849); Henry Barnard's *American Journal of Education* (1840–1880); the *New England Journal of Education* (1875–1900); *Educational Review* (1891–1900); *School Review* (1895–1900); and others for selective topics. I also benefited from the *Alabama Teachers Journal* (1885–1888); *Carolina Teacher* (1886–1888); *Common School* (Grafton, North Dakota, 1893–1894); *Dakota Educator* (1888–1891); *Dakota School Journal* (1885); *Dixie School Journal* (1894–1895); *Educational Weekly* (Chicago, 1877–1881); *Educational Weekly* (Indianapolis, 1883–1886); *Indiana School Journal* (1881–1900); *Mississippi Journal of Education* (1895); *North Carolina Journal of Education* (1897–1900); *North Carolina Teacher* (1883–1885); *Pennsylvania School Journal* (1879–1900); *Teacher at Work* (Huntsville, Alabama, 1889–1891); and the *Wisconsin Journal of Education* (1879–1900). Particularly useful information on numerous topics appeared in Henry Kiddle and Alexander J. Schem, eds., *The Cyclopaedia of Education: A Dictionary of Information for the Use of Teachers, School Officers, Parents, and Others* (1877).

In addition to the numerous publications of the U.S. Bureau of Education in the post–Civil War era, nineteenth-century school reformers often left an impressive paper trail for historians. Indispensable for this study were the annual reports of Horace Mann during his tenure as secretary to the Massachusetts State Board of Education (1837–1848) and the annual reports (1868–1880) and other writings by William T. Harris during his years as school superintendent in St. Louis. For fuller references on Harris, see my essays entitled "The Philosopher-King of St. Louis," in Barry M. Franklin, ed., *Curriculum and Consequence: Herbert M. Kliebard and the Promise of Schooling* (2000), 155–177; and "Public Education in Nineteenth-Century St. Louis," in Eric Sandweiss, ed., *St. Louis in the Century of Henry Shaw: A View beyond the Garden Wall* (2003), 167–87. The thoughts of lesser-known figures lie buried in state and local periodicals and other documents. The original writings of the English, German, and American romantic poets and educators similarly help recapture their distinctive world views, and Raymond Williams locates major concepts in time and place in *Keywords: A Vocabulary of Culture and Society* (1976).

There are numerous references to primary and secondary sources on child-centered education in my article "The Origins of Progressive Education," *History of Education Quarterly* 41 (Spring 2001): 1–24. In particular, I was influenced by the following: Florence Bernstein Freedman, *Walt Whitman Looks at the Schools* (1950); Arthur O. Lovejoy, *Essays in the History of Ideas* (1960); Gerald Lee Gutek, *Pestalozzi and Education* (1968); Bernard Wishy, *The Child and the Republic: The Dawn of Modern American Child Nurture* (1968); George Dykhuizen, *The Life and Mind of John Dewey* (1973), on Dewey's high school teaching; Robert B. Downs, *Friedrich Froebel* (1978); Hugh Cunningham's masterful *Children and Childhood in Western Society since 1500* (1985); Barbara Beatty's definitive, *Preschool Education in America: The Culture of Young Children from the Colonial Era to the Present* (1995); Norman Brosterman, *Inventing Kindergarten* (1997); and Robert D. Richardson Jr., *Emerson: The Mind on Fire* (1995). On the remarkably diverse expressions of early childhood education in different times and places, see Roberta Wollons, ed., *Kindergartens and Cultures: The Global Diffusion of an Idea* (2000). On teachers, see Barbara Finkelstein, *Governing the Young: Teacher Behavior in Popular Primary Schools in Nineteenth-Century United States* (1989).

As public schools formed in the nineteenth century, they became grist for the mill of public debate, and this volume depended upon the availability of a plethora of books, pamphlets, speeches, debates, and other written sources on educational theory and practice. While many additional sources are cited in the endnotes of *The Origins of the American High School*, antebellum education and reform are illuminated in James G. Carter, *Letters to the Honorable William Prescott, LL.D., on the Free Schools of New England, with Remarks on the Principles of Instruction* (1824); James G. Carter, *Essays upon Popular Education* (1826); Benjamin O. Peers, *American Education* (1838); John Orville Taylor, *Satirical Hits on the People's Education* (1839); Orestes A. Brownson, *The Laboring Classes* (1840); Samuel Wadsworth Gold, *Education for the Millions: Physical, Intellectual, and Moral* (1850); Ira Mayhew, *Popular Education* (1852); Per Adam Siljestrom, *Educational Institutions of the United States* (1853); S. S. Randall, *Mental and Moral Culture and Popular Education* (1855); and Hiram Orcutt, *Hints to Common School Teachers, Parents, and Pupils; Or, Gleanings from School-Life Experience* (1859). On the McGuffey Readers, see Ruth Miller Elson, *Guardians of Tradition: American Schoolbooks of the Nineteenth Century* (1964) and Elliot J. Gorn, ed., *The McGuffey Readers: Selections from the 1879 Edition* (1998).

On public schools in the Civil War era, see Edward A. Sheldon, *Lessons on Objects* (1863); and C. F. Childs, *Essays on Education and Culture* (1867). On the postwar era, read Albert N. Raub, *Plain Educational Talks with Teachers and Parents* (1869); William N. Hailmann, *Kindergarten Culture in the Family and Kindergarten* (1873), among his many important writings; Francis Adams, *The Free School System of the United States* (1875); Robert William Dale, *Impressions of America* (1878); Charles F. Adams Jr., *The New Departure in the Common Schools of Quincy and Other Papers on Educational Topics* (1879); Gail Hamilton (pseudonym), *Our Common School System* (1880); J. G. Fitch, *Notes on American Schools and Training Colleges* (1890); Richard Harcourt's caustic *Conspiracy: The American Public Schools* (1890); and Louisa Parsons Stone Hopkins, *The Spirit of the New Education* (1892).

FROM THE PROGRESSIVE ERA THROUGH WORLD WAR II

The Progressive Era (circa 1890–1920) and, to a lesser extent, the New Deal era (1933–1945) have been the subjects of an explosion of books and articles on the history of reform movements and educational change. Most influential have been Richard Hofstadter, *The Age of Reform: From Bryan to FDR* (1955), particularly in its claims about the symbolic nature of reform; Robert H. Wiebe's *The Search for Order, 1877–1920* (1967) for its emphasis on the bureaucratic and professional turn among the "new middle class"; and Robert M. Crunden's *Ministers of Reform: The Progressives' Achievement in American Civilization, 1889–1920* (1982) for reminding scholars of the moralistic, Protestant roots of many reform movements in the early twentieth century. FDR's New Deal primarily aimed to solve the economic problems resulting from the Great Depression, leading to the foundations of the modern welfare state. Despite a few innovative and memorable programs that directly affected the schools, it did not principally focus on educational reform. An extensive bibliography can be found in David M. Kennedy's masterful volume, *Freedom from Fear: The American People in Depression and War, 1929–1945* (1999). The best volumes on the educational developments of the interwar period include David Tyack, Robert Lowe, and Elisabeth Hansot, *Public Schools in Hard Times: The Great Depression and Recent Years* (1984); Paula S. Fass, *Outside In: Minorities and the Transformation of American Education* (1989); and the relevant chapters in Jonathan Zimmerman, *Whose America? Culture Wars in the Public Schools* (2002).

Nearly every aspect of Progressive Era school reform has attracted the attention of historians. David A. Gamson, David P. Setran, Karen Benjamin, and Jeffrey Mirel helped shape my understanding of Progressive Era reforms through their outstanding essays in "American Education in the Twentieth Century: Progressive Legacies," a special issue of *Paedagogica Historica* 39 (August 2003): 417–97. School administrators and administration in particular have received considerable scrutiny from many scholars. An early synthesis was Raymond E. Callahan's *Education and the Cult of Efficiency: A Study of the Social Forces That Have Shaped the Administration of the Public Schools* (1962). David Tyack's analysis in *The One Best System* (1974) of school board reform and the rise of the modern urban administrator has been especially influential. Also see David Tyack and Elisabeth Hansot, *Managers of Virtue: Public School Leadership in America, 1820–1980* (1982); and, for a different perspective, Jackie M. Blount, *Destined to Rule the Schools: Women and the Superintendency, 1873–1995* (1998). On the Country Life movement, consult David B. Danbom, *The Resisted Revolution: Urban America and the Industrialization of Agriculture, 1900–1930* (1979); and on the contemporary defense of the district school, Hal S. Barron, *Mixed Harvest: The Second Great Transformation in the Rural North, 1870–1930* (1997).

Since the cities were the major sites of reform, historians have naturally been attracted to developments there. See, for example, David John Hogan, *Class and Reform: School and Society in Chicago, 1880–1930* (1985); William J. Reese, *Power and the Promise of School Reform: Grass-Roots Movements during the Progressive Era* (1986), which further documents some themes expanded upon in this volume; Marnie Jones, *Holy Toledo: Religion and Politics in the Life of 'Golden Rule' Jones* (1998), a fine biography of the social justice mayor; Bryce E. Nelson, *Good Schools: The Seattle Public School System, 1901–1930* (1988); Ronald D. Cohen, *Children of the Mill: Schooling and Society in Gary, Indiana, 1906–1960* (1990); Judith Rosenberg Raftery, *Land of Fair Promise: Politics and Reform in Los Angeles Schools, 1885–1941* (1992); and Jeffrey Mirel, *The Rise and Fall of an Urban System, Detroit, 1907–81* (1993). Joel H. Spring's *Education and the Rise of the Corporate State* (1972) also contains insightful criticisms of educational policy during the Progressive Era, particularly related to urban developments and business policy. On the vast literature on the origins of the testing movement, see the essays and extensive references in Michael M. Sokal, ed., *Psychological Testing and American Society, 1890–1920* (1987). Henry L. Minton, *Lewis M. Terman: Pioneer in Psychological Testing* (1988) is an outstanding source that shaped my understanding of its subject. On a major critic of testing, see J. Wesley Null, *A Disciplined Progressive Educator: The Life and Career of William Chandler Bagley* (2003).

The controversial question of whether progressive and child-centered ideas actually shaped school practice is the concern of several important books, which reach different conclusions. Arthur Zilversmit is skeptical in *Changing Schools: Progressive Education Theory and Practice, 1930–1960* (1993), Diane Ravitch detects more influence in *Left Back: A Century of Failed School Reforms* (2000), while Larry Cuban offers balance and nuance in *How Teachers Taught: Constancy and Change in American Classrooms, 1890–1980* (1984). Students of John Dewey can choose among numerous biographies, none more accessible or insightful than Robert B. Westbrook's *John Dewey and American Democracy* (1991). Westbrook persuasively locates Dewey's ideas in their time and place and reemphasizes the philosopher's importance to democratic theory and his distance from many erstwhile followers. Different aspects of the lives of teachers and nature of the teaching profession come to life in Donald Warren, ed., *American Teachers: Histories of a Profession at Work* (1989); and Kathleen Weiler, *Country Schoolwomen: Teaching in Rural California, 1850–1950* (1998). On oral histories of teachers, see Kate R. Rousmaniere, *City Teachers: Teaching and School Reform in Historical Perspective* (1997). On how teachers interpret and adapt innovative ideas, examine David B. Tyack and Larry Cuban, *Tinkering Toward Utopia: A Century of Public School Reform* (1995).

There is a burgeoning literature on African American educational history, and a revisionist account can be found in Eric Anderson and Alfred A. Moss Jr., *Dangerous Donations: Northern Philanthropy and Southern Black Education, 1902–1930* (1999). On Booker T. Washington, especially read Louis R. Harlan's two-volume biography: *Booker T. Washington: The Making of a Black Leader, 1856–1901* (1972) and *Booker T. Washington: The Wizard of Tuskegee, 1901–1915* (1983); on W. E. B. Du Bois, David Levering Lewis, *W. E. B. Du Bois: Biography of a Race, 1868–1919* (1993). Also read the still valuable Horace Mann Bond, *The Education of the Negro in the American Social Order* (1939). On state-level reform and local developments, see James L. Leloudis, *Schooling the New South: Pedagogy, Self, and Society in North Carolina, 1880–1920* (1996). On immigrant experiences, see Susan Cotts Watkins, ed., *After Ellis Island: Newcomers and Natives in the 1910 Census* (1994), especially the essay by Jerry A. Jacobs and Margaret E. Greene, "Race and Ethnicity, Social Class, and Schooling," 209–55, the primary source of my description of differential school achievement among the various immigrant groups; the essays in Stephan Thernstrom, ed., *Harvard Encyclopedia of American Ethnic Groups* (1980), especially Michael R. Olneck and Marvin Lazerson, "Education," 303–19; Stephan F. Brumberg, *Going to America, Going to School: The Jewish Immigrant Public School Encounter in Turn-of-the-Century New York* (1986); David K. Yoo, *Growing Up Nisei: Race, Generation, and Culture among Japanese Americans of California, 1924–49* (2000), for details on school achievement and the extracurriculum; and Yoon K. Pak, *Wherever I Go, I Will Always Be a Loyal American: Schooling Seattle's Japanese Americans during World War II* (2002). Barry M. Franklin has pioneered in the study of children with learning problems, evidenced in his major contribution, *From "Backwardness" to "At Risk": Childhood Learning Difficulties and the Contradictions of School Reform* (1994).

How work and the conditions of labor shaped educational policy has attracted many scholars, including Arthur G. Wirth, *Education in the Technological Society: The Vocational-Liberal Studies Controversy in the Early Twentieth Century* (1972); Harvey Kantor and David B. Tyack, eds., *Work, Youth, and Schooling: Historical Perspectives on Vocationalism in American Education* (1982); and John L. Rury, *Education and Women's Work: Female Schooling and the Division of Labor in Urban America, 1870–1930* (1991). Herbert M. Kliebard's *Schooled to Work: Vocationalism and the American Curriculum, 1876–1946* (1999) recaptures the tensions underlying movements for practical education and vocationalism's broad impact in the schools; it also presents some important case studies, coauthored with Carol Judy Kean, on reform in one industrial city, Milwaukee. As adolescents were displaced from the workplace, high schools expanded enormously, and their changing nature is analyzed with insight and wit in Edward A. Krug's *The Shaping of the American High School, 1880–1920* (1964) and *The Shaping of the American High School, 1920–1940* (1972), which remain indispensable. Also read Selwyn K. Troen, "The Discovery of the Adolescent by American Educational Reformers, 1900–1920: An Economic Perspective," in Lawrence Stone, ed., *Schooling and Society: Studies in the History of Education* (1976), 239–51. For an excellent synthesis, see Jurgen Herbst, *The Once and Future School: Three Hundred and Fifty Years of American Secondary Education* (1996). The story of declining academic standards in the twentieth-century high school is central to David L. Angus and Jeffrey E. Mirel's *The Failed Promise of the American High School, 1890–1995* (1999). For a sketch of Ellwood P. Cubberley, begin with Lawrence A. Cremin, *The Wonderful World of Ellwood Patterson Cubberley: An Essay on the Historiography of American Education* (1965), supplemented by the fuller treatment by Jesse B. Sears and Adin D. Henderson, *Cubberley of Stanford and His Contribution to American Education* (1957).

Even the very best scholarship in print pales in excitement when compared with contact with primary sources. As schools rose in importance during the first half of the twentieth century, the number of written sources grew exponentially, adding to the difficulties scholars face in hunting their quarry. Much of what I learned derived from case studies of particular school systems, as demonstrated in my book *Power and the Promise of School Reform* (1986). Similarly, references on Indiana and its urban school system, mentioned at different points in this volume, can be gleaned from the relevant essays in my edited book, *Hoosier Schools: Past and Present* (1988), and from my essay entitled "Education," on the history of the Indianapolis public schools in David J. Bodenhamer and Robert G. Barrrows, eds., *The Encyclopedia of Indianapolis* (1994), 72–85.

Most important in my research were contemporary books and articles as well as numerous special reports published under the auspices of the U.S. Bureau of Education. In addition to reading the annual reports of many school boards and superintendents in various towns and cities, I also learned a considerable amount from professional educational periodicals. Especially helpful were the *Alabama School Journal* (1923–1941); *Atlantic Educational Journal* (1911–1918); *Complete Education* (Toledo, Ohio, 1900–1902); *Educational Exchange* (Birmingham, Alabama, 1889–1919); *High School Journal* (1918–1941); Pennsylvania's *School Journal* (1905–1918); *Mississippi Educational Advance* (1911–1942); *School Life* (1918–1941); *Southern School and Home* (1902–1903); and *Wisconsin Journal of Education* (1900–1945). The original writings of leading educational theorists and main actors in various school reforms are essential, including Leonard P. Ayres, William Bagley, Boyd H. Bode, George Counts, Ellwood Cubberley, John Dewey, Isaac Kandel, Charles Prosser, George D. Strayer, Edward L. Thorndike, and Edward J. Ward.

In the first half of the twentieth century, countless volumes were written on the nature of elementary and secondary education, but especially see Paul H. Hanus, *Educational Aims and Educational Values* (1900); Charles B. Gilbert, *The School and Its Life: A Brief Discussion of the Principles of School Management and Organization* (1906); John Louis Horn, *The American Elementary School: A Study in Fundamental Principles* (1922); Isaac L. Kandel, ed., *Twenty-Five Years of American Education* (1924); Leonard V. Koos, *Trends in American Secondary Education* (1926); Abraham Flexner, *Do Americans Really Value Education?* (1927); Henry John Otto, *Elementary School Organization and Administration* (1934); Isaac L. Kandel, *Conflicting Theories of Education* (1938); I. B. Berkson, *Education Faces the Future: An Appraisal of Contemporary Movements in Education* (1943); and Walter S. Monroe, ed., *Encyclopedia of Educational Research* (1950).

FROM THE POSTWAR ERA THROUGH THE EARLY 1980S

The widening embrace of the public schools after World War II led to a proliferation of written sources on the history of education. Again, secondary sources are essential to understand the context in which schools grew ever important. All students of postwar America are indebted to James T. Patterson's impressive and hard-hitting synthesis, *Grand Expectations: The United States, 1945–1974* (1996). Invaluable surveys of the 1950s and the 1960s increasingly abound, as do biographies of presidential administrations, reform movements such as the Great Society, and the conservative reaction of the 1970s. Especially helpful on presidential politics in the 1950s are Stephen E. Ambrose, *Eisenhower: Soldier and President* (1990); on youth culture and delinquency, James Gilbert, *A Cycle of Outrage: America's Reaction to the Juvenile Delinquent in the 1950s* (1986); on civil rights and the freedom movement, Mario T. Garcia, *Mexican Americans* (1989); Pete Daniel, *Lost Revolutions: The South in the 1950s* (2000); on Appalachian out-migration, Jacqueline Jones, "Southern Diaspora: Origins of the Northern Underclass," in Michael B. Katz, ed., *The "Underclass" Debate: Views from History* (1993), 27–54; John Dittmer, *Lo-*

cal People: The Struggle for Civil Rights in Mississippi (1994); Ruben Donato, *The Other Struggle for Equal Schools: Mexican Americans during the Civil Rights Era* (1997); two volumes by Guadalupe San Miguel Jr., *"Let All of Them Take Heed": Mexican Americans and the Campaign for Educational Equity in Texas 1910–1981* (1987) and *Brown, Not White: School Integration and the Chicano Movement in Houston* (2001); and James T. Patterson, *Brown v. Board of Education: A Civil Rights Milestone and Its Troubled Legacy* (2001). References to demography, careers in teaching, public opinion polls, and other facets of the African American experience are easily accessible thanks to Stephan Thernstrom and Abigail Thernstrom, *America in Black and White: One Nation, Indivisible* (1997). On the 1960s, I similarly drew upon the work of Dominick Cavallo, *A Fiction of the Past: The Sixties in American History* (1999); Robert Dallek, *Lone Star Rising: Lyndon Johnson and His Times, 1908–1960* (1991) as well as *Flawed Giant: Lyndon Johnson and His Times, 1961–1973* (1998); David Farber, *The Age of Great Dreams: America in the 1960s* (1994); and Robert M. Collins, "Growth Liberalism in the Sixties: Great Societies at Home and Grand Designs Abroad," in David Farber, ed., *The Sixties: From Memory to History* (1994), 11–44; Hugh Davis Graham, *The Uncertain Triumph: Federal Education Policy in the Kennedy and Johnson Years* (1984); and Allen J. Matusow, *The Unraveling of America: A History of Liberalism in the 1960s* (1984). Bruce J. Schulman, *The Seventies: The Great Shift in American Culture, Society, and Politics* (2001) is a valuable synthesis.

On school reform generally, the two leading interpretations of postwar educational policy are still Joel Spring, *The Sorting Machine: National Educational Policy since 1945* (1976) and Diane Ravitch, *The Troubled Crusade: American Education, 1945–1980* (1983). Richard A. Gibboney offers insightful and passionate appraisals of several reform movements in *The Stone Trumpet: A Story of Practical School Reform, 1960–1990* (1994). For developments in special education, read Thomas Hehir and Thomas Latus, eds., *Special Education at Century's End: Evolution of Theory and Practice since 1970* (1992). The idea of cultural deprivation is seen with greater clarity thanks to the historical perspective provided by Alice O'Connor, *Poverty Knowledge: Social Science, Social Policy, and the Poor in Twentieth-Century U.S. History* (2001). Great Society reforms are analyzed in Julie Roy Jeffrey, *Education for Children of the Poor: A Study of the Origins and Implementation of the Elementary and Secondary Education Act of 1965* (1978); Milbrey Wallin McLaughlin, *Evaluation and Reform: The Elementary and Secondary Education Act of 1965, Title I* (1975); Harvey Kantor, "Education, Social Reform, and the State: ESEA and Federal Education Policy in the 1960s," *American Journal of Education* 100 (November 1991): 47–83; and Harvey Kantor and Barbara Brenzel, "Urban Education and the 'Truly Disadvantaged': The Historical Roots of the Contemporary Crisis, 1945–1960," in Katz, ed., *The "Underclass" Debate*, 366–402. An outstanding case study of the urban crisis is Jerald E. Podair, *The Strike That Changed New York: Blacks, Whites, and the Ocean-Hill Brownsville Crisis* (2002). On an ill-fated curriculum reform based on the ideas of Jerome Bruner, read Peter B. Dow, *Schoolhouse Politics: Lessons from the Sputnik Era* (1991); and on the influence of the cold war, also see the exemplary volume by John L. Rudolph, *Scientists in the Classroom: The Cold War Reconstruction of American Science Education* (2002), as well as Barbara

Barksdale Clowse, *Brain Power for the Cold War: The Sputnik Crisis and National Defense Act of 1958* (1981).

The literature on testing is vast. See especially Nicholas Lemann, *The Big Test: The Secret History of the American Meritocracy* (1999). Historical perspective on contemporary reforms of the 1970s incisively informs Daniel P. Resnick, "Minimum Competency Testing Historically Considered," *Review of Educational Research* 8 (1980): 3–29; and Daniel P. Resnick and Lauren B. Resnick, "Standards, Curriculum, and Performance: A Historical and Comparative Perspective," *Educational Researcher* 14 (April 1985): 5–20. Handy guides to public opinion are Stanley M. Elam, *A Decade of Gallup Polls of Attitudes toward Education, 1969–1978* (1978); and Craig Norback, ed., *The Complete Book of American Surveys* (1980). The impossible goal of grasping the research literature on educational policy and social change in its entirety is aided by the dozens of learned essays found in a succession of encyclopedias sponsored by the American Educational Research Association. See Chester W. Harris, ed., *Encyclopedia of Educational Research* (1960); Robert L. Ebel, ed., *Encyclopedia of Educational Research* (1969); and Marvin C. Alkin, ed. *Encyclopedia of Educational Research* (1992, 4 volumes).

The published works of the people who shaped educational policy debates and practices in the postwar era remain the best guides to understanding their world views and educational ideas. A short list includes the principal writings of Arthur Bestor, Ernest Boyer, Benjamin Bloom, Jerome Bruner, James B. Conant, Herbert Kohl, Jonathan Kozol, Frank Reissman, Charles Silberman, and Theodore R. Sizer. My indebtedness to Michael Young, *The Rise of the Meritocracy* (1958) is enormous. My interpretation of the nature of elementary and secondary schools also derived from some key periodicals, including the *Elementary School Journal* (1956–1980); *High School Journal* (1950–1980); *Bulletin* of the National Association of Secondary-School Principals (1950–1980); *School Life* (1950–1964); and the numerous other magazines and periodicals cited in the text. Articles in *Commentary, Time, Newsweek,* and *U.S. News & World Report* were especially valuable in reconstructing particular policy debates that affected the schools.

Countless volumes appeared after midcentury to explain the nature of elementary schools to future teachers and to the wider reading public. Especially read Harold G. Shane, ed., *The American Elementary School* (1953); John L. Goodlad and Robert H. Anderson, *The Non-Graded Elementary School* (1959); Frank Riessman, *The Culturally Deprived Child* (1962); John I. Goodlad, *School Curriculum Reform in the United States* (1964); Jeanne S. Chall, *Learning to Read: The Great Debate* (1967); and John I. Goodlad, *A Place Called School: Prospects for the Future* (1984), a monument to a lifetime of distinguished scholarship; and Goodlad's memoir, *Romances With Schools: A Life in Education* (2004). Similarly, books proliferated that described the character of high schools, including Harold Spears, *High School for Today* (1950); Franklin Jefferson Keller, *The Comprehensive High School* (1955); William Marshall French, *American Secondary Education* (1957); James S. Coleman, *The Adolescent Society: The Social Life of the Teenager and Its Impact on Education* (1961); Alvin C. Eurich et al., eds., *High School 1980: The Shape of the Future in American Secondary Education* (1970); and Ernest L. Boyer, *High School: A Report on Secondary Edu-*

cation in America (1983). Also read Robert L. Hampel, *The Last Little Citadel: American High Schools since 1940* (1986), the best one-volume history of the modern high school; William Graebner, *Coming of Age in Buffalo: Youth and Authority in the Postwar Era* (1990); Sherman Dorn, *Creating the Dropout: An Institutional and Social History of School Failure* (1996); and John L. Rury, "Democracy's High School? Social Change and American Secondary Education in the Post-Conant Era," *American Educational Research Journal* 39 (Summer 2002): 307–36, which offers a thoughtful appraisal of the modern high school and includes a superb bibliography.

FROM *A NATION AT RISK* TO "NO CHILD LEFT BEHIND"

To most historians, the past quarter-century still constitutes current events, yet my attempt to understand contemporary history benefited from a number of specific sources. Especially important were the essays in Philip W. Jackson, ed., *Handbook of Research on Curriculum* (1992); and Marvin Alkin, ed., *Encyclopedia,* previously cited. Also, public opinion polls provided me with a sense of the unreal expectations that citizens sometimes have for their schools. I also systematically read popular publications such as *Time* and the daily *New York Times* to help track policy debates. The innumerable reports of the U.S. Department of Education, along with the hundreds of state and local documents generated in the wake of *A Nation at Risk* (1983), will some day be mined more thoroughly by an intrepid researcher. Many of these sources are already accessible via the Internet. A starting point in understanding federal policy is Diane Ravitch and Maris A. Vinovskis, eds., *Learning from the Past: What History Teaches Us about School Reform* (1995); Thomas C. Hunt, *The Impossible Dream: Education and the Search for Panaceas* (2002); and David T. Gordon, ed., *A Nation Reformed? American Education 20 Years after "A Nation at Risk"* (2003). On persistence inequalities in school funding and the gap between city and suburb, read Jonathan Kozol, *Savage Inequalities: Children in America's Schools* (1991); on testing, Linda M. McNeil, *Contradictions of School Reform: Educational Costs of Standardized Testing* (2000). On high school sports, see H. G. Bissinger, *Friday Night Lights: A Town, a Team, and a Dream* (1990). A huge literature on school choice, vouchers, desegregation, and market choices in education will keep scholars busy in their study, as will competing interpretations of "No Child Left Behind" that are already proliferating.

Index